SECOND EDITION

Economic Issues and Policy

SECOND EDITION

Economic Issues and Policy

Jacqueline Murray Brux

University of Wisconsin-River Falls

Janna L. Cowen

University of Wisconsin-River Falls

SOUTH-WESTERN
™
THOMSON LEARNING

Australia · Canada · Mexico · Singapore · Spain · United Kingdom · United States

Economic Issues and Policy, 2e, by Jacqueline M. Brux and Janna L. Cowen

Vice President/Publisher: Jack W. Calhoun
Acquisitions Editor: Michael W. Worls
Developmental Editor: Maria T. Accardi
Senior Marketing Manager: Lisa L. Lysne
Media Technology Editor: Vicky True
Media Development Editor: Peggy Buskey
Media Production Editor: John Barans
Production Editor: Daniel C. Plofchan
Design Manager/Internal Design: Rik Moore
Cover Design: Liz Harasymczuk, Liz Harasymczuk Design
Sponsoring Representative: Susanna C. Smart
Manufacturing Coordinators: Charlene Taylor, Sandee Milewski
Production House: UpperCase Publication Services, Ltd.
Printer: R.R. Donnelley & Sons Company, Crawfordsville Manufacturing Division

Printed in the United States of America
1 2 3 4 5 05 04 03 02 01

For more information, contact South-Western Publishing, 5101 Madison Road, Cincinnati, Ohio 45227, or find us on the Internet at http://www.swcollege.com

For permission to use material from this text or product, contact us by
• **telephone: 1-800-730-2214**
• **fax: 1-800-730-2215**
• **Web: http://www.thomsonrights.com**

Library of Congress Cataloging-in-Publication Data
Brux, Jacqueline Murray.
  Economic issues and policy / Jacqueline Murray Brux, Janna L. Cowen.–2nd ed.
    p. cm.
  Includes bibliographical references and index.
  ISBN 0-324-10856-7 (pbk. : alk. paper)
  1. Economics. 2. Economic policy. I. Cowen, Janna L., 1942- II. Title.
HB171.5 .B8 2001
330–dc21
                              2001020812

BRIEF CONTENTS

101923

TABLE OF CONTENTS

FOREWORD

TO THE INSTRUCTOR

This text is intended for a nontechnical, issues-oriented economics course, usually a 100-level course in four-year universities. The book is also appropriate for two-year colleges and other institutions, as well as economic education programs for elementary and secondary schoolteachers. Chapters are designed so that they can be taught in any order (with the exception that Chapter One must come first). Each chapter includes references to other chapters that mention similar topics.

The authors together have approximately 40 years' experience in teaching issues-oriented economics. Usually our students are not economics majors, although many have decided to major in economics after taking this course. Some of our students are recent high school graduates and incredibly naive about the workings of the economy. Others are nontraditional students who know only too well how the economy works. They also understand how disadvantaged they are without a college degree. The primary objective of this book is to reach both groups plus those in between.

Our goals in writing the book were to make students aware of economic issues in the world around them and to facilitate their understanding of these issues and related policy perspectives. Students are often unaware that so many important issues of our day, including ones that directly affect them, are rooted in economics: issues pertaining to our environment, our health care, and our educational system, and matters as weighty as war and peace. Furthermore, students often set aside as too complex the issues that *are* recognized as economic, such as unemployment and inflation or trade and budget deficits. They believe that these issues are better left for the experts. Students need to know that these issues are indeed relevant, interesting, and within their ability to understand. They need to comprehend these issues to make sound choices and form intelligent opinions.

Recent studies suggest that today's youth are disinterested in the world around them and focused instead on more personal concerns such as getting good grades, paying for education, and acquiring a job. Students must be shown the connection between themselves and their world. In a functioning democracy, they need to understand the relevance of social issues to their lives, and the impact their lives can have on these issues. This book is an effort to demonstrate that relevance and suggest that impact. Indeed, its epilogue, "You and the World around You," invites the student to address some of the matters raised in the text.

The discussion of issues in this book is lively and current. We have made an effort to include issues of gender, race, and ethnicity. Because the world is so rapidly becoming interdependent, we also have provided plenty of discussion of the international economy. Even if you rarely have time to include international topics in your course, we encourage you to read all three chapters addressing such topics before deciding to skip them. We think you will find them quite relevant and interesting, and the issues are presented in such a way that students can understand them.

In this book we use economic theory to analyze economic situations and the implications of possible policies. The economic theory is basic: supply and demand, aggregate supply and aggregate demand, production possibilities, and so on. The level of technicality in the book is deliberately appropriate for an economic issues course with no prerequisites, unlike the level in other texts on the market that attempt to incorporate all relevant principles and theory into pages better focused on the issues themselves. The material is written in a clear and student-friendly manner. Occasionally more technical material or additional examples are placed in appendices to the chapters. Graphs are clear and each usually illustrates only one concept. A careful explanation of the concept appears with most graphs. We generally use only two basic types of graphs: production possibilities and demand and supply (and aggregate demand and supply). Every effort has been made to place the graph and the discussion of the graph on the same or adjacent pages.

We generally present economic theory in a simple, market-oriented framework, but we don't limit policy discussion to such a narrow context. Rather, we offer diverse policy perspectives. As a result, the book contains a more liberal orientation than one that would rely on market analysis only, but the text is carefully balanced to reflect both the conservative and the liberal views.

Indeed, the careful presentation of conservative and liberal viewpoints is one of the unique characteristics of this book. Students often have opinions, and they often consider themselves to be either conservative or liberal, but they rarely have the sophistication to understand the economic meaning of these terms and how their viewpoints tie into one or the other general philosophy. The Viewpoint section at the end of each chapter clarifies these notions, giving students a framework within which to understand their own economic philosophies. Please point out to your students the importance of reading the Foreword to the Student, which clarifies the conservative versus the liberal economic views.

Changes in the Second Edition

The second edition of the text is extensively updated. First, it has a new design and artwork that should be more appealing to the student. This artwork includes a "roadmap" at the beginning of each chapter that shows how topics from previous chapters tie into the current chapter, and how topics in the current chapter tie into future chapters. As a result of a reorganization of chapters, two of the international chapters appear earlier in the second edition than in the first. The renamed chapter "International Trade" now appears directly after "Market Power" (extending the concept that competition is enhanced by trade), and the renamed chapter "World Poverty" appears directly after "U.S. Poverty" (extending the concept of poverty worldwide). Because of exciting additions to "International Trade," the topic of international finance is now relegated to an appendix. Because discrimination is certainly one of the causes of poverty, the chapter on "Discrimination" now directly precedes "U.S. Poverty." The chapter "Globally Free Markets for the Twenty-First Century?" remains at the end of the book, inviting students to synthesize all they have learned about economic conservative and liberal philosophies and put it to the test of predicting the future of the world economy. The epilogue "You and the World around You" follows this chapter as before.

Second, the new edition contains the latest data available, as well as new, current topics. These topics include the conservative Bush agenda, our newly designed welfare program, the employment effects of immigration, the controversy over the minimum wage, the new era of government budget surpluses, indigenous people's rights to land, AIDS in Africa, the Seattle protests, sweatshop labor, (an expanded discussion of) housing segregation, and the controversy underlying our trade relationships with Cuba and China.

Third, Internet exercises are now included in the Discussion Questions in each chapter, as well as Web links directing students to further information. You have the option of providing your students with the *New York Times Economic Issues Guide*. This guide can be used formally in the classroom or informally for life-long learning. All articles are accompanied by exploratory exercises and probing questions developed by experts in the field. Previews provide context for each chapter of articles and link them to key economic topics. Because the guide is divided into six sections highlighting critical factors in economics today, it can easily be integrated into any economics course. You and your students are also invited to use the South-Western Web site at http://economics.swcollege.com, where you can find summaries of the latest economics news stories, indexed by topic, as well as commentary on today's most crucial economic policy debates, and a variety of economic data.

Ancillaries

Two ancillary volumes, *Instructor's Manual with Test Bank* and *Study Guide,* are available with this book. These volumes are newly revised to complement the second edition of the text. As authors of the text, we also wrote the instructor's manual and the study guide, thereby ensuring that the ancillaries are consistent with the second edition in both vocabulary and intent.

In *Instructor's Manual with Test Bank,* we reveal our purpose and objectives on a chapter-by-chapter basis. The manual contains teaching and lecture suggestions (based on our long-term education in how students think) as well as additional examples that you can use in class. It also contains sample short-answer, multiple-choice, true-and-false, and critical thinking exam questions. As such, it provides instructors with plenty of choices in the types of exam questions they wish to use. The manual also includes suggested Web sites for instructors.

Study Guide also presents our purpose and learning objectives. In it we've included, on a chapter-by-chapter basis, study suggestions and practice exercises that reflect our experience with students. We also provide a self-test of multiple-choice and true-and-false questions.

This book focuses on economic issues. It includes those issues that you would normally consider to be economic issues, such as unemployment and inflation. But it also includes a variety of other social issues that you might not ordinarily think of as economic ones: crime, the plight of our nation's homeless, the degradation of our environment, and the problems of public education. These and many other issues are addressed in this book.

The book is intended to be student-friendly. The graphs are straightforward and clear. You may be relieved to know that most of the graphs in this book boil down to just two basic types: production possibilities and demand and supply. The definitions of economic vocabulary help you cut through the economic jargon. The issues are current. The text is clear and to the point, with a minimum of technicality. The material is presented in a way that you should find relevant to your personal life.

The book is intended to get you to think. As you acquire a basic understanding of economics, you also acquire a basic framework within which to form and justify your personal opinions about social issues. Are you a conservative or a liberal? Are you conservative on some issues and liberal on others? Do you even know what these terms mean in the context of economics? In economics, and from a U.S. perspective, conservative generally means believing in only a limited role for government in the economy. In the conservative view, the free market operates relatively well by itself; therefore, little government intervention in the form of regulations, taxes, and programs is needed. Indeed, conservatives believe that if left alone, the market will solve most economic problems. The conservative view is on the right end of the economic philosophical spectrum. Liberal, on the other hand, generally means support for far greater government involvement in the economy. In the liberal view, the marketplace may often be efficient, but it is not necessarily equitable—that is, the marketplace is not always fair, and it does not ensure an adequate education, health care, housing, and income for all. Government intervention in the marketplace is thought to be necessary to overcome problems such as discrimination, poverty, and pollution. The liberal view is on the left end of the economic philosophical spectrum.

Keep in mind that these notions of what it means to be conservative or liberal specifically apply to *economics*. On the other hand, from a *social* perspective, conservative often means resistance to change, whereas liberal means support of social experimentation and change. Social conservatives may therefore support more government involvement in the social aspects of our individual lives than a liberal would. Social conservatives are more likely to favor, for example, government censorship of music, movies, and magazines than are liberals. *Do not confuse the economic and social perspectives!*

This textbook covers viewpoints that are conservative or liberal from an economics standpoint. The Viewpoint section at the end of each chapter clarifies the positions of both liberals and conservatives to help you formulate your own beliefs. Keep in mind that this section is intended to show opposite viewpoints; often economists and policymakers find themselves closer to the middle. On many issues, agreement among economists is widespread.

Basic economic tools can be used as a framework for understanding the various social issues in the world around us. They can provide greater insight into issues such as crime, education, housing, poverty, and discrimination. They can help us understand government policy within our nation. They can help us understand economic events in other countries, including those countries making a transition from socialism to capitalism in Eastern Europe and those countries struggling to develop in the less-developed world.

Finding solutions to economic problems is not easy. People of different philosophies can hold very different viewpoints, despite a common understanding of economic concepts. Here is where you, the student, come in. This book will provide a basic economic framework for discussing social issues and problems, but you must determine your own viewpoint on these issues and problems.

The second edition of the text is extensively updated from the first. First, it has a new design and artwork that should be appealing to you. This artwork includes a "roadmap" at the beginning of each chapter that shows how topics from other chapters are linked to topics in the current chapter. Second, the new edition contains the latest data available, as well as new, current topics. These topics include the conservative Bush agenda, our newly designed welfare program, the employment effects of immigration, the controversy over the minimum wage, the new era of government budget surpluses, indigenous people's rights to land, AIDS in Africa, the Seattle protests, sweatshop labor, housing segregation, and the controversy underlying our trade relationships with Cuba and China. Finally, you will benefit from the Internet exercises included in the Discussion Questions in each chapter, and Web links, which direct you to further information.

An updated study guide is available with this textbook to aid you in your study of economic issues and policies. It presents our purpose and learning objectives for each chapter. It includes, on a chapter-by-chapter basis, many study suggestions and practice exercises that reflect our experience with students. Multiple-choice and true-and-false questions are provided.

Finally, as a student using a South-Western textbook, you have access to an excellent Web site (http://economics.swcollege.com) that includes data summaries of the latest economic news, and commentary on today's most crucial economic policy debates.

Now enjoy your discovery of the world of economic issues!

ACKNOWLEDGMENTS

We owe a debt of gratitude to many people. First we wish to thank the thousands of students who allowed us to experiment on them. Without them, we would still fail to understand why they always believed that economics was *so* difficult and boring! We would never know how we could make it relevant for them.

Second, we would like to thank all the reviewers who made suggestions on early drafts of this book: Robert L. Gordon, San Diego State University; Alan

Grant, Eastern Illinois University, Eric R. Hake, Eastern Illinois University; Emily P. Hoffman, Western Michigan University; George Monsma, Calvin College; and Raymond A. Pepin, Stonehill College. They critiqued our pedagogy and our English usage, and the book is significantly stronger because of their efforts. Its remaining weaknesses are, of course, our responsibility.

Third, we appreciate the support provided by our department chair and interim director, Glenn Potts, and our program assistant, Eunice Filkins.

And finally, we are grateful for the support of family and friends. Thank you, Corey and Christina, for providing enough joy in my life to see me through any project.

Jacqueline M. Brux
Janna L. Cowen

ABOUT THE AUTHORS

Jacqueline Murray Brux received her Ph.D. in economics in 1983 from the University of Michigan in Ann Arbor, and is a professor of economics at the University of Wisconsin-River Falls. Her areas of expertise are economic development and international economics. Her research encompasses the area of economic development of less-developed countries, with special focus on women in development and structural reforms. Dr. Brux's international experience includes work and research in the countries of Burkina Faso and Ghana in West Africa; Mexico, Chile, and Cuba in Latin America; Russia; and Vietnam.

Janna L. Cowen received her Ph.D. in economics from the University of Nebraska-Lincoln in 1979; she has been at the University of Wisconsin-River Falls (UW-RF) ever since that time. Her teaching and research interests are in the areas of government regulation of business and labor economics. Dr. Cowen was recognized as the 1987 Teacher of the Year at UW-RF and the 1988 Outstanding Teacher in the Social Sciences.

CHAPTER 1

Introduction

In economics, hope and faith coexist with great scientific pretension and also a deep desire for respectability.

John Kenneth Galbraith, U.S. economist, *New York Times Magazine* (June 7, 1970)

WEB LINK

http://economics.
swcollege.com
A unique, rich, and robust
online resource for economics students. This site provides
product information, learning tips and tools, information about careers in economics, access to all of South-
Western's text-supporting
Web sites, and other cutting-
edge educational resources.
You, the student, will find this
site invaluable.

Welcome to Economics! Welcome? To the dismal science? To the colorless pages of the *Wall Street Journal*? To the realm of boring statistics, intimidating jargon, complex graphs, and middle-aged men in three-piece business suits carrying leather briefcases?

Welcome? To terms like budget deficit, balance of trade, national debt, inflation, money supply, unemployment rate, labor force, and market equilibrium? Do we really want to know what these phrases mean? Do we really want to look at the graphs, charts, numbers, and newsprint? Can these possibly have meaning for our lives? Can they possibly be understood by average citizens such as those of you right here in this classroom?

Perhaps surprisingly, the answer to all of the above is a resounding yes . . . not because we enjoy jargon and numbers, but because we want answers to important questions. Will I be able to get a job when I graduate? Why does a marketing professor make more than an English professor? Will I be helped or hurt by a raise in the minimum wage? Why are college costs so high? And should students receive greater financial aid? Why have we encouraged farmers to produce huge surpluses through government subsidies? Why does hunger persist in a world of plenty? Why does poverty exist in the midst of affluence? Who will eat, and who will not? Who will find jobs, and who will not? Why does the average female worker earn only about three-quarters as much as the average male worker? Whose children will have education and health care, and whose children will not?

Scarcity
Limited resources relative to wants and needs.

If you've wondered about these or similar questions, *you are interested in economics*. This is because economics deals primarily with **scarcity:** how shall we allocate our limited resources to satisfy seemingly unlimited human wants and needs? Once you understand a little economic reasoning, you will be able to answer the world's (and your) pressing questions better than most of the politicians, newscasters, and opinionated people who persistently tell you what to believe. Survival in the face of scarcity is what economics is all about. Understanding a few economic concepts allows you to analyze these issues yourself and come up with your own answers to these questions. So let's get started.

ECONOMICS AND SCARCITY

Resources
Land, labor, machinery, and other inputs used to produce goods and services.

Let us begin by discussing scarcity. **Resources** (land, labor, factory buildings, timber, minerals, machinery, and the like) are the basis for producing the food, shelter, medical care, and luxury goods that we want. These resources are scarce in the sense that there are not enough of them to produce everything we desire. Even when using all resources as efficiently and completely as possible, and using all modern technology to its fullest extent, there is some limit to the amount we can currently produce. Scarcity forces us to choose among competing uses for society's resources. What to produce and how to distribute this output to society's citizens are the most basic economic choices to be made.

Production possibilities curve
An economic concept explaining scarcity and the need for choices; a graph showing alternate combinations of the maximum amounts of two different goods that can be produced during a particular time period if the economy's resources are efficiently and fully employed.

The easiest way to think about the problem of societal choice is by looking at a basic economic concept and graph called the **production possibilities curve.** (We promise that only two basic graphs will be used to analyze almost all the issues in this book.) The production possibilities curve shows the maximum amount of two different goods that can possibly be produced during any particular time period using society's scarce resources. Because reality is complex, economists try to simplify it by making assumptions about the basic elements involved in analyzing an issue. In examining production possibilities, we must make these simplifying assumptions about our economy:

1. All available resources will be used fully.
2. All available resources will be used efficiently.
3. The quantity and quality of available resources is not changing during our period of analysis.
4. Technology is not changing during our period of analysis.
5. We can produce only two goods with our available resources and technology.

Let's consider the implications of these simplifying assumptions. First, all available resources are used fully, so that no workers are unemployed, no factory buildings sit idle, and so forth. (This does not mean that we fail to conserve some of our resources for the future. If we think that the habitat of the snowy owl is important ecologically, we simply do not make that part of the available resources.) Second, efficiency means that we use our knowledge and technology to produce the maximum amount of output with these resources. These first two assumptions mean that our economy is doing the best that it can; it is operating fully and efficiently. Third, the quantity and quality of our resources is not changing. This means that over the current time period, workers do not begin new training programs to make them more productive, new natural resources are not discovered, and so on. The next assumption is similar. Technological change—which might give us a better means of producing more goods with the same resources—is not occurring. We make these last two assumptions to deal with the world as it is right now, and not how it might become over the future. And finally, to simplify our analysis (and because we can graph in only two dimensions), we assume that we can produce only two goods with our resources. Let's pick bread and roses as the goods.

One of our choices is to put all of our resources and technology into the production of bread. This choice might give us 150 units of bread. Whether these bread units are loaves, cases, truckloads, or tons is irrelevant here. Let's suppose they are tons.

Two old adages suggest that man (and woman) cannot live by bread alone and that life is richer if we stop and smell the roses. So let's allow another choice and take some resources and some technology out of bread production and use them to produce roses. Now we might end up with 20 units of roses and only 130 tons of bread. Again, the nature of the units is irrelevant; our rose units might be bouquets, boxes, truckloads, or tons. Let's suppose they are tons. (Note, however, that we had to give up 20 tons of bread production in order to produce the 20 tons of roses.)

Another alternative might be to give up even more bread, leaving us with bread production of only 105 tons, in order to produce 40 tons of roses. (Note that this time we had to give up 25 tons of bread production in order to get the additional 20 tons of roses.) The alternatives could go on and on and might be summarized in a production possibilities table such as Table 1-1. Note that each alternative A through F represents one possible combination of bread and roses that we could produce.

The information in Table 1-1 can be easily displayed in a production possibilities curve, or graph. Don't let graphs intimidate you. They can be very useful. Every graph has just two axes, and each axis shows the amounts of one variable. As you move along the axes away from the origin, the amounts of the variables

WEB LINK

http://www.amosweb.com
This economics education site covers economics with a touch of whimsy. Check out "production possibilities" or any other topic of your choice.

TABLE 1-1	Production Possibilities Table	
ALTERNATIVE	**BREAD (TONS)**	**ROSES (TONS)**
A	150	0
B	130	20
C	105	40
D	75	60
E	40	80
F	0	100

FIGURE 1-1   Production Possibilities Curve

Points *A* through *F* show alternative combinations of bread and roses that the economy can produce, whereas point *U* represents unemployed resources.

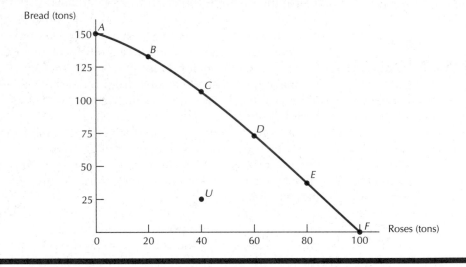

increase. In Figure 1-1 the horizontal axis represents tons of roses, and the vertical axis represents tons of bread. Each point in the graph represents a row in the table, and the labeling of the points corresponds to the alternatives in the table. Connecting all points gives us a production possibilities curve, which shows the alternative combinations of maximum quantities of bread and roses that our country is capable of producing.

A number of important concepts are illustrated by the production possibilities curve. The most basic concept is that there is some limit to what we can produce. Thus to produce more of one good, we must give up production of something else. This reality is what economists refer to as opportunity cost. **Opportunity cost** is the best alternative that is forgone in order to produce or consume something else. The opportunity cost of producing roses is not measured in dollars but in the bread that we give up when we produce these roses. And the opportunity cost of producing bread is the roses we give up when we produce this bread. As economists are fond of saying, there is no free lunch! There is an opportunity cost to everything!

Furthermore, note that as we produce larger quantities of roses, we must give up *larger and larger* quantities of bread. This is another way of saying that opportunity cost increases as we produce more of a particular good. It increases because we ultimately use resources that are less well suited to producing more of a particular good. In our example, we would begin production by using those resources that are best suited for each product. As we produce more roses, we would need to use resources that are more suitable for bread production, so that we would need to use larger quantities of these resources to make up for their lower productivity. Consequently, we would have to give up more bread, our alternative good. And this means that the opportunity cost of rose production increases as we produce more and more of it. The same would be true for the production of bread.

Opportunity cost
The best alternative forgone to produce or consume something else; what you give up to get something else.

The second economic concept that is illustrated by production possibilities is that of **unemployment.** Realize that our alternative combinations of the two products represent *possible* quantities. We have explicitly assumed the full use of our resources, knowledge, and technology; hence the phrase production *possibilities.* In actuality, we rarely if ever produce to our full potential. In reality, some resources may go unused: factories are idle and workers are laid off. Nor do we always use resources in the most efficient manner. In these cases we will not be on the production possibilities curve, but at some point inside (below) it, such as *U* (representing unemployment) in Figure 1-1. At point *U* we are producing only 40 tons of roses and 25 tons of bread, though we could produce more of both if we had full employment. Clearly we could do much better by putting idle resources to work and moving our way back out to the production possibilities curve.

Finally, it is evident that our country need not be restricted to a single production possibilities curve forever. Economies may grow, and the variables that we assumed are unchanging (resources and technology) certainly *do* change. **Economic growth** may occur if the quality or quantity of society's resources increase, or if new technologies are developed so that we can produce more output with our available resources. Such growth would be reflected in an forward shift of the entire production possibilities curve, as illustrated in Figure 1-2. Such a shift would enable us to move to a point such as point *G* (representing growth) on the new production possibilities curve. Clearly point *G* (with 60 tons of roses and 105 tons of bread) is superior to point *D* (with 60 tons of roses and only 75 tons of bread) on the original curve. Such growth is possible only *over time,* and not in the current time period illustrated by the first production possibilities curve.

FIGURE 1-2   Production Possibilities with Economic Growth

Note that more of both bread and roses can be produced when the production possibilities curve shifts outward as the result of economic growth.

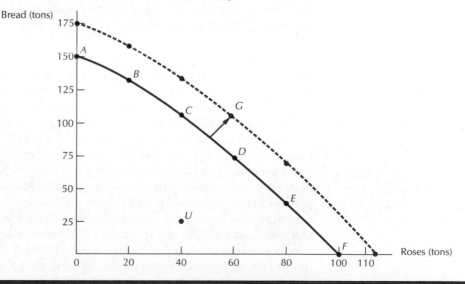

Of course our country and world are capable of producing more than just two goods. We produce trucks, spaghetti, gasoline, VCRs, swimming suits, and a bewildering array of merchandise that fills our shopping centers. We also produce **services** such as health care, education, road repair, and telephone installation. We can easily imagine infinite combinations of all the goods and services that an economy can potentially produce. We cannot graph these infinite combinations, however, because a graph has only two axes. So bread and roses simply represent one of an infinite set of choices. We can make our graph a bit more realistic by redefining the axes. We might redefine the horizontal axis as staple goods and the vertical axis as luxury goods. Or we could divide our economy's output into agricultural goods and manufactured goods, or **consumer goods** (goods that are purchased by consumers) and **capital goods** (goods such as factory buildings and dump trucks, which are themselves resources for further production). We may examine the choice between military goods and civilian goods. Or we may look at the production possibilities for **private goods** (such as CD players and hamburgers, which are provided by businesses) and **public goods** (such as police and fire protection, which are provided by government). Thus we can realistically consider many choices involved in the production of various types of output.

We hope you don't suspect that the purpose of the production possibilities exercise was merely to illustrate some economic concepts and drawings. It wasn't. It has very important real-world relevance. It suggests to us first of all that we can never be absolutists when it comes to our nation's spending priorities. If we wish to devote more of the country's current resources to environmental protection, for example, we may have to give up part of our space program. If we wish to expand public education, we may have to give up some of our national defense. Or if we wish to have more government goods and services overall, we must give up some private goods. We can't have more of everything. We can't insist on any spending priority without limit, because there are always opportunity costs to consider.

The production possibilities curve also helps us realize that the costs of unemployment are not limited to personal hardships experienced by the unemployed person and his or her family, although these personal costs may be severe. Costs are also borne by our nation and our world as a whole in the form of reduced production. If we waste our resources through inefficient production techniques, output is similarly reduced. In a world of scarcity, emphasis on economic growth is not enough. We must see to it that our resources are fully and efficiently employed in the present before seeking to expand our productive potential in the future.

And the problem of scarcity is real. Worldwide, some 15 children die every minute from lack of adequate nutrition and health care. The world's citizens lack basic education, shelter, clothing, clean water, and hygiene as well. Many of the world's nations lack basic infrastructure in the form of communications, transportation, sanitation, and electricity. Even in a prosperous country such as ours, some 12 percent of the population is poor. As we shall see in Chapter Seven on poverty, these people receive inadequate food, shelter, health care, clothing, and other necessities. Our nation as a whole lacks sufficient environmental protection, first-rate educational opportunities, and quality health care for all. Choices as to what we produce and how much we produce can easily become matters of life and death to some of our citizens.

Although production choices are important, they really tell us only half of the story. At least as important are choices relating to the distribution of goods and services. Who shall receive the bread and roses, and everything else, after they are produced? Shall the decision be based on equality, so that everyone receives the same amount of every good that everyone else does? Shall people receive a share of the goods and services that is proportional to their contribution to producing those goods and services? Shall the government make the distribution decisions, perhaps giving higher rations to those most "deserving" (however that might be determined)? On what basis shall distribution choices be made?

As we shall see, in a market-based economy such as ours, the choices of distribution as well as production are based primarily on prices. And prices are determined by demand and supply.

Demand and Supply

Demand

No one can be good for long if goodness is not in demand.

Bertolt Brecht (1898–1956), German dramatist, poet
First God, in *The Good Woman of Setzuan,* scene 1a

Have you ever had to hire a tutor to help with your coursework? (We hope you haven't had to in economics, at least not yet!) What would be some of the factors that would determine the number of tutoring hours you would wish to purchase? Probably the degree of difficulty of the coursework is important, and so is your income, which will determine how much tutoring you can afford. Most likely the price of tutoring services is important to you as well. All other things being equal, you would probably be inclined to purchase more tutoring service hours at $1 per hour than at $5 per hour. Most of us tend to behave in the same way. At very high prices we tend to be frugal in our use of tutoring services. We will ask more questions in class, or study with a friend, or visit the teacher during office hours, or generally work harder (or take the consequences) rather than pay the fee for many hours of tutoring if the price is high. At lower prices, we are willing and able to purchase more hours of tutoring. Let's focus on the price variable for a moment.

Let's assume that you attend a large university where there are many students who want tutors as well as many students willing and able to tutor. Suppose we consider all your school's students and their desire to purchase tutoring services. Let's assume that the time period is one week and that all factors other than price (such as course difficulty and income) are held constant. (Economists usually say "all other things equal" to specify that all other factors that might influence the quantity demanded are unchanging.)

To illustrate this example further, let's put this information into a tabular format. Let's consider people's willingness to buy tutoring services, where *P* stands for

TABLE 1-2	Demand Schedule for Tutoring Services, One Week	
ALTERNATIVE	P ($ PER HOUR)	Q_d (HOURS)
a	$1	100
b	$2	80
c	$3	60
d	$4	40
e	$5	20

Demand schedule

A table showing the quantities that consumers are willing to buy at alternative prices during a specified time period.

Law of demand

There is an inverse (negative) relationship between price and quantity demanded.

Demand curve

A graph showing the quantities that consumers are willing to buy at alternative prices during a specified time period.

alternative possible prices of tutoring services and Q_d (quantity demanded) stands for the amounts of tutoring that students are willing and able to purchase at these various prices. This is reflected in Table 1-2, which shows alternative prices and the quantities that people are willing and able to purchase at these prices. This is called a **demand schedule.** It is clear that if tutoring prices are low (say $2 per hour), the quantity demanded will be high (80 hours). If tutoring prices are high ($4 per hour), the quantity demanded will be lower (40 hours). This simple commonsense idea that people will be willing and able to buy more of a good or service at low prices than at high prices is a fundamental economic principle, the **law of demand,** which is usually stated as follows: *Price and quantity demanded are inversely related, all other things equal.* This means that when price goes up, quantity demanded goes down, and vice versa.

We can place the information from Table 1-2 into a graph of demand, illustrated in Figure 1-3. A graph of demand is referred to as a **demand curve** (even though demand curves are often drawn as straight lines). The price of tutoring services (P) is on the vertical axis, and the quantity of services demanded (number of hours) is on the horizontal axis, which is labeled Q for quantity. Plotting the

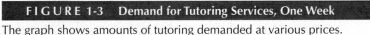

FIGURE 1-3   Demand for Tutoring Services, One Week

The graph shows amounts of tutoring demanded at various prices.

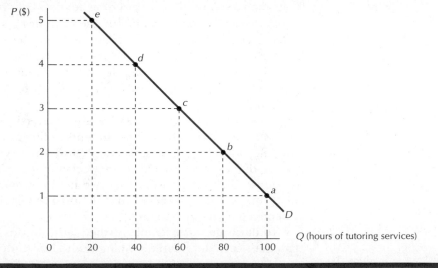

TABLE 1-3   Increased Demand Schedule for Tutoring Services, One Week

ALTERNATIVE	P ($ PER HOUR)	Q_d (HOURS)
a′	$1	140
b′	$2	120
c′	$3	100
d′	$4	80
e′	$5	60

information in each of the rows *a* through *e* in the table gives us points *a* through *e* in the graph. Connecting these points gives us the demand curve in Figure 1-3. The demand curve (labeled *D* for demand) indicates all possible combinations of alternative prices and quantity demanded, assuming that all factors except price that could affect quantity demanded are held constant.

Note that the demand curve is downward sloping, reflecting the law of demand. A higher price is associated with a lower quantity demanded ($4, 40 hours), whereas a lower price is associated with a larger quantity demanded ($2, 80 hours.)

What if one of the other factors affecting demand were to change? Course difficulty might increase, for example. Or student incomes might increase, making students better able to afford tutoring. Each of these examples would increase the demand for tutoring services. You can probably add to the list of things that would increase the demand for tutoring.

An increase in the demand for tutoring services will result in an entirely new demand schedule, such as the one in Table 1-3.

We can plot this new information in the same graph as before, and we end up with an entirely new demand curve, *D′*. (See Figure 1-4.) Demand has increased so

FIGURE 1-4   Increased Demand for Tutoring Services, One Week

Demand curve *D′* represents larger quantities demanded at each price than does demand curve *D*.

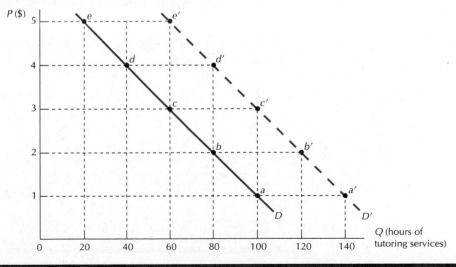

the demand curve has shifted forward, or to the right. Note that for every price that existed before, a higher quantity demanded now exists.

If an event causing a decrease in demand were to occur (say a decrease in student incomes), the demand curve would shift backward or to the left. A decrease in demand is shown in Figure 1-5. Note that for every price on both demand curves, a smaller quantity is shown on D'' than on the original demand curve D.

Supply

> The sinews of war, a limitless supply of money.
>
> Cicero (106–43 B.C.), Roman orator, philosopher
> *Phillippics*, Oration 5, sct. 5

Now let's consider the other side of the market for tutoring services, the supply side. Imagine the students at your school who not only don't need tutoring, but are actually able to tutor. This is the group of students who might supply tutoring services for a fee. What are the factors that influence these students' willingness to offer their tutoring services for sale? Probably the costs associated with providing the service are important. The most obvious cost is the value of the tutor's time. Remember that opportunity costs are always important. The opportunity costs of a tutor's time may be quantified easily if an adult tutor hires a baby-sitter while he or she tutors or if the tutor forgoes income from alternative employment. Some costs that are less easy to quantify are just as real. The tutor might be giving up precious

FIGURE 1-5   Decreased Demand for Tutoring Services, One Week

Demand curve D'' represents smaller quantities demanded at each price than does demand curve D.

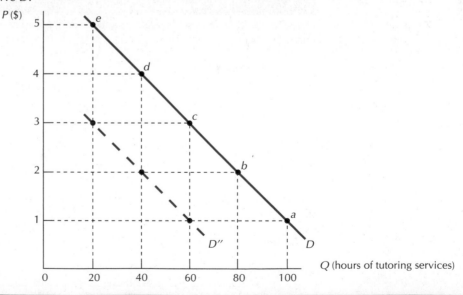

study time, quality time with friends and family, or simply valued leisure time. Although it's hard to attach a dollar value to these costs, they remain important. Remember that there is no free lunch; every choice has an opportunity cost; every activity chosen entails another activity given up.

Another factor affecting the total quantity of tutoring services supplied will be the number of tutors available. If we experience an increase in enrollment of top-notch students who are dying to become tutors, we can expect more tutoring services suddenly to be supplied.

The price that tutors can receive for their services will also be an important determinant of their willingness to supply these services. Let's focus our attention on this price variable for a moment. Let's look at the supply of tutoring services in a one-week time period, when all the factors except price that might affect the number of tutoring hours supplied are held constant. It is realistic to assume that individual tutors will be more willing to provide tutoring services at a high price than at a low price. The higher price will allow them to cover their baby-sitting expenses more easily or serve as a stronger inducement to give up leisure or time with friends and family. It will compensate them better for other job prospects they don't pursue because they are tutoring. In simple terms, the higher the price, the greater the incentive to provide tutoring services. Tutors (and business firms) will offer for sale a larger amount at higher than at lower prices. This is known as the **law of supply,** which is usually stated as follows: *Price and quantity supplied are directly related, all other things equal.* This simply means that price and quantity supplied (the amount offered for sale) change in the same direction. If price goes up, so does quantity supplied; if price goes down, so does quantity.

The behavior of all tutors as a group might be summarized in Table 1-4, which is a **supply schedule** showing different quantities of tutoring hours supplied (Q_s) at the alternative prices that the tutors might receive. The quantities represent the *total* number of hours supplied by the group as a whole at each alternative price over the specified one-week time period. All the factors other than price that might affect the tutors' willingness to tutor do not change. Thus the only thing changing is the price determinant.

We can place the information from the supply schedule in Table 1-4 into a graph of supply or **supply curve.** The axes are identical to those in the demand graphs with price on the vertical axis and quantity on the horizontal axis. Plotting the information in each of the rows v through z gives us points v through z on the

Law of supply
There is a direct (positive) relationship between price and quantity supplied.

Supply schedule
A table showing the quantities that suppliers are willing to sell at alternative prices during a specified time period.

Supply curve
A graph showing the quantities that suppliers are willing to sell at alternative prices during a specified time period.

TABLE 1-4	Supply Schedule for Tutoring Services, One Week	
ALTERNATIVE	P ($ PER HOUR)	Q_s (HOURS)
v	$1	20
w	$2	40
x	$3	60
y	$4	80
z	$5	100

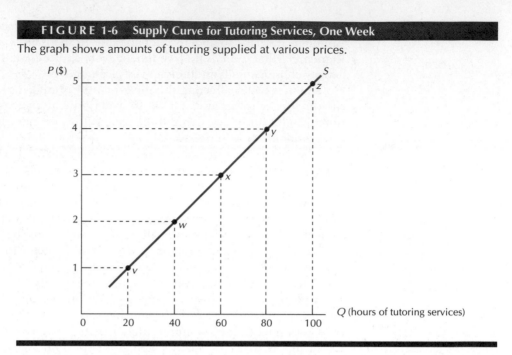

FIGURE 1-6 Supply Curve for Tutoring Services, One Week

The graph shows amounts of tutoring supplied at various prices.

graph. Connecting these points gives us the supply curve *S* in Figure 1-6. The supply curve indicates all possible combinations of quantity supplied and alternative prices with the assumption that all other factors affecting supply are held constant. Note that the supply curve is upward sloping, reflecting the law of supply: price and quantity supplied increase together.

What if one of the other factors affecting supply were to change? Baby-sitting costs might decrease so that some tutors would be more willing to provide tutoring services, for example. This would increase the supply of tutoring services. You can probably list other factors that would increase the supply of tutoring.

An increase in the supply of tutoring services will result in an entirely new supply schedule, such as the one shown in Table 1-5. Note that for each price, a larger quantity supplied now exists.

If we plot this new information on the same graph as the original supply curve, we have an entirely new supply curve *S'*, as indicated in Figure 1-7. Supply has increased, and the supply curve has shifted forward or to the right, showing increased quantities supplied at each of the given prices.

TABLE 1-5 Increased Supply Schedule for Tutoring Services, One Week

ALTERNATIVE	P ($ PER HOUR)	Q_s (HOURS)
v′	$1	60
w′	$2	80
x′	$3	100
y′	$4	120
z′	$5	140

If an event (such as an increase in baby-sitting costs) causing a decrease in the supply of tutoring were to occur, the supply curve would shift backward or to the left. Figure 1-8 shows a decrease in supply. The original supply curve is S. Note that there is a smaller quantity supplied at every price on supply curve S″ than on S.

FIGURE 1-7   Increased Supply of Tutoring Services, One Week

Supply curve S′ represents larger quantities of tutoring supplied at each price than does supply curve S.

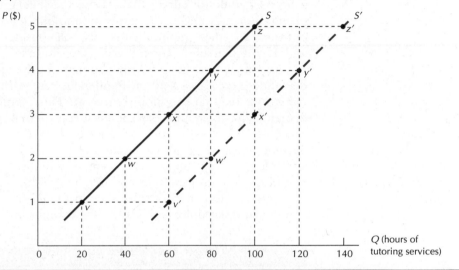

FIGURE 1-8   Decreased Supply of Tutoring Services, One Week

Supply curve S″ represents smaller quantities supplied at each price than does supply curve S.

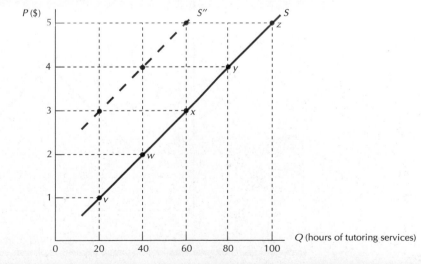

Putting Demand and Supply Together

The supply of words in the world market is plentiful but the demand is falling.

Lech Walesa, Polish trade union leader, politician,
Newsweek (November 27, 1989)

We can now consider the entire market for tutoring services at your school for the time period of one week. We have a demand schedule (or curve) that reflects the buyers' (students') attitudes toward purchasing tutoring services. And we have a supply schedule (or curve) that reflects the sellers' (tutors') attitudes toward supplying tutoring services. We simply have to put demand and supply together. Let's put them together graphically first. We will consider the original demand curve *D* and the original supply curve *S*, which are shown together in Figure 1-9.

As you can see, there is only one point in the graph (point *E*) where quantity demanded (which we read off the demand curve *D*) is equal to quantity supplied (which we read off the supply curve *S*). This point occurs at the intersection of demand and supply and corresponds to a price of $3 and quantities demanded and supplied of 60 hours a week. At point *E* the market for tutoring services is in **equilibrium,** or a state of balance, because the amount of tutoring services that students are willing and able to purchase is identical to the amount that tutors are willing to provide.

This equilibrium can also be seen in Table 1-6, which shows the original supply and demand schedules and (italics) the equilibrium price and quantity.

Equilibrium

A state of balance; a point at which quantity demanded equals quantity supplied.

FIGURE 1-9   Market for Tutoring Services, One Week

The market will clear at point *E*. At $3, quantity demanded equals quantity supplied.

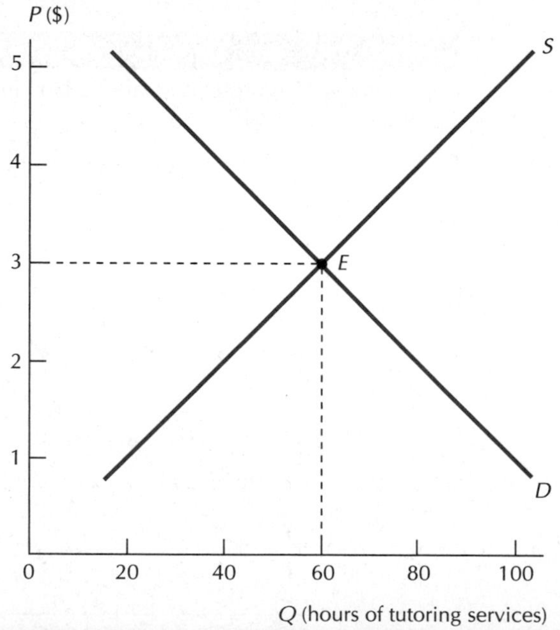

TABLE 1-6	Supply and Demand for Tutoring Services, One Week	
P ($ PER HOUR)	Q_s (HOURS)	Q_d (HOURS)
$1	20	100
$2	40	80
$3	*60*	*60*
$4	80	40
$5	100	20

Shortage
A situation in which quantity demanded is greater than quantity supplied.

The market for tutoring services naturally tends to move toward the equilibrium point. To illustrate this tendency, consider what would happen if tutors were charging less than the equilibrium price of $3 an hour. Suppose that the tutors were charging only $1 an hour. At $1 the quantity demanded (100) exceeds the quantity supplied (20) by 80 hours. There would be a **shortage** of tutoring services of 80 hours, because at $1 buyers regard tutoring as a bargain, whereas sellers have little incentive to provide tutoring. Students will bid for the tutoring services that are available, and in the process the price will be bid up. Put yourself in the position of a student who needs tutoring. You would quite likely offer slightly more than $1 to a tutor so that you would receive the tutoring instead of your friend. Your (former) friend would probably be trying to do the same. In this process the average price of tutoring would be pushed up. The bidding up of the price will continue only so long as the shortage exists, and as the price rises the shortage will disappear. Two things happen as price increases: (1) buyers decrease the quantity they demand, and (2) sellers increase the quantity they offer for sale. This process of rising price, decreasing quantity demanded, and increasing quantity supplied is shown in Figure 1-10 on page 16. The process will come to a screeching halt when equilibrium is reached at point *E*. Because the shortage no longer exists, the price will rise no higher. Economists usually refer to this phenomenon as the "rationing function of price." This means that the movement of the price has ultimately rationed away the shortage. Without the ability of prices to adjust by moving upward, the shortage would have persisted indefinitely. Socialist countries have often done just that—they have prohibited prices from adjusting upwards. As a result, shortages have been commonplace.

Now consider the opposite possibility. Tutors might be charging a price—say $5—that is above the equilibrium price. Perhaps they feel that they can make a lot of income at this high price. There is, however, a problem in the market at this price. At $5 an hour, the quantity (20 hours per week) of tutoring services demanded will be very small. But tutors will be willing to supply a large quantity (100 hours per week) because they have so much incentive. The difference between the quantity that tutors supply and the amount that students actually buy (quantity demanded) is a **surplus** of unsold services in the market. Surpluses cause price to fall. Tutors will undercut one another's price to get some business, and the price will fall until it reaches the $3 equilibrium. As the price decreases, quantity demanded will increase, quantity supplied will decrease, and the surplus will

Surplus
A situation in which quantity supplied is greater than quantity demanded.

FIGURE 1-10   Response to a Shortage of Tutoring Services

At a price of $1, quantity demanded exceeds quantity supplied by 80 hours. The 80-hour shortage will cause price to rise to the equilibrium price of $3.

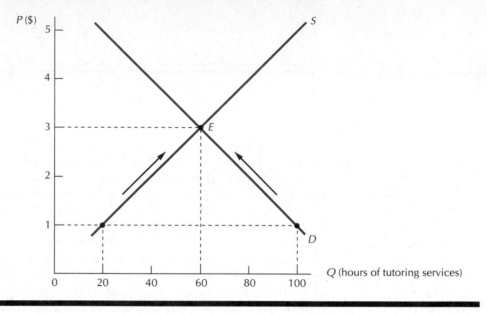

disappear. This process is illustrated in Figure 1-11. The process comes to a halt when equilibrium is reached. The falling price has rationed away the surplus.

Shifts in Demand and Supply

The market for tutoring services will remain in equilibrium at point E unless some other factor affecting the market changes. Because things rarely remain unchanged, it is important to consider what might happen if the variables affecting either the demand for or the supply of tutoring services were to change.

Consider our earlier example in which an increase in student incomes caused an increase in the demand for tutoring services. The only thing that we are doing differently now is considering this shift in demand in the context of demand, supply, and equilibrium. The demand curve will shift forward to D', as illustrated in Figure 1-12. Note that the supply curve *will not* shift.

The old demand curve D becomes irrelevant, and a new equilibrium E' exists at the intersection of the new demand curve D' and the old supply curve S. By reading the new equilibrium price and quantity, we see that price has increased to $4 an hour and that quantity has increased to 80 hours per week. Because demand has increased, the market price has increased, and suppliers have moved up their supply curve and increased the amount that they are willing to offer for sale (the quantity supplied). The increased demand curve and the unchanged supply curve have thus caused an increase in both equilibrium price and equilibrium quantity.

FIGURE 1-11   Response to a Surplus of Tutoring Services

At a price of $5, quantity supplied exceeds quantity demanded by 80 hours. This 80-hour surplus will cause price to fall to the equilibrium price of $3.

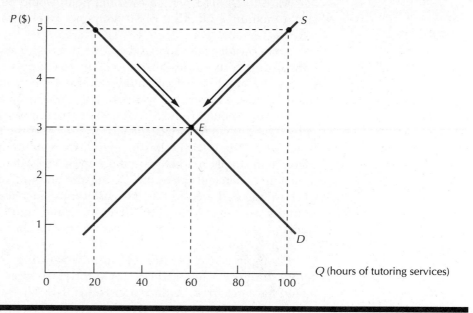

FIGURE 1-12   Effects of Increased Demand for Tutoring Services

The increase in demand from D to D' causes equilibrium price to increase from $3 to $4 and equilibrium quantity to increase from 60 to 80 hours.

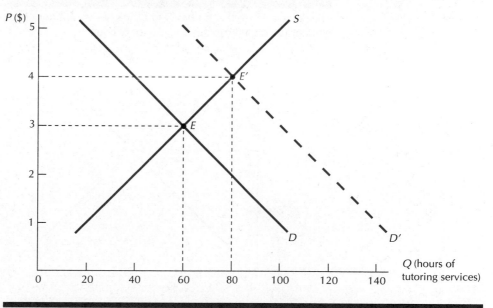

The opposite phenomenon would have occurred if there had been a decrease in demand. Such a decrease is shown in Figure 1-13. If student incomes had decreased, causing a decrease in demand, the demand curve would have shifted backward to D''. The new equilibrium point would be E'' at a price of $2 an hour and a quantity exchanged of 40 hours per week. Both price and quantity would have decreased.

Now consider the supply side of the tutoring market. Recall that a decrease in baby-sitting costs causes an increase in the supply of tutoring. If this increase occurs, the supply curve will shift forward but the demand curve will not shift. This phenomenon is illustrated by the shift of supply from S to S' in Figure 1-14.

The new equilibrium E' is found at the intersection of the original demand curve D and the new supply curve S'. We see that the price has decreased to $2 an hour, while the quantity has increased to 80 hours per week. As a result of an increase in supply, market price went down, so students (consumers) moved down along their demand curve, increasing the amount of tutoring services that they were willing and able to buy. Because supply increased, price decreased and the quantity exchanged increased. The increased supply curve and the unchanged demand curve have caused a decrease in equilibrium price and an increase in equilibrium quantity.

If supply had decreased because baby-sitting costs had increased, causing tutors to desire a higher price for tutoring services, the opposite phenomenon would have occurred. As shown in Figure 1-15, the supply curve would shift backward to S'' resulting in a new equilibrium E''. The price would be $4 an hour, and the quantity bought and sold would be 40 hours per week. The market price would be higher, but the equilibrium quantity would be lower.

FIGURE 1-13   Effects of Decreased Demand for Tutoring Services

The decrease in demand from D to D'' causes equilibrium price to fall from $3 to $2 and equilibrium quantity to fall from 60 to 40 hours.

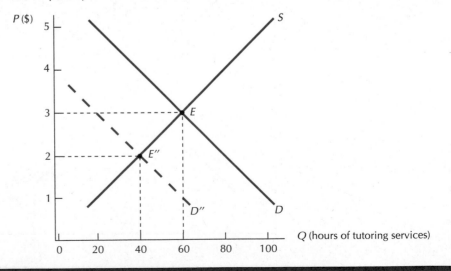

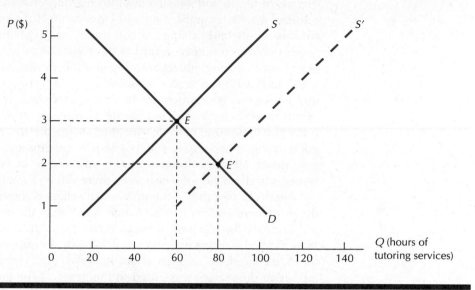

FIGURE 1-14   **Effects of an Increased Supply of Tutoring Services**

The increase in supply from S to S' will increase equilibrium quantity from 60 to 80 hours but decrease equilibrium price from $3 to $2.

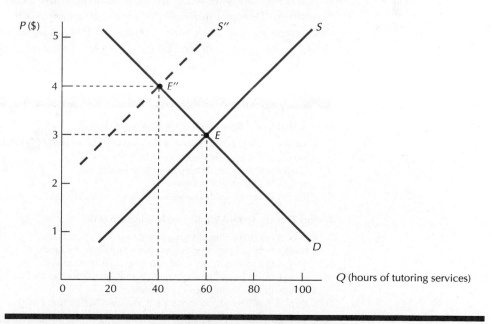

FIGURE 1-15   **Effects of a Decreased Supply of Tutoring Services**

The decrease in supply from S to S'' will increase equilibrium price from $3 to $4 and decrease equilibrium quantity from 60 to 40 hours.

The Real World

You now have learned the basic tools to answer many of life's economic questions. All markets have a demand (buyer's) side and a supply (seller's) side. And the things that affect supply and demand are the commonsense sorts of things described in the tutoring market example. Demand curves shift if the number of buyers changes, if consumers' incomes change, if consumers' tastes change, or if the prices of other goods that the consumers regard as substitutes or complements change. In our tutoring example, a substitute for tutoring might be buying and using the study guide that goes along with the textbook. Substitute relationships occur when the consumer uses less of one good whenever he or she uses more of the other. A classic example of substitutes is butter and margarine. Complements are the opposite of substitutes. If the consumer uses more of one good, he or she will also use more of the other. A good example of complementary goods is cameras and film. If the price of cameras goes down, all other things constant, more cameras will be purchased. With more cameras in the hands of consumers, there will be a greater demand for film.

Supply curves shift if the number of sellers changes or if the factors that affect the producers' (sellers') costs change. So a rise in the energy costs of a manufacturer will decrease the supply of manufactured goods. If businesses must pay higher wage rates to produce the same amount of output, the supply of output will decrease. On the other hand, if the price of raw materials goes down, the supply of the product for which the materials are used will increase. If the government taxes the production of a good or service, the supply of output will decrease; if the government provides subsidies (which lowers costs), however, the supply of the product will increase. Technological change that increases business efficiency and lowers the cost of producing each unit of output will increase the supply of output. Figure 1-16 shows the factors that commonly cause real-world demand or supply curves to shift.

Assume that you wake up some morning and read the following newspaper headlines: "Drought in Brazil destroys coffee crop. Coffee prices skyrocket!" "Pokemon craze sweeps the country. Prices of Pokemon toys soar!" "Boycott of grapes drives grape prices down. Grape growers dismayed." "Great weather results in

---

FIGURE 1-16   Factors That Cause Real-World Demand and Supply Curves to Shift

Factors That Cause Real-World Demand Curves to Shift

1. Changes in the number of consumers who wish to purchase the product.
2. Changes in the tastes of the consumers in the market.
3. Changes in the prices of complements or substitutes.
4. Changes in consumers' incomes.
5. Changes in consumers' expectations about the product's future price or availability.

Factors That Cause Real-World Supply Curves to Shift

1. Changes in the number of sellers in the market.
2. Changes in the prices of resources used to produce the product.
3. Changes in the technology used to produce the product.
4. Changes in the prices of other products that could be produced with the same resources.
5. Changes in government taxes or subsidies.
6. Changes in sellers' expectations about the product's future price.

bumper crop of pumpkins. Pumpkin prices plummet!" How would you explain these price changes?

If you follow a step-by-step procedure, it is not hard to answer this question. First, draw a graph showing the particular market (coffee, Pokemon merchandise, etc.) in equilibrium. Always label your equilibrium price and quantity. Second, consider the situation that is occurring. Decide whether its first and primary effect is on consumers or suppliers. Your answer will determine whether the demand or supply curve will shift. *You will shift only one curve in each graph!* Determine whether this curve should increase or decrease, and shift the curve accordingly. Third, find the new point of equilibrium and label the new equilibrium price and quantity. Finally, compare the new quantity with the old quantity and the new price with the old price. It's as easy as pumpkin pie when there is a bumper crop of pumpkins. See Figure 1-17 for the analysis of these newspaper headlines.

FIGURE 1-17   Newspaper Headlines: Demand and Supply

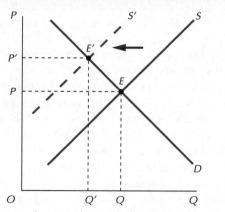

Drought in Brazil causes coffee supply to decrease, which causes a rise in coffee prices.

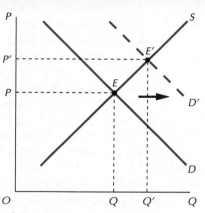

Pokemon craze causes demand to increase, raising the price of Pokemon toys.

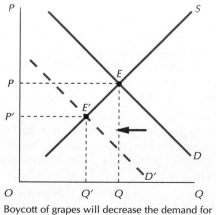

Boycott of grapes will decrease the demand for grapes, which causes the price of grapes to fall.

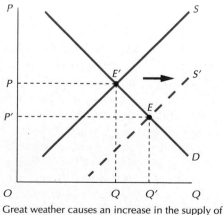

Great weather causes an increase in the supply of pumpkins, which causes a decrease in their price.

http://netec.wustl.edu/
JokEc.html
This site contains numerous
economics jokes.

Which Comes First?

Which came first, the chicken or the egg? Which comes first, the price or the quantity? We know that price determines both quantity demanded and quantity supplied. Yet demand and supply together determine the market price of the product. In a market economy it is the simultaneous interaction of all prices, quantities, demands, and supplies that ultimately determines the final market price and the market quantity exchanged.

THE MARKET: EFFICIENT BUT INEQUITABLE?

Understanding demand and supply gives us greater insight into the working of the market economy and its production possibilities, because demand and supply determine how much of each particular good or service is produced. High prices encourage frugality. Only those most willing (with the greatest desire) or most able (with the greatest income) will purchase the product at high prices. High prices also encourage producers to offer more for sale. The marketplace sifts out those with lesser preferences or lesser ability to afford the product, and the market thus serves as an allocating mechanism.

In many ways this function of market prices is desirable. Prices encourage thrift and careful choices among competing goods. Goods and services are allocated to those most willing to pay. Thus the market is an effective allocative device. Without prices, products might go to people who do not strongly desire them and be wasted. Shortages of highly desirable goods and surpluses of less desirable ones might occur. But in the market, prices ration away these shortages and surpluses, suggesting that the marketplace is very **efficient** as a means of allocation and distribution.

Efficient
Using resources in such a way as to maximize the output from them.

In other ways the distribution of goods and services may not be **equitable.** Equity is a value-laden concept, and economists cannot say whether a particular distribution is fair. But some of the results of market activity may not seem fair to some of us. A student may truly need tutoring services but not be able to afford them and thus fail the course. Children may go without milk, the homeless without shelter, and poor pregnant women without prenatal care because their low incomes render them unable to pay the prices that these things command. We might summarize by saying that the market entails both positive and negative aspects. It is often efficient, but not necessarily equitable.

Equitable
Fair.

Poverty is an issue of equity. We may argue that the inability of some people to meet their basic needs because they have low incomes is unfair. Housing is one example of a basic need that is often unmet, hence the growing numbers of people who are homeless or living in overcrowded or substandard housing. Also important is the issue of discrimination. To the extent that racism and sexism exist in our society, some people have less opportunity than others to receive their fair shares of our nation's income and output. The topics of discrimination, poverty, and homelessness are addressed in Chapters Six, Seven, and Eleven, along with the many policies that the government may use to address these problems.

In many ways our market-based economy serves us well. In some ways it does not. In addition to questions of equity, there are specific sets of circumstances—

http://economist.com
This is the site of the British periodical *The Economist*. Its articles on various topics can usually be understood by beginning students of economics.

economists call them "market failures"—in which the market does not result in an optimum outcome. Let us look at some of the failures of the market.

Public Goods and Services

Public goods and services have unique characteristics that make it unlikely that the market will provide enough of them. Therefore the government often provides them. Public goods and services include national defense, police and fire protection, roads and highways, and the like. At least to some point, the use of public goods and services by some of us does not keep others from using them. Your driving on the highway does not keep others from using it, for example.

Public goods and services are unlikely to be provided by the marketplace because they cannot be divided into small segments and offered for sale. Furthermore, they are usually subject to the "free rider problem." This means that if the private market provides them, it is difficult to keep people who do not pay for them from using them. Take fire protection, for example. Suppose the 100 merchants in the downtown section of your town decide to assess themselves each $500 annually to pay for fire protection. Ninety-nine of them pay their assessment, but one does not. The nonpayer's business catches on fire. Although this business has not paid its assessment, the other businesses cannot afford to let it burn. If it burns, it will endanger the properties of the other businesses. Fire protection is provided, and the nonpayer becomes a free rider. An alternative solution is to allow the government to provide fire protection and to pay for it through taxes.

Most economists agree that the provision of public goods and services is an appropriate role for government. Our disagreement concerns just what goods and services these will be, and how much of them we want. These disagreements are not trivial; they are taken up in the chapters addressing three important goods and services that some consider public goods: health care (Chapter Nine), education (Chapter Ten), and crime prevention (Chapter Thirteen).

In addition to markets for public goods, other markets in the U.S. economy are often considered too important to be left to the marketplace alone. A prime example is the market for agriculture. Food is basic to life, and we tend to see the farm family as the backbone of America. Issues pertaining to agriculture are considered in Chapter Two.

Spillovers

Spillovers
Costs or benefits of private market activity shifted onto society at large.

Economic efficiency and equity cannot occur when **spillovers** exist. An economic spillover occurs when some cost (or benefit) related to production or consumption "spills over" onto people not involved in the production or consumption of the good. Pollution of our environment is the most obvious example. If a manufacturer pollutes our air and water in the process of production, we will bear the costs of this pollution even if we don't own the company, work for the company, or buy its products.

We bear the costs in terms of greater risk of illness, less aesthetic beauty, and lower-quality environment. The manufacturer has shifted part of the costs of production to society at large. Our natural resources are not being used appropriately, and our economy is not addressing our real needs and concerns. Our own dissatisfaction with the degraded environment will not remedy the problem unless collectively we are able to channel our concern through active government involvement. Issues surrounding pollution and government response are addressed in Chapter Three.

Other goods and services provide spillover benefits to society. Education, discussed in Chapter Ten, provides significant spillover benefits to society. The educated person is likely to be a more productive worker and to contribute more than the uneducated person to the economy. The educated person is more likely to vote and otherwise participate in government and public affairs. The educated person is less likely to be chronically unemployed or to commit a violent crime. He or she is more likely to pay taxes and less likely to be on welfare. The market will not, by itself, provide sufficient levels of education, because the market does not reflect these spillover benefits.

Market Power

Pure competition
A market in which many independent producers compete to sell a standardized product to many independent buyers.

Our example of the demand and supply of tutoring services at a large university was one that approximates **pure competition.** There were many suppliers of tutoring services, so that no single tutor could dictate the market price. If 1 of 100 tutors were to charge an exorbitant price, students would seek the services of the other 99. Competition protects us from unreasonable prices.

We would not be protected if there were only one tutor. This monopoly supplier of tutoring services could charge a high price and consumers would be forced to pay it. Even if there were a few more tutors available, this small group could hold back-alley meetings and fix the price of their services at a very high level. Without competition, we would be at the mercy of this group. We would say that the individual supplier and the price-fixing group possess **market power,** which is the ability to influence the market price of its product. It is only with a large number of tutors—so many that it is unrealistic for them all to come to agreement about prices and so many that no individual supplier produces for a large share of the market—that market power is absent.

Market power
The ability to influence the market price of a product.

To the extent that many industries in the United States consist of just a few dominant producers (examples are the automobile, steel, and breakfast cereal industries), competition is reduced and society's well-being suffers. This problem of market power is discussed in Chapter Four.

Imperfect Information

For markets to operate efficiently, both buyers and sellers must have sufficient information to make rational decisions. But sometimes one or the other lacks necessary information. Prescription drugs may have harmful side effects of which the consumer is not aware. A producer may not be aware of all the properties of chemicals used to produce the firm's product. The consumer, worker, and health movements are intended to remedy the market failure of imperfect information.

Stability

Consumer price index (CPI)
A measure of the average price level.

Inflation
A rise in the average price level in the economy.

We have already considered the topic of production possibilities and employment. The factors that determine whether our nation will be *on* the production possibilities curve (operating at full employment) or *below* the production possibilities curve (with resources unemployed) are very volatile. Thus at times we may have very low unemployment, and at other times we may have high unemployment. Closely related are the factors affecting the average level of prices throughout our economy. One tool for measuring the average price level is the **consumer price index (CPI).** If the consumer price index in the economy rises, we say that we have **inflation.** Because prices and employment tend to fluctuate a great deal, we say that our market economy is inherently unstable. As we shall see in Chapter Fifteen, our government and the Federal Reserve System can intervene in many ways to ensure greater stability of prices and employment.

THE GOVERNMENT VS. THE FREE MARKET

We have already discovered that although the marketplace (demand and supply) tends to be efficient, it may not be equitable. We've recognized that many market failures exist and that many areas are considered too important to leave solely to the market. All of these indicate a proper role for government. Nevertheless, there is probably no debate more contentious in our economy than the relative importance of government versus the free market. As explained in the Foreword to the Student, liberals in the United States prefer to see a broader role for government in our economy. They feel that only then can the shortcomings of the marketplace be addressed. Conservatives, on the other hand, prefer to see a smaller role for government. The marketplace overall operates well, they argue, and government intervention may well make circumstances worse. You will have the opportunity to discover your own opinions about the government versus the market in the Viewpoint sections in each chapter of the text.

Closely related to this topic is the issue of how government activities will be financed. Certainly it costs to educate our public, ensure adequate housing and health care, assist farmers, control pollution, and monitor business to ensure competition and fairness. Government acquires financing in two basic ways. It receives tax revenues from the public, and it borrows by issuing government securities. Both methods raise a variety of issues and controversy, not the least of which is their effect on the national debt. These topics are considered in Chapter Sixteen.

MICROECONOMICS AND MACROECONOMICS

Microeconomics
The study of individual areas of activity within the total economy.

We've examined the production possibilities curve as a means of discussing scarcity. And we've studied the graphs of demand and supply to understand distribution. We will use these topics throughout the text to analyze a variety of microeconomic and macroeconomic issues. **Microeconomics** deals with individual areas of activity

Macroeconomics
The study of the total economy.

Gross domestic product (GDP)
Total output of an economy.

within the economy, whereas **macroeconomics** deals with the economy as a whole. Microeconomics covers topics such as the distribution of income within the country and the output within each individual market, whereas macroeconomics covers topics such as total income and total output in the economy. When we speak of total output, we are really referring to gross domestic product. More specifically, **gross domestic product (GDP)** is the value of an economy's total output of goods and services produced within a particular year.

GDP will be a very useful concept throughout the textbook because we often use it as a frame of reference. It is somewhat meaningless to talk of the millions of dollars spent on health care when a more meaningful topic of discussion is expenditures on health care relative to GDP, because GDP is really the nation's capacity to generate income that can be spent on health care or on any other good or service. Similarly, we find it useful to talk about the budget deficit as a share of GDP, or the national debt relative to GDP, and so on. Remembering just what we mean by GDP is therefore important.

PRIVATE VS. PUBLIC

Private
Individual people and businesses.

Public
Government.

The terms private and public are used throughout the text. The term **private** refers to individual people and businesses. It relates to *private* markets, which reflect consumer demand and producer supply. We speak of *private* spending (by people and businesses) and *private* ownership (by people and businesses). On the other hand, the term **public** refers to the government. Thus we can speak of *public* spending and *public* ownership. Recall that we have already used these terms as we considered private and public goods.

THE INTERNATIONAL ECONOMY

As our world becomes increasingly internationalized, awareness of the economics of domestic social issues is insufficient. We must also be aware of our international economy. We must enter into the exciting world of international trade and finance, the devastating world of international poverty, and the fascinating world of international issues addressed in Chapters Five, Eight, and Seventeen. The world is alive on our TV sets and computer screens, in our travels and contacts with international students and faculty, and in our jobs of the future. We must be aware of our world.

YOU AND THE WORLD AROUND YOU

We've come back to the topic we started with: that is *you*, the student. How do *you* fit into this world of economic problems and issues? What do these problems and issues mean for *your* life and well-being? And how can *you* affect the world around you? The Epilogue tackles these questions.

The way to begin making changes is to educate ourselves. With that in mind, let's begin to address our social and economic concerns!

Economics deals primarily with scarcity: how shall we allocate our limited world resources to satisfy our seemingly unlimited human wants? Limited resources translate into limited production possibilities. The production possibilities graph shows us the alternative combinations of the maximum amounts of two different goods that can be produced during any particular time period, assuming full use of our technology and resources. Unemployment of resources will result in production levels lower than those possible. Economic growth over time will result in increasingly higher levels of production of all goods.

Actual output and distribution decisions are made in the markets for individual goods and services. Demand for a product by consumers and supply of a product by producers both hinge on the prices that must be paid or received. Demand and supply together determine the market equilibrium, establishing the "going market price" and the quantity exchanged. Our market economy ensures that goods and services will be distributed only to those most willing and able to pay the market price. Markets are often considered to be efficient, but inequitable.

Market failures include the inadequate provision of public goods and services, the existence of spillovers, the presence of monopolies and imperfect information, and the lack of stability of our economy. An important issue is the role of government versus the free market. Economic liberals prefer a large role for government in the economy, and economic conservatives prefer a small role. As you continue your reading, you will make your own decisions about whether you are liberal or conservative on certain issues. Finally, you will consider your role within our world economy.

DISCUSSION QUESTIONS

1. *Suppose your friend is a hawk on defense and insists that we must bolster our national defense, whatever the cost. How can you use economic logic to make him aware of the opportunity costs associated with his objective?*

2. *Unemployment imposes serious hardship on out-of-work individuals and their families. What are some of the costs of unemployment to society as a whole? (Keep in mind the production possibilities curve.)*

3. *Why, in a rich nation, is it important that we fully use our resources and technology to maximize our nation's output? Is it only the level of total output that is important, or are the types of output that we produce also important? Do you think that the distribution of this output is just as important as its total amount?*

4. *How do you think our nation's output should be distributed—according to income, or according to some other standard?*

5. *Equilibrium implies that quantity demanded equals quantity supplied at a particular price. Must consumers and producers actually sit down to discuss and decide on an equilibrium market price? Why or why not?*

6. *Does the efficiency of the price mechanism ensure that our market-based economy is an equitable one? Why or why not?*

7. *The schedules below are for bushels of apples in a local market. Graph the supply and demand curves. What are the equilibrium price and quantity?*

Quantity Demanded	Price	Quantity Supplied
200	$20	1,000
400	$18	800
600	$16	600
800	$14	400
1,000	$12	200

Now assume that an early freeze has decreased the apple harvest, and the new supply schedule is as shown below. Has supply increased or decreased? What are the new equilibrium price and quantity?

Price	Quantity Supplied
$20	600
$18	400
$16	200
$14	0

CHAPTER 2

Agriculture

When the farmer comes to town with his wagon broken down,
Oh, the farmer is the man who feeds them all.
If you'll only look and see, I am sure you will agree
That the farmer is the man who feeds them all.
The farmer is the man lives on credit till the fall.
With the interest rate so high, it's a wonder he don't die,
For the mortgage man's the man who gets it all.
When the banker says he's broke, and the merchant's up in smoke,
They forget that it's the farmer feeds them all.
It would put them to the test if the farmer took a rest,
Then they'd know that it's the farmer feeds them all.

American folk song, from Alan Lomax, *Folk Songs of North America,* Doubleday, 1960

Indeed, as the folk song says, the farmer is the one who feeds them all. And in the United States, a relatively small body of farmers feeds a multitude of non-farmers. One person engaged in agriculture feeds about 130 nonfarmers. Less than 2 percent of the country's population is engaged in farming, but the country is well fed. Yet one hears of farm bankruptcies, and Willie Nelson holds FarmAid concerts to help the endangered farmer.

What is happening in agriculture? Should we worry about our food supply? In this chapter we will discuss the unique characteristics of American agriculture, the history and effects of government policy toward agriculture, and the outlook for agriculture in the future.

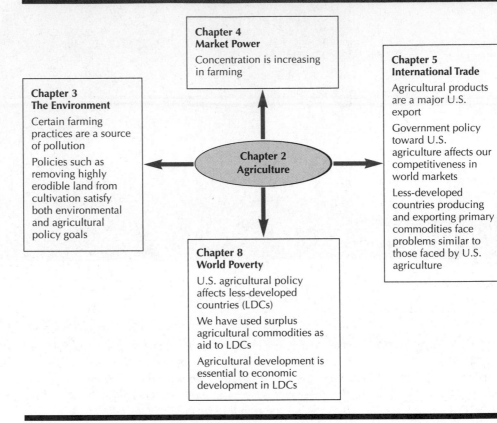

Chapter 4
Market Power

Concentration is increasing
in farming

Chapter 5
International Trade

Agricultural products
are a major U.S.
export

Government policy
toward U.S.
agriculture affects our
competitiveness in
world markets

Less-developed
countries producing
and exporting primary
commodities face
problems similar to
those faced by U.S.
agriculture

Chapter 3
The Environment

Certain farming
practices are a source
of pollution

Policies such as
removing highly
erodible land from
cultivation satisfy
both environmental
and agricultural
policy goals

Chapter 2
Agriculture

Chapter 8
World Poverty

U.S. agricultural policy
affects less-developed
countries (LDCs)

We have used surplus
agricultural commodities as
aid to LDCs

Agricultural development is
essential to economic
development in LDCs

CHARACTERISTICS OF AGRICULTURE

Certain characteristics of agriculture distinguish the farm sector from the remainder of the economy. The characteristics are

1. an inelastic demand for farm products,
2. extensive technological change in the past half-century, and
3. immobile resources.

Let's see how these characteristics affect farmers.

Inelastic Demand for Farm Products

Inelastic demand
Demand in which buyers
are relatively unresponsive to changes in price.

When we say that a product has **inelastic demand,** we mean that its buyers are relatively unresponsive to changes in its price. This means that buyers show little variation in the quantity they are willing to buy when the price changes. This is the case for most farm commodities, and the inelasticity of demand has considerable significance for farm prices and farmer's incomes. (A more complete discussion of elasticity is in the appendix to this chapter.)

Price Instability

Let's begin by looking at the significance of the inelastic demand for farm products. First, this inelasticity affects the stability of farm prices in the short run. If demand is inelastic, the small fluctuations in supply that might result from either exceptionally good or exceptionally bad weather will have a resounding effect on the prices that farmers receive for their product. Figure 2-1 illustrates this effect. Note that the demand curve shown is relatively steep. As will be explained in the appendix, inelastic demand is represented by relatively steep demand curves.

The graph in the figure shows a hypothetical demand curve for corn with an initial equilibrium price of $3 per bushel and an initial equilibrium quantity of five million bushels. Now consider an increase in supply from S to S' due to exceptionally good weather. The equilibrium quantity increases to six million bushels. Due to the relatively inelastic demand, the effect of the supply shift on market price is great. The increase in supply causes the price to fall all the way to $2 per bushel. Similarly, a decrease in supply due to poor weather (from S to S") would cause a large increase in price (all the way up to $4 per bushel). The combination of

---

FIGURE 2-1   The Effect of Inelasticity on Price and Farm Incomes

Because the demand for farm products is inelastic, an increase in supply from S to S' will cause a sharp decrease in price, as well as a decrease in farmers' incomes. Note that price falls from $3 to $2, while incomes decrease from $15 million to $12 million. Conversely, a decrease in supply to S" will increase price to $4 and increase total farm incomes to $16 million.

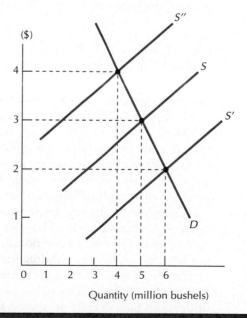

Quantity (million bushels)

weather-related supply fluctuations and inelastic demand results in large fluctuations in agricultural prices. (Note: Try drawing the same graph with a flatter demand curve. When demand is not inelastic, identical fluctuations in supply will cause much less price variation than when demand is inelastic.)

Farm Income

Now let's consider how farmers' incomes are affected by this inelastic demand. If demand is inelastic and price decreases, so will overall farm income. Income from a corn crop is equal to the number of units sold times the price at which they are sold. Refer again to Figure 2-1. At the initial price of $3, farmers sold five million bushels, earning income of $15 million from their corn crop. (Five million bushels times $3 per bushel is $15 million.) After the increase in supply, farmers sold six million bushels at a price of $2 per bushel. They earned only $12 million for their corn crop. Because the farmers have an inelastic demand, price decreases result in decreased farm income.

A factor that strongly influences the size of the total crop harvested by farmers is the weather. Sometimes the farm sector produces an unexpectedly large crop, so prices fall and farm incomes decrease. This is the classic farm problem of the **bumper crop,** or crop that turns out larger than planned because growing conditions are great. When better-than-usual weather causes supply to increase, price plummets, farm incomes fall, and consumers enjoy a windfall of low-cost food. Note that crop failures decrease supply and drive up prices, and overall farm incomes increase. But also note that we are referring to total farm income, not the income of individual farmers. The farmer who has lost an entire crop certainly will not have higher income.

Extensive Technological Change in the Past Half-Century

In the long run, technological change and slow growth in demand have caused the real prices of farm products to fall. Commercial farmers have not only adopted new techniques, but also use new, efficient (and expensive) machinery. New high-yield crop varieties exist. Intensive use of fertilizers and pesticides increases yield per acre. Artificial insemination and other improved breeding techniques have resulted in more reliable growth in cattle herds. Center-pivot irrigation systems dot the Great Plains. The results of these technological changes are a trend toward capital- and chemical-intensive agriculture, a movement toward large-scale farming enterprises, and a pronounced increase in the supply of farm products. Although the number of Americans engaged in agriculture is much smaller than a half-century ago, the supply of farm products has increased markedly.

Compared with the large increase in supply, the increase in Americans' demand for food over time has been relatively small. That increase is attributable mainly to an increase in our population. We have grown more affluent over time, but we have spent our additional income on things other than food. As a people we have been well fed for a great many years.

The combined effects of the huge increase in supply and the modest increase in demand have greatly decreased the **real price** of farm products. This change is

Bumper crop
Unexpectedly large crop resulting from good growing conditions.

Real price
Price adjusted for the effects of inflation.

not a year-to-year price fluctuation of the sort caused by agriculture's inelastic demand, but a long-run trend instead. The real price is the actual price adjusted for the effects of inflation in the economy. As inflation occurs, the dollar is worth less. So if a farmer is receiving the same actual number of dollars for a bushel of wheat in 2000 that was received in 1975, the farmer is receiving a lower real price. Those same dollars will buy fewer other goods, so the farmer receives less purchasing power per bushel of wheat.

In the 1960s the average U.S. family spent one-third of its income on food. Now we spend less than one-fifth of our income on food. One reason is the lower price of farm commodities compared with other goods. Figure 2-2 shows the effects of a small increase in demand and a large increase in supply on the market for farm commodities. Note that the equilibrium quantity is larger but that the real price has decreased.

Immobile Farm Resources

The principal resource used in farming is, of course, land. With the exception of land near rapidly growing cities, which can be developed, there are few alternative uses for most farm land. So although one farmer may leave farming and find a job in the city, land tends to remain in agriculture. Some other farmer buys the land

FIGURE 2-2   Effects of a Large Increase in Supply and a Smaller Increase in Demand on the Market for Farm Commodities

The larger increase in supply, coupled with the relatively small increase in demand, has caused the real prices of agricultural commodities to fall in the past 65 years.

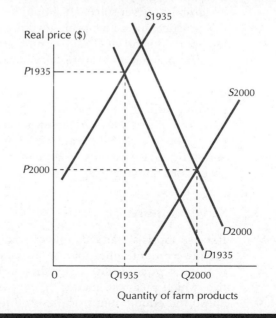

and continues to farm it. If real prices fell as precipitously in other sectors as they have in farming, resources would rapidly flow out of these markets into other markets that investors believe are more profitable. But land is not removed from agriculture. Either farm land lies fallow or someone farms it. Agriculture's main resource is slow to respond to adverse industry conditions.

Although the limited use to which farm land can be put undoubtedly contributes to this resource immobility, it can also be argued that the government's past agricultural policies have kept in agriculture resources that should have been transferred to other lines of production. Legislation in the 1990s, however, has reversed many of these policies.

GOVERNMENT POLICY TOWARD AGRICULTURE

The U.S. government has been extensively involved in agriculture since the Great Depression of the 1930s. The entire country (indeed, much of the world) was in distress during the 1930s, but agriculture suffered more than other sectors. The demand for farm exports declined greatly, as other countries imposed **protective tariffs** (taxes placed on imported products to protect domestic producers) in an unsuccessful attempt to keep the depression outside their own borders. Farm prices fell, and net farm income plummeted. Furthermore, the prices that farmers received for their crops decreased more than the prices that they paid for their inputs.

Because the price of farm products was too low to cover farmers' costs, the government initiated a variety of policies to assist farmers. Congress passed the Agricultural Adjustment Act in 1933 to restore income parity between farming and the rest of the economy. This was one of the first pieces of Franklin D. Roosevelt's New Deal legislation to be enacted. The government has been extensively involved in agriculture ever since. (It should be noted that the United States is not alone in this practice; most European governments also subsidize agriculture.) Next we will look at the history of U.S. government involvement in agriculture.

The objectives of farm policy have been to stabilize conditions in farming and to increase real farm incomes. Raising agricultural prices would serve both objectives. Accordingly, programs were devised to affect both the supply of agricultural products and the price received by farmers. Two policy instruments were used early on. These were **price supports** and **programs to restrict supply.** As time passed, price supports became less important policy instruments, and target prices and deficiency payments became more important. Let us discuss each of these policy options and its effect.

Price Supports

Price supports are an example of **administered prices**—that is, prices regulated by the government rather than set by market supply and demand. Price supports are minimum prices below which the market price is not allowed to fall. To be effective, which means to matter in the market, these minimum price floors must be above the equilibrium price level. Prices therefore cannot fall to the equilibrium level when surpluses occur in the market, and the price supports interfere with the

Protective tariffs
Taxes placed on imported goods to protect domestic producers.

Price supports
Legally fixed minimum prices.

Programs to restrict supply
Policies to decrease the amount produced and offered for sale.

Administered prices
Prices regulated by government.

TABLE 2-1	Demand and Supply of Wheat (hypothetical data)	
QUANTITY DEMANDED (MILLION BUSHELS)	PRICE	QUANTITY SUPPLIED (MILLION BUSHELS)
1,500	$4.50	4,500
2,000	$4.00	3,500
2,500	$3.50	2,500
3,000	$3.00	1,500
3,500	$2.50	500

Rationing function of price
Ability of flexible market price to clear the market of shortages and surpluses.

rationing function of price. As we discussed in Chapter One, markets tend to clear at an equilibrium price and quantity. In the process, shortages and surpluses are rationed away. This is the rationing function of price in a competitive market. Because price supports cannot fall to the equilibrium price, they cannot perform a rationing function. Look at the hypothetical data for the U.S. wheat market shown in Table 2-1, for example.

The equilibrium price is $3.50, at which both quantity demanded and quantity supplied equal 2,500 million bushels of wheat. At this equilibrium price, 2,500 million bushels will be exchanged and the market will clear. If price is temporarily above equilibrium, at $4, a surplus will exist in the market. Figure 2-3 shows the supply and demand data graphically, indicating the surplus at $4.

FIGURE 2-3   Wheat Market with Price Support

When a price support keeps the price of wheat from falling below $4, a surplus of 1,500 million bushels of wheat is created.

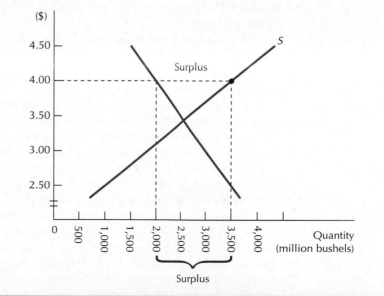

At the price of \$4, farmers produce and offer 3,500 million bushels for sale, but consumers are willing to buy only 2,000 million, so only 2,000 million bushels are exchanged. The remaining 1,500 million bushels are an unsold surplus in the market. If the price is free to fall, the surplus will cause it to decrease. It will fall as long as there is a surplus to push it down. As price falls, a message is sent to buyers: increase the amount you demand, because price is falling. An opposite message is sent to sellers: decrease the amount you supply, because price is falling. Buyers and sellers each move down their respective demand or supply curve. When the equilibrium price (\$3.50) is reached, quantity supplied equals quantity demanded, and there is no more surplus to drive the price down further. The falling price has rationed away the surplus. This process is what economists mean when they refer to the rationing function of price, which makes markets efficient means to allocate goods and services.

Now assume that the government had set the legal minimum price at \$4, so that price could not fall in response to the surplus. The surplus would *not* be rationed away. Instead, the market would have a persistent surplus of wheat. And that is what happens when the government supports the prices of farm commodities. The price supports actually create surpluses.

The method by which U.S. farm prices are supported is somewhat indirect, but the result is a minimum legal (support) price. Prices are supported by granting farmers loans on their stored commodities through the Commodity Credit Corporation (CCC), which was established in 1933 for this purpose. Farmers can get loans on the value of their commodities at a rate established by the government. They put up their commodities as collateral. If the market price is above the loan rate, the farmer can withdraw the commodity from storage, pay the storage, repay the loan, and sell the commodity. On the other hand, if the market price is below the support price, the farmer simply surrenders the commodity to the government instead of repaying the loan. The loan rate is therefore the effective price support. The government is the buyer of the surplus, and it is the government that bears the losses.

By means of price supports, income is redistributed to the farm sector from taxpayers in general. Whenever income is redistributed, some groups gain and others lose. Let's look at the losers and the gainers. Taxpayers, who are also consumers, are obvious losers. Their taxes are used to buy and store the surplus at artificially high prices, and the higher prices lead to at least slightly higher food prices. (We say "slightly" because most of the price you pay for food results from the costs of processing and distributing the food, not from the cost of the farm products themselves.) The support price makes U.S. farm commodities more expensive on world markets, so our farm sector is less competitive internationally. This comparative lack of competitiveness doubtless decreased our exports in the years when we had many high price supports.

The farm sector is the gainer, but in a manner that many taxpayers do not understand. The lion's share of the support goes to large farmers, because the subsidy is paid on a per-unit-of-output basis. Large-scale farmers produce more bushels (units of output), so they receive bigger subsidy payments from the government. This reality undoubtedly conflicts with the average citizen's vision of government farm programs helping small, struggling American farmers. Most of us picture small-scale production on the "family farm" when we think of farmers. Agricultural economists Willard W. Cochrane and C. Ford Runge refer to the average citizen's false image of agriculture as the "Little House on the Prairie" image.[1] The average voter is far more likely to support farm programs that he or she believes guarantee a decent living to the hard-pressed, hardworking small farmer than to support programs that offer huge subsidies to large farms.

Programs to Restrict Supply

Price supports have been combined with efforts to reduce supply. Refer again to Figure 2-3. Assume that government analysts believe that a "fair" price for farm commodities is $4. This price would cover the costs of production, including a **normal profit** for the average farmer. (A normal profit is the minimum profit needed to keep the farmer in business, and economists regard the normal profit as an element of cost.) One way to ensure that farmers receive $4 per bushel is to support the price at $4 and create a surplus in the process. Another method would be to shift the supply curve back to the point at which supply intersects demand at $4. The effects of this method are shown in Figure 2-4.

After the decrease in supply, the equilibrium price is $4, and the market clears with 2,000 million bushels of wheat being exchanged. There is no surplus for which the government is the buyer of last resort. There are no storage charges. There is no loss of the stored grain from rodents or simple deterioration with age. Programs to reduce the supply of farm products appeared preferable to rigid price supports in the 1930s, and these programs remain preferable today.

Normal profit
Minimum profit needed to keep a farmer in business.

http://www.cnic.org/nle/ag-2.html
This is the Congressional Research Service agriculture site. It contains good policy data.

FIGURE 2-4   Effects of a Supply Restriction Program on the Wheat Market

If the supply of wheat can be decreased from S to S' by a government program, the market price will increase from $3.50 to $4.

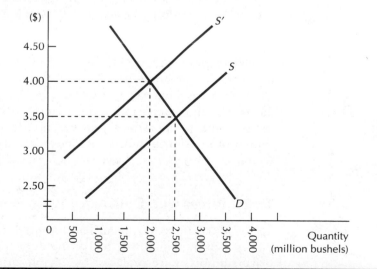

Accordingly, the history of farm policy in the United States is filled with efforts to reduce supply. Early efforts were voluntary and often involved land rent payments on acres taken out of the production of specific crops coupled with support prices on crops grown on the individual farmer's remaining land. Despite these attempts to control supply, the surpluses grew. The 1955–1956 Commodity Credit Corporation wheat inventory exceeded more than a year's production, for example. Commercial warehouses were filled. Abandoned schoolhouses and (in some cases) churches were used for storage. Consequently, efforts to restrict supply became more formal and far-reaching.

In 1956 the Soil Bank was instituted. It encouraged the long-term withdrawal of farmland from production of any crops and stricter compliance with acreage controls on specific crops. Farmers were paid for not farming. In subsequent legislation, supply restriction programs were continued under other names: the Set-Aside program, the Payment-in-Kind (PIK) program, and the "ten-year plan," which encourages farmers to put highly erodible acres in a long-term supply restriction program. Under the Set-Aside program, farmers were paid for setting aside and not farming a proportion of their total acres. They were guaranteed support prices on crops grown on their remaining acreage. Under the PIK program, they were given surplus commodities from the government's storehouses instead of cash, but PIK resembled the Set-Aside program in other respects. The ten-year plan (CRP) required a longer commitment to not farming acres and restricted alternative uses more than the two prior programs had done, but otherwise the programs were similar.

These supply restriction programs have not worked. Acres were taken out of cultivation, but supply continued to increase, pushing down market prices. Why? Put yourself in the place of the American farmer. Would you put your best or your worst land in the Set-Aside program? Of course you would put aside those swampy, poorly drained acres on which you get your tractor stuck every spring! You would be foolish to set aside well-drained, fertile acres in favor of your less productive land. And that is what farmers have done: they have put their poorest land into supply restriction programs and then farmed the remaining acres more intensively. If rows of corn are planted closer together, and irrigation and fertilization of the crop is increased, the supply of corn increases despite acreage reduction programs. Simply by behaving in an economically rational way, the farmer dooms supply restriction programs to failure.

Like price supports, supply restriction programs favor large farms over small farms. The more acres put into the supply restriction program, the larger will be the payment to the farmer. And like price supports, supply restriction programs represent a redistribution of income from taxpayers at large to the agricultural sector.

Target Prices with Deficiency Payments

By the 1960s the government had acquired huge surpluses under the price support program. Something had to be done. In many commodity markets, rigid price supports were replaced by flexible price supports based on past market

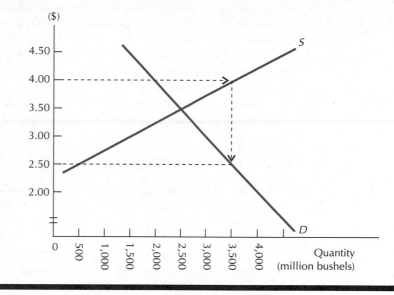

FIGURE 2-5   Effects of Target Pricing on the Wheat Market

With target prices, price is allowed to fall to the level that clears the market ($2.50); farmers receive deficiency payments for the difference between the target price ($4) and the market price ($2.50).

prices. These price supports (loan rates) were markedly lower than those used previously. They became a less important instrument of farm policy for most commodities, whereas **target prices** became a more important instrument. Under target pricing, farmers received direct payments. These payments were called **deficiency payments.** They covered the gap between the target price and the actual market price.

Figure 2-5 illustrates how target pricing works. Suppose that policymakers determine that a $4 target price is justified by the costs of producing wheat, but the market price is below $4. They establish $4 as the target price for wheat. At a target price of $4, farmers will offer 3,500 million bushels (quantity supplied) of wheat for sale.

Follow the arrow in the graph. The price at which buyers are willing to buy (quantity demanded) 3,500 million bushels is $2.50. So the price will fall to $2.50, and the entire quantity supplied by farmers will be purchased. Farmers will receive $2.50 from the market for a bushel of wheat, but the government will send them a check for the difference between the target price ($4) and the market price ($2.50). So for each bushel sold, the farmer will receive a government deficiency payment of $1.50. A farmer selling 10,000 bushels will receive a check for $15,000.

Target prices differ from the previously discussed price supports in a number of important ways. First, because the market price is much lower than the target price, the cost of farm commodities does not drive up the cost of food. Indeed, because target prices drive down the market price for farm products to below the

Target prices
Support program in which farmers will be paid the difference between the target and the market price.

Deficiency payment
Target price minus market price, times the number of units sold.

free-market equilibrium, food is made cheaper for buyers. Second, because prices are lower for consumers whether they are in the U.S. or the export market, American farm products are more competitive on world markets at the lower prices. Third, the market is less distorted by target prices than by price supports, because no surplus is created. Finally, the costs to taxpayers of target prices and deficiency payments are easier to count because the costs associated with surpluses are not incurred.

There are, of course, some similarities between price supports, target prices, and supply restriction programs. They all result in a transfer of income from taxpayers to farmers. They all favor large-scale farmers over small farmers. And all of these programs are aimed at the farm sector, or the supply side of the market. Other programs have been aimed at buyers, or the demand side of the market.

Efforts to Increase Demand

Efforts to decrease supply have been accompanied by various efforts to increase domestic and export demand. You are undoubtedly familiar with some of the programs used in an attempt to increase demand. Surplus commodities are distributed to the public school system for use in the school lunch program. (This practice explains some of the strange menus you encountered as an elementary-school student.) Food stamps are distributed to poor families so that they can purchase more food. Surplus commodities such as cheese have been distributed directly to the poor through various welfare agencies. The objectives of these programs are both humanitarian and pragmatic. Feeding the poor and seeing that schoolchildren receive a free or subsidized lunch are worthy humanitarian aims, but the pragmatic purposes of these programs are to increase the demand for agricultural products and to get rid of our surpluses.

Foreign demand for U.S. farm commodities has been affected by two types of programs: foreign food assistance programs (such as Food for Peace) and export subsidies. The foreign food assistance programs have been a means of disposing of surplus commodities abroad. When surpluses accumulate, distributions abroad increase. When surpluses are smaller, we send less humanitarian food aid to less-developed countries. In the world food crisis of the early 1970s, millions died of famine while the United States cut off food aid because surpluses had been drawn down. In many cases our Food for Peace program has done more harm than good to Third World residents, as is discussed in Chapter Eight.

Dumping
Exporting goods at prices below the cost of production.

The U.S. government has paid export subsidies to grain exporters and similar firms to lower the cost of exporting American commodities. This practice creates an increase in foreign demand for our agricultural products, because our prices are lower. Indeed, we have lowered the world price of some commodities so much that we have been accused of **dumping,** or selling our farm products abroad at prices well below cost. The decrease in the price of these commodities has greatly upset the other grain-producing and -exporting countries of the world, such as Canada and Australia, as you may imagine.

Efforts to increase the price of farm products to assist farmers by increasing demand have not been very effective. In most cases we have merely disposed of

accumulated surpluses. There is, however, some evidence that these programs meet their humanitarian objectives better than their farm program objectives. For instance, the Food Stamp program increases poor families' access to food.

Recent Changes in Agricultural Policy

In recent years the United States has attempted to coordinate and to change these various farm programs. In 1990, for example, farmers were first required to put some of their acreage in a supply restriction program if they were to participate in the deficiency payments program. Attempts were made to decrease farmers' incentives to continually increase yields and thereby receive more government payments by linking one year's eligible crop to the previous years. Finally, in 1996, Congress passed the so-called Freedom to Farm bill, which eliminated the target prices and deficiency payments on feed grains and wheat, although it did not affect such crops as peanuts and sugar. It replaced deficiency payments with income support payments based on acreage. Restrictions on what farmers could plant and remain eligible for government farm programs were virtually eliminated, an action that was viewed as a major step toward "getting the government out of farming." The income support payments were scheduled to last for seven years, after which these changes would be reviewed by Congress.

The effects of the Freedom to Farm Act have been what you probably would have predicted from reading the previous sections. At first farmers were delighted to have less government interference with their decisions about what (and how much) to plant. But the supplies of grains and other crops affected by the act have increased markedly, causing the market prices of corn and many other commodities to fall to historically low levels. Many farmers' incomes do not cover their costs. More farmers have left agriculture. And in response to a number of natural disasters, such as floods and droughts, as well as the adverse market conditions mentioned above, Congress passed emergency farm aid measures in 1998, 1999, and 2000.

AN EVALUATION OF U.S. FARM POLICY

Government policies have not solved the core farm problem of declining real incomes, and they have had some unforeseen side effects: by treating a symptom rather than a cause, they have contributed to an increasingly concentrated agricultural sector, promoted productive techniques that have harmful environmental consequences, and indirectly affected Third World nations in a disadvantageous manner.

Treating a Symptom

The low real price of farm products is a symptom of a resource allocation problem in the economy. We simply produce too many farm products in comparison with other goods. The solution to the problem is to decrease the resources devoted to farming. As long as prices are supported artificially, there will be an incentive to continue to overproduce. Indeed, government policies are a part of the farm problem because they encourage the retention in agriculture of resources that would otherwise leave farming and be used for other purposes.

Increasing Concentration in Agriculture

http://www.nass.usda.gov
This site has the *1997 Census of Agriculture,* the latest of the agricultural censuses.

A market is said to be concentrated if it contains a relatively few large firms. There is a trend toward greater **concentration** in agriculture. As we discussed previously, the "Little House on the Prairie" image of American agriculture is a false one today, but it was a more accurate image in the 1930s, when government involvement in agriculture began. The average farm was much smaller, and 25 percent of the population resided on farms.[2] Now less than 2 percent of the population is engaged in farming, and the average size of farms has greatly increased. In 1997 there were fewer than two million farms in the United States. But 3.6 percent of these farms produced 57 percent of our farm output, as measured by sales revenues.[3] The majority of farms are incorporated as businesses. The effects of concentration are discussed in more detail in Chapter Four.

Most farm subsidies have gone to a relatively few large farms, because subsidies have been designed to be paid on output or acres. In 1997 the largest 2 percent of farms that had sales of $10,000 or more received an average government payment of $75,142, whereas the smallest 73 percent of these farms (many of which were at least partially supported by off-farm earnings) received an average government payment of $3,322.[4] Over time these subsidies have led to fewer and larger farms, because the larger farms have been most helped by the government.

Harmful Environmental Effects

Another false image of American agriculture noted by Cochrane and Runge is that farmers are "stewards of the land" or protectors of the land and environment.[5] Farming is viewed as a healthy, wholesome way of life. In fact, modern farming has been reliant on chemical fertilizers to increase yield per acre to thereby obtain more government payments. It relies on pesticides to decrease insect damage and maximize yield. Nitrate pollution of wells in farm states is common. Studies have found 20 percent of wells in Kansas, Nebraska, and South Dakota to have nitrate levels considered unsafe. An Environmental Protection Agency study found 46 pesticides from agricultural use in the groundwater of 26 states.[6]

As people have left farming, they have been replaced by machines that are both expensive and dangerous. Farming is now one of the most dangerous sectors of the economy as measured by workplace accidents and deaths. Irrigation in the lower Midwest has damaged aquifers (underground water supplies serving large areas) but increased bushels per acre on which deficiency payments were earned. Commodity programs have encouraged the production of crops that are particularly likely to cause erosion, because these crops often have had high target prices. Farm life is neither particularly healthy nor environmentally benign. And our government programs have contributed to these adverse effects.

Conservatives have argued for a long time that price supports, target prices, and supply restriction programs have contributed to our farm problem instead of solving it. Because of these programs, our country simply allocates too many resources to agriculture, and we simply produce too much on our farms. Conservatives would therefore end virtually all farm programs and let market forces determine the outcome for farmers.

Liberals, on the other hand, do not see these programs as total failures. They point out that since the Great Depression of the 1930s, nearly one-fourth of our population has transferred from agriculture to other fields. They believe that our farm programs have made the exodus from farming more orderly and humane. Liberals do not wholeheartedly endorse the programs, however, and many believe that they should be gradually phased out. Their major objection to the programs is that the bulk of government payments go to large farms rather than small family farms.

Some economists argue that the increasing concentration of agriculture worsens the environmental problems associated with large-scale production. Huge cattle feed lots, factory hog farms, and dairies with 1,200 cows on relatively few acres create significant problems of odor and waste disposal. Realistically, we will never return to the idealized nation of small, family farms. We can, however, preserve the 500,000 or so medium-sized farms that remain if we adjust our national farm policy so that it no longer favors the largest producers. Policies that promote the greatest possible yield have proven self-defeating because they worsen the resource allocation problem and in the process increase concentration. Policies that promote a more diverse and less chemical-dependent agriculture appear to make more sense.

Effect on Third World Countries

Some economists argue that our heavily subsidized agriculture produces commodities that compete unfairly with those of less-developed countries (LDCs). The LDCs often rely on agricultural exports for much-needed foreign currency. If, for example, the price of rice produced in Arkansas is artificially low because of target pricing, Thailand's rice exports to the United States and our trading partners will be diminished. This is an especially serious problem because European countries, another major market for Third World agricultural exports, have policies similar to our own.

SUMMARY

Agriculture is characterized by inelastic demand, fluctuations in short-run supply, immobile resources, and such rapid technological change that supply has increased far more rapidly than demand. Thus agriculture has long been a troubled sector of the U.S. economy. Since the 1930s, government policies aimed at the farm problem have promoted the overallocation of resources to the agricultural sector. Furthermore, despite these policies, the proportion of our population engaged in farming has shrunk to below 2 percent. Supply restriction programs, price supports, and target prices have not saved the small American farm but instead have contributed to the farm problem. Concentration has increased in agriculture, in part because of our farm policies. Policies that promote the greatest possible yield have proved self-defeating because they worsen the resource allocation problem and in the process increase concentration.

Our farmers compete in an international arena. To compete effectively, they need to be efficient and produce low-cost products. Thus they need government policies that will not hamper their competitiveness by increasing their costs or prices.

Finally, our farm policies affect the rest of the world.

NOTES

1. Willard W. Cochrane and C. Ford Runge, *Reforming Farm Policy* (Ames, IA: Iowa State University Press, 1992), p. 21.
2. Ibid., p. 22.
3. *1997 Census of Agriculture Highlights,* Figure 2.
4. Calculated from the *1997 Census of Agriculture,* Table 5.
5. Cochrane and Runge, p. 24.
6. Testimony of Justin Ward, *The Intersection of Agricultural and Environmental Interests,* Hearings, U.S. Congress Joint Economic Committee (Washington, DC: U.S. Government Printing Office, 1992).

DISCUSSION QUESTIONS

1. *How does demand inelasticity affect farm prices and farmers' incomes?*

2. *How do target prices differ from price supports? Do different groups win or lose from these programs?*

3. *What is the direction of the trend in concentration in farming? How have government programs contributed to this trend?*

4. *How do administered prices interfere with the rationing function of price? Use price supports as an example.*

5. *Why don't supply restriction programs work to increase farm prices and incomes?*

6. *Do you believe that the government should be involved in agriculture? What kinds of policies would you suggest?*

7. *Has the Freedom to Farm Act solved the problems in U.S. agriculture? Why or why not?*

8. *(See the appendix to answer this question.) For what nonfarm products is demand likely to be inelastic? Why is this the case? For what types of products is demand more likely to be elastic?*

9. *Go to the Bureau of the Census Web site (http://www.census.gov). Click on A for agriculture. Go to the Agricultural Census. Look under "farm count" for the number of farms in your state.*

Chapter Two Appendix: Elasticity

Elasticity of demand is simply the responsiveness of buyers in the market to changes in the price of the product. When buyers are responsive to changes in the product's price, we say that demand is elastic. When buyers are not responsive to changes in the price of the product, we say that demand is inelastic, as described earlier in the chapter.

When we say that buyers are not responsive to a change in price, we mean that a change in price has little effect on the quantity that they are willing to buy. If demand were elastic, and buyers were responsive to changes in price, a change in price would have a significant effect on quantity demanded. Economists frequently describe elasticity by calculating an elasticity coefficient. The formula for the coefficient is:

$$\frac{\textit{Percentage Change in Quantity Demanded}}{\textit{Percentage Change in Price}}$$

If demand is elastic, the coefficient will have an absolute value greater than one, indicating that a relatively small percentage price change causes a larger percentage change in quantity demanded. However, if demand is inelastic, the coefficient's absolute value will be fractional, or less than one, indicating that a relatively large percentage change in price causes a smaller percentage change in quantity demanded.

The graphs in Figure 2-6 show the theoretical extremes of elasticity: perfect elasticity and perfect inelasticity. The demand in the graph on the left is perfectly

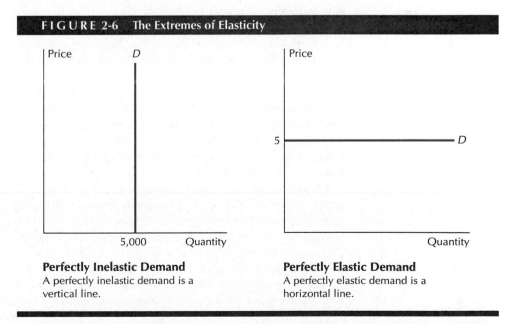

FIGURE 2-6   The Extremes of Elasticity

Perfectly Inelastic Demand
A perfectly inelastic demand is a vertical line.

Perfectly Elastic Demand
A perfectly elastic demand is a horizontal line.

FIGURE 2-7 Two Demand Curves of Varying Elasticity

D_1 is less elastic than demand curve D_2 at prices near their $4 intersection.

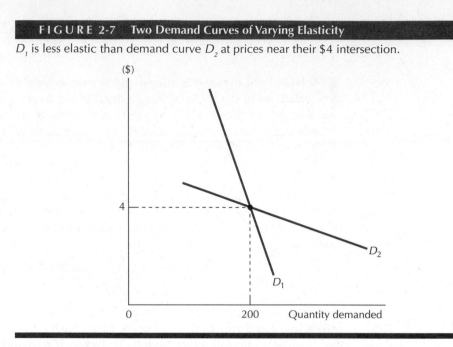

inelastic. Whatever happens to price, quantity demanded does not change, but remains at 5,000. There is absolutely no response to a change in price so we say that demand is perfectly inelastic. Perfectly inelastic demand curves are always drawn as vertical lines. The graph on the right in Figure 2-6 is a perfectly elastic demand curve. Perfectly elastic demand curves are always horizontal lines. Although price does not vary from $5, quantity demanded varies infinitely. This is the ultimate in elasticity (responsiveness).

Most demand curves are neither perfectly elastic nor perfectly inelastic. The more typical case of elasticity is related to both the location of the curve on the graph and its slope. If two demand curves intersect so that their location on the graph is very close, we can compare their elasticity in the region near their intersection by comparing their slopes. The flatter (closer to horizontal) curve will be more elastic. The steeper (closer to vertical) curve will be more inelastic.

Figure 2-7 shows two demand curves that intersect at $4 and a quantity of 200 units. Demand curve D_1 is more inelastic at prices near $4 and quantities near 200 than is D_2, which is flatter.

Elasticity has significant implications for changes in price and income when supply changes. The same increase in supply will result in a greater decrease in price if demand is inelastic than if demand is elastic. Figure 2-8 illustrates this phenomenon. The graph on the left illustrates that if demand is relatively inelastic, an increase in supply will cause a large decrease in price and a decrease in farmers' incomes. The graph on the right of the figure shows a more elastic demand. When an increase in supply increases the market equilibrium quantity to 6 million in both cases, price falls to $2 if demand is relatively inelastic, but only to $2.75 if

FIGURE 2-8   Two Demand Curves of Varying Elasticity

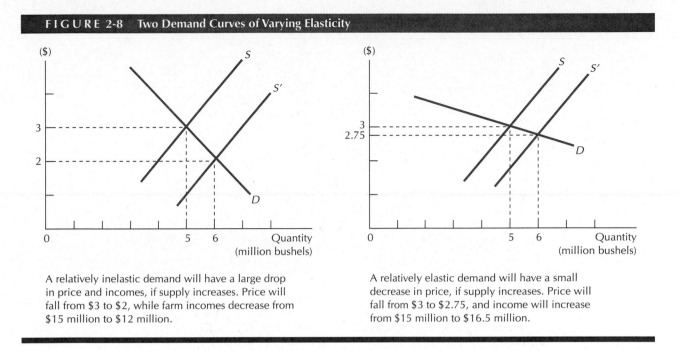

A relatively inelastic demand will have a large drop in price and incomes, if supply increases. Price will fall from $3 to $2, while farm incomes decrease from $15 million to $12 million.

A relatively elastic demand will have a small decrease in price, if supply increases. Price will fall from $3 to $2.75, and income will increase from $15 million to $16.5 million.

demand is relatively elastic. Income, which is the price of the product times the quantity sold, is also affected. When demand is relatively inelastic, income falls from $15 million to $12 million. When demand is relatively elastic, income increases from $15 million to $16.5 million.

CHAPTER 3

The Environment

The one who dies with the most toys wins.

Bumper sticker

Are you concerned about global warming? Acid rain? Ozone depletion? Deforestation of the rain forests? Desertification of once productive land? Pollution of our air and water? Extinction of species of animals and plants? Do you recycle some things? Do you try to conserve our natural resources? Do you support government policies to protect the environment?

Most (probably all) of us are concerned to some degree about environmental issues. In this chapter we will consider the economics of the environment. Let's start by saying that economic activity affects the environment, often in a harmful manner. Production of goods often causes pollution. Consumption of goods can also pollute. We often use our scarce resources inefficiently and unwisely.

In this chapter we will discuss the pollution created as a by-product of production. We will also discuss policies to limit pollution caused by industry; the environmental effects of consumption, conservation, and recycling; and the international dimensions of the environmental problem.

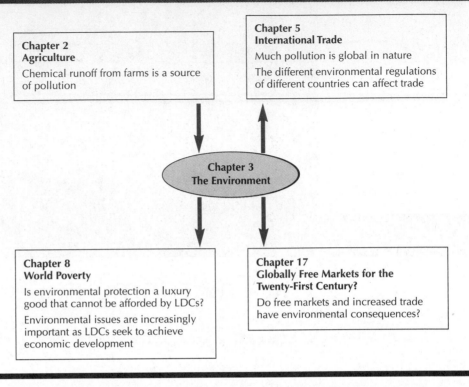

Chapter 2
Agriculture

Chemical runoff from farms is a source of pollution

Chapter 5
International Trade

Much pollution is global in nature

The different environmental regulations of different countries can affect trade

Chapter 3
The Environment

Chapter 8
World Poverty

Is environmental protection a luxury good that cannot be afforded by LDCs?

Environmental issues are increasingly important as LDCs seek to achieve economic development

Chapter 17
Globally Free Markets for the Twenty-First Century?

Do free markets and increased trade have environmental consequences?

THE PROBLEM OF POLLUTION

Pollution
Waste that is not recycled.

Let us define **pollution** as waste that is not recycled. Motor vehicles and industrial plants emit carbon monoxide, sulfur oxides, nitrogen oxides, and other hazardous compounds into the atmosphere, thereby polluting our air. The burning of fossil fuels releases carbon dioxide, which, along with other greenhouse gases, traps heat within the earth's atmosphere, thereby contributing to global warming. Deforestation of the rain forests causes the loss of precious biodiversity, while removing vegetation that could otherwise absorb the carbon dioxide that leads to global warming. Desertification occurs when deforested areas no longer prevent the shift of desert sands onto previously fertile soil. The release of certain chemicals, primarily chlorofluorocarbons (CFCs), damages the ozone layer of our atmosphere, thereby allowing in dangerous levels of ultraviolet radiation from the sun. Industrial wastes, leaking septic tanks and landfills, and pesticides contaminate aquifers and threaten our water supply.

In all of these cases, environmental damage is an unplanned and harmful by-product of economic activity. The problems caused by pollution are twofold: spillover costs and inefficient resource allocation. These problems are discussed in the sections that follow.

Spillover Costs and Benefits

Pollution is the classic example of an economic externality. An **externality** is simply a cost or benefit of an economic activity that spills over onto the rest of society. Externalities can be positive or negative. Pollution represents a negative externality, or **spillover cost.** Although firms that pollute incur the private costs of production such as wages and energy costs, they do not bear the entire cost of production. A portion of the production costs, specifically the pollution, spills over onto society. The polluter's accounting books do not take into account the effects of pollution. Instead, society bears the burden of this pollution cost in the form of poorer health and productivity, higher health care expenses, greater cleaning costs, damage to buildings and forests, aesthetic displeasure, and so on. Other businesses bear the burden of the pollution cost in the form of damage to capital structures and machinery, damage to crops and needed resources, and so forth. We, as a society, either tolerate the environmental degradation or clean up someone else's mess with our tax dollars. This inequitable burden of costs is one of the chief economic characteristics of pollution. All negative externalities involve costs created by an economic activity and shifted to other firms or individuals outside that economic activity. This situation is not an equitable one.

Pollution is not the only negative externality that is common in our lives. Consider your dismay if you live near a newly constructed airport or highway. You will bear the burden of the noise pollution that results. Or imagine living in a heavily populated area, driving on heavily congested streets and freeways, and experiencing time delays and a greater probability of accidents. You would bear costs of congestion. These too are negative externalities.

Not all spillover costs are caused by businesses. We consumers create some negative externalities. A good example is our use of the automobile. As you know, Americans love their cars, and as a result are reluctant to carpool or take public transportation. We incur private costs associated with driving: car payments, insurance, gas, oil, maintenance costs, taxes and license fees, and parking expenses. Society, however, bears a portion of the total costs of our driving in the form of the air pollution caused by auto emissions. Another example might be our use of throwaway bottles and cans. We consumers pay for the product, but society bears a burden in the form of litter, solid waste, and an inefficient use of scarce resources. All negative externalities involve costs imposed on others who do not benefit from the production or consumption of the product.

Externalities can also be positive. We call positive externalities **spillover benefits.** Education is a classic example of a service that yields spillover benefits. You, the student, will benefit most directly from your education. You are likely to earn a higher income, to have a job you enjoy, and to have a richer intellectual life if you are educated. But society also benefits. College graduates tend to be better-informed citizens. They are less likely to be chronically unemployed. They are more likely to vote. They are less likely to commit crimes, or at least violent crimes. They are often more productive workers. So spillover benefits are conferred on society. Because society receives these benefits, most people feel that society is justified in bearing part of the costs of education through tax revenues.

Another spillover benefit comes to society through immunization of your children against common childhood diseases. You pay for the shots and vaccinations, and your family receives most of the benefits in the form of decreased risk of measles, smallpox, and polio. Others in society benefit as well, however. Other children, even if not immunized, are less likely to contract these diseases because the diseases will not be so prevalent. The families of nonimmunized children benefit without bearing any of the cost. Society benefits in terms of lower medical expenses. The burden of costs is inequitable if you are not in some way compensated for the benefits you provide society.

Inefficient Resource Allocation

As we have noted, externalities can shift costs to groups that did not incur them, and benefits to groups that did not earn them. In addition, externalities can cause resources to be inefficiently allocated. Simply put, we produce and consume too much (overallocate resources) if negative externalities are present, and we produce and consume too little (underallocate resources) if positive externalities (such as benefits to nonimmunized children) exist. Let's look at the effects of pollution on the market for a good produced by firms that hypothetically pollute the environment. Let's use spring vacation air travel to the Bahamas during one week in March as the product.

The Effects of Pollution in a Single Market

First consider the hypothetical market demand curve for air travel to the Bahamas. Remember that demand reflects the value of the product to consumers in society, because it represents the prices that consumers are willing to pay for a ticket to the Bahamas. D is the market demand curve in Figure 3-1.

Now let's consider the supply of air transportation to the Bahamas. Remember that we defined pollution as waste that is not recycled. The amount of pollutants emitted by firms will increase proportionately with output. But low levels of output will not result in spillover costs, because the natural processes of the earth can absorb and reprocess a certain amount of waste (pollutants). If production increases beyond the level that natural processes can handle, we incur pollution and spillover costs.

Suppose that natural processes can absorb the hypothetical air and noise pollutants that we create if we provide 2,000 units of output (passenger tickets), but that if we provide more than 2,000, we exceed the earth's capacity to cleanse itself. (Pretend that college students flying to the Bahamas during this particular week in March represent the *only* people traveling by air.) After the production of 2,000 units of output, then, we have a negative externality.

Curve S_p in Figure 3-1 is the hypothetical private market supply curve. This curve is based on firms' (airlines') private costs of production but does not reflect the full **social costs of production** when pollution occurs. These social costs of production include both the private costs to the producer and the spillover costs borne by society. Curve S_s is the hypothetical social supply curve. This curve is higher in the graph (in terms of the dollar axis) than the private supply curve,

Social costs of production
The total costs of production, including private costs and spillover costs.

Hypothetical air and noise pollution increase the social costs above the private costs of
providing air travel. This rise in social costs causes the private market equilibrium price to be
too low, resulting in the overallocation of resources to air travel.

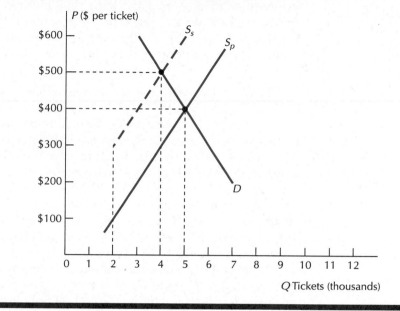

reflecting the higher social costs of production. The vertical distance between S_p
and S_s at each level of output is the hypothetical amount of the spillover cost.

The private-market supply curve intersects with the demand curve at a quantity of 5,000 units (tickets to the Bahamas) and a price of $400 per person. Note,
however, that the social supply curve intersects with demand at only 4,000 units
and a price of $500. The free-market supply curve results in output that is too
high, because it is based on a cost that is too low. (Markets base their output levels
on the private costs of production only, whereas the socially optimal level of output is based on the full social costs of production. This is because we wish to balance our desire for the product with the full social costs of production.) Because
the free market results in too much output, we say there is an **overallocation of
resources** to the production of this product. Too much output may not sound like
a problem, but remember that society has scarce resources. Too much production
of a product that society doesn't want (especially when it causes pollution) means
too little production of products that society does want. Inefficient allocation of
resources means that society's preferences are not being met.

Note an essential difference between the economist's view of the market and
the environmentalist's. The socially correct quantity in Figure 3-1 is 4,000 units,
and at this quantity we will have some pollution. The environmentalist's goal
would be to eliminate all pollution, but if we do that we have to cut production to
2,000 units. Most economists believe that if all costs are accurately reflected in the

**Overallocation of
resources**
The production of more
than the socially opti-
mum amount of a good
or service.

supply curve, and society's values are accurately reflected in the demand curve, the market output is efficient and desirable. Society values those extra 2,000 units enough to be willing to bear the cost of the pollution that accompanies them. In the region between 2,000 units (no pollution) and 4,000 units (socially desirable output), the demand curve is above the social supply curve, indicating that society values these units of the good more than it costs to manufacture them, including the costs of pollution. Thus economists would not recommend cutting back production to 2,000 units to eliminate all pollution. (And students heading for the Bahamas during spring break can breathe a collective sigh of relief!)

The Effects on One Market of Pollution in Another Market

Now let's consider a hypothetical case of resource allocation between two industries, the paper industry and the beer industry, to understand how the actions of firms in one industry can affect those in others. To simplify, the demand and supply curves for the two industries are drawn identically in Figure 3-2. Initially we assume no pollution and no spillover costs. The market equilibrium of price P_1 and quantity Q_1 in each market is the socially desirable price and quantity. Now suppose that firms in the paper industry decide it is too expensive to prevent pollution, and they begin to dump by-products and waste into the river nearby. They save on production costs, but cause water pollution. Decreased private costs of production will shift the firms' supply curve forward to S_2 (for the firms' private costs will not include the costs of pollution). The market equilibrium price and quantity are now P_2 and Q_2, respectively. Too much paper is being produced and consumed at a price that does not reflect the costs of pollution.

FIGURE 3-2   Effects of Water Pollution in the Hypothetical Markets for Paper and Beer

Pollution causes overallocation of resources to the polluting industry (here the paper industry). As a result, resources are underallocated to other industries (here the beer industry).

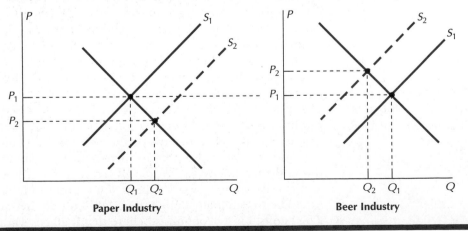

Paper Industry   Beer Industry

The beer industry, which uses water as an input to beer production, will be adversely affected by the paper companies' actions. Assume that the beer industry has breweries located downstream on the river. Because polluted water will not produce beer that is safe and good-tasting, beer-producing firms in the land of sky blue waters have to clean up the water before they use it for brewing. The beer industry therefore incurs private costs in purifying the water, shifting the beer industry's supply curve back to S_2. This decrease in the supply of beer causes an increase in equilibrium price to P_2 and a decrease in equilibrium quantity to Q_2. We consume less beer at higher prices.

Thus the externality in the paper market not only shifts the pollution costs to society at large, but also causes a distortion of resource allocation in other markets, namely the **underallocation of resources** in the beer market. We are consuming more paper and less beer than we would if not for the pollution. To most economists, an essential problem with pollution (or any other externality for that matter) is that it causes resource allocation to be distorted.

Underallocation of resources
The production of less than the socially optimum amount of a good or service.

ENVIRONMENTAL POLICIES AND POLITICS

Air and water pollution are certainly not new phenomena. In 1858 London was stricken by the "Great Stink" caused by the dumping of wastes and garbage into the Thames River. We tend to romanticize the past as a cleaner, better environment, but this view ignores much of our environmental history. The horse-drawn carriage left its own brand of pollution behind it.

Widespread concern about environmental quality is a recent phenomenon, despite our history of environmental problems. It began in the 1960s and was confined mainly to the United States and other economically advanced countries. Why did environmental concern occur so late, and why was it localized in these countries? First, growth in population, accompanied by increases in output, has greatly increased the amounts of pollutants released into the air and water. Inevitably, the quantity of these pollutants has exceeded the natural cleansing abilities of the earth. And the effects are pervasive. The cities of Victorian England may have been grimy, unpleasant, and possibly hazardous to inhabitants' health, but the middle and upper classes could easily avoid these effects by moving to the pleasant, agrarian countryside. This strategy no longer works. Pollution follows us to our rural hideaways.

Second, the degree of peril occasioned by pollutants is greater today than it was in preceding centuries. Nuclear wastes and PCBs are significantly different from the pollutants that plagued our grandparents. Complex technologies have produced pollutants of which they never dreamed. The news that the polar icecap seems to be melting and the very real threat of global warming are problems of a different magnitude than those experienced by previous generations.

Luxury good
A commodity for which demand is highly sensitive to changes in income.

Finally, we have become more affluent, and the demand for environmental quality has increased markedly. Environmental quality is a **luxury good,** or a commodity with a demand extremely sensitive to increases in income. Once society's basic needs for food, clothing, and shelter have been met, citizens begin expecting other things, such as a healthier and higher-quality environment. These three factors explain why the environmental movement is both recent and a product of affluent, economically advanced countries.

ENVIRONMENTAL LEGISLATION

Environmental legislation is based on the fact that spillover costs and misallocation of resources result from externalities unless the government takes a role in controlling the situation. We cannot expect business firms, which are motivated by profit maximization, to take a strong stand against pollution if they are not compelled to do so through regulation or encouraged to do so by economic incentives. Nor will most consumers make major efforts to reduce their pollution unless forced to do so or provided with economic incentives.

http://www.epa.gov
The Environmental Protection Agency site contains information about EPA policy and environmental issues. Most of the issues are not discussed from an economic perspective.

Environmental regulation grew out of a grassroots movement, and therefore many initiatives were at the local level. Chicago and Cincinnati enacted laws to control smoke emissions from factories and power plants in the 1880s, before there was an environmental movement as such. Many other cities subsequently followed their lead. In fact, the federal government did not become involved in controlling air pollution until the 1950s. The Air Pollution Act of 1955 was a federal call for research into the problem. This call was followed by the Clean Air Act of 1963 to control air pollution and the Clean Air Act of 1970 to enforce national clean air standards. Of special concern were automobile emissions, which contributed greatly to the smog plaguing the nation's cities.

The Environmental Protection Agency (EPA) was formed by executive order in 1970 to administer all the environmental laws and to do whatever was necessary to achieve healthy air by 1975. (The deadline was later extended.) The Federal Water Pollution Act of 1972 mandated the EPA to eliminate discharges into the nation's waterways by 1985.

The environmental disaster of the Love Canal made the nation aware of the problem of hazardous waste. Throughout the 1950s, the Hooker Chemical and Plastics Company, as well as certain federal agencies, put waste into an old canal excavation near Niagara Falls, New York. Eventually the landfill was sealed, and a school and housing development were built in the area. Toxic wastes bubbled to the surface and ended up in storm sewers, gardens, basements, and the school playground. In response to the environmental disaster of the Love Canal, the Comprehensive Environmental Response, Compensation, and Liability Act of 1980 established the Superfund to clean up hazardous waste. It also gave the EPA significant enforcement authority to hold identified responsible parties liable for the cost of cleanup.

Because the federal government as well as state and local governments have been involved in regulation for environmental protection, it is important to address the issue of the proper level of government to handle environmental regulation. Some people argue that the federal government is characterized by a huge bureaucracy that is far from the people it governs and unresponsive to the people's needs. The EPA, they argue, is slow to respond to local needs and insensitive to local opinion. They feel that local, or regional, regulation would be more sensitive and responsive. Conservative representatives to Congress have generally taken a strong stand against federal regulations, including those that protect the environment.

Although local regulation keeps government closer to the governed, the federal level may be the more appropriate level of government to regulate the environment. One reason is that whatever the source of air and water pollution, the problem affects neighboring communities, states, and even countries. Acid rain originating in the United States but damaging property in Canada has become a heated issue between the two nations. Global warming and ozone depletion are also global phenomena.

At the same time, local communities, acting in their own perceived self-interest, may be lax in setting standards to control air and water pollution. By tolerating pollution they may attract industry and increase the jobs available for their citizens. As long as some pollution affects other jurisdictions, localities have an incentive to underregulate their own pollution sources. Indeed, a major cause of acid rain is the sulfur dioxide emitted into the atmosphere by the tall smokestacks of coal-burning electric utilities. The smokestacks were built to conform with local standards for air pollution, and they protect the local community but emit pollutants that damage distant communities. They were (and are) considerably less expensive than scrubbers, which are designed to eliminate most of the pollutants at the source. The localities export the problem rather than solve it. Federal legislation helps minimize the disparity of pollution control standards that would exist if regulation were left to individual localities and states.

Furthermore, the states have widely differing resources. The federal government has a larger tax base than any state, and it has greater ability to finance pollution control activities. It can also mitigate the burden of pollution control by transferring income from affluent states to poorer states. Although pollution control policy might be administered at a variety of government levels, the jurisdiction for setting pollution control standards should be large enough to capture all the negative spillovers. Thus decisions about pollution control are most appropriately made at the national, or even international, level.

METHODS OF REGULATION

Government agencies, at any level, use the following methods to limit adverse environmental effects: (1) standards, (2) pollution fees, and (3) pollution permits.

The Standards Approach

Let's look at the standards approach to pollution control first. This approach is the easiest to understand and the one originally used by environmental agencies.

Using the Standards Approach

Standards
Acceptable levels of performance.

With the **standards** approach, maximum acceptable levels of pollutants are established, and firms that exceed these levels are punished, usually by fines. Firms can thus be forced into compliance with the standard.

The logic of the standards approach is clear, and the process appears simple. But this approach is more complex than it at first appears. The agency must first set the standards, then enforce them. In addition, it should continually explore new technical possibilities and evaluate its programs.

Standards may be broad or narrow. A broad water-purity standard might be "swimmable rivers." A narrow standard might be "less than 0.5 percent lead" in paint. The broad standard is vague and general, a statement of what is desirable. As a result, it is not possible to enforce on an individual-firm basis. For enforcement and prosecution, narrow standards are necessary. A firm producing paint that contains more than a half a percent of lead is obviously in violation of the narrow lead-content standard.

Performance standard
Specifies the required level of performance but not the means of compliance.

Standards may also be classified as performance standards or design standards. A **performance standard** specifies a certain level of performance or compliance that must be met. It does not specify the means by which that level must be reached. The regulating agency might require the firm to reduce the pollutants emitted in a combustion process by 10 percent, without specifying the means by which this standard will be met. A **design standard,** on the other hand, specifies not only the required level of performance but also the means to reach that level. Control of auto emissions by the installation of catalytic converters is an example of a design standard. A performance standard leaves the compliance method up to the regulated firm. It is more flexible than the design standard and may encourage research into new technologies and lower-cost methods to meet pollution reduction goals. In practice, both types of standards are used.

Design standard
Specifies both the required level of performance and the means of compliance.

Certification
License to produce a product that meets pollution standards or to use a technique that meets an environmental goal.

Once narrow enforceable standards are set, they must be put into operation. Implementing the standards may begin with **certification,** or the issuance of a permit for the firm to use a technique or produce a product variant. An example would be the issuance of a permit to an automobile company to produce a new engine design that has been shown to meet pollution performance standards. Certification is in the best interests not only of the public but also of the regulated firm. The firm learns that the engine design either meets or does not meet the environmental performance standard before it invests vast sums of money in the engine's production.

Monitoring
Testing to check that standards are being met.

Enforcement also involves **monitoring** firms' compliance by sampling and testing the samples. Are gases or particulates being emitted into the air at a greater level than that permitted by the standard? Is a plant's "purified" sewage clear enough to be dumped into the nearby river? The only way to answer these questions is by sampling the wastes emitted by the plant. Tremendous numbers of enforcement personnel are required for this task. Budgets limit the number of employees and therefore the number of samples taken.

Field surveillance
Inspections for compliance with standards.

Field surveillance is the third enforcement activity. It is a means of double-checking or confirming the results of the sample monitoring. An example would be the annual automobile inspections required in some states. These inspections are meant to catch catalytic converters that are no longer functioning to neutralize carbon monoxide emissions, as well as other environmental and safety hazards. Field surveillance includes the regulatory agency's response to complaints from the public. It also involves follow-up by qualified inspectors, whether they are employed by, or merely approved by, the agency.

Finally, **remedies** must be imposed on those who do not meet the standards. Violators must be forced into compliance. The most common remedy is fines for noncompliance. If the fine is significantly lower than the cost of compliance, the firm may pay the fine without changing its actions. If the fine is unreasonably high, the firm may appeal its imposition to the courts, adding to both the firm's and the government's costs. Litigation is expensive as well as time-consuming.

Instead of being charged a fine, a plant may be temporarily closed until it reaches compliance with the standard. While the plant is closed it will continue to incur the costs of inventory. It may be unable to fill orders for its products. Valued employees may find other jobs. Individual corporate officers can be held liable and prosecuted for particularly harmful and hazardous environmental activities. To force the firm to comply, the remedy cannot be trivial. At the same time, it should not be so severe that it forces the firm out of business. The goal is to eliminate pollution, not businesses.

Issues in Using the Standards Approach

There are many issues involved in using the standards approach to environmental regulation. Since this is the most common means of regulating pollution, it is useful to consider the most controversial of these issues: uniform standards and technology forcing.

Uniform Standards. **Uniform standards** are fairly general standards that cover a wide range of situations and firms. An example might be that all firms reduce their discharges of waste into a river by 70 percent. Uniform standards are attractive to regulators because they are simple to administer; there is one standard to worry about rather than fifty. On the surface, uniform standards appear equitable. It seems fair that everyone is treated the same.

For a number of reasons, however, technical and economic factors require more **specific standards** to effectively control pollution. First, pollutants interact. Thus a pound of waste discharged into already polluted water will do more harm than a pound discharged into relatively clean water. Second, the rate of water flow will affect the amount of harm done by a pound of waste. The faster the stream runs, the more rapidly a waterway can cleanse itself. Thus a pound of waste discharged into a sluggish, slow-moving stream will do more harm than a pound dumped into a fast-flowing waterway. A 70-percent reduction in waste discharges by a firm that dumps waste into a relatively unpolluted, fast-flowing river will decrease environmental degradation by a smaller amount than the same reduction by a firm that dumps waste into a sluggish, polluted waterway. Technical factors such as the interaction of pollutants and rates of water flow suggest that specific standards for particular situations are needed.

Economic factors also mandate that standards be specific to the situation. Efficiency requires that the environmental objective be reached at the least possible cost. However, pollution control technology is characterized by rising marginal cost. **Marginal cost** is the cost of removing an additional pound or other unit of waste. Rising marginal cost means that it costs more to remove each extra pound of waste when much waste has already been removed than it costs to remove each extra pound of waste when very little has already been removed. Thus the cleaner the operation already is, the higher the cost to achieve further purity. Cost also varies considerably depending on the source of pollution. To remove an additional pound of waste from a food manufacturer's discharges might cost less than to remove an additional pound of waste from an oil refinery's. Efficiency therefore requires that firms with the lowest marginal cost make large reductions in pollution rather than that all firms reduce pollution by the same percentage amount. This strategy will minimize the costs of pollution control. In other words, specific standards are more efficient than uniform ones. A number of studies have compared the two approaches and reached the consensus that uniform standards inflate the costs of pollution control somewhere between 10 and 30 percent. Given the magnitude of our environmental problem, this percentage increase would amount to many billions of dollars.

Despite the obvious cost savings provided by specific standards, uniform standards are far more often used. Setting standards for particular firms, industries, and situations is extremely difficult—in part because of the shortage of sound, timely environmental information. For example, we simply do not know the state of our groundwater basins or their ability to cleanse themselves. Furthermore, environmental regulators do not know the marginal costs of cleanup borne by all the firms out there in the real world. Firms have good reasons to overstate these costs, and they control most of the cost information that is available.

Technology Forcing. Agencies are criticized for setting standards that force firms to use specific pollution control technologies. This is the situation when design standards, rather than performance standards, are used. A good example is the emissions standard for automobiles. It requires the installation of catalytic converters, which are expensive bits of technology. Emissions could be cut by the use of diesel engines or other experimental engine designs, but because car emission standards require the use of catalytic converters, research into other emissions control methods has been stymied. The general problem in pollution control is that techniques that could control pollution more cheaply are not being encouraged, developed, or used.

Given the very real problems with the standards approach to environmental regulation, many economists propose that we use pollution fees or pollution permits instead. Both methods are more flexible than standards and rely on the market to control pollution more efficiently than standards regulation can. Let us look now at how these methods of regulation can achieve our environmental goals at less cost than can standards regulation.

Pollution Fees

Effluent fee
A tax on production causing water pollution.

Emissions fee
A tax on production causing air pollution.

There are two types of pollution fees. **Effluent fees** are taxes on production that causes water pollution, whereas **emission fees** are taxes on production that causes air pollution. If the amount of the pollution fee is at least equal to the social spillover cost, the imposition of tax will correct the overallocation of resources that results from pollution. It does this by giving firms an incentive to change their behavior. They can either pay the fee or find a new process of production that is less harmful to the environment.

Refer back to the polluting paper company in Figure 3-2. If the company continues to pollute, it must pay the effluent fee, which can be viewed as an additional cost of production. Supply will decrease in the direction of the original curve. Consumers will pay a higher price for the polluters' products because of the effluent fee. They will also consume less. In these ways they will bear some of the burden of pollution control. If the company chooses to eliminate its pollution, the higher costs of doing so will also cause supply to decrease. The important point is that fees do not force technology. Instead, they give firms an incentive to look for least-cost techniques to cut pollution and fees. From the view of enforcement and administration, pollution fees are easier to administer than are standards. From society's view, they result in least-cost—and thus more efficient—pollution control.

Marketable Pollution Permits

Pollution permit
Tradable permit to produce a given amount of pollution.

Under the **pollution permits** approach, the maximum level of pollution acceptable to society is divided into units, and permits to produce a unit of pollution are issued. These permits can be bought and sold. They will eventually wind up in the hands of firms for whom the costs of reducing pollution are the highest. (Recall from the earlier discussion that firms causing the least amount of pollution have the highest marginal costs of pollution control.) These firms prefer to purchase a permit rather than reduce their levels of pollution. Purchasing the permit will raise their costs of production, thereby increasing the price of their product. Consumers will then buy less of this product that causes pollution.

On the other hand, firms that can reduce pollution relatively cheaply (that is, those firms causing the greatest amount of pollution) will choose to reduce their pollution rather than purchase a high-priced permit. In both cases the pollution is decreased, and the resource misallocation is corrected as well. Society receives greater pollution control in a least-cost process of doing so.

In 1979 the EPA established on an experimental basis its first marketable pollution permits. The earliest experiments focused on individual firms that caused pollution at various points in each of their production processes. Amendments made to the Clean Air Act in 1990 extended the concept industrywide, creating pollution permits for coal-burning utilities.

Pollution permits and pollution fees are incentive-based regulation schemes. Studies indicate that these schemes do work. They are less expensive than standards regulation and do not stifle technological change. Instead they encourage research and the development of new pollution control technologies.

EVALUATION OF ENVIRONMENTAL POLICIES

Pollution affects our lives. And policies to prevent or reduce pollution also affect our lives. Whatever the method used by regulators, regulation raises the firm's production costs and increases the price we pay for the products we buy. These policies also, of course, result in air, water, and soil of higher quality. It is important that the policies used are efficient. The framework for evaluating public policies of all types is cost-benefit analysis.

Cost-benefit analysis is the systematic comparison of all the costs of a program with all of the benefits. The program should be undertaken only if the benefits are greater than the costs. From the perspective of the environment, let's look at the costs and benefits of environmental protection programs. The costs of these programs are the costs incurred by government in regulating business, in running public recycling programs, and in any other activity that cuts down on or cleans up pollution. Business firms also incur costs of environmental protection. If they adopt a more expensive but less polluting process, their increase in cost is an environmental protection cost. If they use less polluting but more costly raw materials, the difference in cost is also an environmental protection cost. If they install and maintain pollution control equipment, such as scrubbers in smokestacks, they incur an environmental protection cost. Consumers can also incur environmental protection costs if they install high-efficiency, less-polluting furnaces and other appliances, or if they incur the expense and inconvenience of recycling. The environmental protection costs are the total of all these costs, whether incurred by government, businesses, or households.

The benefits of environmental protection are the improvements in our environmental quality that result. Some of these benefits are quantifiable. We save on cleaning costs if air pollution is reduced. Businesses save on repair costs when acid rain no longer damages their structures. We save on medical costs when people no longer suffer the ill health that results from pollution.

However, many of the benefits of environmental programs cannot be calculated in monetary terms. The personal benefits of improved health and longevity go far beyond the savings on medical costs. The biodiversity of our rain forests is expected to yield yet-undiscovered products to benefit humankind. And there is no way to place a price on a stream used for trout fishing or a lake used for swimming that might otherwise be too polluted for use.

In reconciling the costs with the benefits of environmental protection, we must take a wide view and a long view. We must consider the monetary and nonmonetary benefits of environmental protection, and we must consider the benefits to future as well as current generations.

CONSERVATION AND RECYCLING

Pollution by producers is an important facet of our environmental problem, but consumers also contribute to the problem. As the world's population increases, we exhaust nonrenewable resources such as copper, oil, and coal at an increasing rate. The danger is that supplies will be depleted to the point at which these resources cannot be extracted economically from the earth.

Population creates environmental strain in two ways. From an ecological viewpoint, a country is overpopulated if (1) its people outnumber its ability to sustain them, or (2) its people consume so great an amount of resources that they stress the global environment. The first condition is the problem of many countries in Asia and Africa, where resources are often inadequate to meet the needs of a growing population. The second condition applies to our own country, which, on a per capita basis, uses an inordinate share of the world's resources. With only 4.7 percent of the world's population, the United States produces 29 percent of all goods and services, uses 23 of the world's energy, and produces 22 percent of the world's carbon dioxide emissions.[1] Given its consumerism, U.S. society stresses the environment far more than does an overpopulated less-developed country. The attitude reflected in the bumper-sticker quotation that opened this chapter, "The one who dies with the most toys wins," results in wasteful consumption of resources and energy. We live in a society characterized by a throwaway mentality, planned obsolescence, and the production of unnecessary and ecologically harmful products. The antithesis of this attitude is one of conservation and recycling. Let us look first at the economics of conservation, then that of recycling.

Economics of Conservation

As a starting point, let us review the law of demand from Chapter One. Price and quantity demanded are inversely related. Consumers will buy more at low prices than at high ones. It therefore follows that raising the price of a product will result in less consumption of it, whereas lowering the price will cause greater consumption. The market can act as a mechanism to encourage conservation. And the government can influence the market by taxes or by subsidies, which are payments to producers or consumers of the product.

Let's look at a few examples of such policies, beginning with a hypothetical market for gasoline. The United States is castigated by environmentalists for being the world's largest importer of oil. Much of the oil we consume is in the form of gasoline to power cars, sport utility vehicles, and light trucks. Despite having only 4.6 percent of the world's population, the United States has 35 percent of the world's cars.[2] The price per gallon of gasoline in the United States is unrealistically low because it is not fully adjusted to account for pollution costs and depletion of natural resources. When the price of gasoline is adjusted for the effects of inflation, we see that it has not changed much since 1940. Further, gas prices in the United States are much lower than in the rest of the industrialized world, where countries impose gasoline taxes higher than those in the United States. Such taxes increase the price of a gallon of fuel, giving consumers an incentive to conserve gas. The U.S. gasoline tax is about 30 cents per gallon.

Let's consider two hypothetical countries, illustrated in Figure 3-3. Let's assume identical demand and supply curves in each hypothetical market. These identical curves result in an initial equilibrium price of $1 per gallon, and an initial equilibrium quantity of four million gallons in each country.

Now suppose that the first country (the low-tax country) imposes a gasoline tax of 50 cents per gallon, and the second country (the high-tax country) imposes a tax of $1 per gallon. In either case the gasoline tax will decrease (shift upward) the supply of gasoline, because the tax is a cost that must be paid to the government by the sellers of the product. The supply curve in the low-cost country shifts upward by 50 cents per gallon to S'. The new equilibrium price to consumers is $1.25 per gallon, and the new equilibrium quantity is three million gallons. The

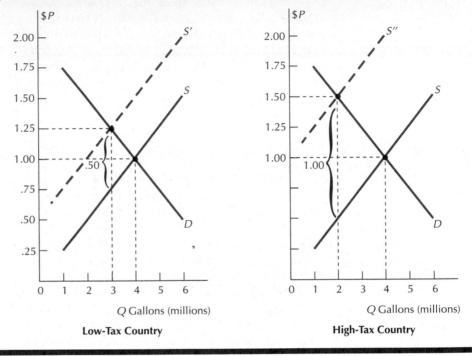

The higher ($1.00 per gallon) gasoline tax results in the consumption of only two million gallons of gas, and thus encourages greater conservation than the lower ($.50 per gallon) tax.

Low-Tax Country

High-Tax Country

imposition of the tax has increased price slightly and resulted in a decrease in consumption of one million gallons of gasoline.

In the case of the high-tax country, the supply curve shifts upward by $1 per gallon to S''. The new equilibrium price is $1.50 per gallon, and the new equilibrium quantity is two million gallons. The imposition of the tax has increased price greatly and has resulted in a decrease in consumption of two million gallons of gasoline. In both cases consumption decreases, but far more significantly where gasoline taxes are higher.

How does this conservation occur? In many ways. Drivers are less likely to make unnecessary trips. They are more likely to take public transportation if it is available. They carpool. When purchasing a car, they compare the gas efficiency of various models and weigh this information heavily in their decision to buy. Higher gasoline prices give individuals an incentive to make many independent decisions that result in conservation of oil supplies. Conversely, a low price encourages us to waste gasoline. (Americans do not vote for politicians who campaign on the promise to raise gasoline taxes, although it might be in our long-run best interest to do so.)

Other examples of using economic incentives to conserve scarce resources come from our agricultural policy. Recall from Chapter Two that one aspect of farm policy is to reduce the supply of farm products by taking land out of production. We pay farmers not to farm land. It makes ecological sense to require that highly erodible land be taken out of production, and it makes sense for the farmer to be paid to leave such land uncultivated. It also makes sense to eliminate subsidies to farmers who cultivate wetlands or other environmentally fragile acreage.

The bottom line with regard to conservation is that taxes increase market prices and therefore lead to efforts to conserve, whereas subsidies usually decrease price and lead to greater consumption. The market, combined with taxes and subsidies, is an effective tool for implementing conservation policy.

Economics of Recycling

It is also possible to save and reuse some of our natural resources. Many communities and business firms have established recycling programs in an effort to reduce the strain on our landfills and resources. Recycling has many dimensions and many economic aspects.

Recycling programs vary throughout the nation. Communities commonly recycle aluminum and newspapers. Some communities also recycle cardboard, magazines, tin cans, glass, plastics, scrap metal, and used oil. Recycling keeps these commodities out of landfills. As our population has grown, so have the wastes we produce. Landfills have filled up. Old landfills, in which everything (including hazardous waste) has been dumped, are recognized as environmental hazards that pollute the land and water supply.

The problem of garbage was brought home to many of us in 1987 as we followed the news story of the barge named *Mobro*, which was loaded with 3,190 tons of garbage at Long Island, New York, and sent out to find a garbage dump that would accept its cargo. It was refused permission to unload in North Carolina, Florida, Louisiana, the Bahamas, Mexico, and Honduras. After a six-thousand-mile journey lasting about half a year, the barge returned to New York City, where it was refused permission to dock. After three months in the New York harbor, the garbage was incinerated in Brooklyn, and the ash was shipped back to the originating community, which buried it in its landfill.

Although modern, state-of-the-art landfills are environmentally safe if located and monitored properly, their use is nevertheless controversial. If you have ever followed the local political wrangling over the site of a proposed new landfill, you are aware of this. No one wants the landfill anywhere near his or her property, and citizens' groups form to fight landfill siting projects. Reducing the bulk of our garbage through recycling is therefore a popular alternative to landfilling.

The two most pressing problems faced by recycling programs are motivating consumers and businesses to recycle and developing markets for recyclable goods.

Motivation to Recycle

Studies have found that people are more willing to recycle if it is convenient for them to do so. Collecting recyclables at consumers' homes (curbside recycling) or establishing numerous neighborhood drop-off points makes recycling easier and more convenient for people.

Although some people recycle because they are environmentally conscious, others will be willing to do so only if they are given sufficient economic incentives. These incentives can take a variety of forms.

Most households pay for waste disposal services by a fixed fee to a public or private garbage collection service. A family might pay $10 a month to have its garbage collected. The charge is the same whether the family has one bag or twelve bags of garbage per week. There is no incentive to reduce the amount of waste that is collected.

On the other hand, some communities have begun to charge households for each bag or can of garbage they discard. A charge of $2 per bag of garbage provides an incentive to decrease the number of bags disposed of. Households can save money by buying products with less packaging, or by recycling or composting their waste. Although such programs hold much promise for motivating consumers to recycle, they also may create some less desirable effects. They may motivate some people to dispose illegally of their garbage by dumping it in vacant lots or along the road or by burning it themselves.

Under other incentive programs, producers are taxed according to the cost of disposing of the goods they produce, whereas firms that use recycled goods are subsidized. Idaho has such a program for tires. A $1 tax is collected from producers for each tire that is sold. This revenue is earmarked to subsidize recycling. Firms that retread old tires are subsidized up to $1 per tire, and firms that process old tires for other uses receive $25 per ton. These types of tax and **subsidy** schemes are particularly appropriate for items such as old tires, car batteries, and motor oil, which create severe disposal problems.[3]

Subsidy
A payment from the government for some given action, such as recycling.

Under another type of incentive system, the government sets a target for recycling a product, and producers are responsible for ensuring that their product is recycled. Producers are required to buy "credits" from firms that recycle their type of product. For example, if a 50 percent recycling target were set for newspaper, the local newspaper company would be required to buy 500 pounds of credits for every 1,000 pounds of newspapers it produces. It would buy its credits from firms such as cardboard box producers that can use old newspapers in producing their product. Because the box producer is paid for using old newspapers, it has an incentive to use recycled newsprint instead of new paper pulp.

The price of the recycling credit is set by market forces. If the box manufacturer can use the newspapers at low cost, the price of the credit will be low. If a second firm can use old newsprint at a still lower cost, it will sell the credits to the newspaper at a still lower price. The old newspaper will go to the firm with the lowest use costs, and society's recycling costs will be minimized. As with taxes and subsidies, recycling credits are most appropriate for particularly troublesome items in our waste stream.

A final example of an economic incentive to reduce waste by recycling is the beverage container deposit, which is legally required in ten states. Consumers pay a deposit of five or ten cents per can or bottle when they buy beer or soda pop. Their money is returned when they bring the containers back to the store or a redemption center. A similar situation exists for plastic milk and water containers. The bottom line is that economic incentives can motivate us to recycle and reuse materials, which extends the life of our resources and landfills.

Markets for Recyclable Products

A serious problem faced by recycling programs is lack of markets for recyclable materials. Old newspapers can be used to make paper or cardboard, or they can be shredded for animal bedding. Glass can be used as an additive for asphalt paving. Other recyclable materials have similar uses. But the firms that produce recycled products often face an uncertain demand. They may therefore suspend the purchase of the recyclable materials, and recycling centers will build up inventories of these articles. When we drop off our recyclables at the recycling collection point, we assume that these articles will be put to some appropriate use. In fact they sometimes go to landfills because there is no user for them. The EPA has awarded numerous grants to local governments so they can develop additional markets for recyclables. Further uses of recycled products need to be found, and consumers, governmental units, and business firms need to be given incentives to choose products made with recycled material, if such a choice is available. Many people are averse to buying products made with recycled materials (for example, retreaded tires) because they view the products as inferior to those made with new materials. If there are quality differences between recycled products and new ones, price differences should be consistent with the quality differences.

CRITICISMS OF U.S. ENVIRONMENTAL POLICY

The environmental movement and our environmental policies are not uncontroversial. Environmental regulation has increased the costs of American business and has therefore been accused of the following adverse effects on the U.S. economy. Critics argue that by increasing costs, environmental regulation has contributed to inflation, which is a general increase in the average level of prices. They also argue that environmental regulation has increased unemployment because the equilibrium output sold by firms is lower (and fewer workers are needed to produce it). Moreover, they argue that because output is lower, economic growth, which is the increase in national production, will slow down. U.S. firms will be less competitive than their international competitors because they face stricter environmental regulations than many firms abroad.

Several studies have estimated the effect of pollution control on these macroeconomic variables. The consensus is that inflation is only slightly affected by environmental regulation, and that employment has actually increased as a result of the regulation because the decrease in jobs in polluting firms has been offset by an increase in jobs at firms formerly harmed by pollution (remember the paper and beer industries?) and by the creation of jobs in pollution control. Furthermore, our competitive position in the world has not been harmed by our environmental protection.[4] Studies indicate that there may be some additional social costs (and benefits) of environmental regulation beyond the ones previously considered. However, any analysis of the costs of environmental protection must be balanced by the benefits of pollution control.

More specific criticisms of the Environmental Protection Agency are that it makes too much use of uniform standards and standards that force the use of a particular technology, as we discussed previously. Furthermore, its administration of the Superfund to clean up hazardous waste is highly controversial. A staff report to Congress noted in late 1993 that 13 years after the establishment of the Superfund program, 1,270 sites were on the National Priorities List to be cleaned up. Twelve billion dollars had been spent, but only 49 sites had been fully cleaned up and taken off the list.[5] The EPA has consistently underestimated the costs of cleaning up environmental hazards, and it has had difficulty defining cleanup goals (how clean is clean?). Rather than look at the future use of the contaminated site, and how clean the site must be for that use, the EPA has defined clean in absolute terms (clean enough for any use). This action has greatly increased the costs and the time required for cleanup. The agency also has been reluctant to use innovative technologies that are not fully developed but might be less expensive than the technologies already in use.

INTERNATIONAL ASPECTS OF THE ENVIRONMENTAL PROBLEM

http://ens.lycos.com
At this site, you can find links from the environmental news service.

Just as local governments do not effectively control local pollution that affects the nation, individual nations do not effectively control national pollution that affects the world. As we have seen, environmental policy should be made by decision-making groups that include all those affected by negative spillovers. Environmental problems such as loss of biodiversity, ozone depletion, and global warming are international issues. International action is therefore necessary. Many experts believe that the major environmental issue of the twentieth century was pollution, but the principal issue of the twenty-first will be global warming.

Several international environmental summits have attempted to deal with some of these problems. These include the Rio Earth Summit in Brazil in 1994, and the Rio Follow-up Summit in Kyoto, Japan, in 1997. Proposals have been made to enter into environmental treaties modeled after our international trade treaties and to reform and strengthen the United Nations' powers with regard to the environment. The Kyoto treaty, which would require industrial countries to substantially reduce industry-generated heat-trapping gases that cause global warming, has not yet been ratified by Congress (or, for that matter, by any other industrial nation). In 2000, 160 nations met at The Hague, Netherlands, to try to arrive at a workable treaty based on the Kyoto treaty. The effort was not successful, and the meeting adjourned without participants reaching an agreement. Some environmental activists argue that some provisions of the World Trade Organization interfere with and weaken environmental protection standards in developed countries. Other problems may be more specific to developing countries as well as to those countries engaged in the transition to capitalist economic systems. Many people are concerned about pollution caused by the maquiladoras (U.S.-owned assembly operations) along the Mexican side of the U.S. border. Pesticides banned by the United States but exported by U.S. corporations to Central America contaminate groundwater and harm the health of farm workers. U.S. waste and environmentally harmful products are often shipped to other countries.

One of the most notorious examples of industrial pollution occurred in 1984, when a Union Carbide subsidiary plant accidentally released toxic emissions in

VIEWPOINT: Conservative vs. Liberal

Economists often make decisions about environmental matters on noneconomic grounds, as they do with certain other issues (such as crime) discussed in this book. It is possible for both liberal and conservative economists to care deeply about the environment.

Because conservatives want to limit the role of government in the economy, they are more likely than liberals to oppose environmental regulation. They will be more likely to favor pollution control policies that utilize market forces rather than other methods. Thus they favor pollution fees and permits over the regulation of pollution by means of standards. Conservatives may also prefer state and local solutions to environmental problems over policies developed at the federal and international levels.

Liberals, on the other hand, are less averse to government intervention in the economy and the regulation of private businesses. As such, liberals are also more likely to favor standards regulation. They may also be more favorable to policies drafted at the national and international levels. Liberals may well take the position that we should do whatever it takes to get the job done and not worry about the government's expanding role in the economy.

Bhopal, India. More than 1,000 people were killed, and more than 200,000 were injured. It was the worst industrial accident ever recorded. The official death toll of the1986 Chernobyl nuclear accident in Russia is 3,576, but Greenpeace Ukraine, an environmental organization, estimates that by 1995 the total death toll from the accident approached 32,000. Many people were killed, many more were injured, women are still bearing deformed children, and contamination in the Ukraine and neighboring countries continues to this day.

SUMMARY

Economic activity causes pollution. Pollution is a spillover cost of production that distorts the allocation of resources in the economy. Pollution causes resources to be overallocated to the market where it occurs and underallocated to other affected markets. Government therefore regulates private business by the standards approach, pollution fees, or pollution permits.

Conservation and recycling programs reduce pollution. Such programs are most effective when they give individuals and businesses some economic incentives for participation. Environmental programs should be evaluated by cost-benefit analysis, and these programs should be used only if benefits are greater than costs. Benefits must be broadly considered and include the monetary and nonmonetary benefits to current and future generations.

Many environmental problems are, in fact, international in nature. Thus international cooperation will be necessary to solve these problems.

NOTES

1. United Nations Development Program, *Human Development Report 2000* (New York: Oxford University Press, 2000).

2. G. Tyler Miller, Jr., *Living in the Environment,* 8th. ed. (Pacific Grove, CA: Brooks/Cole, 2001), p. 227.

3. Terry Dinan, "Solid Waste Incentives That Could Lighten the Load," *The Environmental Protection Agency Journal,* May/June 1992, pp. 13–14.

4. For a discussion of these studies, see Adam B. Jaffe, Steven R. Peterson, Paul R. Portney, and Robert Stavins, "Environmental Regulation and the Competitiveness of U.S. Manufacturing," *Journal of Economic Literature,* March 1995, pp. 132–163; Michael Porter and Claas van der Linde, "Toward a New Conception of the Environment-Competitiveness Relationship," *Journal of Economic Perspectives,* vol. 9, no. 4 (Fall 1995); and Robert Repetto, "U.S. Competitiveness Is Not at Risk in the Climate Negotiations" (Washington, DC: World Resources Institute, 1997).

5. Administration of the Federal Superfund Program, "Report of the Subcommittee on Investigations and Oversight of the Committee on Public Works and Transportation," Washington, DC: U.S. Government Printing Office, November 1993.

DISCUSSION QUESTIONS

1. *Why do polluters pollute? Consider various reasons for both individuals and businesses.*

2. *How does pollution distort resource allocation in the economy? Consider both overallocation and underallocation of resources.*

3. *What are some of the costs of pollution control? Should we be willing to pay anything and sacrifice everything to eliminate all pollution?*

4. *What do you think is the appropriate level of government to deal with pollution? Why?*

5. *Can you think of examples of negative or positive externalities not mentioned in the text?*

6. *Compare the various incentive-based environmental policies to the standards approach. What are the strengths and weaknesses of each?*

7. *Do you think it is appropriate that the consumer bears part of the burden of effluent or emission fees in the form of higher prices? Why or why not?*

8. *Explain cost-benefit analysis. Would the results of cost-benefit analysis ever be different in the short run than in the long run? Why or why not?*

9. *Do you think that we are a throwaway society? Are your attitudes toward consumption the same as your parents'? Your grandparents'?*

10. *Keeping in mind that environmental regulation is a luxury good, would you expect American attitudes to be the same as attitudes of citizens of Third World countries?*

11. *Are you conservative or liberal when it comes to environmental issues?*

12. *Go to the Environmental Protection Agency Web page (http://www.epa.gov). Click on the map to find current environmental issues in your area.*

CHAPTER 4

Market Power

The monopolists, by keeping the market constantly understocked, by never fully supplying the effectual demand, sell their commodities much above the natural price. . . .

Adam Smith, *The Wealth of Nations*, 1776

Do you ever worry about the effects of powerful firms? Have you ever written your senator about the high price of the medicine you must take? Have you ever protested the operating practices of the one cable television system in your area? Have you ever questioned how the electric company is regulated?

Our guess is that you probably have not. Perhaps you haven't realized that the way markets are structured has serious implications for prices, level of output, efficiency, income distribution, and political influence. Much of the American public seems uninterested in, or at least unaware of, the effects of market power in America. Some people naively assume that because we have antitrust laws and economic regulation of natural monopolies, we do not have a problem. Others argue that regulation decreases business efficiency and should be eliminated. But consumer advocate and Green Party presidential candidate Ralph Nader has noted that the general public views antitrust matters as "too complex, too abstract, and supremely dull."

In this chapter we will look at the effects of market power on the American economy. The implications for consumers are significant. We hope we can do this in a way that is neither complex, abstract, nor dull. To gain an understanding of the problem of market power, you must learn something about three market structures: pure competition, monopoly, and oligopoly.

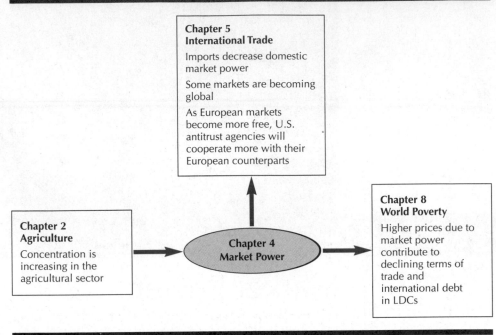

**Chapter 5
International Trade**

Imports decrease domestic market power

Some markets are becoming global

As European markets become more free, U.S. antitrust agencies will cooperate more with their European counterparts

**Chapter 8
World Poverty**

Higher prices due to market power contribute to declining terms of trade and international debt in LDCs

**Chapter 2
Agriculture**

Concentration is increasing in the agricultural sector

**Chapter 4
Market Power**

PURE COMPETITION

Recall that the markets in Chapters One and Two were described as competitive. Because there were many small buyers and sellers, no one producer could dictate the going market price. The examples suggested that if one tutor or one farmer out of many decided to charge an exorbitant price, consumers would simply buy from competing sellers. Thus competition protected consumers from potentially unreasonable prices.

A market structure in which the seller cannot influence price is what economists call **pure competition.** A purely competitive market has three characteristics:

Pure competition
Market in which many independent producers compete to sell a standardized product to many independent buyers.

1. many small buyers and sellers,
2. a standardized product, and
3. no barriers to entry or exit.

Let's consider each of these characteristics separately. As we noted above, the first characteristic has bearing on the relative reasonableness of the going market price. Because many small buyers constitute the total demand in the market, no individual is powerful enough to extract a lower price on the product. Because there are so many small firms selling the product compared with the total supply, no one firm can charge a higher price for the product. If it has occurred to you that the terms "many" and "small" are relative, you are correct. Firms can be large in absolute terms and do many million dollars of business annually, but if a large number of similar firms exist, no one firm will be able to control the market price.

Second, in a purely competitive market the products of all producers are standardized or roughly identical. Most agricultural products, if we carefully specify the grade, are standardized. So are the markets for standard-sized rubber bands, pencils, and floppy disks. See if you can think of other standardized products. The importance of this standardization is that the buyer will not care which seller she buys from, because the products are roughly the same. Therefore she will not develop brand loyalty to one particular firm's product and be willing to pay a higher price for that firm's version of the product. She will base her buying decision only on price because there are no other pertinent factors to consider.

Third, there are no barriers to entry into the purely competitive market. A **barrier to entry** is some condition that makes it difficult or expensive for a new producer to enter the market. Perhaps start-up costs are so huge that a great deal of capital must be raised before a new firm begins operations. Or the government may require a firm to obtain a license before starting operations. Or the products of existing firms may be protected by patents, so that production of a similar product carries the risk of a patent infringement lawsuit. These barriers to entry are *not* present in a purely competitive market. If they were present, there would not be "many small firms."

An important implication of these characteristics is that the purely competitive firm will be a **price taker.** That is, it will take the market price as given but individually will have no influence over this price. Any level of output that it could possibly produce is too small to affect the market price. Consider Figure 4-1, which shows the market for fresh fish offered for sale in one week by fishing boat operators in a

Barrier to entry
Market characteristic that prevents new firms from entering the market.

Price taker
Firm that is not able to influence its own price.

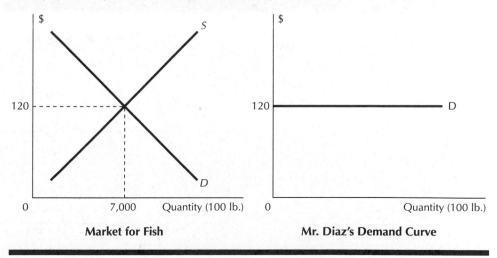

FIGURE 4-1   Demand Under Conditions of Pure Competition

The competitive market sets the price per unit of fish, and the individual commercial fishing boat operator is a price taker with a horizontal, or perfectly elastic, demand curve.

Market for Fish

Mr. Diaz's Demand Curve

northwestern U.S. port, as well as the demand curve of one individual operator, Mr. Diaz.

The market price of $120 per hundredweight (100 pounds) is established by the interaction of total market demand and supply. At this price 7,000 hundredweight of fish will be sold in the port's commercial fish market. Mr. Diaz can offer for sale any quantity between 0 and 50 hundredweight this week, but any of these quantities is too small to influence the market price. Therefore the demand curve faced by Mr. Diaz is a horizontal line at the going market price ($120). A price taker's demand is always horizontal, because whatever quantity the firm offers for sale, there will be no effect on price.

Why doesn't Mr. Diaz just charge a price higher than $120? The answer is simple. If he does, his customers will buy from other producers. His fish are no different from fish caught by other fishing boat captains. If he tries to get a higher price, he will lose all his business.

Profit
Total revenues minus total costs.

Mr. Diaz can adjust the amount that he offers for sale this week. And he will do so to try to maximize his **profit** from the sale of fish. He has an upsloping supply curve, which is based on the cost of the fishing operation. (Recall from Chapter One that the factors that influence supply are the factors that affect business costs.) Mr. Diaz's individual demand and supply curves are shown in Figure 4-2. At the market price of $120, Mr. Diaz will sell 20 hundredweight of fish. His profit will be the difference between the total revenue he receives from selling the fish and the total costs of catching and marketing them. The 20 hundredweight that Mr. Diaz sells is insignificant compared with the total market sales of 7,000 hundredweight.

The competitive price is a reasonable one; the market demand curve reflects the value of fish to all the buyers in the market, and the market supply curve reflects the costs per hundredweight of all the producers in the market. Furthermore, the producers' costs include a **normal profit,** which is just enough of a profit

Normal profit
Minimum profit needed to keep resources invested in a firm (an opportunity cost of production).

FIGURE 4-2   Demand and Supply Curves for Mr. Diaz's Fish

Mr. Diaz will sell 20 hundredweight at the market price of $120.

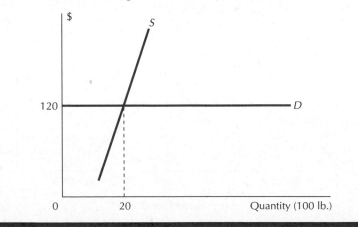

to make continuation of the producers' businesses worthwhile. The competitive firm therefore makes a normal profit, but no excess profits above the normal profit. This outcome is one of the great advantages of competitive markets.

MONOPOLY AND OLIGOPOLY

Monopoly
Market in which one firm produces a product with no close substitutes.

Price maker
Firm that can influence its own price.

The opposite of a purely competitive market is a **monopoly.** A monopoly is a market with only one seller. The product produced by the monopolist has no close substitute, so if buyers want the product they have no choice: they must buy it from the monopolist. The monopolist is not a price taker but a **price maker.** That is, the firm has the ability to influence its own price. The essence of market power is having the ability to impose a price on buyers. This ability does not mean that the firm simply sets the highest possible price; it means that the firm can raise its price by decreasing the quantity that it sells. Unlike the purely competitive firm, which simply accepts the market price and adjusts its quantity, the monopolist determines its price when it determines the quantity that it will offer for sale. The monopolist faces the entire downsloping market demand curve. When it offers for sale a particular quantity, it simultaneously establishes the market price, which is its price as it is the only firm in the market.

Consider Figure 4-3, which shows a market demand for cable television service. The price is the monthly fee for basic cable services, and the quantities are the numbers of subscribers in the area in the month. There is only one cable supplier in the area. Note that if the cable television company sells 25,000 units, it can

FIGURE 4-3   Cable TV Demand

Because the cable TV company's demand curve is downsloping, the company simultaneously establishes a price when it sells a certain quantity.

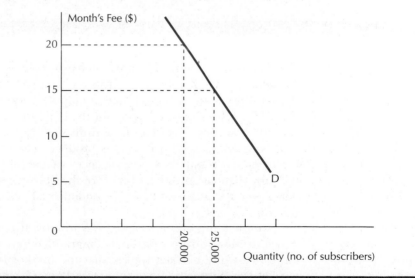

get a price of $15, but if it decides to sell only 20,000 units it can charge a price of $20. The way that the firm controls its price is by controlling its quantity. By selling fewer units it can charge a significantly higher price for those units it does sell. Note also that its revenue will be greater if it sells only 20,000 units. A firm's total revenue is always the product price times the quantity sold. If the cable television company sells 20,000 units at $20, its revenues will be $400,000. But if it sells 25,000 units at $15, its revenues will be only $375,000.

Now compare the demand curves of the individual producers in the purely competitive and the monopoly markets. Mr. Diaz's demand curve is horizontal so that quantity will not affect price, whereas the cable television company's demand curve is downsloping so that quantity establishes price. A price maker always faces a downsloping demand curve. Such a curve is the prerequisite for market power.

When a monopoly dominates the market, the competitive supply curve based on the costs of many small producers simply no longer exists. Instead, the monopolist will choose to supply a lesser amount of the product to get a higher price and receive a larger profit. So compared with a competitive market, a monopoly with the same production costs will produce less, charge a higher price, and receive larger profits.

There are few true monopolies, or markets where only one firm sells a product, in the United States. Most of the monopolies that exist are regulated by some agency of the government (we will look at the controversy over regulation later). Nonetheless, we have a monopoly-type problem. We do have many markets that are oligopolies. An **oligopoly** is a market in which only a few large firms exist. These firms produce a large enough share of the total market supply to perceptibly influence the market price. Indeed, if they agree to limit their output, they can get as high a price as a monopoly. When we speak of the "big three" automobile companies or the "big four" ready-to-eat cereal companies, we are referring to oligopolies. When we speak of the "monopoly problem," we are referring to the market power wielded by these firms.

Oligopoly
A market in which only a few large firms exist.

MEASURING BIGNESS AND CONCENTRATION

The American economy contains some extremely large firms. One interesting way to consider the size of these large firms is to compare their sales (value of output) with the gross domestic product (value of output) of the world's countries. Table 4-1 (on page 77) makes this comparison for the largest U.S. firms and several countries. We can see from this table that large firms such as General Motors and Wal-Mart sell more output than many countries produce. The examples in the table are mostly industrialized countries. Certainly sales by General Motors and Wal-Mart far surpass the gross national product of most of the developing countries of the world. These data suggest that a great deal of economic and political clout is held by large industrial firms.

Concentration
The existence of only a few relatively large firms in a market.

Another, and perhaps better, way to look at bigness is to measure the level of **concentration** within a particular market. When there are only a few relatively large firms in a market, we say that the market is concentrated. Concentration implies the existence of market power. We often measure concentration by means

TABLE 4-1	Value of Output of the Largest U.S. Firms and Selected Countries in $ Billions, 1998. (Firms are in bold.)

FIRM OR COUNTRY	SALES OR GDP
General Motors	**161.3**
Poland	158.6
Norway	145.9
Ford Motors	**144.4**
Wal-Mart	**139.2**
South Africa	133.5
Saudi Arabia	128.9
Exxon	**100.7**
New Zealand	52.8

Sources: Data from *Fortune,* April 26, 1999, and http://www.worldbank.org/data.countrydata

Concentration ratio
The percentage of output produced by the four largest firms in an industry.

http://www.census.gov/epcd/www/concentration.html This Census Bureau site contains the most recent concentration ratios.

of the **concentration ratio,** which is usually defined as the percentage of output produced by the four largest firms in the industry. (An industry differs from a market in that it includes all firms that produce the same product, whereas a market includes all competing firms, even if they do not produce the same product but do produce substitutes for the product.) The higher the concentration ratio, the greater is the concentration in the industry. If there are four or fewer firms in the industry, the concentration ratio will be 100. That is, the four largest firms produce 100 percent of the output. If the industry contains many small firms, the concentration ratio will be very low. A concentration ratio of 10 would mean that the four largest firms produce only 10 percent of the output and that the industry probably contains many competing firms. Table 4-2 (on page 78) shows the concentration ratios for a number of U.S. industries in 1987.

Most economists consider a concentration ratio above 60 to indicate a tight oligopoly in which firms have significant market power. A concentration ratio of 40 or less would indicate little market power. Approximately 60 percent of U.S. manufacturing is done in industries in which concentration ratios exceed 60.

But when using concentration ratios, we must be careful. Although they are useful indicators of possible market power, they are not perfect measures of market power. Some cautions are therefore in order.

First, concentration ratios are based only on domestic (U.S.) production and exclude foreign competition. Some industries face significant competition from imports. The American automobile industry is a case in point. Although there are only three domestic car manufacturers, imports account for more than 30 percent of U.S. sales. American automobile markets are therefore more competitive than the concentration ratio implies. As U.S. industries face increasingly more global competition, U.S. concentration ratios tend to overstate their market power.

Second, the concentration ratios in Table 4-2 are calculated for the entire nation, yet many markets are in fact regional. Take newspapers, for example. The concentration ratio of 25 significantly understates the real market power in the newspaper field. Most cities have only one or two local newspapers, and these firms have significantly more power than the lower concentration ratio suggests.

TABLE 4-2　Concentration Ratios for Selected Manufacturing Industries, 1992

INDUSTRY	CONCENTRATION RATIO
Household laundry equipment	94
Electric lamps	86
Cereal breakfast foods	85
Motor vehicles and car bodies	84
Greeting cards	84
Small arms ammunition	84
Tires and inner tubes	70
Roasted coffee	66
Soaps and detergents	63
Primary aluminum	59
Women's hosiery	55
Household audio and video equipment	39
Mens' and boys' suits and coats	39
Soft drinks	37
Mobile homes	35
Bread, cake, and related products	34
Book printing	32
Upholstered household furniture	25
Newspapers	25
Mattresses and box springs	22
Metal doors, sash, and trim	14
Commercial printing, lithography	7

Source: U.S. Department of Commerce, Bureau of the Census, *1992 Census of Manufactures: Concentration Ratios in Manufacturing* (http://www.census.gov/mcd/mancen/download/mn92cr.sum).

Third, the concentration ratios are defined for industries rather than markets and thus ignore interindustry competition. The concentration ratio of 66 for the coffee industry probably overstates the coffee industry's market power. Coffee is only one of many beverages consumed in U.S. households. Tea, soda pop, and bottled spring water are a few of the products that compete with coffee for the consumer's dollars.

These problems do not mean that concentration ratios are useless as approximations of market power. They do mean, however, that concentration ratios are not perfect measures of market power. They should be used carefully and adjusted when necessary to conform to the realities of the market.

BARRIERS TO ENTRY

The principal reason that some markets are dominated by only a few large firms is that there are barriers to entry into these markets. New firms therefore find it difficult, if not impossible, to begin operations. Barriers to entry are the source of the existing firms' market power and the reason that concentrated markets remain concentrated year after year.

Let's consider seven of the most commonly encountered barriers to entry.

Economies of Scale

Economies of scale
Decreasing long-run average costs.

First, some markets are characterized by **economies of scale.** This means that a large amount of the product can be produced in any given time period at a lower per-unit cost than a small amount of the product. Economies of scale arise from the technology used in manufacturing the product, which is often quite capital intensive. Because most firms manufacturing the product will tend to use similar technologies, they will have similar cost curves. A cost curve illustrating economies of scale is shown in Figure 4-4.

Assume that the average cost curve shown in Figure 4-4 is the typical cost curve for car companies producing compact passenger cars. Note that the curve declines as output per month increases until 100,000 cars per month are produced. Because economies of scale are declining average (per-unit) costs, such economies of scale in our example will exist until 100,000 cars are produced in a month. The smallest quantity at which the lowest possible average cost is reached is called **minimum efficient scale.** This scale is 100,000 in our example.

Minimum efficient scale
The smallest quantity at which the lowest possible average cost is reached.

Note that 100,000 cars a month can be produced at a cost of $5,000 each but that 10,000 cars a month will be produced at a cost of $10,000 each. This market is the sort in which it is impossible to start small and grow. If a new firm enters the market and produces only 10,000 cars a month, it will not be able to compete on the basis of price with established large firms that are already producing 100,000 cars a month. Starting small leads eventually to failure, not growth. This lesson was learned by a number of firms that have tried to enter the automobile industry during the past 40 years. Consider the entry of the Bricklin and the DeLorean into the sports-car market. Although both were exciting vehicles, their producers eventually

FIGURE 4-4   Average Long-Run Cost of Compact Cars

Large-scale production is less expensive than small-scale production, so large producers have a cost advantage over small producers.

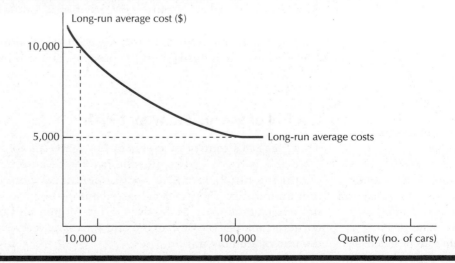

failed because they could not achieve per-unit costs nearly as low as those of the comparable models of established firms.

You may ask why new producers don't start big instead of small. After all, if they were producing 100,000 cars a month, they would have the same low costs as the established auto producers. The answer is that (1) starting big involves a huge capital investment, and (2) large-scale production will affect the market price. The size and type of plant needed to produce the larger output will be significantly more expensive, and investment capital is difficult for new firms to raise. And an increase in production of 100,000 cars a month is large enough to lower the market price. Remember the downsloping market demand curve. A significant increase in quantity offered for sale can only be sold at a lower price. Therefore if the new firm could raise the capital to produce on a large scale, it might well find it unprofitable to do so. Economies of scale therefore are a barrier to entry into the market. The first few firms to enter and achieve output at the minimum efficient scale generally face little competition from new entrants into the market.

Exclusive Franchises

Natural monopoly
Market with significant economies of scale.

Exclusive franchise
Governmental monopoly grant, accompanied by regulation.

Second, sometimes when economies of scale are great or competition simply appears to be unworkable, the market is considered a **natural monopoly.** In such circumstances the government may step in and issue an **exclusive franchise** to one producer. An exclusive franchise gives the firm the sole right to conduct business in a particular geographic area. Because the exclusive franchise is granted to the firm, the firm is usually regulated by an agency of the government to ensure that consumers receive some of the benefits of large-scale production. Examples of regulated natural monopolies are your local telephone company, natural gas company, and electric company. If economies of scale are truly significant in the market, the granting of an exclusive franchise simply recognizes the inevitable. The market will be concentrated with or without the government's action, and regulation will protect the consumer. But the exclusive franchise acts as an additional barrier to entry into the market, because now new firms cannot legally enter the market. A problem arises when natural monopoly-type regulation is imposed on sectors that are potentially competitive. In this situation, regulation is the source of monopoly power within the industry, and the outcome is much inferior to that in a competitive market.

Control of Essential Raw Materials

Control of essential raw materials
Barrier to market entry resulting from a monopoly's ownership or control of an entire supply of a resource needed to produce its product.

Third, a firm's **control of essential raw materials** to manufacture a product will serve as a barrier to entry into the market because new firms will not be able to obtain the raw materials to begin operations. Consider, for example, the aluminum industry. The essential ingredient in the production of aluminum is bauxite. When aluminum was discovered, the Aluminum Company of America (Alcoa) cornered the market on bauxite and for many years had a monopoly on the production of aluminum.

Patents

Fourth, some products are protected by **patents,** which serve as a barrier to entry. Patents are limited-term monopoly grants from the government. (Patents are granted for a uniform worldwide period of 20 years.) We give patents for new products and processes to encourage innovation and invention. After all, firms incur costs in developing new products. If a firm is not guaranteed the benefits of its new inventions because its competitors begin selling the new product shortly after it does, how can we expect the firm to put money into research and development? When a firm has a patent on a product, it can protect itself by bringing a patent infringement suit against any new firm that tries to produce a similar product. Although patents do encourage invention, they also encourage the development of market power in three respects: (1) The holder of the patent will be the sole producer of the product for many years. The patent will enable the firm to establish itself in the minds of consumers as the preeminent seller of the product, giving the firm a competitive advantage even after the patent has expired and other firms can legally begin production of the product. (2) Patents can be misused. Established firms sometimes "blanket" the patent that they intend to use by seeking and obtaining patents that they have no intention of using. In other words, they obtain patents on many more variants of the product than they will actually produce simply to prevent other firms from producing a similar product. Only about one-half of the patents granted are actually used. (3) The common practice of aggressively defending patents with patent infringement lawsuits discourages would-be competitors from producing close substitutes.

Product Differentiation

Fifth, products are frequently differentiated, and **product differentiation** acts as a barrier to the entry of new firms. Product differentiation is any characteristic that makes the product of one firm different from another firm's in the eyes of the buyer. The difference may be real (style, quality, color, taste) or it may be entirely artificial (created solely by labeling and advertising). A good example of a differentiated product is household laundry bleach, which is simply a solution of sodium hypochlorite. Despite the uniformity of the product, Clorox has dominated the bleach market for many years, commanding a higher price than other brands because many consumers are convinced that Clorox is a better product than the other brands on the market. Product differentiation acts as a barrier to entry because new firms must spend a great deal of money on advertising their product in an effort to compete against the established brand name of the firm already in the market. Some highly differentiated products are film, breakfast cereals, and automobiles.

Licensing

Sixth, the government requires new entrants to obtain a **license** before beginning operation in many professions and trades. We license doctors, dentists, lawyers, beauticians, barbers, and undertakers, among others. The reason for licensing is fairly obvious. We accompany the granting of the license with the passing of an examination to ensure some minimum level of competency. But licensing also restricts entry into fields.

Behavior of Established Firms

Limit pricing
Practice whereby established firms take less than the maximum possible profit and thus keep price low enough to retard new entry into their market.

Seventh, the actions of established firms can also deter entry into the market. They may practice **limit pricing,** especially if their costs of production are lower than the costs of new firms that may want to enter the market. Limit pricing is setting the price of the product low enough so that possible new entrants would be unlikely to make a profit and therefore do not enter the market. The established firms accept lower profits in the short term to maintain higher profits in the long term.

Established firms might also behave in a predatory manner toward any new entrant into their market. They might temporarily cut their prices to below cost to drive the new entrant out of the market. A good example of predatory competition comes from the cigarette industry, which was dominated by three large firms back in the 1930s. These firms sold established brands of cigarettes nationally and accounted for about 90 percent of cigarette sales. There were many small local tobacco companies that sold only in a limited geographic region. When one of the small firms would increase its sales, the big three would retaliate by introducing "fighting brands," off-label cigarettes sold at below cost. Evidence presented in a landmark antitrust case in 1945 indicated that the fighting brands sometimes sold retail at prices below the value of the excise taxes stamped on the packs. A market with a history of such predatory competition is not an attractive market for new firms to enter.

Barriers to entry keep markets concentrated over time. Because the firms in the industry will be relatively few and rather large, they will be able to control the supply in the market and to charge a price higher than the competitive market price. They will possess market power.

EFFECTS OF MARKET POWER

We have already discussed some of the effects of market power. The firms will charge a higher price, produce a smaller quantity, and make a larger profit than would competitive producers. Figure 4-5 compares the price, output, and level of profit under conditions of pure competition and monopoly. Assume alternately that (1) only one firm sells long-distance telephone service in the United States, and (2) there are enough firms of relatively equal size to characterize the market as purely competitive. The graph shows the output, price, and profits in one small midwestern town such as Wahoo, Nebraska. S_c represents the supply of the competitive firms. Remember that this supply is based on the cost of providing long-distance telephone service and that the cost of the firms includes a normal profit, or enough of a profit that the firms will continue to provide service. If the market is competitive, the weekly output will be 1,200 long-distance phone calls, and the average charge, or price, will be $1.50. The price will be equal to the costs of production, including a normal profit. If the market is monopolized, the monopoly

FIGURE 4-5   Output, Price, and Profits Under Competition and Monopoly

Note that output is lower and that price and profits are higher under a monopoly than they would be under competition.

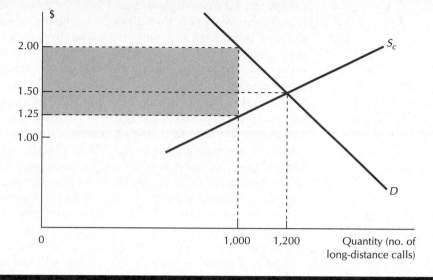

will restrict output below the competitive level, allowing it to charge a higher price. Thus the monopoly will sell only 1,000 phone calls at an average price of $2. Because supply is based on cost, the cost per call is $1.25, so the monopoly will make a profit (in excess of the normal profit) of $.75 on each call. The total monopoly profit is $750 per week. The monopoly profit is shown by the shaded area in the diagram.

In addition to affecting price, output, and profits, market concentration often leads to collusion, inefficiency, and price discrimination. Let's discuss these phenomena one at a time.

Collusion

Collusion
Price fixing.

Collusion is better known as price fixing. It occurs when firms cooperate to restrict the market output and thereby obtain a higher price. For collusion to be successful, all the firms in the market must cooperate. If some firms collude to charge a higher price, while others do not, consumers will simply buy from the noncolluders at a lower price. Collusion is therefore more likely in markets with relatively few firms and substantial entry barriers.

Cartel
Price-fixing agreement and the firms who are party to it.

There are two types of collusion: cartel agreements and price leadership. A **cartel** agreement is an explicit agreement between producers to limit output and to charge a higher than competitive price. Cartels with which you might be familiar are the Organization of Petroleum Exporting Countries (OPEC), an organization of the governments of many of the world's largest oil-producing nations, and the DeBeers diamond cartel, which controls the world's supply of diamonds. A colorful and illegal cartel known as the "electrical equipment conspiracy" existed for many years in the United States. It included 29 electrical equipment companies headed by industry giants General Electric (GE) and Westinghouse. When the conspiracy was uncovered, GE, Westinghouse, and 44 of their executives were charged with conspiring to fix prices over a 25-year period by rigging bids in the sale of billions of dollars worth of heavy electrical equipment. The firms took turns offering the low bid. This low bid had previously been agreed on by the cartel and was at a high level. The colluders had devised ingenious schemes to coordinate their bidding. A firm would know whether to bid high or low, for example, by the phase of the moon.

Price leadership

Form of collusion in which firms follow the price increases of a leading firm.

Price leadership is a more subtle form of collusion. It occurs in markets in which firms never explicitly agree to collude, but instead somehow come to the realization that it is in their best interests to charge similar prices and to restrict output to maintain higher prices. When this happens one of the firms emerges as price leader, and the other firms adjust their price whenever the leader changes its price. American Tobacco was long the price leader in the cigarette industry, Kellogg in the cereal industry, Campbell in the canned soup industry, and General Motors in the automobile industry. (Incidentally, the long-established practice of price leadership in the American automobile industry collapsed in the early 1980s when the industry began contending with substantial competition from imports.)

As you probably know, price fixing is illegal under our antitrust laws. And indeed, firms that form cartels are subject to severe penalties should they be caught. Our antitrust system has been quite effective against cartels. The sad truth, however, is that the system is ineffective against price leadership. Without convincing evidence that firms have met and agreed to collude, proving that they are guilty of price fixing is nearly impossible.

Inefficiency

A second problem with concentration is that firms in concentrated markets have less incentive to be efficient than do firms in competitive markets. A competitive firm must minimize the cost of its product to survive and make a normal profit. But the firm in a concentrated market, protected by entry barriers, has no such incentive. Security breeds laxness, and costs rise. The *Wall Street Journal* and other business publications abound with examples of dominant firms that, suddenly faced with competition, cut costs substantially. Caterpillar Tractor Company, long the leading U.S. producer of construction equipment, found it possible to cut costs by more than 20 percent when suddenly besieged by Japanese competition in the early 1980s. When the American automobile industry was hit hard by foreign competition in the late 1970s, General Motors, Ford, and Chrysler were able to reduce their costs by 20 to 30 percent. When the Harley-Davidson motorcycle company lost its market dominance to Japanese competitors in the 1960s, it first sought protection in the form of import tariffs on motorcycles, which were in place during much of the 1980s but slated to end in 1988. By 1988 Harley-Davidson had cut its inventory by two-thirds, improved productivity by 50 percent, and reduced its rate of defects by 70 percent. As you may have realized as you read these examples, the business publications reported the successful cost-cutting measures, lauding the "lean and mean" American firms. But the firms had substantial excess costs to cut, and it was competition that forced them to do so.[1] Competition, whether domestic or international, promotes efficiency and benefits consumers.

Price Discrimination

Another consequence of market power is **price discrimination,** or charging different prices to different groups of customers when the price differentials are not justified by differences in costs. Firms simply charge "what the market will bear," and different market segments will bear substantially different prices. Price discrimination is profitable for the discriminators, but it is only possible when firms have significant price-making power. Price discrimination is extremely common in the United States.

Let's consider some examples, beginning with the automobile industry, which has a rich history of price discrimination. As you undoubtedly know, American car manufacturers produce a variety of vehicles, ranging from small economy cars to luxury models. The markup over cost varies substantially with the model. Because purchasers of small economy cars tend to be more price conscious than purchasers of Cadillacs and Lincolns, firms take a smaller markup over cost on the economy models. The price differences reflect not only cost differences but also differences in what the market will bear.

Another way that automobile companies discriminate is illustrated in the area of replacement parts and optional equipment. The markup is much higher on parts and options than on the car itself. If your car is not running because it needs a new part, you are not particularly price conscious about the part. You may be horrified when you see the repair bill, but if you consider the car worth keeping, you have little choice other than to pay it. The high markup on options explains why the salesperson pressures you so much to buy many options when you shop for a new car (one of the most frustrating events in American life). The auto industry is, by the way, not the only industry that discriminates in the sale of replacement parts. The practice is exceedingly common. If you don't believe this, price a replacement plate for your microwave oven.

The drug industry, the products of which are usually protected by patents, uses extensive and systematic price discrimination. Drugs that will ultimately be consumed by hospital patients are often priced higher than drugs that will be consumed by retail buyers. Large buyers such as the Veterans Administration can obtain drugs at far lower prices than can retail druggists. The drug industry claims that the huge price differences are the result of differences in the cost of packaging and selling drugs to different groups, but such differences are small, and Senate testimony in the 1970s revealed that druggists often paid prices more than three times that paid by the Veterans Administration for the same patented drug.

FORCES THAT DECREASE MARKET POWER

It is obvious that market power produces some undesirable consequences that harm the consumer, whereas competition benefits the consumer. Let us now consider the forces that constrain or decrease market power. These forces are:

(1) technological change, (2) antitrust actions, (3) deregulation of unwisely regulated sectors, and (4) import competition.

Technological Change

Technology is a major force on market structure in the economy. Economies of scale, which characterize natural monopolies, are often eroded by the forces of technological change. Take, for example, the telephone industry. When phone messages were carried on wire cables, the industry was characterized by extensive economies of scale. Fiber-optic and microwave transmission of phone messages, however, involve lesser economies of scale, and long-distance telephone service, which was once a natural monopoly, is now potentially competitive. Since the divestiture of AT&T, consumers in most localities have had a choice of long-distance carriers, and competition has decreased the price of long-distance calls. Now additional competition is coming from the wireless phone, a still newer innovation.

Consider next the railroads, which had significant market power during the late 1800s and the early part of this century. Technological change since then has resulted in new competitors for the railroads. The invention of the internal combustion engine and the subsequent development of cars, trucks, and airplanes led to a significant level of interindustry competition for the railroads. Once the dominant force in American transportation, railroads are now a slowly declining industry.

The great and deeply conservative economist Joseph A. Schumpeter argued that competition in innovation and technological change was the driving force of the economy and that economic concentration was immaterial when compared to the technological change promoted by large firms. Schumpeter spoke of a process of "creative destruction" whereby temporary monopolies or dominant firms were supplanted by other monopolies or firms as technology changed, and new innovations were diffused throughout the economy. The Schumpeterian cycle suggests that innovation creates market dominance, which creates monopoly profits, which stimulate new innovation, which leads to new dominance, and so forth. The implications are that concentration begets technological change, which ultimately benefits the consumer, and that market dominance is transitory. Despite the attractiveness of the Schumpeterian view, empirical evidence does not indicate that concentration necessarily leads to rapid technological change. Indeed, what evidence we have appears to indicate that dominant firms lag technologically. Furthermore, the rate of erosion of the dominant position of firms is exceedingly slow. Campbell Soup, IBM, and Eastman Kodak have dominated their markets for many decades. Industries with high concentration ratios tend to maintain high levels of concentration over time. Technological change does produce monumental change in some sectors, but market dominance persists for long periods of time in others. In these cases monopoly power needs to be controlled.

The U.S. Antitrust System

Antitrust
Laws, agencies, and court system established to control monopoly in the United States.

Our **antitrust** system is a set of weapons designed to combat market power. It consists of laws passed by Congress, agencies empowered to administer these laws, and a court system to try cases under the laws. The first federal antitrust law ("trust" is simply an old-fashioned word for monopoly) was the Sherman Act, which was enacted in 1890. The Sherman Act's provisions made illegal monopolization and conspiracies in restraint of trade. The law was quite generally written. Congress made known its intent and left it up to the Justice Department and the courts to apply the law to specific cases. As time passed it became evident that the courts and agencies had difficulty interpreting the law, and another more specifically written law was passed. This was the Clayton Act of 1914. The Clayton Act contains many provisions making illegal particular actions that would "substantially lessen competition." The Clayton Act has been amended several times, most notably in 1950, when the passage of the Celler-Kefauver Act strengthened the law against mergers that would adversely affect competition.

http://www.law.com
This site has links to articles on various aspects of the law, including antitrust law. It is very well indexed.

The principal agencies charged with administering the law are the Antitrust Division of the Justice Department and the Federal Trade Commission (FTC). The FTC is also the federal agency with jurisdiction over trade practices such as deceptive advertising and bait-and-switch sales tactics, so its resources—not great to begin with—are split between its two functions. The Antitrust Division is staffed at its lower levels with people who make a career of enforcing the antitrust laws, but its head is a political appointee, as is the attorney general to whom the chief antitrust officer reports. The vigor of antitrust prosecution therefore varies with the presidential administration, not only because the people at the head of the agency set its goals but also because the agency's budget is politically controlled. This is not to say that antitrust is ever abandoned. Every administration prosecutes price fixers when they are apprehended. But prosecution of other antitrust cases, especially mergers (the combining of two or more firms), waxes and wanes.

The position of the Reagan Administration (1980–1988) was that the economy is in fact more competitive than simple examination of concentration ratios would indicate. It argued that even markets with high concentration seldom have barriers to entry so high that they are not subject to the "potential competition" of new entrants. The threat of this potential competition can be expected to constrain the established firms and lead them to behave in a relatively competitive manner. Furthermore, firms must be large and unconstrained to compete effectively internationally. These arguments were used to curb antitrust budgets and decrease antitrust activity. Actions against mergers were virtually eliminated under the Reagan Administration, and as a result one of the heaviest periods of merger activity in U.S. history began in the 1980s.

http://www.usdoj.gov/atr
This is the Department of Justice antitrust page.

Both the Antitrust Division and the FTC have always been small when compared to their job. Their resources, however, grew until the 1980s, when the Reagan Administration cut their budgets by about 30 percent in inflation-adjusted dollars. The number of attorneys employed by the Antitrust Division and the relevant section of the FTC declined from 435 to 221 in the period from 1980 to 1989.[2]

Both the Bush and Clinton administrations were somewhat more activist with regard to antitrust. The budgets and staff of antitrust agencies were increased. A price-fixing case against Archer-Daniels-Midland Co. and the corn processing industry was brought and won by the government. Proposed mergers are examined more closely. The only two acute-care hospitals in Dubuque, Iowa, were prevented from merging. The 1997 merger between McDonnell-Douglas and Boeing, which left the United States with one civilian aircraft manufacturer, however, was allowed because international competition in aircraft manufacturing is substantial. But the proposed merger in 2000 of Sprint and WorldCom, two large telecommunications firms, was blocked by the U.S. Antitrust Division and its European counterparts. The telecommunications market is *global,* and the merger would have significantly decreased competition in telecommunication throughout the world.

The most recent, newsworthy antitrust action undoubtedly was the 2000 decision of District Court Judge Thomas Penfield Jackson that Microsoft Corporation was a monopoly that should be broken up. The case was filed in 1998. The government accused Microsoft of monopolizing the market for operating platforms with its 90 percent Windows market share. Furthermore, the government charged that the company had used its monopoly power to stifle competition by bundling its Internet Explorer into Windows, polluting Sun Microsystems' Java programming language to diminish its competitive threat to Windows, and threatening IBM and Compaq. As a result, innovations that would benefit consumers were never developed. The decision has, of course, been appealed. Microsoft and its defenders are arguing that breaking up the firm will result in slower technological progress in the software industry. Furthermore, they argue that Microsoft's product is admired and used by millions of consumers. The final outcome of the Microsoft case will not be known until all appeals have been completed.

A question facing U.S. antitrust authorities is how and to what extent they should cooperate with similar agencies in the European Union. As the countries of Europe have pursued free trade policies, privatizing some industries that were once owned by the state, they have realized that they must protect competition within their economies. Therefore agencies similar to our antitrust agencies have been established. Furthermore, technological advances in communications have resulted in some markets that are truly global. International cooperation is necessary to protect competition in such markets.

Although antitrust laws do not eliminate all market power, they do constrain the activities of dominant firms. Driven underground, price fixing has undoubtedly been weakened. Past constraints on mergers have kept concentration in many markets from increasing. It can be argued that the antitrust system thus confers important benefits to consumers.

Regulation and Deregulation

Natural monopolies that exhibit substantial economies of scale are generally regulated by state or federal government agencies such as your state public service commission. Regulation involves limitation of market entry by the granting of exclusive franchises to firms. These franchises eliminate any real or potential competition. The natural monopoly is then regulated with respect to rates charged and level of service offered. Rates, or prices, are set after rate hearings in which firms present data on their costs, and citizens groups present testimony about the probable adverse effects of rate increases. The accounting data presented by the firm are scrutinized by the professional staff of the regulatory agency. The result is a compromise between the interests of the firm and those of its customers. Because markets with substantial economies of scale tend to be highly concentrated anyway, regulation can greatly improve the outcome.

WEB LINK

http://www.antitrustinstitute.org
This site contains links to recent news articles about antitrust cases.

The major problem with regulation occurs when a public utility-type of regulation is imposed on industries that are not natural monopolies because they do not have substantial economies of scale. When this happens, regulation shelters the firms from competition and actually causes inefficiency. In markets in which competition is possible, it should be encouraged. Regulation tends to be less flexible than competitive market forces, which would lead to a better outcome in terms of prices, services, and level of output.

Consider, for example, the trucking industry, which is not subject to economies of scale. Small and large trucking firms can compete on a relatively equal basis. However, interstate trucking was regulated by the federal government in 1935 and continued to be strictly regulated until 1980. Firms could not begin operating on particular routes without obtaining licenses to do so from the Interstate Commerce Commission (ICC), the agency given jurisdiction over highway carriers. The ICC limited entry into the industry to protect existing carriers, eliminating potential competition. Many trucking firms' licenses were for specific commodities, so all firms could not carry all commodities. If these firms could not obtain a load of their regulated commodity at the end of a trip, they simply traveled back to their terminal empty. This practice obviously created inefficiency. All similar carriers charged the same regulated price. As they could not compete on the basis of price, they competed on the basis of frequency of service and therefore often hauled loads that were less than their vehicles' capacity. This too was inefficient. Trucking regulation did not benefit consumers. Shippers paid significantly higher rates due to the industry's inefficiency, and these higher rates were passed along to consumers in the form of higher prices. In 1980 the industry was substantially deregulated. Because regulation was unwise in this case, efficiency improved and consumers benefited.

Deregulation simply means lessening regulatory restrictions, either in part or in total. Many formerly regulated industries were deregulated in the late 1970s and the 1980s. Because these industries were quite competitive without regulation, deregulation was appropriate. Among the industries deregulated in this period were natural gas production, airlines, railroads (the monopoly position of which had been eroded by interindustry competition), and, of course, trucking.

The bottom line with regard to regulation is that it can improve the performance of natural monopolies but that it is inferior to competition when competition is possible.

Import Competition

Finally, competition from imported products curbs the market power of domestic firms. The presence of Toyota, Nissan, and Volkswagen provides effective competition for the big three U.S. auto companies. The industry's abandonment of price leadership in the 1980s stemmed not from government action but from competition from abroad. Our domestic producers have been forced to improve efficiency to compete with Japanese firms. Ultimately, American consumers have benefited.

Import quotas and tariffs that limit competition from abroad protect American firms. The powerful firms that lobby Congress to limit imports to protect American jobs are often in concentrated markets. Restricting imports protects

Conservative and liberal economists differ greatly in their attitudes toward market power, antitrust activities, and economic regulation. Conservatives, who believe in a limited government role in the economy, feel that market power is seldom a serious problem. They believe that barriers to market entry are seldom so high as to eliminate the threat of competition from new firms entering the industry. Furthermore, technological change erodes established monopoly positions. Thus conservatives seldom see a need for antitrust or economic regulation, and they believe that such policies usually create inefficiency.

One of the ways in which conservative and liberal economists differ most is in their attitudes toward mergers. Conservatives argue that any increased market power that is created when firms merge will be controlled by potential competition from new entrants into the market and by technological change. Liberals, on the other hand, generally feel that the antitrust system is needed to control excessive market power and that proposed mergers should be scrutinized closely before they are allowed to take place.

Liberals believe that public utilities should be regulated to protect the consumer from monopolistic excesses. Conservatives, however, argue that the government actually creates monopoly power by granting the utility companies exclusive franchises. They argue that the problem is the government monopoly grant, not the economies of scale that result in a natural monopoly. Thus conservatives view economic regulation largely as a source of inefficiency and the expansion of the government role.

their market power, not the American worker. The American automobile industry has been quite successful in increasing restrictions on imports. At the same time, it is building assembly plants abroad, where labor is cheaper. American workers, who are also American consumers, benefit from low or nonexistent import restrictions.

THE TREND IN MARKET POWER

How serious is the problem of market power? The answer is not simple. Overall, the U.S. economy has grown more competitive over time. William G. Shepherd noted a sharp increase in "effective competition" for the period 1958–1980. He credited import competition and vigorous enforcement of the antitrust laws for the decline. He believes that effective competition has been relatively stable—or perhaps increasing slightly—since 1980, with the deregulation of competitive sectors offsetting the lax enforcement of the antitrust laws.[3]

But this overall picture masks the fact that market power remains high in particular markets. Automobiles, soups, newspapers, and many other markets are not effectively competitive. The airlines, which were quite competitive when first deregulated, have engaged in a series of mergers that have created a tight oligopoly. Many economists argue that we still need to support the policies that limit market power.

SUMMARY

Market power exists when there are only a few firms in a market. These firms are sheltered from competition by barriers to entry. The firms can significantly influence their own prices by restricting the quantity of their products. The adverse consequences of market power are often higher prices, lower quantities of goods available, inefficiency, price discrimination, and collusion.

The major factors inhibiting the development and abuse of market power are technological change, our antitrust system, economic regulation of natural monopolies, and import competition. The level of market power in the U.S. economy decreased throughout the 1960s and 1970s and is thought to have been relatively stable since 1980.

NOTES

1. Much of the discussion of inefficiency is based on the work of William G. Shepherd. See, for example, *The Economics of Industrial Organization,* 4th ed. (Englewood Cliffs, NJ: Prentice-Hall, 1997).

2. William G. Shepherd, *Public Policy Toward Business,* 8th ed. (Boston: Irwin, 1991), p. 191.

3. William G. Shepherd, *The Economies of Industrial Organization,* pp. 95–98.

DISCUSSION QUESTIONS

1. *What characteristics are necessary for a market to be purely competitive? Are there many purely competitive markets in the real world?*

2. *What are the disadvantages of market power for society? (Hint: discuss price, output, profits, price discrimination, etc.)*

3. *What are barriers to entry? Why must barriers to entry be present if market power exists in a particular market?*

4. *Discuss the following barriers to entry: (a) economies of scale, (b) exclusive franchises, (c) licenses,* *(d) patents, (e) product differentiation, (f) limit pricing. Describe how each functions as a barrier to market entry by new firms.*

5. *Are you a liberal or a conservative with respect to antitrust and economic regulation?*

6. *How do tariffs and import quotas harm the consumer?*

7. *Open the Department of Justice's antitrust page (http://www.usdoj.gov/atr), and click on What's New. List the new cases that have been initiated.*

CHAPTER 5

International Trade

For to what purpose is all the toil and bustle of this world?

Adam Smith, *Theory of Moral Sentiments,* 1759

WEB LINK

http://www.wto.org
This is the site for the World
Trade Organization. It includes statistics, WTO publications, and a wide variety of
material about world trade.

The year was 1999. The place was Seattle. Widespread protests broke out amid clouds of tear gas in the air and battalions of police in the streets. Environmentalists, human rights protesters, and labor activists were there. The target of the demonstrations? The World Trade Organization, on the occasion of its opening meeting to prepare for the policy discussions of the year.

The time, the place, and the setting were unusual. And just what is the World Trade Organization? Until recently, it was virtually unheard of in the homes of American families. Now suddenly, demonstrations against this international organization were on the nightly news, the daily newspapers, *Time* magazine, and the Internet. Demonstrators were protesting against sweatshops, environmental destruction, unsafe working conditions, child labor, unemployment, firm shutdowns, and a host of other problems perceived to be the result of the global economic system, as "managed" by the international organization responsible for the rules of trade across much of the globe.

Seattle was the location of just the first of many such protests. Since then, the World Trade Organization and other international organizations have been the targets of demonstrations around the world, including the Millennium Summit at the United Nations in New York City; the Economic Summit in Prague, Czech Republic; the Organization of American States meeting in Windsor, Ontario; and

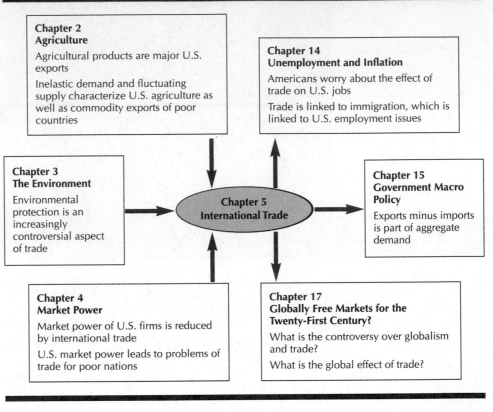

Chapter 2
Agriculture

Agricultural products are major U.S. exports

Inelastic demand and fluctuating supply characterize U.S. agriculture as well as commodity exports of poor countries

Chapter 14
Unemployment and Inflation

Americans worry about the effect of trade on U.S. jobs

Trade is linked to immigration, which is linked to U.S. employment issues

Chapter 3
The Environment

Environmental protection is an increasingly controversial aspect of trade

Chapter 5
International Trade

Chapter 15
Government Macro Policy

Exports minus imports is part of aggregate demand

Chapter 4
Market Power

Market power of U.S. firms is reduced by international trade

U.S. market power leads to problems of trade for poor nations

Chapter 17
Globally Free Markets for the Twenty-First Century?

What is the controversy over globalism and trade?

What is the global effect of trade?

WEB LINK

http://www.worldbank.org
This site of the World Bank presents data, articles, daily news discussions, and a wealth of information about individual countries.

the Economic Summit in Melbourne, Australia. Even the Republican National Convention in Philadelphia and the Democratic National Convention in Los Angeles were sites of demonstrations over issues of globalism and trade.

We know that the world is becoming increasingly internationalized. As communications and transportation improve, we become more and more linked to other parts of the globe. Through imports, we consume products like cocoa and bananas that we could never produce domestically. Through exports, we create jobs for our citizens. The World Trade Organization, the World Bank, and the International Monetary Fund are now becoming household words. International investment takes place at a frantic pace. Multinational corporations locate subsidiaries in remote parts of the world. Chances are good that you will one day work for a company involved in international business. On your own computer, you can communicate around the globe by electronic mail in a matter of seconds. On your own campus, international faculty teach you, and students from abroad share your classes. You are undoubtedly becoming more aware of international issues.

Yet many Americans seem reluctant to *think* "internationally." We see the world as complex and confusing, and sometimes refuse to think of matters beyond our own backyard. Why is international economics so intimidating? Is it because it's so foreign: foreign countries, foreign currency, and foreign terminology? Is it because we feel threatened by the international trade advances of countries such as Japan? It's a mistake for us to retreat to the familiar, for the world will march on without us, and international economics will grow increasingly important in our lives. Finally, international economics is not as complicated as you might think. The next several pages will convince you of that. *And,* by inserting phrases like "the dollar traded high today" into your everyday conversation, you'll soon be impressing your friends and relatives.

In this chapter, we'll focus on issues surrounding international trade. Along the way, we'll discover some of the trade issues that culminated in Seattle. We'll also discover the importance of trade as an offset to the problem of market power discussed in Chapter Four. Finally, in the appendix we'll discover the basics of international finance, which is the means of paying for internationally traded goods. So let's begin. . . .

THE IMPORTANCE OF TRADE

Exports
The value of goods and services sold to foreigners.

Imports
The value of goods and services purchased from foreigners.

Trade balance
The value of a nation's exports minus its imports.

Trade deficit
The amount by which a nation's trade balance is in deficit (imports exceed exports).

Trade surplus
The amount by which a nation's trade balance is in surplus (exports exceed imports).

Over time in the United States we have seen the increasing importance of international trade in terms of the dollar size of our exports and imports. Our **exports** are the goods and services that we sell to foreigners, whereas our **imports** are the goods and services we buy from them. A good way to consider our exports and our imports is in terms of their share of gross domestic product (GDP). Recall that GDP is the value of our nation's production. As a share of GDP, our exports have increased from 4 percent in 1960 to 12 percent in 1999. Our imports have increased from 3 percent of gross domestic product in 1960 to 13 percent in 1999.[1]

Our exports *plus* imports as a share of GDP is 25 percent. This number shows the importance of international trade in our economy. Our exports *minus* imports is our **trade balance,** valued at –1 percent of GDP (12% – 13% = –1%). The negative number means that we have a **trade deficit** of 1 percent of GDP. If a country has more exports than imports, the trade balance is positive. We refer to this as a **trade surplus.** Table 5-1 displays data for a diverse group of countries around the

TABLE 5-1 Exports, Imports, Exports Plus Imports, and Trade Balance (exports minus imports) as a Share of GDP in Selected Countries, 1999

COUNTRY	EXPORTS (AS % OF GDP)	IMPORTS (AS % OF GDP)	EXPORTS + IMPORTS (AS % OF GDP)	EXPORTS – IMPORTS (AS % OF GDP)
Myanmar (Burma)	1	2	3	–1
Laos	4	5	9	–1
United States	12	13	25	–1
Mexico	31	33	64	–2
Canada	41	39	80	+2
Netherlands	56	49	105	+7
Angola	84	59	143	+25
Malaysia	124	111	235	+13

Source: Data from World Bank, *World Development Report 2000/2001* (New York: Oxford University Press, 2001).

world. We have not included a sufficient number of countries to discern any patterns, but column four reveals that international trade plays a very large role in some countries and a much smaller role in others. Column five shows that some countries have a trade deficit, whereas others have a trade surplus.

The statistics show that international trade is important for the United States, and increasingly so. But is this situation good or bad? To answer this question, we must consider the benefits of trade.

THE BENEFITS OF TRADE

Forget about the international environment for a moment, and think about yourself as a producer and consumer. Imagine: what would life be like if you tried to produce everything you need and want? You would grow your own food, build your own house, sew your own clothes, and teach yourself economics! Or you could try to specialize in something you're particularly good at, maybe accounting or computer programming, and then earn a living at this task. You could use your income to purchase all of the other things that you need and want.

Most of us would agree pretty quickly that we are better off specializing in what we are good at and exchanging our income for the things that we want to consume. Why? Because we are simply not very good at producing everything that we need. Some of us would spend so much time figuring out how to bake bread or fix the plumbing that we would never get around to any other activities. Far more efficient for me to teach economics, hire a plumber, and stop at the bakery!

This way of thinking is an appropriate analogy for individual countries trying to determine whether or not to engage in international trade. A country might try to be self-sufficient; that is, to produce everything that its people need and want. Indeed, politicians in many countries have advocated this goal from time to time. It sounds so strong and independent! But like an individual, a country can specialize in the production of a limited number of products that it is especially good at producing. It can then export these products and use the resulting income to import the other things that its people desire. Just like the individual, the country will gain from specialization and exchange.

More specifically, what is the source of these benefits? You now have some idea, but we need to be more precise than simply saying we ought to specialize in the activities at which we are good. Exactly what do we mean by being "good at it"? The answers lie in the concepts of absolute and comparative advantage.

Absolute Advantage

Absolute advantage
A situation whereby a country can produce a good at a lower resource cost than another country.

Absolute advantage is defined as a situation whereby a country can produce a good at a lower resource cost than another country. Resources include labor, land, capital, and so on. Note that we are comparing the resource cost of producing a good in one country with that of producing the good in another country. Consider the United States and Brazil as examples. Brazil has a climate and land type far more beneficial to the growing of coffee than does the United States. Someone might be able to devise a climate control system that would allow coffee to be produced in the United States, but it would be very difficult to do so, and it would entail a high resource cost. Brazil can produce coffee at a lower resource cost.

On the other hand, the United States is better suited for the growing of barley than is Brazil. Proper land, weather, machinery, and technology allow the United States to produce barley at a lower resource cost than Brazil. We say that Brazil has an absolute advantage in coffee production (compared with the United States), whereas the United States has an absolute advantage in barley production (compared with Brazil). It would be far more reasonable for the United States to devote its resources to barley production (rather than to produce both barley and coffee) and then exchange with Brazil to acquire coffee. With the United States specializing in barley, and Brazil specializing in coffee, both countries are producing more total output than if each country tried to produce each good. Larger total output means larger total consumption: each country could benefit from specialization and trade.

Comparative Advantage

The situation we just described presents a fairly obvious example of the benefits of trade. A country need not possess absolute advantage as described above to garner these benefits, however. Consider a situation in which one country enjoys an absolute advantage in the production of two goods, and another country possesses an absolute advantage in none. Suppose, for example, that the United States can produce both floppy disks and shoes at a lower resource cost than Greenland. Should the United States produce both floppy disks and shoes or specialize in production of one good and trade with Greenland for the other good? To answer this question, we need to consider the concept of comparative advantage.

Comparative advantage is defined as a situation whereby a country can produce a good at a lower opportunity cost than another country. Notice the similarity to absolute advantage. We are comparing two countries and two goods. However, the term *resource cost* is replaced with *opportunity cost*. This difference is important. Recall from Chapter One that opportunity cost refers to that which you give up to get something else. That is, to produce some amount of one good, a country must give up the opportunity for some production of another good. Resources are limited; when they are put into one use, they cannot be put into another. Let's be more specific.

Suppose that labor is the only resource used in producing floppy disks and shoes, and that workers receive identical daily wages (two simplifying assumptions). Let's assume that each worker in the United States can produce either eight floppy disks or four pairs of shoes per day (or some combination in between), and that each worker in Greenland can produce either two floppy disks or two pairs of shoes per day (or some combination in between). This information is displayed in Table 5-2 on page 98.

Clearly the United States has an absolute advantage in the production of both floppy disks and shoes. Because each worker in the United States can produce more floppies and more shoes than each worker in Greenland, the resource cost of producing both of these goods will be lowest in the United States.

Comparative advantage A situation whereby a country can produce a good at a lower opportunity cost than another country.

According to the table, each worker in the United States can produce either eight floppy disks or four pairs of shoes per day. Each worker in Greenland can produce either two floppy disks or two pairs of shoes per day. This means that compared with Greenland the United States has an absolute advantage in the production of both floppy disks and shoes.

COUNTRY	FLOPPY DISK PRODUCTION	SHOE PRODUCTION (PAIRS)
United States	8	4
Greenland	2	2

But let's think in terms of comparative advantage. The opportunity cost of producing eight floppy disks in the United States is the four pairs of shoes that will not be produced. Or put another way, the opportunity cost of producing each two floppies in the United States is one pair of shoes (a two-to-one ratio). On the other hand, the opportunity cost of producing two floppy disks in Greenland is the two pairs of shoes that will not be produced (a one-to-one ratio). In terms of forgone shoe production, the United States has a lower opportunity cost than Greenland for floppy disk production. One floppy disk requires that we give up only one-half pair of shoes, whereas Greenland gives up a whole pair of shoes for each floppy disk. Because the United States gives up fewer shoes when producing floppy disks, it has the comparative advantage in floppy disk production.

Now consider the production of shoes. The opportunity cost of producing four pairs of shoes in the United States is the eight floppy disks that will not be produced. Put another way, the opportunity cost of producing two pairs of shoes is four floppy disks (a one-to-two ratio). On the other hand, the opportunity cost of producing two pairs of shoes in Greenland is only two floppy disks (a one-to-one ratio). In terms of forgone floppy disk production, Greenland has the lower opportunity cost for shoe production. That is, Greenland has the comparative advantage in shoe production.

What this means is that if the United States specializes in floppy disk production, and Greenland specializes in shoe production, the two countries will be able to come up with a rate of exchange in trade that will be mutually beneficial. The rate of four floppy disks in exchange for three pairs of shoes would benefit both countries, for example. Greenland could receive four floppy disks from the United States by selling three pairs of shoes in exchange. This is a more effective strategy than Greenland trying to produce the four floppy disks, for it would then have to give up four pairs of shoes in production (the one-to-one ratio). The United States could receive three pairs of shoes from Greenland by selling the four floppy disks in exchange. This is a more effective strategy than the United States trying to produce the three pairs of shoes, for it would then have to give up six floppy disks in production (the one-to-two ratio). Each country can trade at a rate of exchange that is superior to the opportunity costs associated with domestic production.

Why shouldn't the United States produce both floppy disks and shoes? After all, it can produce both goods at a lower resource cost than Greenland. But by specializing in floppy disk production, the United States can obtain more floppy disks *and* shoes than if it tried to produce them both. This outcome can be easily illustrated by the production possibilities curve, a technique with which you are already familiar.

Recall from Chapter One that the production possibilities curve shows alternative combinations of the maximum amounts of two different products that can be produced by one economy, during a particular time period when resources are fully and efficiently utilized. The production possibilities curve in Chapter One was bowed outward, but the one in Figure 5-1 is straight for simplicity. Notice that the production possibilities curve in Figure 5-1 shows that each worker in the United States can produce either eight floppy disks or four pairs of shoes (or some combination in between) per day. (We could multiply these numbers by the number of workers in the United States to obtain the total number of floppy disks and shoes that the United States could produce, and end up with a more conventional production possibilities curve.) In the absence of trade, the United States cannot consume more floppy disks and shoes than it produces.

Now let us introduce the possibility of trade. Suppose the United States decides to specialize in floppy disk production because this is where it has its comparative advantage. Further, suppose that the United States agrees with Greenland to trade at the rate of exchange of four floppy disks for three pairs of shoes. This trade ratio is arbitrary but is chosen as representative of a ratio that will benefit

FIGURE 5-1   Production Possibilities for Each U.S. Worker per Day, No Trade

The production possibilities curve shows alternative combinations of the maximum amounts of two products that can be produced by one country (or one worker in a country) during a particular time period. This graph shows that each U.S. worker can produce either 8 floppy disks or 4 pairs of shoes (or some combination in between) per day.

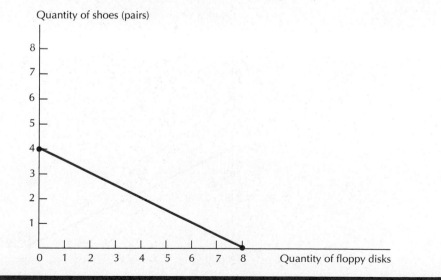

each country. This situation is displayed in Figure 5-2, with the production possibilities curve of Figure 5-1 repeated for convenience. Note that if the U.S. produces at Point A (reflecting specialization in the production of eight floppy disks), it can move to alternative points along a new curve, which we might call a **consumption possibilities curve** with trade.

Consumption possibilities curve
A curve that shows alternative combinations of the maximum amounts of two products that can be consumed within a country during a particular time period.

The United States, for example, may decide to sell four floppy disks to Greenland (back up four floppy disks from point A to A′) in exchange for three pairs of shoes (move up three pairs of shoes from A′), moving its consumption point back up along the consumption possibilities curve to point B (at which the United States ends up with four floppy disks and three pairs of shoes). Alternatively, the United States might sell another four floppy disks (back up four more floppy disks from point B to B′) in exchange for another three pairs of shoes (move up three more pairs of shoes from B′), moving its consumption point back up along the curve to point C (at which the United States ends up with no floppy disks and six pairs of shoes). With the exception of point A, the United States is better off at all points along the dashed consumption possibilities curve made possible through specialization and trade than along the production possibilities curve in the absence of trade. We could draw a similar graph for Greenland, indicating the same types of benefits through specialization in shoe production and trade with the United States for floppies.

FIGURE 5-2   Production Possibilities for Each U.S. Worker, and Consumption Possibilities with Trade, per Day

This graph shows that each U.S. worker can produce either 8 floppy disks or 4 pairs of shoes (or some combination in between) per day. With no trade, the United States would be restricted to consuming amounts indicated along the production possibilities curve. With trade, and a trade ratio of 4 floppy disks for 3 pairs of shoes, the United States can consume along the higher consumption possibilities curve.

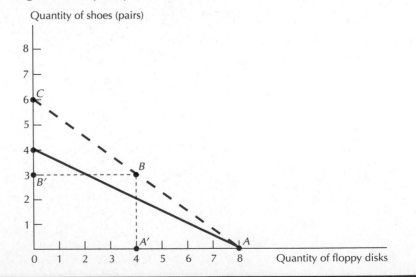

The Basis for Advantage

Why is one country better at producing a good than another country? Whether we're thinking in terms of absolute or comparative advantage, there are some basic reasons why one country will have the advantage. Some obvious factors are weather and climate. Sometimes weather and climate can be overcome (through the use of greenhouses to produce tomatoes, for example), but extraordinary efforts to overcome natural factors may entail a high resource cost. This high cost will give the advantage to the country with the more favorable natural conditions.

Labor is another important factor in determining advantage. A country with higher labor productivity might have an advantage in producing goods that require a large amount of labor input. Factors that contribute to labor productivity include the obvious ones, such as labor training and education, but other factors may be even more important. Sophisticated capital equipment and technology used in conjunction with labor will greatly enhance labor productivity. U.S. workers tend to be very productive because they are well trained and educated and because they often work with modern capital and technology.

When considering labor costs, both productivity and wages are important. Suppose that one worker in the Gambia is paid the equivalent of $5 per hour and can produce five baskets per hour. Suppose that one worker in the United States is paid twice the wage rate, or $10 per hour, but can produce twice the baskets, or ten baskets per hour. Which country has the higher labor cost? Neither! The labor cost of producing each basket is identical in each country ($1 per basket). Labor costs in the United States and the Gambia are identical because the U.S. worker receives twice the wage but is also twice as productive. This productivity factor is important to keep in mind when there is talk about cheap foreign labor. It is cheap *only if* productivity is high and wages remain low. People often complain about U.S. workers losing jobs to cheap foreign labor. Do you see now how this may be untrue?

Other factors determining advantage include the quality and availability of land, capital equipment, technology, and other resource inputs. Singapore, for example, has scarce land, hence extremely high land costs. Such a country would not have an advantage in the production of most agricultural products.

All of the Benefits of Trade

Whew! The most basic benefits of trade are the gains from specialization according to absolute or comparative advantage that we have just discussed. Such specialization leads to greater output from limited resources and to benefits to each trading nation and the world as a whole. Some additional benefits are also important. Consumers receive a greater diversity of products and more choice among competing brands than they would if purchasing only domestic goods. We know you are choosy among brands when buying your compact disk player or your personal computer and that your choices include foreign products!

Furthermore, the increased competition among firms made possible by trade will reduce the likelihood and degree of market power, benefiting society. Recall from the previous chapter that concentration and market power within an industry result in lower output levels (and lower employment), less efficient production, and higher prices to consumers. Increased international competition reduces the probability of these negative outcomes by reducing concentration within the industry. Instead of only three major automakers, many automobile companies sell to the U.S. market. Larger numbers of firms have less ability to raise prices and restrict output.[2]

THE DISTRIBUTION OF BENEFITS

Economic theory clearly indicates that individual nations will benefit from trade as they specialize according to their advantage, but we must realize that *not all people within the country will benefit from trade.* Although the country as a whole becomes better off, there will be some gainers and some losers within the country. That is, the benefits of trade will not be distributed equally. This unequal distribution is one of the concerns about free trade.

We can see the distribution of benefits from trade if we consider a simple graph for a country as it moves from a no-trade situation to a situation in which it begins to import a product (the free trade situation). Let's consider the United States and the market for cotton cloth. The only assumptions we need to make to keep the analysis simple are that (1) all cotton cloth is identical whether produced in the United States or elsewhere, and (2) the United States is a large producer of cotton cloth. Consider Figure 5-3, in which D and S represent the hypothetical domestic demand and supply curves, respectively, for cotton cloth in the United States. Equilibrium at point E (with the corresponding price of $1 per yard and

FIGURE 5-3   The U.S. Market for Cotton Cloth

Domestic demand for cotton cloth is indicated by D, while domestic supply is indicated by S. In the absence of trade, equilibrium is at point E, with the corresponding price of $1 per yard, and quantity of 1,000 yards. As the United States begins to import cotton cloth, D continues to represent domestic demand, while S^T represents the total free trade supply curve. The new equilibrium is E^T. Equilibrium price falls to $.75 per yard, quantity consumed increases to 1,500 yards, and quantity produced domestically falls to 500 yards.

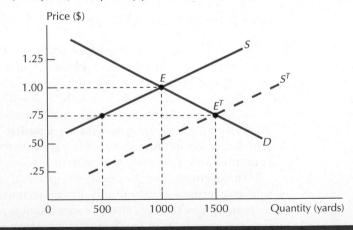

the quantity of 1,000 yards) reflects the situation in which the United States engages in no international trade of cotton cloth.

Now suppose the United States begins importing cotton cloth into the country. D will continue to represent the domestic demand (that is, the demand for cotton cloth by U.S. consumers) and S will continue to represent the domestic supply (that is, the supply of cotton cloth by U.S. producers). But note the new supply curve S^T as well. S^T represents the total free trade supply curve for cotton cloth. It includes all of the supply represented by the domestic supply curve S, plus additional supply by foreign countries. (Hence the curve is drawn by simply shifting the domestic supply curve forward; that is, by increasing it.) The new supply curve S^T now becomes the relevant curve for determining equilibrium price and quantity consumed under the free trade situation. At the new equilibrium point E^T, determined by the intersection of D and S^T, the new free trade price is $.75 per yard, and the quantity consumed is 1,500 yards. This new price is lower, representing an improved situation for U.S. consumers of cotton cloth. The new quantity consumed is higher, indicating that consumers are now purchasing larger quantities of cloth. Clearly, consumers of cotton cloth gain from trade.

Consider U.S. producers of cotton cloth, however. Although the new supply curve S^T is the relevant curve for determining equilibrium price and quantity consumed under free trade, the old supply curve S is still the relevant curve for representing the supply decisions of domestic suppliers. At the new lower price of $.75, domestic suppliers reduce the quantity they produce to 500 yards (the new domestic quantity supplied). Note that U.S. consumers are buying a quantity of 1,500 yards and U.S. suppliers are selling a quantity of 500 yards; the difference between them is made up by imports of cotton cloth into the country. U.S. producers of cotton cloth are harmed by free trade: they receive a lower price for their product, and they now sell a smaller quantity. Both the individual cloth companies and the workers for these companies (who may experience layoffs) lose as a result of trade.

Even though the benefits of trade accrue to the United States as a whole and to U.S. consumers of cotton cloth in particular, U.S. producers of cotton cloth are harmed. The effects of free trade are summarized in Table 5-3. It is the U.S. producers of cotton cloth (firms and workers) who will argue most vehemently in favor of trade restrictions. To the extent that these producers are politically powerful (typically more powerful than unorganized consumers), the U.S. government may respond to their appeals with a variety of trade restrictions.

TABLE 5-3   Effects of Free Trade in Cotton Cloth Imports into the United States

EFFECTS OF FREE TRADE ON:	EFFECT	REASON
The United States as a whole	Gain	Efficiency through specialization and exchange according to comparative advantage, greater diversity of product, reduced market power
U.S. consumers of cotton cloth	Gain	Lower price and increased quantity consumed
U.S. firms producing cotton cloth	Lose	Lower price and decreased quantity supplied
U.S. workers producing cotton cloth	Lose	Jobs lost as cotton cloth production decreases

RESTRICTIONS TO FREE TRADE

Quota
A restriction on the quantity of an imported good.

Tariff
A tax on an imported good.

Two common types of trade restrictions are quotas and tariffs. A **quota** is a restriction on the quantity of an imported good. A quota on sugar, for example, means that only a limited amount of sugar from other countries will be allowed to enter the United States. Once this quota is met, Americans will be forced to buy U.S.-produced sugar, or to go without. A **tariff** does not limit the quantity of an imported good but is simply a tax imposed on the imported product. A tariff on Canadian whiskey coming into the United States would serve to raise the price of the product (in this case, the Canadian whiskey) to American consumers, making them more likely to purchase American whiskey.

The purpose of most U.S. trade restrictions is to force or encourage American consumers to buy more American-made products and fewer foreign counterparts. They are thus designed to protect American producers, despite the fact that the resulting trade barriers reduce the benefits of free trade that would otherwise accrue to our country. Trade restrictions on cotton cloth imports cause the price of cotton cloth to rise, thereby benefiting U.S. cloth producers (firms and workers) and hurting U.S. cloth consumers. (In the extreme case of a trade restriction that would totally prohibit imports of cotton cloth into the United States, we would revert back to the original demand and supply curves in Figure 5-3, a situation in which prices to consumers increase, smaller quantities are consumed, and larger quantities are supplied domestically.) The fact that we have many trade restrictions means either that American producers are more powerful in protecting their interests than American consumers, or that American consumers do not understand the consequences of trade restrictions for their own well-being. Both of these situations probably exist.

Trade restrictions have powerful effects beyond the ones discussed above with respect to producers and consumers. The nation as a whole will lose the benefits of specialization and exchange according to advantage. Competition within protected industries will decrease because foreign competition among producers is lessened. Consequently, domestic producers will have more market power. (As we know, increased market power may cause output within the concentrated industry to fall. If firms produce less output, they may hire fewer workers, suggesting that workers within concentrated U.S. industries, such as the American automobile industry, may have been falsely convinced that trade restrictions would protect their jobs. A graph like that of the cotton cloth industry may not accurately reflect workers' interests in the case of a concentrated industry with market power.)

Retaliation
A situation in which one country responds to the trade restrictions of another country by imposing trade restrictions of its own.

And finally, producers within other industries, in particular our export industries, will likely suffer as a result of trade restrictions. If the United States imposes quotas on imports of cotton cloth, U.S. producers of wheat and corn for export may see their foreign sales decline. This sales drop may occur for a variety of reasons. First, other countries may respond to U.S. trade restrictions with restrictions of their own. This action is called **retaliation.** If the United States limits imports of cotton cloth, Sri Lanka, for example, may limit imports of U.S. corn. Moreover, incomes of foreign producers of cotton cloth may fall as the United States restricts its purchases. As the incomes of Sri Lankans fall, they will be less *able* to purchase

TABLE 5-4   Effects of Trade Restrictions on Imports of Cotton Cloth into the United States

EFFECTS OF TRADE RESTRICTIONS ON:	EFFECT	REASON
The United States as a whole	Lose	Loss of efficiency through specialization and exchange according to comparative advantage, less diversity of product, greater market power
U.S. consumers of cotton cloth	Lose	Higher price and decreased quantity consumed
U.S. firms producing cotton cloth	Gain	Higher price and increased quantity supplied
U.S. workers producing cotton cloth	Gain	Jobs gained as cotton cloth production increases
U.S. producers of export goods	Lose	Loss of export sales

U.S. corn. And finally, U.S. trade restrictions will affect the value of the U.S. dollar relative to foreign currencies. The change in this value will likely reduce U.S. exports, as indicated in the appendix to this chapter. Table 5-4 summarizes the effects of U.S. trade restrictions on cotton cloth imports.

Because U.S. producers (workers and firms) of cotton cloth are the only beneficiaries of trade restrictions and because the rest of the United States suffers, perhaps we should seek better ways to deal with the hardships suffered by these producers when we freely import cotton cloth. If other countries have the advantage in cotton cloth production, encouraging continued production by U.S. firms means supporting relatively inefficient industries. The United States does not really benefit in the long run. But, rather than leaving these U.S. firms and workers to suffer their losses through trade, we might seek solutions that improve the efficiency of U.S. industry (for example, through subsidies for research and development) or that retrain workers for and redirect firms into production of more advantageous goods. The latter solution is pursued under the North American Free Trade Agreement, which is discussed shortly. Do keep in mind the main point, however, that the United States as a whole benefits when importing products in which it does not have a comparative advantage. If a reason for the lack of comparative advantage is cheap foreign labor, then the United States as a whole benefits from cheap foreign labor!

THE REST OF THE CONTROVERSY

The U.S. job and business loss was one of the concerns underlying the Seattle and subsequent protests. It was not the only one, however! Many of the issues are much broader and involve economic justice throughout the world. These global issues involve trade in less-developed countries, the politics of trade, and international trade agreements.

Less-Developed Countries

People of less-developed countries (LDCs) are among those who are sometimes hurt by trade. These poor countries of the world have experienced problems with trade, even when carefully following the economic theory of specialization according to comparative advantage. One problem is related to the lack of diversity in exports. Costa Rica, for example, relies on coffee exports for a large share of its export earnings. Yet if bad weather significantly harms the coffee crop, or if international prices of coffee fall dramatically, the Costa Rican economy could be devastated. It would be better not to specialize so completely. Greater diversity of exports would provide some insurance against problems that might beset one particular product. In the meanwhile, however, poor countries are vulnerable to national and international circumstances that are largely beyond their control.

Another closely related problem concerns the reliance of many LDCs on primary commodities for export. **Primary commodities** are unprocessed raw materials or agricultural products, such as coffee, sugar, tea, cocoa, and rubber. Prices for these types of products are often very unstable, as was discussed in Chapter Two with respect to U.S. agriculture. This instability is related to two common characteristics of primary commodity markets. Consider the hypothetical market for coffee depicted in Figure 5-4. The demand curve is drawn fairly steep, suggesting that demand is inelastic. Recall from Chapter Two that **inelastic demand** exists when consumers are relatively unresponsive to changes in price. That is, they do not alter the quantity they purchase very much when there is a price change. A steep demand curve reflects this small change in quantity relative to price. Compare the change in quantity demanded between points A and B, for example, with the larger change in price between these two points. Quantity demanded falls from 5,000 pounds to 4,000 pounds (a 20 percent reduction) when price rises from $1 to $2 per pound (a 100 percent increase).

Inelastic demand characterizes the markets for many primary commodities. It makes sense in the coffee market, for when coffee prices rise, the coffee drinkers

Primary commodities
Unprocessed raw material and agricultural products.

Inelastic demand
Demand in which buyers are relatively unresponsive to changes in price.

FIGURE 5-4   The Demand for Coffee

In the coffee market, the demand curve D is drawn relatively steep. This reflects an inelastic demand for coffee. Notice that a large increase in price from $1 to $2 (a 100 percent increase) is associated with just a small decrease in quantity demanded from 5,000 to 4,000 pounds (a 20 percent decrease).

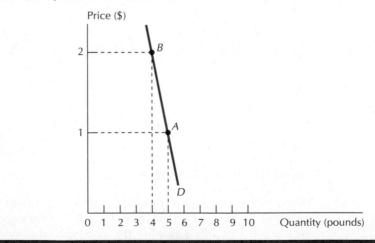

FIGURE 5-5   The Market for Coffee

The demand for coffee D is inelastic, while supply fluctuates from S to S' from one year to the next. The combination of inelastic demand and fluctuating supply results in large fluctuations in price, from $1 to $2 per pound (a 100 percent increase).

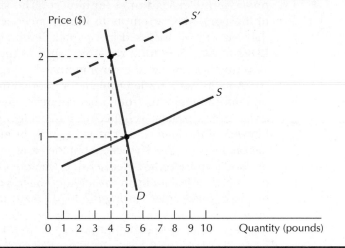

among us will be reluctant to reduce our consumption of coffee by very much. We are creatures of habit, especially when it comes to our caffeine consumption. The same is true for other commodities, such as tea and tobacco.

Another characteristic of markets for primary commodities is a fluctuating supply. The supply of many primary commodities is heavily dependent on weather, and weather tends to fluctuate a lot.

The combination of fluctuating supply and inelastic demand results in a large fluctuation in price, as is evident in Figure 5-5. (Experiment a little: redraw the graph with a relatively flat demand curve, yet identical fluctuation in supply. You will see that the price will no longer fluctuate as much.) Price fluctuation is a short-term phenomenon. That is, prices fluctuate from year to year, just as weather fluctuates from year to year.

This fluctuation in price can be very detrimental for countries producing primary commodities for export. Although prices may average to an acceptable medium, the fluctuation itself is hard to deal with. A producer might go out of business entirely, and a country may have its export earnings plummet in a particularly bad year. These potential outcomes have led to some developing countries' attempts to join together in commodity agreements that seek to stabilize commodity prices. These agreements have met with mixed success.

Declining terms of trade
A situation in which the price of a country's exports declines relative to the price of its imports.

Another problem affecting the trade situation of many poor countries is what is known as **declining terms of trade.** Over time, the prices of poor-country exports (especially primary commodities) have declined relative to the prices of poor-country imports. Declining terms of trade is a long-term phenomenon, whereas price fluctuation is a problem in the short term. Demand for poor-country exports has tapered off (and therefore price of the exports has decreased), due in part to the development of synthetics and developed-country trade restrictions. At the same time, the prices of manufactured goods and petroleum products imported into poor countries have generally increased (due to market power in developed-country industry and the market power of the Organization of Petroleum Exporting Countries). As a result, poor-country export earnings have declined relative to poor-country expenditures for imports. This situation has undermined poor developing countries' attempts to import needed products and repay international debt, as will be discussed in Chapter Seventeen. It has also made it necessary for LDCs to exploit natural resources, such as timber, as a source of export earnings. This practice has led to environmental degradation.

An additional trade problem for poor countries is the possibility of over-reliance on important imports from other countries. According to the theory of comparative advantage, a country is better off importing a good in which it lacks an advantage, but what if the importation of an essential product becomes unreliable? When international food prices skyrocketed in the early 1970s, developing countries dependent on food imports found themselves priced out of the market. Hundreds of thousands of people starved to death throughout the less-developed world. When international oil prices quadrupled during the 1970s, many poor oil-importing countries could no longer afford basic energy inputs. Often, imports may become unreliable for other than economic reasons: supplies may be cut off for political reasons, or shipping and transportation systems may be disrupted due to adverse weather, civil unrest, and war. We have repeatedly observed this dynamic in many African countries today.

Finally, globalization has created opportunities for local and foreign companies to exploit local workers, including children, in the production of goods for export in many LDCs. This practice has especially been publicized in the garment and carpet industries. Many of us are now becoming aware of our role as consumers, when we purchase items produced in so-called sweatshops. Our buying decisions may indeed affect the practices of international companies.

All of these issues suggest that poor nations must be very careful as they plan their development strategies. Comparative advantage ought to be an important element of such strategies, but attention must also be directed to proper diversification and processing of commodity exports because processed goods are less vulnerable to trade restrictions and declining terms of trade. Wealthier countries must ensure that trade is fair, and that their own trade restrictions on poor countries are reduced. In addition, wealthy countries and companies must accept their share of responsibility when their policies and profits encourage environmental degradation and unjust labor conditions.

http://www.dol.gov
This is the site for the Department of Labor; it has links to sites dealing with sweatshop labor.

Politics and Trade

Although international trade is an economic issue, it has often become politicized. The United States became the victim of politics during the Arab Oil Embargo in 1974 and the Iranian Oil Embargo of 1979. In each case, oil was cut off from the United States, causing an energy crisis in our nation.

Sometimes the United States restricts trade to bring about political goals. It commonly restricts trade with communist countries. Cuba is a case in point. In 1959, the Cuban revolution created a socialist economy headed by Fidel Castro, who initiated the nationalization (government confiscation) of U.S. property in

Embargo
Restrictions on trade with
another country for
political reasons.

Cuba. The United States responded with a trade **embargo,** as well as subsequent policies to "punish" some of the countries that trade with Cuba. The embargo has severely harmed the well-being of the Cuban nation and its people. Many people in the United States are opposed to Cuba's socialist economic system and communist political system, and they charge the Castro government with violating the human rights of Cuban people. Many others feel that far from violating human rights, Cuba has provided high-quality health care and education to all of its residents, despite the severe poverty of the country.

Efforts are now underway in the United States to reduce the trade restrictions of the embargo. In June 2000, the U.S. House of Representatives struck a deal to allow the sale of food and medicine to Cuba (under highly restricted conditions) for the first time in four decades. President Clinton signed this bill a few months later. The agreement allows U.S. exports of similar goods to four other countries under embargo by the U.S. government: Iran, Sudan, Libya, and North Korea. In the case of North Korea, the embargo had been in effect since the early days of the Korean War in 1950. The plan allows U.S. firms to sell products, especially farm products, to North Korea and allows that nation to sell raw materials and finished goods to the United States.

China and Vietnam are two other countries whose trade relations with the United States are improving. Both countries have socialist economies in partial transition to capitalism. Vietnam, like Cuba, provides all of its people with health care and education. Yet, both Vietnam and China have communist political systems that are opposed by the United States. China has a long history of human rights violations, which anger many U.S. citizens and make them hostile toward the easing of trade restrictions. Many feel that maintaining trade restrictions is the only leverage that the United States has for improving human rights in China. Others argue that only through normalized relations will improvements be generated. They also argue that free trade would benefit both the United States and China.

Those in the latter camp believe that free trade will improve not only trade relations but also other relations between the United States and foreign countries. Opportunities for foreign investment may open up. In addition, travel restrictions may fade. Fewer restrictions on immigration may encourage greater intercountry mobility of workers, raising some issues addressed in Chapter Fourteen on unemployment. All of these topics arise in the debates and protests over globalization.

International Trade Agreements

**North American Free
Trade Agreement
(NAFTA)**
An agreement between
the United States, Canada, and Mexico allowing
more equal access to one
another's markets. The
agreement went into
effect on January 1, 1994.

The world has been moving in the direction of far-reaching trade agreements. One of the more prominent is the **North American Free Trade Agreement (NAFTA).** This agreement between the United States, Canada, and Mexico went into effect on January 1, 1994. NAFTA allows each of the three trading countries more equal access to one another's markets, along with reductions in trade restrictions. Congress passed the NAFTA Transitional Adjustment Assistance program to provide worker retraining and assistance to American workers displaced from jobs as a result of NAFTA. As we've already discovered, the United States benefits when importing a product from a country with lower labor costs. Indeed, most economists see benefits to all three of the countries. Nevertheless, there have been some concerns.

VIEWPOINT: Conservative vs. Liberal

The lines are drawn fairly clearly between traditional conservative and liberal views when it comes to the international economy, particularly in discussions of international trade. Economic conservatives within the United States generally favor free trade. They feel that free trade results in the efficiencies that arise in general from free markets. Economic liberals, on the other hand, are concerned about the effects of free trade on U.S. workers and businesses. They argue that government intervention in the form of quotas and tariffs is necessary to protect U.S. citizens from "unfair" trade practices in foreign countries. If, for example, foreign businesses keep labor costs artificially low by subjecting their workers to unsafe conditions, they have an unfair cost advantage relative to U.S. businesses. Labor in both the United States and the foreign country suffers.

The line between conservatives and liberals is no longer drawn so clearly. There appears to be much greater consensus that free trade will generally benefit the United States. NAFTA is a case in point. The Clinton Administration lobbied hard for the passage of NAFTA, and the legislation received conservative and liberal support. Liberals are probably a bit more concerned about the effect of the trade agreement on U.S. labor and the environment than conservatives.

Development economists and policymakers have traditionally held the same types of views when it comes to the trade relations affecting poor countries. Liberals have feared the problems facing LDC exports, including many of the economic justice issues that have been raised. Conservatives have traditionally focused more on the inefficiencies associated with trade restrictions. They have promoted freer markets for international trade. Liberals and conservatives have generally come together in their attention to market forces and the promotion of exports.

A major issue is that some of the lower production costs in Mexico are due to unfair circumstances. Mexico has had less restrictive controls on pollution, minimum wages, child labor, and working conditions in its factories. To deal with these circumstances, so-called side agreements were added to NAFTA, whereby businesses in Mexico are required to comply with child labor laws and laws requiring environmental protection, minimum wages, and safe working conditions. Many people believe that these requirements are inadequate and have been widely ignored,[3] leading to concerns about unfair production cost differentials between the United States and Mexico that may be forcing U.S. firms to go out of business or to relocate in Mexico. Ross Perot, former U.S. presidential candidate, once referred to the potential job loss associated with NAFTA as a "giant sucking sound."

In fact, economists believe that very few U.S. workers have lost jobs, and that others have found jobs in our export industries, as a result of NAFTA. First, the job and trade changes that took effect were already well underway when the agreement was signed. Second, very few U.S. workers have applied and been certified as eligible for benefits under the NAFTA Transitional Adjustment Assistance program.[4] Ross Perot's "giant sucking sound" seems more like a moderate whisper.

Nevertheless, the problems of pollution and poor working conditions continue in Mexico. These issues of sweatshop labor and environmental destruction are raised in protests against globalization.

General Agreement on Tariffs and Trade (GATT)
An international trade agreement, first negotiated in 1947, that has included efforts to reduce tariff barriers among member countries of the world. It is now replaced by the World Trade Organization.

World Trade Organization (WTO)
The organization that replaced GATT in 1995 and continues to pursue GATT's agenda to reduce barriers to trade among member countries.

The European Union (EU) has continued to reduce trade barriers and other economic restrictions between member countries in Europe, resulting in more open economic relations among them. The European Union now encompasses most of Europe (rather than just Western Europe). One of the major recent achievements of the European Union was the adoption of a new common currency, called the Euro.

In addition to these regional trade agreements, there are also movements underway to extend NAFTA to Chile, to negotiate a Free Trade Agreement of the Americas, and to initiate or expand other regional trade agreements. The combined effects of these trends in regional trade agreements remain to be seen.

Finally, the **General Agreement on Tariffs and Trade (GATT)** was an international trade agreement in effect since World War II. GATT was replaced by the **World Trade Organization** in 1995. Several rounds of discussions have taken place within the context of GATT, including the "Kennedy Round" completed in 1967, the "Tokyo Round" completed in 1979, and the "Uruguay Round" completed in 1993. These "rounds" have been remarkably successful in reducing tariff barriers among member countries of GATT. The average tariff on manufactured goods decreased from 40 percent in 1947 to 5 percent in 1992. The Uruguay Round reduced tariffs still further. The WTO, as the introduction to the chapter indicated, has recently evolved as a target of the Seattle and other protestors.

SUMMARY

International trade and finance are becoming increasingly important for the United States, as well as for the rest of the world. Our imports provide important products for U.S. consumers, and our exports provide jobs for our workers. Residents of other countries around the globe benefit from trade in this manner as well. Indeed, as long as countries specialize along the lines of comparative advantage and exchange through trade, the world as a whole produces more output, providing higher total consumption levels for all trading countries.

The benefits of free trade are not equally distributed within a trading country. Although consumers and exporters gain from free trade, companies and workers displaced by imports lose. The plight of the latter parties triggers arguments for trade restrictions. Two common restrictions are quotas and tariffs, which both reduce the economic benefits of trade. As an alternative to trade restrictions, governments might provide direct assistance to and retraining programs for displaced workers and companies.

The theory of specialization and exchange sometimes breaks down in practice, especially in the case of many poor countries. Among the problems that these countries frequently encounter are lack of diversity of exports, reliance on primary commodities with unstable prices, declining terms of trade, an overreliance on essential imports, and economic injustice.

Some trade issues are political, as well as economic, such as politically motivated trade embargoes. Yet throughout the world, countries have been moving toward far-reaching regional trade agreements, including the North American Free Trade Agreement. This agreement and the General Agreement on Tariffs and Trade (now the World Trade Organization) are aimed at reducing trade restrictions among member countries.

1. World Bank, *World Development Report 2000/2001* (New York: Oxford University Press, 2000), and previous issues.

2. If mergers of international corporations located in different countries continue, international trade may become less effective in terms of reducing market power.

3. Jackie Brux, "Neo-Liberalism in Mexico," 2000, unpublished.

4. Helene Cooper, "'Experts' View of NAFTA's Economic Impact: It's a Wash," *Wall Street Journal,* June 17, 1997.

DISCUSSION QUESTIONS

1. *How does international economics affect you directly as a consumer and as a future worker? How do international events and circumstances touch you as a student in a U.S. university?*

2. *Find out about the World Trade Organization by checking out its homepage (http://www.wto.org/). Choose The WTO (along the top menu); then choose What is the WTO? Check out the 10 benefits of the WTO trading system, 10 common misunderstandings about the WTO, and frequently asked questions.*

3. *Have you ever considered trying to become self-sufficient, producing for yourself all the things that you need and want? What would be the benefits of this attempt? What would be the drawbacks?*

4. *Look up information about the trade situation of some of the countries listed in Table 5-1 in the* **CIA World Factbook** *Web site (http://www.odci.gov/cia/publications/factbook). Click on the link to the country listing, then choose the letter for the name of the country, then hit the link to the country of interest. After finding the country, hit the link to the economy, and read the Economy Overview and scroll to the trade statistics. Discover the major exports and imports of the country, along with its trading partners. Is the country in deficit or surplus? What is the effect of warfare in some of the countries? Are there any reasons that statistics may be underreported?*

5. *What are some goods in which you think the United States has an absolute advantage in production? What about low-wage countries such as Thailand and Pakistan? What about tropical countries such as Costa Rica and Cuba?*

6. *Based on the information in Table 5-2, and assuming a trade ratio of four floppy disks for three pairs of shoes, what would the production possibilities curve (without trade) and the consumption possibilities curve (with trade) look like for Greenland? Does Greenland benefit from specialization and trade?*

7. *Suppose that the U.S. Congress passes trade restrictions on imports of French wine into the United States. What will be the effect of these restrictions on (a) U.S. consumers of wine, (b) U.S. producers of wine, (c) French producers of wine, (d) U.S. farmers producing agricultural goods for export, and (e) the U.S. as a whole?*

8. *Why do U.S. companies and workers within particular industries that are harmed by trade tend to have more political influence than the consumers who benefit from this trade? Do U.S. consumers have a good understanding of how they benefit from trade? Are they a cohesive political lobby?*

9. *Suppose a concentrated U.S. industry, such as the aluminum industry, is successful in getting trade restrictions on aluminum imports passed through Congress. Because these restrictions will reduce the foreign competition faced by the American aluminum industry, they will also enhance the market power of American firms within this industry. What then is a possible impact of the trade restrictions on U.S. employment within this concentrated industry?*

10. *What are some of the problems of international trade that are faced by less-developed countries? What suggestions would you have for the government of a less-developed country as it plans its trade strategy?*

11. *Draw a graph of a product, such as cocoa, but assume that demand for this product does not have inelastic demand (draw the demand curve relatively flat). Now draw in a supply curve that fluctuates from*

year to year (try to shift the supply curve forward and backward about the same distance as in Figure 5-5). Is the price fluctuation larger or smaller than that depicted in Figure 5-5? What does the answer tell us about less-developed country commodity exports for which demand generally is inelastic?

12. Look up the U.S. Department of Labor Web site (http://www.dol.gov) to learn about its "No Sweat" campaign. What are some things that you can do about sweatshop labor?

13. What benefits do you think the United States receives from the North American Free Trade Agreement? What problems do you think the United States experiences as a result of NAFTA? How do you think the United States can benefit from the economic growth of Mexico, which is an expected result of the agreement?

14. (Refer to the appendix to answer this question.) Why do Japanese residents demand U.S. dollars? Why do U.S. residents demand Japanese yen?

Chapter Five Appendix:
International Finance

When residents of two countries engage in trade or when they transfer funds for other purposes, they must deal with the matter of foreign currency. If a product is worth $500 in U.S. currency, how much is it worth in terms of French francs? If I wish to invest my $1,000 in a Japanese company, how many yen does this amount represent? To answer these questions, we need to understand the concept of exchange rates, and how these rates are determined.

EXCHANGE RATE DETERMINATION

Exchange rate
The price of one country's currency in terms of another country's currency.

An **exchange rate** is simply the price of one country's currency in terms of another country's currency. We can say, for example, that one U.S. dollar is worth seven French francs. This is the exchange rate between dollars and francs.[1] Alternatively, we can say that one French franc is worth $.15 (15 U.S. cents). (This exchange rate is calculated by taking the equation $1 = 7 francs and dividing each side by 7. We end up with $1/7 = 7 francs/7; or $.15 = 1 franc.) The two expressions are identical: we can talk in terms of 7 francs per dollar or 15 cents per franc. Note, however, that an exchange rate always expresses the value of one currency in terms of another. There is no such thing as an absolute value for a currency; exchange rates are always relative.

Flexible (floating) exchange rate system
A system whereby exchange rates are determined on the basis of international demand and supply for a currency.

Most of the industrialized world uses a **flexible (floating) exchange rate system,** in effect since 1973. Under this system, exchange rates are determined on the basis of demand and supply. Using simple techniques with which you are already familiar, we can see how the exchange rate between the dollar and franc is determined.

To simplify matters, pretend that there are only two countries in the world, the United States and France. This oversimplification enables us to use a graph, and does not detract from the analysis. Let's consider the market for the dollar, and determine the value of the dollar in terms of the French franc. This market is portrayed in Figure 5-6.

Note the demand curve D, is the demand for dollars by French residents. (Remember that there are only two countries in the world.) Why would French residents demand dollars? There are a number of reasons. One obvious one is that French people may wish to travel in the United States. They will need to pay their hotel bill and taxi fare in dollars; hence they first need to exchange their French francs for dollars. This process of acquiring dollars represents a demand for dollars.

There are more important reasons for demanding dollars, however. Suppose a French resident wishes to purchase a General Motors car. GM wants to be paid in dollars. Although the French customer won't need to come up with dollars, the French company that imports the GM vehicle into France will. The process of exchanging francs in order to acquire dollars with which to purchase the vehicle represents a demand for dollars. Suppose another French resident wishes to invest

FIGURE 5-6   **The Market for the U.S. Dollar**

The demand curve *D* represents the demand for U.S. dollars by French residents. The supply curve *S* represents the supply of U. S. dollars by U.S. residents, which is synonymous with the demand for French francs by U.S. citizens. The intersection determines the equilibrium price, or exchange rate, between the U.S. dollar and the franc. This exchange rate is 7 francs per dollar.

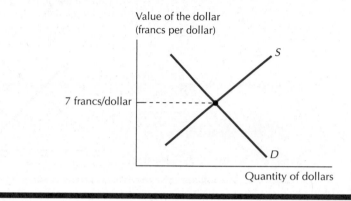

her savings in a U.S. financial market, perhaps by purchasing a U.S. government or corporate bond. She will have to first acquire dollars with which to pay for the bond; this transaction also represents a demand for dollars. Suppose a French company wishes to buy and operate a plant in the United States. The owner will have to purchase the plant and pay the workers with dollars, thereby first exchanging francs for dollars. This transaction again represents a demand for dollars. Although there are other reasons to acquire dollars, these are four important ones: to travel in the United States, to purchase U.S. goods and services, to invest in U.S. financial markets, and to buy and operate plants in the United States.

Now consider the supply curve *S* in Figure 5-6. This curve represents the supply of U.S. dollars by American residents. Why would U.S. citizens wish to supply dollars? The answer to this question is very easy if we recognize that the process of U.S. residents supplying dollars is the same as the process of U.S. residents demanding francs. In a two-country world, our process of acquiring one currency is the same as our process of supplying the other: we exchange our dollars for francs. Consequently, the supply of U.S. dollars by U.S. residents can be simultaneously viewed as the demand for French francs by U.S. residents.

Why do U.S. residents demand francs? For the same reasons that French residents demand dollars! Many of us wish to travel to Paris, or purchase French perfume, or invest in the French stock market. Many of our companies want to buy and operate plants in France. All these desires create a U.S. demand for French francs! And this makes our picture complete. We have a demand for dollars and a supply of dollars (demand for francs). The intersection of the demand and supply of U.S. dollars determines the equilibrium exchange rate between the dollar and franc. This intersection occurs at the exchange rate of seven francs per U.S. dollar in Figure 5-6.

FIGURE 5-7   A Shift in the Demand for U.S. Dollars

Increased advertising of U.S. products in France will probably increase the demand for U.S. products by French residents. This will cause French residents to increase their demand for U.S. dollars with which to pay for the U.S. products, causing the demand for dollars to increase from *D* to *D'*. The new equilibrium exchange rate is 8 francs per U.S. dollar.

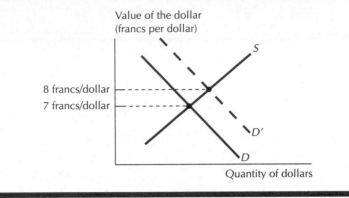

We can extend this analysis by recognizing that either the demand or supply curve of Figure 5-6 can shift in response to changing economic conditions. The demand for U.S. dollars by French residents will increase if advertising of U.S. products increases in France. This relationship is demonstrated in Figure 5-7. Note that the equilibrium exchange rate will change to eight francs per dollar, representing an increase in the value of the dollar relative to the franc (just what we would expect when the demand for dollars increases). Another way of saying this is that the dollar has **appreciated** (increased in value) relative to the franc. Because the value of one currency is always expressed relative to the other, we can also say that the franc has **depreciated** (decreased in value) relative to the dollar.

Is a higher value of the dollar good or bad? You may be used to this answer by now: it depends! In particular, it depends on who you are. For a U.S. consumer of French wine imported into the United States, a high dollar is good. It means that the franc is low, so that fewer dollars are needed to pay for the wine denominated in francs. That is, French products become cheaper for the U.S. consumer. On the other hand, a high dollar is not so good for a U.S. exporter. When the dollar is high, more francs are needed to pay for U.S. wheat denominated in dollars. That is, the U.S. wheat has become more expensive for French residents, who may now be less likely to make the purchase. U.S. exports may fall.

Appreciate
An increase in the value of one country's currency relative to another country's currency.

Depreciate
A decrease in the value of one country's currency relative to another country's currency.

ECONOMIC POLICY

Economic policy in the United States (or any other country) can have an impact on exchange rates. Recall the earlier discussion of U.S. trade restrictions imposed on imports of cotton cloth. These restrictions reduce U.S. purchases of foreign cotton cloth. If our purchases of foreign cloth decline, so too does our demand for foreign currency with which to pay for the cloth. As our demand for a foreign currency falls, the value of that currency decreases (and the relative value of the dollar increases). A rising value of the dollar makes our exports more expensive to foreign consumers, who will likely purchase fewer of them. Now we see the harm to U.S. producers of export goods when we impose trade restrictions designed to protect our cotton cloth industry. We may help one sector of the U.S. economy, but hurt another.

Consider another example of economic policy. Suppose policymakers decide to raise U.S. interest rates. A rise in U.S. interest rates relative to interest rates in other countries of the world means that U.S. financial markets now become more attractive to foreign investors. Why should a British citizen deposit her savings in a British financial institution when she can receive higher interest earnings by depositing the savings in a U.S. financial institution? Of course she would first have to exchange her British pounds (the British currency) for U.S. dollars (thereby creating a demand for dollars). This increase in the demand for dollars with which to make the deposit pushes up the value of the U.S. dollar. Indeed, one of the most important factors affecting the value of a currency is the relative interest rate in different countries.

If nothing else, this discussion should make it clear to you that the world is indeed interdependent. An action by one country has an impact felt around the world. An action by a country as important as the United States can have an especially large impact. It has been said that when the United States sneezes, the rest of the world catches pneumonia. The ripple effects are often particularly significant for the smaller, poorer countries of the world.

INTERNATIONAL MANAGEMENT OF EXCHANGE RATES

Group of Eight (G-8)
A group of eight countries (the United States, Canada, Britain, France, Italy, Germany, Japan, and Russia) that coordinate policies in an effort to influence exchange rates.

Six Markets Group (Asian G-6)
A group of six (original) countries (the United States, Japan, China, Singapore, Australia, and Hong Kong) that coordinate financial policies.

Although much of the industrialized world uses flexible (floating) exchange rates, the real world system is not based entirely on the market forces of demand and supply. Individual countries may intervene, buying and selling currencies, to influence exchange rates. This action is sometimes referred to as a "dirty float." Since 1986, an entire group of countries has coordinated their policies in an effort to influence exchange rates. These countries are now referred to as the **Group of Eight (G-8).** These countries are the United States, Canada, Britain, France, Italy, Germany, Japan, and Russia. A major goal of G-8 is to stabilize exchange rates of major world currencies within an acceptable range of one another. It is felt that all member countries benefit from greater stability among these rates.

Six Markets Group, also called Asian G-6, was formed in early 1997. This group is made up of the United States, Japan, China, Singapore, Australia, and Hong Kong (now part of China). The group is expected to extend to additional Asian countries and to evolve into an Asian counterpart to the Group of Eight.

1. The actual exchange rate between the U.S. dollar and the French franc was 7.2306 francs per dollar on August 3, 2000.

CHAPTER 6

Discrimination

Our nation is moving toward two societies, one black, one white—separate and unequal.

Report of the President's National Advisory Commission on Civil Disorders
(the Kerner Commission), March 1, 1968

Nearly four decades have passed since Dr. Martin Luther King, Jr., delivered his celebrated "I Have a Dream" speech at the foot of the Lincoln Memorial, climaxing the historic August 1963 March on Washington for Civil Rights. And more than 30 years have elapsed since President Lyndon Johnson's Kerner Commission submitted its shocking 1968 report blaming racism and discrimination, poverty, and unemployment for the riots that had besieged the nation's central cities during the 1960s. We have opened this chapter with the Kerner Commission's dire prediction. Was it accurate? The ensuing years have been years of controversy and change. Have we come any closer to realizing Dr. King's dream? Have African Americans and other ethnic and racial minorities in America attained equal access to the prerequisites of our affluent society? Or are doors still closed to some people on arbitrary bases such as race, ethnicity, and gender?

The answers to these questions are not easy. Let us begin by looking at the composition of the U.S. population according to the last census. Then we will look at the sociological meaning of the word "minority" and discuss the concept of discrimination. We will examine the available data on the socioeconomic position of our minorities. Finally, we will discuss the various policies with which we try to eliminate prejudice and discrimination.

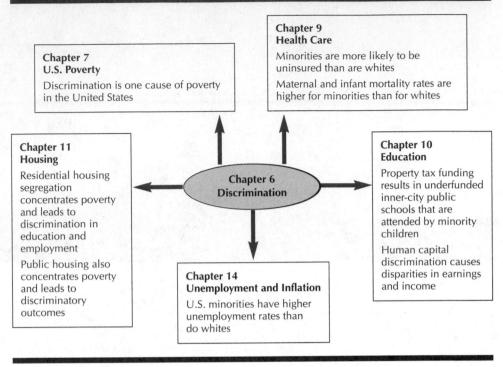

Chapter 7
U.S. Poverty

Discrimination is one cause of poverty in the United States

Chapter 9
Health Care

Minorities are more likely to be uninsured than are whites

Maternal and infant mortality rates are higher for minorities than for whites

Chapter 11
Housing

Residential housing segregation concentrates poverty and leads to discrimination in education and employment

Public housing also concentrates poverty and leads to discriminatory outcomes

Chapter 6
Discrimination

Chapter 10
Education

Property tax funding results in underfunded inner-city public schools that are attended by minority children

Human capital discrimination causes disparities in earnings and income

Chapter 14
Unemployment and Inflation

U.S. minorities have higher unemployment rates than do whites

THE DIVERSITY OF THE U.S. POPULATION

http://www.census.gov
This is the U.S. Bureau of the Census site. It contains up-to-date information on population, poverty, earnings, and income, as well as many other variables.

Our national heritage is one of diversity of race and ethnicity. The Native American Indian population had developed a rich and varied culture before the first nonnative populations journeyed to this country. In the sixteenth century white European settlers began arriving in the United States. They came in search of freedom and a better way of life. More recent immigrants have come for the same reasons. The preponderance of the most recent waves of immigrants has been from Asia and Latin America, but immigrants come from everywhere on the globe.

The data in Table 6-1 illustrate some of this rich diversity. Numbers of people belonging to various racial and ethnic groups, as well as their percentage of the total population, are shown for 1990 and 2000. The largest group of people is white; whites are 82 percent of the total population. The percentage of whites decreased during the 1990s, indicating growing diversity in the population.

African Americans

African Americans, still referred to as blacks by the Bureau of the Census, represent the largest nonwhite group in the United States. Blacks are more than 12 percent

TABLE 6-1   Resident Population, by Race and Hispanic Origin

Numbers in thousands; % refers to percent of total U.S. residents.*

	1990		2000	
	NUMBER	PERCENT	NUMBER	PERCENT
Total	248,709	100.0	281,422	100.0
White	208,741	83.9	211,461	75.1
Black	30,517	12.3	34,658	12.3
American Indian, Eskimo, or Aleut	2,067	0.8	2,476	0.9
Asian or Pacific Islander	7,467	3.0	11,741	3.7
Hispanic**	22,379	9.0	35,306	12.5
Two or more races			6,826	2.4

*Numbers and percentages may not add due to rounding.
**Persons of Hispanic origin may be of any race.
Source: U.S. Department of Commerce, Bureau of the Census, Census 2000 Redistricting Data
(http://www.census.gov/).

of the population. According to the Census Bureau, blacks are largely concentrated in the South and in central cities of the United States.[1] The South was home to 55 percent of all blacks in 1999. In the same year 55 percent of all blacks lived in the central cities of metropolitan areas in both the North and the South. Because only 22 percent of non-Hispanic whites lived in central cities, the percentage of blacks who were central-city dwellers was two and a half times that of whites.

Hispanics

The Hispanic population is the second-largest group in Table 6-1. Hispanic people may be of any race, although about 95 percent are white. Hispanics are persons with origins in one of the Latin American countries. (Many prefer the term Latino to Hispanic.) Nearly two-thirds of U.S. Hispanics are from Mexico or descended from Mexican immigrants. Significant numbers also have roots in Puerto Rico, Central and South America, and Cuba. The percentage of the U.S. population that is Hispanic increased from 9 percent in 1990 to nearly 12 percent in 2000. Hispanics accounted for 38 percent of the nation's population growth from 1990 to 2000, and according to projections, Hispanics will account for the majority of our population growth in the first half of the twenty-first century.

The Hispanic population is highly concentrated in the Southwestern states. Census Bureau data from 1999 show that 51 percent of Hispanics live in Texas and California alone. Outside the Southwest, four states have another 22 percent of the Hispanic population: New York (8 percent), Florida (7 percent), Illinois (4 percent), and New Jersey (3 percent). The states with the highest concentration of Hispanics were New Mexico (41 percent of the total population), California (32 percent), Texas (30 percent), and Arizona (23 percent).[2]

Asian or Pacific Islanders

Asian and Pacific Islanders represent about 4 percent of the population. People in this group have origins in Japan, China, Taiwan, the Philippines, and Korea; 60 percent are foreign-born and 44 percent are naturalized citizens. Fifty-three percent of Asians and Pacific Islanders live in the western United States and 96 percent live in metropolitan areas.[3]

American Indians, Eskimos, and Aleutian Islanders

The group of American Indians, Eskimos, and Aleutian Islanders makes up the smallest share of any single race or ethnic group in Table 6-1. This group comprises the native populations of the United States. It consists primarily of Native American Indians. Slightly more than one-half live outside metropolitan areas, and nearly one-half live in western states.

Trends in Population Growth

It is clear from Table 6-1 that population growth varies for various racial and ethnic groups. Figure 6-1 shows the percent of the U.S. population that was non-Hispanic white, black, and other racial and ethnic minorities in 1990 with Census Bureau

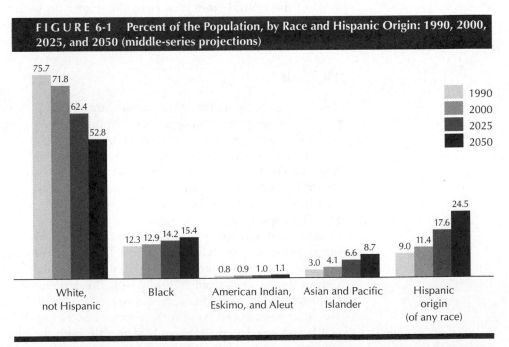

FIGURE 6-1   Percent of the Population, by Race and Hispanic Origin: 1990, 2000, 2025, and 2050 (middle-series projections)

Source: U.S. Department of Commerce, Bureau of the Census, Current Population Reports, Series p25-1130, *Population Projections of the United States by Age, Sex, Race, and Hispanic Origin.*

projections to 2050. As you can see, the percentage of the population that will be non-Hispanic white is expected to decrease. By 2025 Hispanics are projected to be our largest minority by a considerable margin. What causes a group's population to increase? The principal causes are natural increase and net immigration. Natural increase is births minus deaths; net immigration is immigration minus emigration.

The rate of population growth from natural increase is lower for whites than for any of the other groups. This lower population growth is primarily due to the lower birth rate of whites. Blacks and Hispanics have shorter life expectancies (greater death rates), but their higher birth rates more than offset these expectancies so that they have greater population growth from natural increase.

Net immigration is a major source of population growth for Asian and Pacific Islanders and Hispanics. Wars, political repression, and lack of economic opportunity led large numbers of Southeast Asians and Latin Americans to seek asylum and a better life in the United States.

WHAT IS A MINORITY?

Minority
Group with lesser access to the prerequisites of society.

Prejudice
Prejudgment on the basis of stereotypes and hearsay, plus the refusal to credit evidence that conflicts with prejudgment.

Discrimination
Action that treats like individuals differently on the basis of some arbitrary characteristic.

Quite obviously we are a racially and ethnically diverse population. White non-Hispanics outnumber any other group. Indeed, they outnumber all other groups added together. Numerically, nonwhite groups are minorities. But when we are speaking of racism, prejudice, and discrimination, it is perhaps wiser to use the sociological definition of the word "minority," because we are speaking of a phenomenon that is central to that discipline. A **minority** is a group that has lesser access to positions of power, prestige, and status in a society. The term has little to do with numbers and everything to do with power. From this perspective, women, who outnumbered men by 6,000,000 in 2000, are a minority because they do not have equal access to positions of power.

Let us define a few other terms before we go on. **Prejudice** is the prejudgment of individuals or groups on the basis of stereotypes and hearsay, plus the refusal to acknowledge evidence that conflicts with such prejudgment. Prejudiced people might believe, for example, that all Hispanics are lazy, and despite meeting Latinos who are ambitious and conscientious workers, they hold fast to that belief by rationalizing that these ambitious people are the exceptions.

Prejudice is an internal attitude, but *discrimination* involves actions. **Discrimination** means treating people differently for arbitrary, often prejudicial, reasons. We discriminate when we do not rent to a Hmong family because they are Asian immigrants. We discriminate if we refuse to hire a qualified woman to fill a job formerly held by a man. Sociologists and psychologists have much to say about the types of prejudice and discrimination that exist in our world. They can explain the many causes of prejudice to us. We recommend that you take their courses to learn about these things. But some of the causes and many of the effects of discrimination are economic. Lower incomes, inferior educations, higher rates of unemployment, poorer housing, and inadequate medical care may be consequences of discrimination. These are the things we wish to examine in this chapter.

INCOME AND EARNINGS

Income
Money received from
all sources.

Earnings
Money received from
labor market activities.

Let us begin by looking at income. U.S. Census Bureau data indicate that the median incomes of black and Hispanic households are less than 70 percent of the median income of white households.[4] Why the disparities? **Income** is money received from all sources. It includes not only earnings, but also interest on savings accounts and dividends received on stock shares, rents from property and land owned, welfare payments, and so forth. **Earnings** is income received in the form of wages and salaries from labor market activities (working). About 80 percent of total income in the United States is in the form of wages and salaries. Earnings is the principal source of income for most American families. We will focus our attention on earnings in the pages that follow. But let us first note that families and individuals with high earnings are more likely to save and make investments that will provide other forms of income than are low-earnings workers. To eliminate the effects of sources of income other than working, let's focus on earnings.

EARNINGS

http://www.bls.gov
This Bureau of Labor Statistics site has the most current information on employment and earnings, as well as the *Monthly Labor Review* online.

Earnings from labor markets depend on both the wage rate that the worker receives and the number of hours that the worker works. Your earnings are your wage rate times the hours you work. If your family (household) has two, or even three, persons working full time, you will have more earnings than a family with only one person working full time at the same wage rate. So let us look at the weekly *earnings* of full-time workers to eliminate both the effect of part-time workers and the effect of different numbers of workers in the household. A full-time worker works 39 or more hours a week. Table 6-2 compares the weekly earnings of full-time workers.

Note that women working full-time earn about three-fourths of what men working full-time earn, and that minorities working full-time earn less than whites. The disparity between the earnings of whites and minorities is more pronounced for men than for women. These figures are especially interesting because both blacks

TABLE 6-2   Median Weekly Earnings of Full-Time Workers by Race, Hispanic Origin, and Gender, First Quarter 2000

	MALE	FEMALE	FEMALE AS PERCENT OF MALE
White	$672	$497	74.0%
Black	$496	$422	85.1%
Hispanic	$419	$355	84.7%
Black as a percent of white	73.8%	84.9%	
Hispanic as a percent of white	62.4%	71.4%	

Source: Bureau of Labor Statistics, *Employment and Earnings* (http://www.bls.gov/newsrelease/wkyeng.t02.htm).

and Hispanics work more hours per week than whites. Because the government's definition of a full-time worker is one who works 39 or more hours per week, some full-time workers will work only 39 hours per week, and others will work considerably more hours. On average, middle-class black families work 9 percent more than their white counterparts, whereas middle-class Hispanic families work 5 percent more.[5] The earnings differences are not proof of discrimination, although the pattern certainly makes one wonder what the causes of such large differences are.

Several types of discrimination can affect labor market activities. Technically, labor market discrimination occurs when like workers (or potential workers) are treated unequally on the basis of some arbitrary characteristic such as race, gender, or ethnicity. In the context of the labor market, "like" means "equally productive." It is not discrimination when college graduates earn more than high school graduates if the college graduates are more productive because they have developed job-related abilities to a greater extent than the high school graduates. It is not discrimination if a concert violinist has greater innate ability than the rest of us, and the labor market compensates her by paying her a premium for her talent. It *is* discrimination if two equally productive workers are treated differently because one is black and the other white, or because one is female and the other male.

Workers can be treated differently in at least four ways that may affect their earnings. First, they may be paid different wage rates solely on the basis of some arbitrary characteristic. This practice is called **wage discrimination.** Second, they may be last hired and first fired in an economic downturn; hence they will be unemployed more than other groups. This practice is called **employment discrimination.** Third, they may be prevented, or at least discouraged, from working in some fields and encouraged to work in others, resulting in separate black and white occupations and men's and women's occupations. This practice is called **occupational discrimination.** All of these types of discrimination directly affect earnings, and they all occur after the worker has entered the labor market. (One enters the labor market as soon as he or she begins to actively seek employment.)

The fourth type of discrimination is more indirect. It occurs before the worker's entry into the labor market, but it certainly influences how he or she fares in the labor market. This discrimination is **human capital discrimination,** or discrimination with respect to education. If some groups receive more education or better quality education than do others, members of these groups will be rewarded by the labor market for the skills and abilities that they have developed through education and will have higher earnings than workers who are less educated.

Earnings and Education

Let us pose a related question. To what extent do earnings differences reflect differences in education? Table 6-3 on page 126 addresses this question. The data reveal a pattern of higher earnings for whites than minorities even when we control for education. Earnings increase as education increases for whites and minorities and for both men and women. But education seems to pay off more for whites than minorities. Additional years of education add more to white workers' earnings than to black or Hispanic workers' earnings. The differences between men and women's earnings are even more pronounced. Note that the median earnings

Wage discrimination
Paying equally productive workers different wages on the basis of some arbitrary characteristic.

Employment discrimination
Not hiring certain workers on the basis of some arbitrary characteristic.

Occupational discrimination
Not hiring some groups of workers for particular jobs, resulting, for example, in men's jobs and women's jobs or black jobs and white jobs.

Human capital discrimination
Anything that prevents certain groups from acquiring the level or quality of education to which other groups have access.

TABLE 6-3 Median Annual Earnings of Year-Round Full-Time Workers, 25 Years Old or Older, by Gender, Race, and Hispanic Origin, 1998

HIGHEST EDUCATIONAL ATTAINMENT	MALE	FEMALE
Not high school graduate	$21,699	$15,266
High school graduate	30,838	21,963
Some college, no degree	35,949	26,024
Associate degree	38,483	28,377
Bachelor's degree	49,982	35,408
Master's degree	60,168	42,002
Professional degree	90,653	55,460
Doctoral degree	69,188	52,167

	WHITE	BLACK	HISPANIC
Not high school graduate	$19,576	$18,206	$16,525
High school graduate	27,303	22,369	23,154
Some college, no degree	31,637	27,092	27,005
Associate degree	34,636	28,454	30,722
Bachelor's degree	42,412	37,339	35,691
Master's degree	50,693	41,426	49,226
Professional degree	76,308	b	51,373
Doctoral degree	66,987	b	b

b = sample too small to calculate
Source: U.S. Department of Commerce, Bureau of the Census, *Educational Attainment*, Table 9 (http://www.census.gov/population/socdemo/education/p20-528/tab09.txt).

of women with doctoral degrees is only slightly more than the median earnings of men with bachelor's degrees.

Earnings and Unemployment

Your earnings will be lower if you have frequent periods of involuntary unemployment than if you are employed continually. To be considered unemployed, a person must be actively looking for work. The government then calculates the unemployment rate, which is unemployed people as a percentage of people who are either working or actively seeking employment. Let us look at unemployment rates for blacks, Hispanics, and whites and for men and women. Table 6-4 shows these data. Unemployment rates for men and women are similar. But note that both blacks and Hispanics experience far higher rates of unemployment than do whites. Year after year the black unemployment rate is at least twice the white unemployment rate, and the Hispanic rate is between the other two.

SOME EXPLANATIONS OF DISCRIMINATION

Some discrimination may be the result of prejudice, but it is possible for labor market discrimination to occur without any prejudice in the personal, malicious sense. Let us look at the theories of the "taste for discrimination" model, statistical discrimination, and occupational crowding.

TABLE 6-4 Unemployment Rates by Race, Hispanic Origin, and Gender, Selected Years				
	1985	1990	1995	1998
Total population	7.2%	5.5%	5.6%	4.5%
Male	7.0%	5.6%	5.6%	4.4%
Female	7.4%	5.4%	5.6%	4.6%
White	6.2%	4.7%	4.9%	3.9%
Black	15.1%	11.3%	10.4%	8.9%
Hispanic	10.5%	8.0%	9.3%	7.2%

Source: U.S. Department of Commerce, Bureau of the Census, *Statistical Abstract of the United States, 1999,* Table 680.

Becker's "Taste for Discrimination" Model

"Taste for discrimination" model Gary Becker's theory of discrimination as the result of prejudice and "psychic costs."

The first examination of discrimination by an economist was done by Gary Becker in the 1950s, when he developed his famous **"taste for discrimination" model.** Becker hypothesized that prejudiced employers would discriminate in hiring because employing members of those groups they were prejudiced against imposed a "psychic cost" on the employers. The stronger the prejudice, the greater would be the psychic cost. Let's assume that some employers were prejudiced against blacks. These employers would hire blacks only if their wages were lower than whites' by at least as much as the employers' psychic cost. Other employers were not prejudiced, and they would hire white and black workers randomly.

Because the average wage paid to a black worker was lower than the average wage paid to a white worker, the nonprejudiced employer who hired blacks would have lower labor costs than the prejudiced employer. Furthermore, the more prejudiced the employer, the greater would be the cost disadvantage, because the less likely was the employer to have hired lower-wage black workers. Because the prejudiced employer was at a cost disadvantage, Becker believed that discrimination would eventually end without government policy such as affirmative action. Simply put, the discriminator could not long survive in a competitive product market, because the discriminator firm's costs would be higher than the nondiscriminator's.

Statistical Discrimination

Statistical discrimination Judging an individual on the average characteristics of his or her group.

If an employer judges a prospective employee on the basis of the characteristics of the group she belongs to rather than on her own characteristics, the employer is practicing **statistical discrimination.** For example, the employer might believe that a young woman is more likely to need a parental leave than a man is. Or he might believe that married women with children are absent more often than men because they will be the ones to stay home with sick children who cannot be taken to day care. He might believe that women are more likely than men to quit their jobs because their spouses are being transferred. And he would be right on average. He would not be right in each case, however, because individuals do not fit the characteristics of their group in every way. Many men take time off work to care for young children, and they often quit jobs to accompany wives who have been transferred.

But if the employer hires only men, on average he will avoid the characteristics to which he objects in the group. He will save money in the hiring process because screening individual applicants is expensive. So he may see it as simply a good business decision to hire men for the position. Indeed, if the perceived differences between men and women are accurate, the discriminator's costs will be lower than a nondiscriminator's. Young women who would have been equally productive, or even more productive, than the men who are hired in the job therefore are discriminated against. The discriminating employer may pass over extremely productive women workers. Furthermore, if the average labor market characteristics of men and women converge over time, the cost savings from statistical discrimination will disappear.

Occupational Crowding

Occupational crowding
Crowding some groups of workers into a limited number of jobs.

Occupational crowding occurs when there are blacks' jobs and whites' jobs or men's jobs and women's jobs in the economy. Refer again to Table 6-3. The data for men and women are perhaps even more striking than those for whites and minorities. Why do women college graduates have earnings of 71 percent those of their male counterparts? Why do women with master's degrees have earnings of 70 percent those of similarly educated men? The answer to these questions is, at least in part, that in the U.S. economy some occupations are dominated by men and other occupations are dominated by women, and that men's occupations are more highly paid than women's. Women are crowded into relatively few occupations, whereas men have more occupational choices. Women are 80 percent of our elementary schoolteachers and more than 90 percent of our registered nurses. They are our college-educated social workers. They dominate retail sales and the clerical fields. The reasons for this occupational segregation are complex. Some women are in so-called women's fields because they have made a rational choice to teach third grade. It's what they always wanted to do. Others are in such occupations because these traditional women's fields are the only ones they ever really considered working in or the only ones they have been encouraged to enter. Still others wind up in these fields due to discrimination against them in the fields in which they would rather work, or because they lack the education to enter other vocations that they would prefer.

Figure 6-2 illustrates the effects of occupational crowding. Each graph represents a labor market that is similar to other markets we have examined. Instead of the quantity of meat or fish, the horizontal axis shows the number of workers (quantity of labor). The vertical axis shows the wage rate (the price of labor). The supply of labor shows the number of workers willing to work at various wage rates. The demand for labor shows the number of workers that employers are willing to hire at various wage rates.

Assume that there are 30 million workers in the economy, and that one-half are men and one-half are women. Furthermore, there are three occupations at which the workers may work. Two of the occupations are traditionally men's jobs;

FIGURE 6-2   Labor Markets With and Without Occupational Crowding

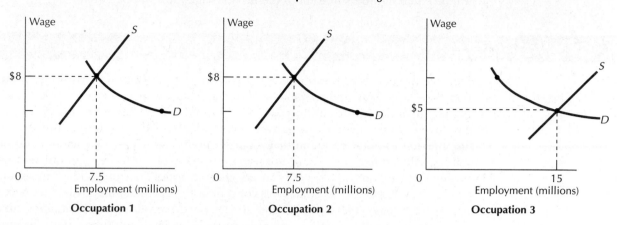

A. With Occupational Crowding

If the 15 million female workers are crowded into Occupation 3, while the 15 million male workers share Occupations 1 and 2, women will earn lower wages ($5) than men ($8).

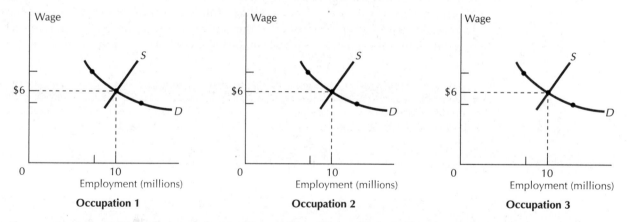

B. Without Occupational Crowding

If occupational segregation is eliminated, the 30 million workers will be randomly distributed among the three occupations and they will earn the same wage ($6).

one is traditionally a women's job. If there is equal demand for workers in all three occupations, the demand curves will look like the demand curves in Figure 6-2. Assume that Occupations 1 and 2 are the men's jobs, and that Occupation 3 is the women's job. In the top panel (A) of Figure 6-2 we have occupational crowding, and all the women are crammed into Occupation 3, whereas the men are divided between Occupations 1 and 2. As a result, men earn higher wages than women. In the bottom panel (B) of the figure, occupational crowding has been eliminated, and there are no men's or women's jobs. The 30 million workers are randomly distributed throughout the labor markets, and because there is equal demand there will be equal numbers in each of them. The wage rates will be equal.

EFFECTS OF LABOR MARKET DISCRIMINATION

Some of the effects of discrimination are obvious; others are not. With discrimination there are always gainers and losers. The groups with higher employment and higher incomes (whites and males) are obvious gainers. The groups with lower employment and incomes (minorities, including women) are losers. But there is another, less obvious loser, and that is our economy as a whole. Our national output will be reduced because we are not using our labor force in the most efficient way possible. Hiring on the basis of arbitrary characteristics does not achieve maximum productivity. Figure 6-3 illustrates this concept using a production possibilities curve.

As we discussed in Chapter One, we are on the production possibilities curve only if we have full and efficient employment of society's resources. With discrimination we are at some point such as *X* inside the production possibilities curve. We are not achieving our maximum potential national output of capital and consumer goods, because we are inefficiently utilizing the labor of the economy. The economist Andrew Brimmer has estimated that eliminating discrimination against African Americans so that they could make full use of their education would have increased the gross domestic product, our national output, by $137 billion, or 2.15 percent.[6] Thus discrimination hurts our society as well as individuals within it.

FIGURE 6-3   Discrimination's Effect on National Output

With discrimination, labor is not utilized as efficiently as possible, and the nation's output of consumer and capital goods is at point *X*, inside the production possibilities curve.

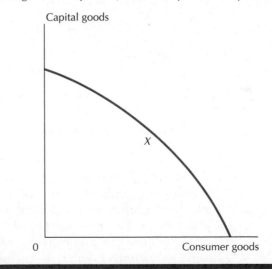

Such systematic patterns as those revealed by the statistics presented earlier certainly raise questions about the presence of discrimination on the basis of gender, race, and ethnicity. But some of the disparities may be attributed to alternative factors. Some economists argue that many of the differences are the result of rational choice, not discrimination. Let us look at this viewpoint before we go on.

Rational Individual Choice

What if the difference between men's and women's earnings results from women choosing to work fewer hours than men on average? The data on men's and women's weekly earnings presented in Table 6-2 were for full-time workers, but the Bureau of Labor Statistics considers 39 hours weekly to be full-time employment. If men, on average, work more than 40 hours, while full-time female employees, on average, work only 40 hours, it might explain a large part of the difference in earnings. Because women are the primary caregivers of children and the chief housekeepers in most marriages, it makes sense that they might limit their time working outside the home. To the extent that this is true, their lower incomes are the result of rational choices on their parts.

Furthermore, some economists and sociologists argue that women *choose* the so-called women's occupations because these are complementary to their primary roles as mothers and wives. The skills learned to teach other people's children to read can be utilized within one's own family. The same is true of nursing skills. Therefore the selection of a traditional women's occupation may be the result of rational choice, not discrimination.

Moreover, the decision not to finish high school may consign a minority worker to low-wage, dead-end jobs throughout his or her life, but it can be argued that this decision was a conscious choice that he or she made. Lower earnings due to unfortunate past choices cannot be categorized as discrimination. In all of these cases, it is difficult, if not impossible, to determine how much of the earnings differentials are the result of rational choices and how much are due to discrimination.

Choice, Discrimination, and Culture Intermingled

Other people question whether either women or minorities make truly independent choices. Culture and tradition play a large part in our lives. We give little girls dolls and dollhouses, but we give boys building sets. Children still appear to leave elementary school believing that boys are good at math and girls are good at English. How much truly individual choice do young women have?

Furthermore, discrimination may be a cause of decisions that, having been made, affect earnings and incomes. If a minority youth sees that his older relatives who finished high school are frequently unemployed and appear to find jobs only near the minimum wage, he will have less incentive to finish high school himself.

If a young woman believes that she will be discriminated against if she trains for the sciences, she will be far more likely to train as an elementary schoolteacher. In short, discrimination can be both a cause and an effect.

Individual choice, discrimination, and culture are intermingled to produce the results we have discussed. All the disparities are not attributable to discrimination, but some portion of them is. The controversy revolves around how large this portion is.

QUALITY OF LIFE VARIABLES

If we look at other measures of socioeconomic well-being, we can see that the same groups that are discriminated against in labor markets occupy an inferior position with respect to other aspects of their life. Ethnic minorities and families headed by women bear a disproportionate share of the burden of our nation's problems. Poverty (see Chapter Seven for a detailed discussion) does not afflict all segments of our population proportionately. Nor do all groups have equal access to quality health care (Chapter Nine), education (Chapter Ten), and housing (Chapter Eleven).

Poverty

Given that women and other minorities earn less in labor markets, it should not be too surprising that these groups bear more than their share of the nation's poverty. We will see in Chapter Seven that ethnic and racial minorities and families headed by women have higher poverty rates than other groups. For example, blacks and Hispanics have a poverty rate more than three times that of the white non-Hispanic population. Single-female-headed families have a poverty rate over three times the national average.

Health Care

Unequal access to quality health care exists in our society. This reality is reflected in higher infant and maternal death rates and lower life expectancies for blacks, Hispanics, and Native Americans than for whites in our society. As we shall see in Chapter Nine on health care, the black infant death rate is more than two times the white rate, and the black maternal death rate is almost four times the white rate. Blacks have a life expectancy six years less than that of whites.

Although infant and maternal death rates for both blacks and whites have decreased since the 1960s, the ratio of black rates to white rates are very similar to those published in the Kerner Report in 1968. Furthermore, white children are more likely to receive immunizations against childhood diseases than are minority children. In 1998, 77 percent of black and 80 percent of Hispanic children aged 19 to 35 months were up-to-date for their age on immunizations compared with 87 percent of non-Hispanic white children.[7]

Housing

Nor are minorities as likely to enjoy adequate housing as are whites. Whites are more likely to own their homes than either blacks or other minorities. In 1999, 73.2 percent of housing units occupied by non-Hispanic whites were owned by the occupants. Only 44.3 percent of black housing units and 45.5 percent of Hispanic housing units were owner-occupied.[8] So minorities are less likely to own and more likely to rent.

Redlining

Lending institutions' refusal to make loans on property in areas dominated by minorities.

Among the reasons for this pattern is, of course, the lower incomes of minorities. Another is discrimination in lending. Until the 1960s, financial institutions commonly practiced **redlining**—that is, refusing to make real estate loans on property in neighborhoods populated mainly by minorities. The term comes from the idea of drawing a boundary line in red ink on a map around the areas in which minorities live. Redlining is now illegal, but whites are still less likely to be turned down for a housing loan than are minorities. A recent study found that a black mortgage applicant in New York City is twice as likely to be rejected for a home loan as a white applicant. Hispanics are also more likely to be turned down for a home loan. Even if blacks or Hispanics have the same or greater income than whites, they are rejected more frequently. For example, 21 percent of blacks with income above $55,000 were turned down for a loan, while only 19 percent of whites with income between $22,900 and $36,200 were rejected.[9] Insurance companies have also been accused of redlining in the sale of homeowners insurance. In 2000, one company, Nationwide Insurance, settled a redlining case by agreeing to pay a fair housing group $17.5 million and to improve service to minority and inner-city customers.[10]

POLICIES TO ELIMINATE DISCRIMINATION

The government can, and does, act to reduce discrimination. Some policies involve direct intervention in markets, whereas others involve indirect intervention. Let us begin with direct labor market policies. Many such policies are a legacy of the civil rights movement of the 1960s. Among these are the following.

The Equal Pay Act of 1963

This landmark antidiscrimination law made it illegal for an employer to pay men and women different wage rates for doing the same job. The law was therefore an important policy against gender discrimination. Prior to its passing, the practice of paying women less than men who did the same job was common; it was justified on the traditional basis that men were the breadwinners of families, whereas women were mainly secondary earners in the family.

Although this important piece of legislation ended the practice of unequal pay, it clearly did not end all gender discrimination. It certainly had no impact on the occupational segregation that persists in the United States. As long as a hospital pays all its licensed practical nurses, male and female, the same wage rate for doing the same job, it is behaving in a lawful manner. But if employees in this traditionally female occupation are poorly paid in comparison to automobile mechanics, the Equal Pay Act will not address that issue.

http://www.eeoc.gov
This is the Equal Employment Opportunity Commission home page.

The Civil Rights Act of 1964

This law is the most important antidiscrimination statute we have. It not only makes discriminatory compensation (including fringe benefits) illegal, but also forbids discrimination in hiring, promoting, and firing. Furthermore, it is broader in coverage than the Equal Pay Act. It forbids discrimination on the basis of race, gender, color, religion, or national origin. The law applies to all employers with 15 or more workers engaged in interstate commerce, to all labor unions with 15 or more members, and to all workers employed by educational institutions and by state, local, and federal government. The Civil Rights Act created the Equal Employment Opportunity Commission (EEOC), which administers it.

Executive Orders

Affirmative action
Mandated program to provide equal access to labor markets.

In 1965 and 1968, executive orders intended to stop discrimination by firms that do business with the federal government were issued. These orders require that all federal contractors whose contracts total $50,000 or more develop **affirmative action** programs. The term implies that firms should be able to demonstrate that they are not discriminating. If, on examination, it is found that a firm underemploys women and minorities, numerical goals to increase the representation of these groups must be established. The objective is for the firm's workforce to reflect that of the available labor force. If the firm is a law practice and 25 percent of the lawyers in the area are women, the firm should strive to hire so that eventually 25 percent of its lawyers are female.

Quota
Rigid numerical requirement in hiring.

Affirmative action programs have been controversial since their inception. Critics argue that they have resulted in **quotas,** or rigid numerical proportions of jobs held for minorities and women. These jobs, they argue, are filled with little regard for the workers' qualifications. Still others argue that affirmative action has resulted in **tokenism,** or the hiring of certain workers solely to demonstrate an attempt to comply with the law. These critics regard affirmative action as a system of preferences that results in **reverse discrimination** against white males. And they maintain that affirmative action programs do not benefit disadvantaged minority workers as much as they benefit middle-class minority workers.

Tokenism
Hiring minorities to comply with law, not for their abilities.

Reverse discrimination
Discrimination against white males.

On the other hand, affirmative action proponents argue that affirmative action is the only way to end historical patterns of discrimination, and that it is justifiable to give preference now to groups that have historically been discriminated against. They point out the disparities in earnings of various ethnic, racial, and gender groups, and maintain that affirmative action is necessary to narrow these gaps over time (or at least to prevent their widening further).

As you undoubtedly know, the Supreme Court interprets our laws. All laws must conform to the U.S. Constitution. The Supreme Court upheld the constitutionality of affirmative action programs in a series of important decisions in the mid-1980s. More recently, however, Supreme Court decisions have seemed to chip away at affirmative action. It declared illegal a program to set aside a portion of the construction work of the city of Richmond, Virginia, for minority-owned firms. It also permitted certain public employees to challenge existing affirmative action programs on the basis of reverse discrimination. Affirmative action appears to be under legal attack as we write.

Some economists argue that direct government intervention in labor markets, such as affirmative action, is unnecessary, or even harmful. Nobel laureates Milton Friedman and Gary Becker have both argued that the employer who hires on any basis other than efficiency, which means finding the most productive worker for the job, will be at a competitive disadvantage compared with other employers. They argue that discriminating employers have higher costs than nondiscriminators, so eventually they will be driven from the market. Direct intervention in labor markets, they argue, is therefore unnecessary.

Thomas Sowell, a black economist, goes still further. He argues that government intervention in favor of disadvantaged groups actually hurts these groups. He cites as an example the Native American. Sowell states that Native Americans have the longest relationship (as a ward of the state) with the federal government of any of our minorities, and Native Americans are consistently at the very bottom of our economic ladder. Sowell argues that minorities such as Japanese Americans, who were not favored by the government, have succeeded far better than the recipients of the government's largesse.

Other economists argue that labor markets clearly have neither solved the problem of discrimination nor, for that matter, even made substantial progress toward eliminating discrimination. Nor do they believe that discriminators are necessarily at a cost disadvantage. Instead, they note that statistical discrimination probably results in short-run cost savings. Therefore they argue that we need programs such as affirmative action. They propose that programs directed at the supply side of the labor market are especially needed. Affirmative action is now directed at the demand side of the market, or at the business firm that hires and promotes. Supply side efforts would attempt to supply these employers with workers who have the proper education and skills for the positions available. What, they ask, is the advantage of an employer's willingness to hire female auditors if none are available? Therefore training women and minorities so that they can supply the needed skills is important. They argue that we need more women accounting majors to fill the auditing positions and that we should be concerned about women's access to such training.

Affirmative action is also the subject of extensive political debate. The state of California has passed a law to eliminate affirmative action considerations in hiring by the state and in admission to state universities. Opponents argue that a "system of preferences" is no longer necessary because our national values, as well as our laws, have changed so as to prevent discrimination from occurring. Others feel that affirmative action programs should be targeted more carefully toward disadvantaged groups. It is quite likely that affirmative action programs will be considerably modified in the future, if they are retained at all.

http://aad.english.ucsb.edu
This site, maintained by the University of California at Santa Barbara, contains extensive material on affirmative action, both pro and con.

Indirect Labor Market Policies

The government can also work in less direct ways to reduce discrimination. Improving educational opportunities for racial and ethnic minorities and women will put them in a better position vis-à-vis the labor market. Many low-income workers with families have child-care problems, which can be alleviated by public day-care programs.

Residential segregation, discussed more fully in Chapter Eleven, institutionalizes discrimination. Inner-city residents usually do not know what jobs are available in the suburbs, and even if they know of job opportunities, they often lack transportation to these jobs. For this reason, Dr. Martin Luther King, Jr., maintained that public transportation was a civil rights issue. The provision of public transportation is still an antidiscrimination policy. Measures to eliminate housing segregation will increase employment opportunities and are also antidiscrimination policies.

Maintaining a healthy economy through appropriate fiscal and monetary policies also can be construed as an antidiscrimination policy. A healthy economy implies job opportunities. If there is a relative surplus of job openings compared to workers, employers cannot afford to discriminate. The truly tight labor markets during World War II opened windows of opportunity for many female and minority workers.

Various Equal Opportunity Laws

Since the 1960s we have passed many laws to end discrimination and provide legal recourse for those who are discriminated against. Citizens are ensured the right to vote by the Voting Rights Act of 1965. Other laws have made it illegal to discriminate in housing. Redlining by mortgage lenders is illegal under the Fair Housing Act. No longer can a landlord refuse to rent to people solely because they are members of a minority group. Despite the disparities that remain between minorities and whites, there is no question that the legal environment has changed since the 1960s.

EDUCATIONAL DESEGREGATION AND SCHOOL FINANCING REFORM

It has been more than 45 years since the U.S. Supreme Court struck down the "separate but equal" doctrine in *Brown v. Topeka Board of Education* (1954). In that case the court ruled that segregated schools were in fact unequal and did irreparable harm to minority children. Since then our country has proceeded to integrate its schools at a pace that varies by state and region. Many large urban areas of the South have had metropolitanwide desegregation plans since the early 1970s, and some have had no segregated schools for years. Two Supreme Court orders in the 1970s created mandatory desegregation across the entire metropolitan areas of Wilmington, Delaware, and Louisville, Kentucky. These orders have produced much higher levels of integration throughout the two states.

Many conservatives argue that remaining disparities between the earnings of minorities and whites and between those of men and women are the result of rational choice, not discrimination. They point out that gaps between these groups have narrowed somewhat since the 1960s. Conservatives oppose government intervention in markets, including labor markets. They see affirmative action as misguided and a source of great inefficiency. They believe that changing social values and the passage of antidiscrimination laws have alleviated the problem of discrimination and that affirmative action is no longer needed.

Liberals believe that affirmative action programs have done some good but that they have not completely solved the problem of discrimination. Therefore they see a need to continue affirmative action programs. Many, however, argue for "means-tested" affirmative action programs. The beneficiaries of such programs would have to be economically disadvantaged, not middle-class women or minorities.

In contrast, the Supreme Court's 1974 Detroit decision in *Milliken v. Bradley* blocked desegregation across Detroit's metropolitan population. The central city was to desegregate separately from the suburban fringe. The ruling prevented effective desegregation, and Detroit is now one of the nation's most segregated metropolitan areas. With a high concentration of racial minorities within many of our country's central cities, and a high concentration of whites in the suburbs, desegregation must be carried out at the metropolitan level. As a result of the precedent set, as well as a failure of leadership on the issue, there has been little or no progress toward school desegregation since 1974.

Evidence indicates that large-scale school desegregation works not only to improve objective measures of achievement such as test scores but also to increase the probability of college attendance. It also positively affects type of college, college major, and types of employment as an adult. Recent research by the University of Chicago's Metropolitan Opportunity Project, however, shows an extremely strong pattern of continued educational segregation for blacks and increasing segregation for Hispanics in our central cities. Furthermore, minority high schools in almost all cases have large numbers of low-income students. There are strong positive correlations between predominantly minority schools, high proportions of poor children, and low educational achievement. Far too many black and Hispanic students are trapped in schools where dropout rates are high and opportunities for success minimal.[11]

One important reason for the dismal record of many inner-city schools is that they are often underfunded. A major source of finances for education in the United States is property taxes. This means that school districts in affluent, growing suburbs are extremely well financed, while inner-city schools are poorly financed. There is a current movement to explore new ways of financing public education in the United States. These issues are discussed in more detail in Chapter Ten.

As the diversity of our population increases, we will naturally turn our faces toward a broader exposure to other cultures. The movement toward multiculturalism in our schools and colleges reflect the changes in our broader society. Schools attempt to reflect the diversity of the population in their faculty and students. The purpose of the multicultural teaching methods and materials is to spread greater knowledge of other cultures and to foster tolerance. An important objective of multiculturalism is to increase the respect with which we treat people of all races, genders, and ethnicities.

SUMMARY

The United States has a rich diversity of people of different races and ethnicities, including those who are black, Hispanic, Asian, and Native American. The quality of life for people of minority race, however, may be substantially below that of white Americans. Furthermore, women are in a position similar to racial and ethnic minorities. All face lower earnings and income and greater likelihood of poverty, with all the implications of poverty for poorer health care, housing, education, and other quality of life variables.

The past 40 years have seen changes in our legal environment. Many overtly discriminatory practices are now illegal. But the relative positions of minorities and whites are still greatly unequal. Reduced discrimination in our society would increase our economy's efficiency and thus benefit us all.

NOTES

1. U.S. Department of Commerce, Bureau of the Census, Current Population Survey, March 1999, Racial Statistics (http://www.census.gov/population/socdemo/race/black/tabs99/tab16.txt).

2. U.S. Department of Commerce, Bureau of the Census, http://www.census.gov/Press-Release/www/2000cb00ff11.html

3. U.S. Department of Commerce, Bureau of the Census, http://www.census.gov/Press-Release/www/2000/cb00ff05.html

4. Calculated from U.S. Department of Commerce, Bureau of the Census, Statistical Abstract of the United States, 1999, Table 742.

5. Mishel, Laurence, Jared Bernstein, and John Schmitt, The State of Working America, Economic Policy Institute (http://www.epinet.org).

6. Andrew F. Brimmer, "The Economic Cost of Discrimination Against Black Americans," in Margaret C. Simms (ed.), Economic Perspectives on Affirmative Action (Washington, DC: Joint Center for Political and Economic Studies, 1995), p. 19.

7. Centers for Disease Control, National Immunization Survey 1999, Table 7 (http://www.cdc.gov/nip). Statistical Abstract of the United States, 1993, Table 49, p. 46, and Table 53, p. 49. The data for Hispanic children are from 1991.

8. U.S. Department of Commerce, Bureau of the Census, Housing Vacancies and Homeownership Annual Statistics: 1999 (http://www.census.gov/hhes/www/housing/hvs/annual99/ann99t20.html).

9. "Widespread Redlining Exposed," New York Amsterdam News, August 20, 1998, p. 30.

10. "Nationwide Settles Redlining Case," Associated Press Online, April 24, 2000.

11. Much of this material is taken from Gary Orfield, "Have the Kerner Warnings Come True?," in Fred R. Harris and Roger W. Wilkins (eds.), Quiet Riots (New York: Pantheon, 1988) and "Education in the Twenty-first Century," Christian Science Monitor Service (http://www.nabe.org/press/reprint 990504b.htm).

DISCUSSION QUESTIONS

1. Go to the Census Bureau Web site and look up more recent data on the diversity of the U.S. population. Hint: Go to http://www.census.gov and click on Population.

2. Is it possible to be a member of a minority when, in fact, your group has greater numbers than another group?

3. What factors explain the disparities in earnings between men and women? Blacks and whites? Are the factors different for race and gender?

4. What is the relationship between education and earnings? Does this relationship explain all the earnings differences among various groups? Why or why not?

5. Explain statistical discrimination. Do you think such discrimination is widespread?

6. Do you think occupational crowding is widespread? Is the pressure for young women to enter traditional women's fields as great as it used to be?

7. Affirmative action began in the late 1960s. It has been accused of amounting to reverse discrimination. Do the data in the chapter support this view?

8. In the nineteenth century, secretaries were generally male, and the occupation was prestigious and well-paid. Is this true today? Can you explain the change in attitudes?

9. Why is measuring the extent of discrimination in our culture so difficult?

U.S. Poverty

I went to college so that I can earn a living wage for my children and me. I want my children to play safely and have opportunity to be educated. I want to raise socially responsible, morally responsible and psychologically sound children who are capable of coping and dealing with society and its ills. They must have a mother who isn't totally stressed out over every penny so that when clothes are accidentally ruined I don't flip out over how I am going to provide for that expense and rip unjustly on the unfortunate child. This comes with a livable income.

From *In Our Own Words: Mothers' Perspectives on Welfare Reform*[1]

Most of us are concerned about the poor, but we tend to think that poverty is not a problem that will ever affect us personally. We picture the poor as people in central cities, possibly women with too many children or people whose families have always been dependent on welfare. The poor live on the reservations or in the hills of Appalachia or on the urban streets. We imagine that the poor are drug addicts or alcoholics. They are mentally or physically ill or disabled. They are the very old or the very young. But they are never ourselves.

These stereotypes are misleading. Many poor adults are people much like us. They are people who never imagined they would someday be poor. They are people like the single mother in the chapter introduction. They are people who have become poor as a result of some life crisis: the loss of a job, the death or desertion of a spouse, an unplanned pregnancy, or an unexpected illness. These are normal events that could alter the lives of any of us.

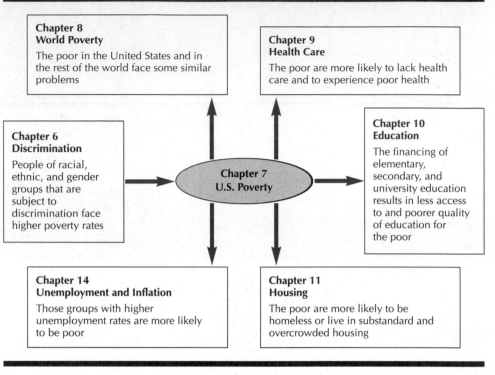

Chapter 8
World Poverty
The poor in the United States and in the rest of the world face some similar problems

Chapter 9
Health Care
The poor are more likely to lack health care and to experience poor health

Chapter 6
Discrimination
People of racial, ethnic, and gender groups that are subject to discrimination face higher poverty rates

Chapter 7
U.S. Poverty

Chapter 10
Education
The financing of elementary, secondary, and university education results in less access to and poorer quality of education for the poor

Chapter 14
Unemployment and Inflation
Those groups with higher unemployment rates are more likely to be poor

Chapter 11
Housing
The poor are more likely to be homeless or live in substandard and overcrowded housing

Relative poverty
A situation in which people are poor in comparison with other people.

Absolute poverty
A situation in which people experience the hardship of poverty according to some objective criterion.

As of 1999, 32.3 million Americans, representing 11.8 percent of the total U.S. population, were poor by government definition.[2] This means that they live in a household with total cash income falling below some level that is considered necessary to satisfy their basic needs. Poverty in the midst of plenty is an issue of equity. Recall from Chapter One that our market-based economy tends to be efficient, though not necessarily equitable. The poverty statistics appear large for one of the richest countries of the world. But what do the numbers mean? Who are these poor? And what can be done about the problem of poverty in the United States?

There are two ways to look at poverty. One is by considering **relative poverty**—a situation in which people are poor in comparison to other people. The other is by considering **absolute poverty**—a situation in which people experience actual hardship according to some objective criterion. We will consider both of these in turn, beginning with relative poverty.

RELATIVE POVERTY

Because relative poverty focuses on comparisons among people in different income classes, the standard measure of relative poverty is the income distribution.

Measuring Relative Poverty

Income distribution
The division of total income in an economy among people of different income groups.

Money income
All household income from any source, including income transfers, calculated before taxes.

Income transfer
A cash transfer from the government to an individual, for which no good or service is provided to the government in return.

In-kind transfer
A transfer of goods or services (or access to goods or services) from the government to an individual, for which no good or service is provided to the government in return.

The **income distribution** refers to the division of total income in the economy among different income groups. Statistics on the income distribution are based on the U.S. Bureau of the Census concept of **money income:** that is, all household income received from working, interest, rent, dividends, or any other source before payment of taxes. Included as money income are any government **income transfers** such as Social Security payments, veterans' cash benefits, and unemployment compensation. Not counted as part of money income, however, are **in-kind transfers,** which are government transfers of goods or services (or direct access to these goods or services) such as food stamps, health care, housing assistance, and free legal aid.

For the purpose of analyzing the income distribution, the total population of the country is ranked according to income and then divided into fifths. That is, the percent of total money income going to the poorest 20 percent of the population is determined, as well as that going to the second-poorest 20 percent of the population, and so on. If income was distributed perfectly equally, each 20 percent of the population would receive 20 percent of total money income. Table 7-1 indicates that the income distribution in the United States is far from equal, with the richest one-fifth of the American population receiving 49.3 percent of total money income in 1999, and the poorest group receiving only 3.7 percent. The income distribution is also displayed for the year 1981.

Trend in the U.S. Distribution of Income

The U.S. income distribution is becoming increasingly unequal. Comparisons between 1981 and 1999 in Table 7-1 indicate that the poorest four-fifths of the population have seen their share of total money income decrease, whereas the richest one-fifth has enjoyed an increased income share. In a relative sense, the rich are becoming richer, while the poor are becoming poorer.

TABLE 7-1   Distribution of Total Money Income in the United States by Fifths of the Total Population: 1981 and 1999

	PERCENT OF TOTAL MONEY INCOME RECEIVED	
FRACTION OF TOTAL FAMILIES	1981	1999
Poorest fifth	5.0	3.7
Second fifth	11.3	9.0
Third fifth	17.4	15.0
Fourth fifth	24.4	23.0
Richest fifth	41.9	49.3

Source: U.S. Department of Commerce, Bureau of the Census, Current Population Survey, March 2000 and earlier (http://www.census.gov/hhes/income/income99/99tablef.html).

It is important to point out that a perfectly equal income distribution is not necessarily the ideal. Most people, economists included, argue that some degree of income inequality is essential to preserve incentives. If you didn't think you would eventually have a higher income, you might have no incentive to work hard, study well, invest wisely, take necessary risks in business, and so on. Productivity and economic efficiency would suffer. On the other hand, many people also argue that the income distribution can be *too* unequal. Poor people may have very little incentive to try when income is so low and the odds of reaching the top of the ladder are *so* poor. Poverty also results in poor health and nutrition, which may sap energy and harm labor productivity. Finally, the argument goes, inequality of income to the degree experienced in the United States is hardly necessary to provide adequate incentives to work and produce.

As we begin to think of the reasons why the income distribution has become less equal over the 1980s and 1990s, we need to recognize that certain factors have not played a role. Important changes in our nation's tax system since 1981, for example, served to place more income into the hands of upper-income people. These changes in the nation's tax system do not directly affect the Census Bureau statistics on the income distribution, however, because these statistics are based on money income *before* taxes. Similarly, changes in certain government in-kind transfers since 1981 do not alter statistics on the income distribution because the benefits of these transfers are also excluded from the calculation of money income. Thus, although changes in taxes and government in-kind transfers to the poor will indeed alter the well-being of people, they will not directly affect the statistics on the income distribution.

Other factors must account for the changes in the income distribution observed in these data. One of these factors would be the indirect effect of tax cuts for the rich. While the higher after-tax income that results from the tax cuts does not show up in the income statistics, certainly higher incomes permit greater financial investment by the rich, thereby *indirectly* raising their future incomes. One other obvious factor affecting the changes in income distribution is structural change in the economy. Such change is characterized by the loss of blue-collar manufacturing jobs and the creation of low-wage service-sector jobs. We will consider these matters shortly when we turn to the topic of absolute poverty. But first let's compare the income distributions across different countries.

International Comparisons

It is interesting to compare statistics on income distributions across different countries. The task is complicated, however, by the fact that data are not always accurate or comparable. Furthermore, statistics on the income distribution for other countries of the world are generally not calculated as frequently as for the United States. Nevertheless, the World Bank does provide some such information. These numbers suggest that the United States has the *least* equal income distribution of all the Western industrialized nations for which data are available. (Of the remaining nations, including the less-developed countries, approximately one-half have greater equality and one-half have less equality of income distribution than the United States.[3])

Finally, graphs can be used to compare the income distribution in one country over different time periods or to compare the income distributions of two countries. These graphs are discussed in the appendix to this chapter.

ABSOLUTE POVERTY

Because the poor are on the lower rungs of the income distribution ladder, the concepts of relative poverty and absolute poverty are intricately linked. Recall that absolute poverty refers to a situation in which people experience actual hardship according to some objective criterion.

Measuring Absolute Poverty in the United States

Poverty line
A level of income below which a household is considered poor.

The **poverty line** is the official criterion for determining absolute poverty. The poverty line is simply a level of household income that delineates an amount considered adequate to cover basic needs for survival: food, clothing, housing, and so on. The concept of money income that was used in the statistics on the income distribution is used in calculating poverty statistics as well. The poverty line is adjusted for family size. Larger families have a higher poverty line. If household money income falls below the poverty line, all members of the household are considered poor.

Origins of the Poverty Line
The poverty line was initially based on the Department of Agriculture's 1961 "economy food plan," later refined and renamed the "thrifty food plan." A minimum food budget was determined and multiplied by three, because the cost of food was considered to represent about one-third of consumer expenditures, according to studies of consumer spending patterns in the 1950s. In each subsequent year, the poverty line has been adjusted upward to reflect inflation, which is a rise in the average price level.

Meaning of the Poverty Line
It is important to realize that the concept of official poverty is not a measure of those who would be poor in the absence of government income transfers, because "money income" *does* include these cash transfers. Rather, it includes all those who are officially poor *despite* these transfers. It is equally important to realize that official poverty does not necessarily confer eligibility for government programs, either now or in the past. States may require that families have income much lower than the federal poverty line to qualify for certain welfare programs. Official poverty reflects a statistical measure only.

Measurement Problems with the Poverty Line
This measure of official poverty has been the target of much controversy. Some economists and politicians have argued that this indicator exaggerates the true extent of poverty in the country because it ignores the receipt of in-kind transfers.

Because these benefits are ignored in calculating a family's money income, the family may be classified as officially poor, even though its actual well-being is enhanced by transfers such as food stamps and Medicaid health coverage.

Another problem arises when adjusting the poverty line for inflation. Many economists believe that the consumer price index, which is used to measure inflation, actually overstates the extent of inflation. (This issue is discussed in Chapter Fourteen.) In this case, inflation adjustments would result in an artificially high poverty line and an overstatement of the extent of poverty.

Others have argued that official poverty statistics do not exaggerate the actual extent of poverty in this country, but rather underestimate it. They argue that the concept of household income used to measure poverty ought to be after-tax income because this is the income that can actually be used by households for their personal needs. (As a case in point, the poor pay a very large share of their income in the form of Social Security taxes.) They also argue that the poverty line itself is inadequate. The threshold was established when food expenses actually *were* one-third of a consumer's budget; since then increases in fuel, housing, and health care costs have increased the importance of these items relative to food expenditures in a typical budget. Recent studies indicate that U.S. families spend closer to one-fifth than one-third of their incomes on food. This statistic would suggest that food expenses perhaps ought to be multiplied by some number larger than three (such as five) to arrive at an official poverty line. Furthermore, the Department of Agriculture's minimum food budget was never intended to represent a long-term adequate diet.

Life at the Poverty Line

Consider the implications of life at the poverty line. Imagine that you live in a family of four, and household money income is at the 1999 poverty line of $16,895. Assuming that your family spends one-fifth of its income on food, your family would have $3,379 for food and the remaining $13,516 for all other expenditures for the year. Each *person* would have $16.24 per week, or $2.32 per day for food. Have you tried to live on that? The family as a whole would have $1,126 per month to cover rent, fuel, utilities, insurance, transportation (including auto maintenance), clothing, medical and dental needs, educational expenses, entertainment, and taxes. Existence is frugal, to say the least.

Trends in Poverty Statistics

Poverty rate
The percentage of the population that is poor.

A comparison of poverty statistics over recent years shows fairly dramatic trends. When measuring the number of poor people as a percentage of the total population, poverty was very extensive in the 1950s and up to 1960. Indeed, this **poverty rate** was 22.2 percent in 1960 (see Table 7-2). (Certainly the nostalgia that many people have for the 1950s is misguided. The 'wonder years' were not so wonderful for the fifth of our population that was poor.) However, this poverty rate declined substantially throughout the 1960s and the early 1970s with the economic prosperity of the period, as well as the antipoverty programs that began with the Johnson

TABLE 7-2   Poverty Rates: The Percentage of the Population Living Below the Poverty Line, Selected Years 1960–1999

DATE	POVERTY RATE	DATE	POVERTY RATE
1960	22.2	1991	14.2
1965	17.3	1992	14.8
1970	12.6	1993	15.1
1973	11.1	1994	14.5
1980	13.0	1995	13.8
1983	15.2	1996	13.7
1989	12.8	1997	13.3
1990	13.5	1998	12.7
		1999	11.8

Source: U.S. Department of Commerce, Bureau of the Census, 2000, http://www.census.gov/hhes/poverty

WEB LINK

http://www.bread.org
This is the site of Bread for the World, a Christian citizens' lobby on issues of domestic and international hunger and poverty. It includes information on current legislative issues involving hunger and poverty, as well as addresses for legislators who are considered key contacts. This site has links to other antipoverty organizations' Web sites.

Medicaid
A government program providing medical coverage for eligible low-income people.

Medicare
A government program providing medical coverage largely to elderly people.

Administration. The national poverty rate reached a low of 11.1 percent of the total population in 1973, and climbed to 13.0 percent in 1980. The poverty rate rose to 15.2 percent by 1983, reflecting the recession of the early 1980s. Poverty rates recovered, then rose again in the early 1990s, again reflecting recession. Poverty rates declined steadily during the 1993–1999 period, reaching 11.8 percent in 1999. The latter period corresponds to one of the longest periods of steady economic growth in U.S. history. A national poverty rate close to 12 percent is nevertheless very troublesome.

The Implications of Poverty

It has been said that poverty statistics are just people with the tears washed off. What is the real meaning of poverty as it affects people's lives? Certainly hunger is a problem for the poor. Bread for the World, a national citizens' lobby on hunger issues, recently cited a 1999 U.S. Department of Agriculture study reporting that more than 31 million people in the United States—12 million of whom are children—lived in households that were either hungry or at risk of hunger. That means that 1 in 10 families had to skip meals, rely on emergency food, or eat less because they could not afford the food they need. Bread for the World also cited a 2000 U.S. Conference of Mayors report stating that 25 cities across the country reported an increase in demand for emergency food assistance of 17 percent.[8]

Homelessness is also an implication of poverty, and families with children represent the fastest-growing group among the homeless. Homelessness is discussed in more detail in Chapter Eleven. In addition, adequate health care is often not available to our nation's poor. As we will see in Chapter Nine, many of the poor are not covered by **Medicaid** (the government medical program for low-income Americans). Also, despite the presence of **Medicare** (the government medical program for the elderly), many poor older people find themselves unable to afford the costs of medications, Medicare premiums and deductibles, and uncovered medical expenses.

The Incidence of Poverty

Incidence of poverty
Who the poor are, and
which groups of people
have a greater likelihood
of being poor.

Equally important to consider is the **incidence of poverty.** That is, who are the poor in this country, and which groups of Americans have a greater likelihood of being poor? There are two ways to look at statistics describing the poor. Both are correct, but they reflect very different perceptions of the poverty problem. We can examine the composition of the poor (that is, who the poor are), or we can look at the percentage of each group of people that is poor (telling us the likelihood that someone within each group will be poor). We shall consider both approaches to the statistics and analyze their implications.

Who Are the Poor?

First, let's consider the total number of people who are considered officially poor in the United States and see who belongs to this group. Table 7-3 breaks down the population of the poor into groups based on race and ethnicity, age, residence, and family type.

Of a total of 32.3 million poor persons in the United States in 1999, the majority are white (68 percent) and nearly two-fifths are children (37 percent). (Keep in mind that children are considered poor if they live in a household with income below the poverty line.) The largest percentage of the poor lives in central cities (41 percent). Additional statistics on poor families, as opposed to poor persons, indicate that more than half of poor families has a female householder (with no husband present). (Householder refers to the person filling out the census form for the family.)

Although statistics such as these show who the poor are in the United States, they do not adequately show which groups bear a disproportionate burden of the nation's poverty. To identify these groups, we must approach the statistics from the other perspective of poverty; that is, we must analyze which groups in the United States have higher *poverty* rates.

Which Groups Have Higher Poverty Rates?

The proportion of all persons in the United States who are poor is 11.8 percent (see Table 7-4 on page 150). However, if we make comparisons among different racial and ethnic groups, we see enormous disparity. At 9.8 percent, the poverty rate for white people is well below the national average. Perhaps more significantly, the poverty rate for non-Hispanic whites (Hispanics may be of any race) is only 7.7 percent. The poverty rate for black people is approximately three times this rate, at 23.6 percent. The poverty rate for Hispanics is just slightly lower than that for blacks, at 22.8 percent. Asian and Pacific Islanders have a relatively low poverty rate of 10.7 percent. Thus although most of the poor in the United States are white, a black or Hispanic person has a far greater *likelihood* of being poor than does a white person.

What is surprising to many is that older people (age 65 and over) have a poverty rate of 9.7 percent, which is well below the national average. This relatively low rate is due in large part to the Social Security program, which is discussed in Chapter Twelve. The war on poverty among old people has not been won, however.

TABLE 7-3   Composition of the Poor, 1999

GROUP	MILLION	PERCENT OF TOTAL POOR
Persons	**32.3**	**100**
Race and Ethnicity		
White	21.9	68
Non-Hispanic White	14.9	46
Black	8.4	26
Asian and Pacific Islander	1.2	4
Hispanic*	7.4	23
Age		
Age under 18	12.1	37
Age 18–24	4.6	14
Age 25–34	4.0	12
Age 35–44	3.7	11
Age 45–54	2.5	8
Age 55–59	1.2	4
Age 60–64	1.0	3
Age 65 & over	3.2	10
Residence		
Inside metropolitan areas	24.8	77
Inside central cities	13.1	41
Outside central cities	11.7	36
Outside metropolitan areas	7.4	23
Families	**6.7**	**100**
Married couple	2.7	40
Female householder, no husband present	3.5	52
Male householder, no wife present	0.5	7.5

*Hispanics may be of any race. Thus figures do not add up to 100.
Source: Based on information from the U.S. Department of Commerce, Bureau of the Census, Poverty 1999: Poverty Estimates by Selected Characteristics, 2000 (http://www.census.gov/hhes/poverty/poverty 99/pv99est1.html).

According to earlier evidence from the Department of Commerce, poverty among elderly women is far more prevalent than poverty among elderly men.

Equally disconcerting is the fact that children have a greater likelihood of being poor than any other age group in the United States. Children under the age of 18 have a poverty rate of approximately 17 percent. That is, more than one of every six children in America suffers from poverty. Consider the words of one woman in poverty:

> (I am concerned) that my children will be strong healthy people, and not have to go through what I have; my daughter to be able to think clearly about things; my son to never abuse any woman in his life. For me—just to provide what my kids and I need and a little extra to survive; that I finish school someday—to be able to work where I

TABLE 7-4 Poverty Status of Persons and Families, 1999, by Race and Ethnicity, Age, and Type of Family

CHARACTERISTIC	POVERTY RATE, %
Persons	**11.8**
Race and Ethnicity	
White	9.8
Non-Hispanic White	7.7
Black	23.6
Hispanic*	22.8
Asian and Pacific Islander	10.7
Age	
Age under 18	16.9
Age 18–24	17.3
Age 25–34	10.5
Age 35–44	8.3
Age 45–54	6.7
Age 55–59	9.2
Age 60–64	9.8
Age 65 & over	9.7
Residence	
Inside metropolitan areas	11.2
Inside central cities	16.4
Outside central cities	8.8
Outside metropolitan areas	14.3
Families	**9.3**
Married couple	4.8
Male householder, no spouse present	11.7
Female householder, no spouse present	27.8

*Hispanics may be of any race.
Source: U.S. Department of Commerce, Bureau of the Census, Poverty 1999: Poverty Estimates by Selected Characteristics, 2000 (http://www.census.gov/hhes/poverty/poverty 99/pv99est1.html).

want to work—because the way that I see it is if you're not happy doing what you're doing, it won't last long. I hope my kids will not inherit my poverty; they deserve much more.[4]

Poverty rates also vary by residence. People living in our central cities have a poverty rate of 16.4 percent. The poverty rate for people living outside metropolitan areas is 14.3 percent. The likelihood of poverty is lowest for people living in metropolitan areas but outside the central cities. In other words, the likelihood of poverty is lowest for people living in the suburbs (8.8 percent). Because blacks and other ethnic minorities are likely to live in the central cities and whites in the suburbs, these figures are consistent with the previous figures on race and ethnicity. The concentration of poverty from residential segregation is further discussed in Chapter Eleven, and the effects of residential segregation on public education are discussed in Chapter Ten.

Finally, families with a female householder and no husband present have almost a 28 percent chance of being poor. Contrast these families with families with a male householder and no wife present. These families have less than a 12 percent chance of being poor. All of these statistics imply quite clearly that poverty in our country is a children's issue; it is also a women's issue, and it is a racial and ethnic issue.

The Feminization of Poverty

The statistics show that women bear the greatest burden of poverty. Many have suggested possible reasons for this feminization of poverty.[5] Historical reasons include the growth in the number of female-headed households, discrimination in the labor market, and domestic violence toward women. Racial and age discrimination may exacerbate the gender discrimination faced by these women. In particular, teenage girls who drop out of school for the birth and care of a child find it difficult to complete their education and eventually find remunerative employment. For those who do manage, additional factors may complicate their lives. For example:

> I think I did things right even at the time I was only sixteen, . . . I married, finished high school, went on to college, and worked, got divorced . . . but haven't received one child support payment.[6]

Insufficient and inadequate child care, inadequate educational and training programs, limited assistance, and insufficient or nonexistent child support prevent many single mothers, and especially teenage mothers, from participating successfully in our economy and achieving independence from the forces of poverty. Other women have forgone educational and career opportunities to remain at home to care for children and family. They frequently find themselves in poverty if their husbands die or desert them. Finally, recent research suggests that 20 to 30 percent of all welfare recipients are current victims of domestic violence. This threat to safety and well-being can prevent many women from entering the labor force, retaining jobs, and supporting their families.[7]

Causes of Poverty

As already indicated, the national poverty rate rose substantially during the early 1980s and again during the early 1990s. Analysis of these and other trends can help uncover some of the causes of poverty.

Recession

Recession
A decline in a nation's gross domestic product (output) associated with a rise in unemployment.

Recessions were an important factor in the high poverty rates of the early 1980s and the early 1990s. A **recession** is a reduction in our nation's output. When businesses are producing lower output levels, the need to hire workers lessens, and lower employment levels result. (Recession is discussed in more detail in Chapter Fifteen, which examines macro policy.) With almost 10 percent of the labor force unemployed in 1982 and 1983, and more than 7 percent unemployed in 1992, one would expect a higher incidence of poverty as income decreased for laid-off workers and as new entrants to the labor force were unable to find jobs. Furthermore, many employed workers find their hours of employment reduced during a recession. However, national unemployment rates are only part of the explanation of poverty.

Subsequent to the recessions of the early 1980s and 1990s, poverty rates did not fall to the degree one might expect in a recovery. Other factors must be considered. These factors include labor productivity, structural changes in our economy, personal factors, demographic trends, and budget cuts for antipoverty programs.

Labor Productivity

People with few skills, limited experience, and little education often have a difficult time finding employment at a satisfactory wage because their labor productivity is considered to be low. As a result, these people are more likely to be poor than are those who are better trained and educated. Many of you are still in school because you expect that your higher education will enhance your productivity and therefore your future income. Low labor productivity also ties in closely with structural changes in the economy as a cause of poverty.

Structural Changes in Our Economy

Changes in the structure of our economy contribute to unemployment and poverty. Technological change (such as robotics in the automobile industry) has enabled machines to replace workers. Furthermore, the lower-wage service sector (child care, restaurant service, health care, and so on) has grown at the expense of the higher-wage manufacturing sector. Finally, the flight of businesses and jobs to the suburbs has left poverty-stricken inner cities in its wake.

These structural changes relate directly to the issue of labor productivity. The point is that the number of good, high-wage, blue-collar jobs has decreased greatly, and the economic gap between high school graduates and workers with higher education has widened. There are simply few well-paying jobs with stable employment left for relatively unskilled and uneducated people.

Personal Factors

People without adequate skills and education are more likely to be poor. But these are not the only factors constraining their incomes. Many individuals lack what we refer to as *job readiness,* or the capacity to show up ready to work, on time, on a daily basis. This lack of readiness may be due to mental disability, inexperience, immaturity, or other factors. Many families, especially single-parent families, lack adequate child care that would enable parents to work. If parents do work, they must miss work when their child is sick or their child care provider is on vacation, or other circumstances exist that make for spotty attendance at work. Still other workers lack adequate transportation to their job sites. Poorer individuals tend to have less-reliable cars, and when their cars break down they may not be able to afford repairs. At the same time, public transportation may be time-consuming or unavailable in the locations where workers need to travel to work and to take their children to child care. Many poor families experience all of these difficulties. Clearly the oft-quoted query, "Why don't they just get a job?" reflects a vast oversimplification of the problem.

TABLE 7-5 Number and Percentage of Families with a Female Householder, No Husband Present, Selected Years 1960–1998

DATE	FAMILIES WITH A FEMALE HOUSEHOLDER, NO HUSBAND PRESENT	
	NUMBER (1000S)	PERCENT OF TOTAL FAMILIES
1960	4,422	9.8
1970	5,500	10.7
1980	8,705	14.6
1990	10,890	16.5
1994	12,406	18.1
1995	12,200	17.6
1996	12,514	18.0
1997	12,790	18.2
1998	12,652	17.8

Source: U.S. Department of Commerce, Bureau of the Census, 2000, http://www.gov/population/socdemo/hh-fam/

Demographic Trends

Demographic statistics indicate that the number of households with a female householder (and no husband present) has increased dramatically and steadily from 1960 to 1994, as is evident in Table 7-5. These families include those with a never-married mother, as well as those in which the father has died or left the family.

Until recently, birth rates for unmarried women aged 15 to 19 were increasing. Just as the term "feminization of poverty" suggests, it is very difficult for these young single mothers to provide adequate incomes for their families when they lack access to good jobs and education, and quality child care is unavailable. The high unemployment rate faced by young unskilled fathers is a contributing factor in their absence from the family and their lack of support.

There may be reason for optimism, however. The data in Table 7-5 show that that both the number and percentage of households with female householders and no husband present has stabilized and may be decreasing. Even more importantly, the National Center for Health Statistics reports that birthrates for teenagers decreased by 18 percent from 1991 to 1998.[9]

Budget Cuts

Many people mistakenly believe that our government spends an enormous amount of money on programs designed to improve conditions for the poor. Many others believe that these programs are ineffective, at best. As a result of these attitudes, support for cuts in government programs for the poor has been widespread since the 1980s. The budget cuts that took place early in the Reagan Administration (1981–1983) were a case in point and were particularly harmful to the poor. Many families, particularly those headed by single mothers, lost eligibility for or received lower benefits from government cash assistant programs. Their children also lost food stamps, access to Medicaid health coverage, eligibility for government school lunch and breakfast programs, and the benefits of a host of other services. Bear in mind that these expenditure cuts occurred during a period when unemployment and poverty rates in the country were high and increasing.

Controversy over government programs continued throughout the 1980s and early 1990s, as rising concern over government budget deficits created pressure for reduced government spending on social programs. Now that we have entered an era of government budget surpluses, there is considerable disagreement over how the surplus should be used. We will return to this issue with the topic of welfare reform. We will see that there are those who believe that government programs effectively decrease poverty and those who feel that government poverty programs are wasteful and even contribute to the poverty problem.

Additional Causes of Poverty

Additional causes of poverty are related to specific aspects of the labor market within our economy. Having a job does not necessarily preclude poverty. A person working for the federal minimum wage of $5.15 per hour for 40 hours per week and 52 weeks per year will earn only $10,712 annually, well below the $16,895 poverty line for a family of four, as noted earlier. The $10,712 is also below the poverty line for a family headed by a single parent with two children ($13,423) and the poverty line for a single parent with one child ($11,483). A minimum wage job clearly does *not* pull these families out of poverty!

We also know that women, on average, earn less than men, at least in part due to labor market discrimination. This discrimination was discussed more extensively in Chapter Six. Racial and age discrimination also serve to lower the average wages of various minority groups, older people, and teenagers. In addition, poverty-stricken individuals include those who for various reasons could not work even if adequately paying jobs were available.

Solutions to Poverty

Solutions to poverty are subject to considerable controversy: witness the continual stream of editorials and letters to the editor in your daily newspaper concerning welfare reform, welfare abuse, government spending, and the like. Let us analyze various solutions that might be used to confront the problem of poverty.

Macroeconomic Policies to Relieve National Unemployment

Given that recession was seen to be a cause of poverty, it is useful to know that the government and Federal Reserve System can undertake various fiscal and monetary policies designed to increase national employment. These policies are discussed more fully in Chapter Fifteen. For the moment it should suffice to say that although national economic prosperity cannot alleviate all poverty, it can work hand in hand with other poverty reduction programs. Certainly it makes little sense to train, educate, and provide work-support services to the hard-core poor and unemployed in an attempt to help them obtain gainful employment, only to find that national unemployment rates dictate that jobs will be unavailable. Requiring the poor to work when jobs do not exist makes even less sense!

Callslip Request   8/16/2014 12:11:36 PM

Request date:8/16/2014 10:31 AM
Request ID: 46065
Call Number:330 B913
Item Barcode:

34711001585902

Author: Brux, Jacqueline Murray.
Title: Economic issues and policy / Jacqueline
Enumeration:c 1Year:
Patron Name:Arveal Drummer
Patron Barcode:

21224060067501

Patron comment:

Request number:

48065

Route to:
I-Share Library:

Library Pick Up Location:

Microeconomic Policies to Improve Labor Productivity

We can address the problems of poverty associated with low labor productivity, structural changes in the economy, and some of the personal factors that we've mentioned by investing in people. We often think about business firms investing in various forms of capital, such as factories and machinery. We can also talk about investment in human capital. An **investment in human capital** is any spending that improves the productivity of people. Obviously, spending on education and job training can improve the skills and abilities of people and make them more productive, enhancing their ability to get jobs and their likelihood of receiving higher incomes.

In addition to job training and education, various programs can improve the job readiness of workers who have difficulty finding or keeping jobs. Transportation and child care needs must also be addressed. The government has addressed some of these needs. At the same time, recent low unemployment rates have left many businesses desperate to hire workers. As a result, these businesses have begun to recognize their need to provide training, child care, and transportation for their workers. Unfortunately, when the economy shifts to a position of scarcity of jobs rather than scarcity of workers, businesses tend to cut back any responsibility for providing these services.

Universal Entitlements

Many of those concerned about poverty have called for expanded systems of **universal entitlements.** These types of programs are not necessarily directed toward the poor. They are targeted to all people meeting various types of criteria. All school-age children in our country, for example, are entitled to a public education. Thus certain standards of education are ensured for all children, regardless of income. Many would expand these types of provisions and guarantees to other areas of importance: child care, medical coverage, maternity and paternity leaves, and child or family allowances. These types of programs are taken for granted in many other Western industrialized countries, and they certainly would address some of the problems associated with the feminization of poverty.

The arguments against universal entitlements center on their expense and their potential for disincentives. Opponents ask, for example, why the government should fund child care for all, rather than just for low-income families in need. And if child allowances provide cash income based on the number of children per family, won't the allowances cause the birth rate to increase?

Proponents reject these claims. They argue that the political likelihood of enacting and maintaining programs and policies is much greater if such programs benefit all, rather than just the poor. Furthermore, only if programs providing benefits such as medical care and child care are targeted to all will quality be ensured; programs for only the poor have often been of substandard quality. Finally, universal entitlements would avoid the stigmatizing of the poor and the pitting of various groups of citizens against one another in their quest for important services.

A Negative Income Tax

A **negative income tax** has been proposed by politicians and economists in a variety of forms but would typically tax income earners at various positive rates as long

---

Investment in human capital
Spending that is designed to improve the productivity of people.

Universal entitlements
Payments (or programs) to which eligible citizens have a right by law.

Negative income tax
A taxation system that taxes people with incomes above a certain level and pays people with incomes below that level.

as income lies above some guaranteed level—for example, the poverty line. At this specified level, income would not be taxed. Below this level, people would actually receive payments from the government, amounting to a negative tax. Actual payments could be automatic, could work through our current income tax system, and could depend on family size.

Proposals vary considerably as to the size of payments as well as the overall intent of the program. For some proponents, the negative income tax would entirely replace all current government programs, including farm price supports, student loans, Social Security, and so on. For others, it would replace only government poverty programs; other programs would remain intact. Milton Friedman, an early advocate of the negative income tax, believed that it should replace a large number of government programs. Other proponents have suggested that the tax be used in conjunction with various other government poverty programs; indeed, they suggest that the beauty of the negative income tax is that it would free up funds and personnel currently involved in the bureaucracy of our cash assistance programs. These resources could be put to work meeting the various social needs of low-income clients.

The proposal has a number of other attractive elements. It is simple and probably efficient. It could be designed to cover the cash needs of all Americans, not just those in specific categories. There would be no incentive for family breakup. And, if properly run, it could minimize disincentives for work effort. As long as individuals receive at least some substantial portion of each additional work dollar, and always are better off working than not, the incentive to work will remain. The actual feasibility and desirability of any such negative income tax proposal will depend on actual payment levels, the types of government programs that complement it, and the minimization of any potential work disincentives.

Despite the many positive aspects of the negative income tax, few politicians are willing to seriously consider it. However, the 1986 tax reform has taken some steps toward the goals envisioned in the negative income tax plan. Various exemptions, deductions, and credits have virtually eliminated the obligation of very-low-income families to pay federal income taxes. Furthermore, increases in the federal **earned income tax credit (EITC),** a tax credit originally geared to low-income working families with children, reduces the tax burden of these poor families. The EITC is actually a limited form of the negative income tax insofar as it returns money to low-income families even if they paid no federal income taxes. President Clinton increased the EITC and expanded it to low-income single individuals and couples without children in 1993. As of 1999, workers who are raising more than one child in their home and have family income of less than $30,580 can get a tax credit of up to $3,816. Workers with one or no children receive a smaller amount. If they paid no income taxes, they would simply receive a check from the government. If they have already paid taxes, they would be reimbursed by this amount. However, they must first file a federal personal income tax form to be eligible.

Because the earned income tax credit works so well to help low-income working families without diminishing their incentive to work, many people have argued for expanded use of the credit at both the federal and the state government levels.

Earned income tax credit (EITC)

A federal tax credit for low-income individuals and families. The credit is available whether or not the worker pays federal personal income taxes.

Miscellaneous

Because discrimination plays a role in poverty, it is important that our nation strive to provide equal opportunities to all people in the areas of education, housing, and employment. Equal opportunity legislation and affirmative action are discussed in more detail in Chapter Six. In addition, financing of public education must be addressed to ensure quality schools for all children. This issue is discussed in more detail in Chapter Ten on education. Our nation's health care system and housing programs must also address the needs of the poor. Finally, we need to consider an increase in the minimum wage. Because there are costs and benefits associated with the minimum wage, we need to carefully consider the issues that are discussed in Chapter Fourteen on unemployment and inflation.

Welfare and Other Government Programs

Social (public) assistance
Any government program that is targeted to aid low-income people.

Several government programs are designed to help the poor. These programs include food stamps, general assistance, Medicaid, Supplemental Security Income, the Special Supplemental Nutrition Program for Women, Infants, and Children, and Temporary Assistance for Needy Families. These programs are described as **social (public) assistance** programs in Table 7-6.

TABLE 7-6   Explanation of Government Programs

PROGRAM	EXPLANATION
Public Assistance Programs	
Food Stamps	Federal government program providing vouchers (coupons) to low-income people, accepted as payment by stores for food.
General Assistance	Local government assistance designed to meet local needs and fill gaps in state and federal government programs.
Medicaid	Combined federal and state government program providing medical coverage for eligible low-income people.
Supplemental Security Income (SSI)	Combined federal and state government program providing cash income to low-income aged, blind, and disabled people.
Special Supplemental Nutrition Program for Women, Infants, and Children (WIC)	Federal government program providing nutritious food to needy pregnant women and young children when special health needs exist.
Earned Income Tax Credit (EITC)	Federal tax credit for low-income working people.
Temporary Assistance to Needy Families (TANF)	Block grants from the federal government to state governments for use in state welfare programs that comply with the Personal Responsibility and Work Opportunity Reconciliation Act.
Social Insurance Programs	
Medicare	Federal government program providing medical coverage largely to elderly people.
Social Security	Federal government program providing cash benefits to retired workers, survivors of deceased workers, and the disabled.
Unemployment Compensation	Combined federal and state government program providing benefits to eligible unemployed workers.

Social Security

A federal program that provides income transfers to retired workers, the survivors of deceased workers, and disabled workers.

Social insurance

Any government program funded by payroll taxes of employers, employees, or both. A person need not have low income to qualify.

Although **Social Security** has removed many people from poverty, it is not considered an antipoverty program because it is available to all who are eligible, regardless of income. Social Security is an example of a **social insurance** program, which individuals pay into while they work and receive benefits from when they become eligible. Thus the public assistance programs in Table 7-6 are targeted to low-income people, whereas social insurance programs are not. Other social insurance programs include Medicare and unemployment compensation.

Temporary Assistance for Needy Families (TANF) is a **block grant** from the federal government to state governments for use in state welfare programs. It is the public assistance program that we will consider in detail momentarily. It replaces **Aid to Families with Dependent Children (AFDC),** which had been our nation's most important public assistance program for many years. The AFDC program provided cash assistance to poor families with children. This program generated controversy in the United States for decades and was revised many times. The controversy culminated in the passage of legislation that eliminated AFDC and replaced it with work programs. The issues that motivated this action are discussed in the next section.

WELFARE REFORM

Temporary Assistance for Needy Families (TANF)

A block grant from the federal government to state governments to be used in state welfare programs in compliance with federal guidelines.

Block grant

A lump sum of money given by the federal government to state governments to use as they wish within broad federal guidelines to develop programs to meet a broad category of need.

Liberals and conservatives alike agreed on the need for welfare reform, as was evident in the Republican "Contract with America" (the 1990s blueprint guiding conservative proposals for our nation's economy), and in President Clinton's election promise to "end welfare as we know it." Dialogue culminated in the passage of the welfare reform bill called the **Personal Responsibility and Work Opportunity Reconciliation Act (PRA).** This legislation, signed into law by President Clinton in October 1996, called for the phase-out of the AFDC program. It is useful to examine the controversy that created the call for welfare reform.

Controversy over Welfare

Disincentives

Many people were concerned about possible disincentives built into the AFDC program. Although individual state programs varied, the federal program was such that if a recipient (usually a mother) took a job and began earning income, she lost AFDC benefits dollar for dollar of the income earned. Although she may have received benefits to cover the additional costs of working (transportation, childcare, and so on), often these were inadequate. If income rose and Medicaid benefits were lost (as well as eligibility for child nutrition programs and other services), the family may well have been placed in a far more precarious situation than before the mother went to work. Thus economic disincentives were said to exist for work effort. Furthermore, severe restrictions on benefits had often been placed on families with a father present in the home. In many cases these restrictions may have encouraged the father to leave the family so that the mother and children could receive benefits. Others argued that the program encouraged illegitimacy. Thus disincentives were said to exist for family stability.

Aid to Families with Dependent Children (AFDC)
Our nation's former welfare program providing cash assistance to eligible low income families with children.

Personal Responsibility and Work Opportunity Reconciliation Act of 1996 (PRA)
Legislation that eliminated AFDC and replaced it with state programs that require work. It also tightened eligibility for and reduced the benefits offered by other social assistance programs.

Welfare Dependency

Another concern was that government programs encouraged people to develop long-term dependence on welfare. Research results on this issue are mixed. Various studies reported different percentages of families remaining dependent on welfare. Despite the discrepancies in findings, the data suggested that most people did not become persistently dependent on welfare but used such assistance to get through a difficult financial period resulting from a divorce, an unplanned birth, an illness or death, a lost job, or other factors. Even though the percentage of families persistently dependent on welfare may have been small, it was significant. The dependent recipient was the stereotype in the minds of people as they railed against AFDC.

Welfare Expense

Finally, people were concerned about the expense of welfare programs. Here it is important to maintain a correct perspective. Census Bureau data reveal that in the last several years of the AFDC program federal spending on this program represented only about 1 percent of the federal budget. (Food stamps and other nutrition programs combined represented only about 2 percent.) Although it is always important to use funds wisely, many people held the mistaken opinion that welfare was draining the federal budget.

The Personal Responsibility and Work Opportunity Reconciliation Act

The 1996 PRA phased out the AFDC program and replaced it with Temporary Assistance to Needy Families block grants to individual states for use in their welfare programs. States were given until July 1997 to develop these welfare programs. The PRA allows the states wide discretion in determining their programs, eligibility standards, and benefit levels. States must comply, however, with some broad federal guidelines. These guidelines specify that (1) states must contribute matching money to their welfare programs, (2) adults must cease to receive benefits if they fail to work within two years of joining the welfare rolls, and (3) states may not use federal money to provide assistance to adults for more than five years in their lifetimes (although 20 percent of each state's welfare recipients can be exempted from this requirement).

In addition to these restrictions, states may also add their own stipulations. They may require, for example that minor, unmarried parents live with an adult and attend school in order to be eligible for benefits. They may deny additional assistance to children born to mothers already receiving benefits. They may also provide lower benefits to people moving to their state if the previous state's benefits were lower.

In addition to the AFDC program, the PRA eliminated many benefits for legal immigrants who are not citizens and have not already worked in the United States for 10 years. (*Illegal* immigrants were already ineligible for most programs.) Some, but not all, of these benefits have since been restored for some, but not all, of those immigrants. Food stamps and federal cash assistance provided through the

PRA are still denied to many legal immigrants. The PRA also eliminated low-income entitlement to child care, tightened eligibility for benefits to disabled children, and allowed states to deny Medicaid to adults who lose cash assistance for failure to comply with work requirements.

Partly as a result of the new legislation, welfare caseloads have fallen dramatically in almost every state since the early 1990s. Only 2.4 million families received welfare cash assistance nationally in mid-1999, a 52 percent reduction from the level of 5 million in early 1994. Cash assistance spending has also fallen. Federal and state expenditures for cash assistance benefits in fiscal year 1999 totaled $12.4 billion, or $10.6 billion less than in fiscal year 1994.[10] The reduction in caseloads is touted as a sign of the program's success, but many people are concerned about what has become of the former clients. Have they become employed with adequate wages? Have they dropped out of the system, overwhelmed by requirements and restrictions, or are they simply unwilling to work?

According to the Center on Budget and Policy Priorities, most people leaving welfare for work earn too little to adequately support their families. Their jobs are typically short-lived, low-wage jobs that lack health or other benefits and offer little room for advancement or wage growth. Other families have left or been dropped from the welfare rolls without work, and many of the people remaining on welfare have very serious unmet needs. The final outcomes of the new welfare program will not be evident until the years 2001 and 2002, when the five-year time limits come into play for early participants in the system. Whether these clients can be placed in secure jobs with adequate incomes remains to be seen.[11]

Although results to date are discouraging, there is some optimism about the capacity of states to improve their programs. Within the context of the broad federal guidelines, states have considerable discretion, flexibility, and financing for developing their own welfare programs. In an ideal situation, the state will take into account the complexity of poverty among its citizens and seek to provide solutions that incorporate training and education, child care, health care, nutrition, transportation, counseling, and other forms of assistance. They might also provide state earned income tax credits and subsidies to employers to cover the costs of hiring welfare clients. In other situations, unfortunately, states will put forth only the minimal effort needed to comply with federal law.

An Example of a PRA Program: Wisconsin Works

Wisconsin had long been a leader in welfare reform and was one of the first states to implement its program in September 1997. This new program is entitled Wisconsin Works (W-2), and it provides various forms of assistance to needy families with children, along with job preparation and job support services for needy parents. Wisconsin is more generous in providing various supports for the transition from welfare to work than are most states. Nevertheless, applicants must have lived in Wisconsin for 60 consecutive days before they are eligible for W-2, though they may be entitled to food stamps, Medicaid, child care assistance, and other services before that time. W-2 requires that all participating parents be placed in one of four tiers of "work" as soon as he or she is able to work or has received assistance under the program for 24 months, whichever comes first. (A single parent caring

WEB LINK

http://www.cbpp.org
This is the site of the Center on Budget and Policy Priorities, a liberal research and advocacy group based in Washington, DC. It posts welfare studies and policy recommendations.

WEB LINK

http://www.heritage.org/issues/chap8.html
This is the site of the Heritage Foundation, a conservative research institute in Washington, DC.

for a child who is less than 12 weeks old is exempt from the work requirement). These four tiers of "work" extend from unsubsidized employment at the top (the program goal) to a work training and education tier at the bottom. This lower tier represents work training and education for individuals who have been determined to have multiple barriers to employment. This work training and education may consist of high school completion, technical courses, English as a Second Language, parenting and life skills, mental health counseling, caring for an incapacitated family member, and volunteer activity. The individual receives a monthly benefit of $628, reduced by $5.15 for each hour that the participant fails without good cause to participate in assigned activities. An individual is eligible for income from any of the three tiers of work activity (excluding unsubsidized employment) for a period up to 24 months, with possible extensions.[12]

The Wisconsin program emphasizes community involvement in the program and includes subsidies to employers who hire W-2 participants. The program also emphasizes pregnancy prevention and includes child care and transportation assistance, food stamps, Medicaid, and emergency assistance for those who are eligible. Minor parents are not eligible for cash assistance but may receive case management services, cash assistance for child care, and health care. Minors without a high school diploma must attend school to receive child care assistance. W-2 payments are not adjusted for the number of children in a family, and W-2 participants receive health benefits in the form of a new insurance plan using health maintenance organizations. Wisconsin also has a state earned income tax credit, and extends food stamps and W-2 services to eligible legal immigrants.

Many people living in and outside Wisconsin are watching the Wisconsin program carefully. A major question concerns the status of people who have ceased to participate in the W-2 program. In response, the Wisconsin Department of Workforce Development commissioned a study to examine the status of every participant who left the program between September 1997 and September 1999. The results of this study indicate that among participants who had not reentered the program by September 1999, 75.9 percent had left the program because they had obtained household income through employment, other government cash assistance, child support, or some combination of these. Other participants left the program because they chose not to enroll or to have an eligibility review (9.4 percent), they chose not to meet program requirements (7.9 percent), they no longer met other eligibility requirements (4.3 percent), or they chose options other than receiving assistance (2.5 percent). The study was able to obtain monthly earnings statements for 13,428 of the families that left the program after becoming employed. Of these, 10.7 percent earned less than $800, 9.6 percent earned $800 to $899, 11.1 percent earned $900 to $999, 21.6 percent earned $1,000 to $1,199, 26.0 percent earned $1,200 to $1,499, 12.7 percent earned $1,500 to $1,999, and 8.4 percent earned more than $2,000. The majority of these incomes are at poverty levels. A second study to be released in July 2001 will include data on more recent participants in the program.[13]

Just as at the federal level, W-2 participants are limited to five years' lifetime participation in the program, though some may be eligible for extensions. Since participation began as early as October 1996 (before the program was implemented nationwide), the earliest participants will reach their five-year time limits in

October 2001. At that time, we will have more information available about clients who lose their eligibility for the Wisconsin program.[14]

Concerns about the PRA

There are many issues surrounding the PRA. One controversial element of welfare reform is whether mothers of young children should be required to work outside of the home. Many feel that work is better for mother and child. Others fear that child care for infants will be inadequate and believe that the choice to work should reside with the mother, as it does for higher-income families. Another issue involves child care for all children in the family. When funds are not made available for child care, many people fear that children will be poorly cared for by an older sibling or by a neighbor or relative already overworked with children of her own. Regardless of viewpoints, child care should be perceived as a valuable form of work in our society.

A second issue involves the level of cash assistance benefits to welfare recipients who are not yet working for a variety of reasons. Currently, the maximum monthly welfare benefit for a family of three in the median (middle-paying) state is just one-third of the federal poverty line. As a result, many welfare families run out of food at some point during the year and are vulnerable to utility shutoffs, evictions, and homelessness. Clearly, the level of assistance is inadequate.

Another issue involves the importance of training and educational opportunities that would ultimately give a client access to jobs providing adequate wages and benefits. According to federal law, participation in vocational education can count toward a state's work participation requirement for up to 12 months for any individual, but for no more than 30 percent of the state's welfare recipients. The federal government does allow some additional flexibility, if states are willing to take advantage of it. Many people feel that the guidelines are very restrictive because although each client needs to meet specific work requirements, any education and training beyond the minimal amount supported by the program must come out of the client's free time. There is little if any free time for a single parent of young children who is working full time. As one single woman explained at the beginning of the program:

> I will complete the higher education degree I am currently seeking. . . . I am told that as of next semester, I will no longer be eligible for childcare assistance and will also be forced to work a minimum of thirty hours per week. School will no longer be a consideration in my case. My sons are three and one-half, and four and one-half, and will need to be in daycare for another year and a half at least. I am eligible for student loans, which will cover the cost. However, my main concern is the work requirement. It will be extremely difficult to keep up a good grade point, work, and still be able to be a mother to my children. This will mean that we will be together as a family less than we are now. That's what frightens me.[15]

Another potentially serious problem of a welfare system centered on work responsibility concerns business cycles. Our economy alternates between periods of growth and decline in GDP, or in other words, between expansions and recessions. Our new welfare system is initiated during a period of steady economic growth and prosperity. What happens when the next recession hits and jobs are no longer available? It is one thing to require people to work; it is another thing to require them to work when jobs do not exist.

One final controversy centers on the transfer of responsibility for welfare programs from the federal government to the states. Many have long contended that individual states know and understand their welfare needs better than does the federal government, which is perceived as distant and bureaucratic. Others believe that federal responsibility is essential to provide consistent benefits to all citizens. Affluent states can provide additional funding for generous benefits and eligibility, but poorer states with high unemployment rates and low property values find it difficult to raise additional tax revenue to meet the needs of their distressed population.

THE ROLE OF ECONOMIC GROWTH VS. GOVERNMENT PROGRAMS

Because recession—which is a decline in national output—causes unemployment rates to go up, we might expect that economic growth—which is an increase in national output—would cause unemployment rates to go down. Higher output levels mean more people working, which means fewer people in poverty. This is, in fact, the essence of **trickle-down philosophy:** the benefits of economic growth and prosperity eventually trickle down to all.

Trickle-down philosophy
The view that the benefits of economic growth and prosperity will "trickle down" to all.

Certainly greater national prosperity does reduce poverty and is one reason for the falling poverty rates we observed during the 1990s. However, there are three particular problems with the trickle-down philosophy. First, some of the policies that are designed to generate economic growth may directly increase absolute and relative poverty, as well as worsen the standards of living of the poor. This phenomenon is discussed in greater length in the section on supply-side policy in Chapter Fifteen, in which examples include cuts in government programs and in personal income tax rates. Second, the newly created jobs that result from economic growth benefit those who are hired into these jobs. Remember that many others are left behind in the labor market, including those who are ill or disabled, the elderly, the young, those who face labor market discrimination, and single parents of young children, as well as people without adequate job skills, education, experience, and transportation. The benefits of economic growth fail to trickle down to these people. Finally, a job does not guarantee a living wage. Recall that the minimum wage may well leave a family below the poverty line. Government programs will always be necessary to help those who cannot achieve success through economic growth alone.

COMPLEXITY OF POVERTY

The problem of poverty is very complex and without simple solutions. If there were only one cause and one type of poverty, solutions would be readily found. Instead, there are a variety of circumstances affecting different individuals. The

People generally adopt either a liberal or a conservative approach to the poverty issue. Liberals are more inclined to stress the need for government involvement in antipoverty efforts; they believe there are equity issues that are not dealt with by the market economy. Conservatives are much more leery of government involvement and are concerned that too many programs or too much assistance creates inefficiencies and disincentives for work effort. Liberals tend to prefer extensive federal involvement in poverty programs, whereas conservatives prefer greater responsibility by state governments (such as with the new welfare reform) and private charities. Liberals favor a direct approach to dealing with the problem of poverty; conservatives often favor an indirect, trickle-down approach.

On the other hand, many economists believe that solutions to poverty should not be viewed as alternative courses of action. Indeed, an effective solution might combine elements of each alternative. A prosperous economy with high employment is an important—but only a partial—solution. Universal entitlements may ensure more adequate standards for many, as would a negative income tax (or expansion of the earned income tax credit). Efforts to improve the productivity and job readiness of workers are lauded by liberals and conservatives alike. Given the complexity of poverty and the individual needs of people, many economists believe that solutions to poverty must be varied and individualized.

solutions to poverty among elderly women will be far different from the solutions to poverty among unskilled and uneducated 18-year-olds. The needs of single women with children will be far different from the needs of the disabled. The problems of poverty in inner-city ghettos are far different from the problems in the suburbs and the countryside.

Many students who work hard to finance their education find it difficult to be sympathetic to the poor. They work hard, so why don't the poor? We must remember that it is one thing to be successful at work, but it is another thing to be successful at work while caring for young children, coping with a disability, or lacking transportation or opportunities for employment. Some Americans have adopted a punitive attitude toward the poor, but many others are sincere in their concern for the poor, though they have different views about how to approach the issue of poverty. What we must do is try to understand the complexities of poverty and avoid stigmatizing and stereotyping the poor. At the same time we must seek common ground for solutions to poverty that work. We cannot expect these solutions to be simple.

SUMMARY

Relative poverty is a situation in which people are poor in comparison with other people. Relative poverty is measured by the distribution of total money income to different income groups. Recent U.S. statistics on the income distribution indicate that the poorest fifth of the population receives less than 4 percent of total income, whereas the richest fifth of the population receives nearly 50 percent. The income distribution in the United States has become less equal since 1981. The United States has the least equal income distribution of all the Western industrialized nations.

Absolute poverty is defined through the use of the poverty line. If a family's money income falls below the poverty line, all members of that family are defined by the government as being poor. The poverty line varies depending on family size and is adjusted annually for inflation. The 1999 poverty line for a family of four is $16,895.

The U.S. poverty rate exceeded 20 percent in 1960. This rate fell dramatically during the 1960s and 1970s, reaching a low of approximately 11 percent in 1973. Poverty rates increased once again in the early 1980s and early 1990s, reaching more than 15 percent in 1983 and 1993. Although most poor people in the United States are white, blacks and Hispanics have considerably higher poverty rates. Households with single female parents have higher poverty rates than other households, and children have the highest poverty rate of all age groups. The implications of poverty include hunger, homelessness, and poor health.

Causes of increased poverty include recession, low labor productivity, structural changes in our economy, personal factors, demographic trends (such as numbers of female-headed households), and cuts in government programs that assist the poor. Proposals to reduce poverty have taken a variety of approaches and include macroeconomic policies to reduce national unemployment, microeconomic policies to improve worker productivity, a system of universal entitlements, a negative income tax and the earned income tax credit, antidiscrimination policies, the minimum wage, and welfare. The debate over welfare reform culminated in the passage of the Personal Responsibility and Work Opportunity Reconciliation Act of 1996, which eliminated Assistance to Families with Dependent Children and replaced it with Temporary Aid to Needy Families. The new program emphasizes work and time limits for assistance.

NOTES

1. These words, and the words of other women throughout the text, are actual quotations of women who were involved in a project of the Women and Poverty Public Education Initiative, funded by the Charles Stewart Mott Foundation. The source is *In Our Own Words: Mothers' Perspectives on Welfare Reform,* The Women and Poverty Public Education Initiative, 1997. Major portions of the report were prepared by Laura Wittmann, Anne Statham, and Katherine Rhoades, as well as Loretta Williams, Jean Verber, Julie Elliott, Selina Vasquez, Kathe Johnson, Nancy Bayne, Ethel Quisler, May Kay Schleiter, Diana Garcia, Iredia Seiler, Mary Ellen Lemke, Michelle Graf, Bets Reedy, Jean Radtke, Kim Noyd, Susan Taylor-Campbell, and Davida Alperin. (Quotations may contain slight grammatical alterations made by the authors.)

2. U.S. Department of Commerce, Bureau of the Census, 2000, http://www.census.gov/hhes/income/

3. World Bank, *World Development Report 1999/2000* (New York: Oxford University Press, 2000), pp. 238–239. Comparisons are based on the Gini coefficient, a measure of distribution of income or consumption expenditures, for the most recent year available (generally in the 1990s).

4. Laura Wittmann, et al., *In Our Own Words: Mothers' Perspectives on Welfare Reform.*

5. The phrase "feminization of poverty" was first used by sociologist Diana Pearce, "The Feminization of Poverty: Women, Work, and Welfare," *Urban and Social Change Review,* Feb. 1978. It also appears, along with an extensive discussion of the feminization of poverty and its causes, in Ruth Sidel, *Women and Children Last: The Plight of Poor Women in Affluent America* (New York: Viking, 1986). In her book, Sidel emphasizes the point made in the introduction to this book—namely, that women are often just one normal life crisis away from poverty. She also makes the arguments in favor of universal entitlements that are discussed subsequently under Solutions to Poverty.

6. Laura Wittmann, et al., *In Our Own Words: Mothers' Perspectives on Welfare Reform.*

7. Center on Budget and Policy Priorities, "Windows of Opportunity: Strategies to Support Low-Income Families in the Next State of Welfare Reform" (http://www.cbpp.org/3-30-00wel.htm).

8. Bread for the World, "Hunger Persists, But Eases Somewhat," *Bread* (The Bread for the World Newsletter), January 2001.

9. The data represent an estimated value for 1999. National Center for Health Statistics, Centers for Disease Control and Prevention, U.S. Department of Health and Human Services, http://www.cdc.gov/nchs/data/sr21_56.pdf

10. Center on Budget and Policy Priorities, "States Have Substantial Unspent Welfare Funds, But Low-Income Families Continue to Need Key Supports," (http://www.cbpp.org/1-12-00wel-pr.htm).

11. Center on Budget and Policy Priorities, "States Have Substantial Unspent Welfare Funds." Subsequent data on levels of cash assistance are also from this source.

12. Information in this paragraph and the next paragraph is from the Wisconsin Department of Workforce Development, *Wisconsin State Plan for the Administration of the Block Grant to States for Temporary Assistance for Needy Families,* June 1, 2000 (http://www.dwd.state.wi.us/desw2/Witamfpl.htm).

13. Department of Workforce Development, *Welfare Closure Study: A Study of All AFDC and W-2 Closures (September 1997 Through September 1999),* March 2000 (http://www.dwd.state.wi.us/des/w2_closure/transmittal.htm). Note that some of the participants in the study had started with AFDC funds and transitioned into W-2. Separate data are available for participants who left W-2 and were subsequently reinstated. The earnings data cited for participants who left due to subsequent employment do not include other forms of government cash assistance or child support.

14. Check the Web site of the Wisconsin Department of Workforce Development (http://www.dwd.state.wi) after October 2001 for information regarding participants terminated due to the five-year time limit.

15. Laura Wittmann, et al., *In Our Own Words: Mothers' Perspectives on Welfare Reform.*

DISCUSSION QUESTIONS

1. *Should incomes in the United States be distributed equally? If not, should there be at least a greater degree of equality than we presently have? What are the advantages and disadvantages of greater equality? How might greater equality be achieved?*

2. *Is the official government definition of poverty an adequate one? Does it understate the true extent of poverty? Does it overstate it? How might the measure of poverty be improved? The Census Bureau (http://www.census.gov) has begun recording poverty statistics with alternative definitions of poverty. Check the site.*

3. *Many people would be surprised by the information on declining teenage birthrates. Does this information surprise you? Does it mean than young people are less likely to become pregnant, or does it mean that abortion rates are increasing? Look up the reasons for lower birth rates at the National Center for Health Statistics (http://www.cdc.gov/nchs/data/sr21_56.pdf).*

4. *Are you eligible for the earned income tax credit? Find out if you're eligible by reading about the earned income (tax) credit on the Web site for the Center on Budget and Policy Priorities (http://www.cbpp.org).*

5. *Should mothers of young children be required to work in return for government assistance? Does the age of the child make a difference? What about the number of children? What are the issues involved?*

6. *Should states or the federal government be given more responsibility for poverty programs? What are the implications of placing greater responsibility for these programs on the states? Think about the financing of programs, the extent of poverty in different states, and problems relating to different eligibility criteria and benefit levels across different states.*

7. *The Center on Budget and Policy Priorities (http://www.cbpp.org/3-30-00wel.htm) provides many suggestions about how state governments can improve their welfare programs. How do these suggestions address poverty-related issues, such as housing, health care, and nutrition?*

8. *The textbook uses 1999 statistics for poverty rates and income distribution. Update these figures by using the Census Bureau Web site (www.census.gov). Search under Income and Poverty.*

9. *Which do you feel is more effective in reducing poverty: government poverty programs or economic growth of the nation? Are you conservative or liberal when it comes to addressing poverty?*

Chapter Seven Appendix:
Graphing the Data on the Income Distribution

It is useful to have a "picture" of the income distribution that can readily be used to compare different time periods or countries. In other words, we need to be able to graph the data on the income distribution.

In Figure 7-1, information from the 1999 statistical table (Table 7-1 in the text) is presented graphically in a **Lorenz curve.** In a graph with the percent of population on the horizontal axis and the percent of total money income on the vertical axis, the 45-degree diagonal line would indicate perfect equality of income among the various income groups. For example, the poorest 20 percent of the population

Lorenz curve
A graphical technique that exhibits the income distribution.

FIGURE 7-1   Lorenz Curve Based on 1999 Distribution of Total Money Income in the United States by Fifths of the Total Population

The Lorenz curve displays the distribution of total money income among fifths of the total population. According to this curve, the poorest 20 percent of the population received 3.7 percent of total money income in 1999 (see Table 7-1). Because the second-poorest 20 percent of the population received 9.0 percent of total money income, the poorest 40 percent of the population received 12.7 percent of total income (3.7 percent plus 9.0 percent). Additional points on the Lorenz curve are calculated similarly. The 45-degree line represents perfect income equality. The larger the area between the actual Lorenz curve and the 45-degree line, the less equally is income distributed.

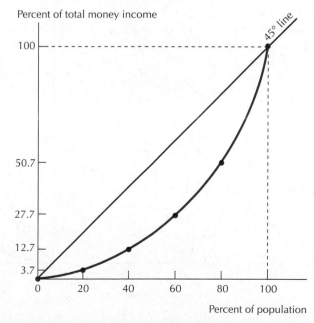

Source: Based on information presented in Table 7-1.

would receive 20 percent of total money income in the United States, the next 20 percent of the population would receive 20 percent of total money income, and so on. This 45-degree line is useful as a reference line.

The Lorenz curve shows the *actual* income distribution. Note that the Lorenz curve is based on cumulative distributions derived from numbers in Table 7-1. First, the poorest 20 percent of the population received 3.7 percent of total money income. The poorest 40 percent of the population (the two bottom income groups) received 12.7 percent of total money income (3.7 percent to the poorest 20 percent of the population plus 9.0 percent to the next poorest 20 percent of the population). The poorest 60 percent of the population (the three bottom income groups) received 27.7 percent of total money income (3.7 percent plus 9.0 percent plus 15.0 percent). Continuing this process completes the Lorenz curve.

The larger the area between the actual Lorenz curve and the diagonal, the less equally is income distributed (since a Lorenz curve directly on the diagonal would mean perfectly equal income distribution). One nice feature of the Lorenz curve is that it can visually represent differences in the income distribution among different time periods or different countries, allowing easy comparisons.

For example, the Lorenz curves in Figure 7-2 show the increasing inequality of the income distribution in the United States. The 1999 graph shows a larger area

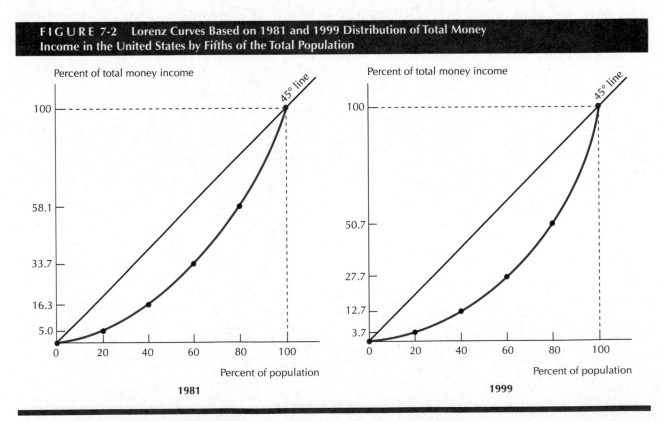

FIGURE 7-2   Lorenz Curves Based on 1981 and 1999 Distribution of Total Money Income in the United States by Fifths of the Total Population

Source: Based on information presented in Table 7-1.

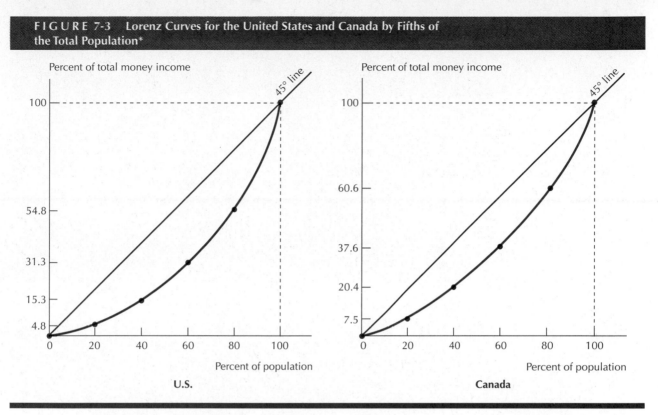

FIGURE 7-3 Lorenz Curves for the United States and Canada by Fifths of the Total Population*

U.S.

Canada

*To maintain comparability, both graphs are based on 1994 data.
Source: Based on data from the World Bank, *World Development Report 1999/2000* (New York: Oxford University Press, 2000), p. 238.

between the 45-degree line and the Lorenz curve than the 1981 graph. (Both graphs are based on information in Table 7-1 of the text.)

As another example, compare the graphs of the Lorenz curves for the United States and Canada in Figure 7-3. (To maintain comparability, 1994 data are used for both countries.) Clearly, Canada has a more equal income distribution than the United States.

CHAPTER 8

World Poverty

Yesterday I ate that macaroni from the garbage with fear of death, because (I remembered the) little black boy. . . . Someone had thrown meat into the garbage, and he was picking out the pieces. He told me "Take some, Carolina. It's still fit to eat." He gave me some, and so as not to hurt his feelings, I accepted. I tried to convince him not to eat that meat, or the hard bread gnawed by the rats. He told me no, because it was two days since he had eaten. He made a fire, and roasted the meat. His hunger was so great that he couldn't wait for the meat to cook. He heated it and ate. So as not to remember that scene, I left thinking: I'm going to pretend I wasn't there. This can't be real in a rich country like mine. . . . The next day I found that little black boy dead. His toes were spread apart. The space must have been eight inches between them. He had blown up as if made out of rubber. His toes looked like a fan. He had no documents. He was buried like any other "Joe." Nobody tried to find out his name. The marginal people don't have names.

Carolina Maria de Jesus, in *Child of the Dark*[1]

In Chapter Seven we considered the problem of poverty in the United States. Although U.S. poverty is a very serious matter, we must remember that the problem of poverty is far more serious for the "marginal people" in many other parts of our globe. Consider the boy in the Brazilian favela (slum), described in the quote that opens this chapter. The poor countries of the world go by a variety of terms: developing countries, less-developed countries (LDCs), low-income countries, and Third World countries are but a few. Throughout this discussion, these terms will be used interchangeably.

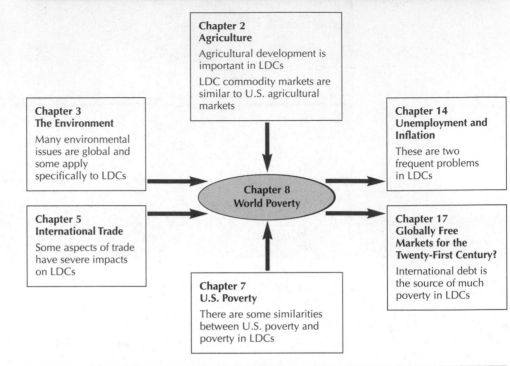

Chapter 2
Agriculture

Agricultural development is important in LDCs

LDC commodity markets are similar to U.S. agricultural markets

Chapter 3
The Environment

Many environmental issues are global and some apply specifically to LDCs

Chapter 5
International Trade

Some aspects of trade have severe impacts on LDCs

Chapter 8
World Poverty

Chapter 7
U.S. Poverty

There are some similarities between U.S. poverty and poverty in LDCs

Chapter 14
Unemployment and Inflation

These are two frequent problems in LDCs

Chapter 17
Globally Free Markets for the Twenty-First Century?

International debt is the source of much poverty in LDCs

http://www.worldbank.org This World Bank site presents data, articles, daily news, discussions, and a wealth of information on less-developed countries. Click on Countries, chose the country of your choice, and select Go to find information and current data specific to that country.

The less-developed countries are located in three geographical regions of the world: Latin America, Africa, and Asia. Table 8-1 lists most of the less-developed countries by region. As the name of a country appears in our discussion, you should reinforce your knowledge of geography by checking the region to which it belongs.

The World Bank recently published statistics indicating the enormous poverty of many people around the world.[2] In the poorest countries of the world (those with a GNP per capita of less than $755 in 1999), more than 10 of every 100 babies born will die before reaching the age of five. Life expectancy is 60 years, and 49 percent of females age 15 or older cannot read and write. These statistics have *worsened* over the last few years.

GNP PER CAPITA

Economists have traditionally measured the prosperity of a country according to its gross domestic product (GDP) per capita or gross national product (GNP) per capita. Because we use both terms interchangeably to represent a country's total output throughout this text, and because international data are frequently presented using GNP statistics, we'll focus our attention on GNP per capita for the moment.

TABLE 8-1   The Less-Developed Countries of the World, by Region

LATIN AMERICA & THE CARIBBEAN	AFRICA		ASIA
Argentina	Algeria	Namibia	Afghanistan
Barbados	Angola	Niger	Bahrain
Belize	Benin	Nigeria	Bangladesh
Bolivia	Botswana	Rwanda	Bhutan
Brazil	Burkina Faso	Senegal	Cambodia
Chile	Burundi	Sierra Leone	China
Colombia	Cameroon	Somalia	India
Costa Rica	Central African Republic	South Africa	Indonesia
Cuba	Cape Verde	Sudan	Iran, Islamic Republic of
Dominican Republic	Chad	Swaziland	Iraq
Ecuador	Comoros	Tanzania, United	Jordan
El Salvador	Congo, Democratic	Republic of	Korea, Democratic
Grenada	Republic of	Togo	Republic of
Guadeloupe	Congo, Republic of	Tunisia	Korea, Republic of
Guatemala	Cote d'Ivoire	Uganda	Kuwait
Guyana	Djibouti	Zambia	Laos, People's Democratic
Haiti	Egypt	Zimbabwe	Republic
Honduras	Equitorial Guinea		Lebanon
Jamaica	Eritrea		Malaysia
Mexico	Ethiopia		Mongolia
Nicaragua	Gabon		Myanmar
Panama	Gambia		Nepal
Paraguay	Ghana		Oman
Peru	Guinea		Pakistan
Suriname	Guinea-Bissau		Papua New Guinea
Uruguay	Kenya		Philippines
Venezuela	Lesotho		Qatar
	Liberia		Saudi Arabia
	Libyan Arab Jamahiriya		Singapore
	Madagascar		Sri Lanka
	Malawi		Syrian Arab Republic
	Mali		Thailand
	Mauritania		United Arab Emirates
	Mauritius		Viet Nam
	Morocco		West Bank & Gaza
	Mozambique		Yemen

Source: United Nations Development Program, *Human Development Report 2000* (New York: Oxford University Press, 2001).

GNP per capita
Gross national product, per person, on average. Calculated by dividing total gross national product by total population.

The phrase "per capita" simply means per person. Thus **GNP per capita** means GNP per person, on average, and is calculated as follows:

$$\text{GNP per capita} = \frac{\text{Total GNP}}{\text{Total Population}}.$$

In addition to measuring production, GNP roughly represents the income generated from the production of GNP. Thus GNP per capita can be thought of as income per person, on average. The phrase "on average" is important. It refers to

TABLE 8-2 1999 GNP per Capita in U.S. Dollars for Richest, Poorest, and Select Countries	
COUNTRY	GNP PER CAPITA ($)
Switzerland	38,350
Norway	32,880
Japan	32,230
Denmark	32,030
United States	30,600
Brazil	4,420
Mexico	4,400
Botswana	3,240
Costa Rica	2,740
China	780
Zimbabwe	520
Vietnam, Laos	370
Angola	220
Nepal	220
Chad	200
Eritrea	200
Malawi	190
Niger	190
Sierra Leone	130
Burundi	120
Congo, Democratic Republic of	110*
Ethiopia	100

*The year for Congo is 1998.
Source: Data from http://www.wto.org

http://www.odci.gov/cia/ publications/factbook This is the Web site of the U.S. Central Intelligence Agency's *World Factbook*. It presents current statistics and information about individual countries of the world.

the typical person in the country, *if* (and this is a *big* if) this income is distributed to all people equally. As we will see, equal distribution *is not* an appropriate assumption.

If GNP per capita is used to measure the prosperity of a country, then it is interesting to compare the prosperity of different countries throughout the world. In doing so, we are struck by the enormous differences, and the incredible poverty of the least prosperous ones. Table 8-2 shows comparisons of GNP per capita for the richest and poorest countries of the world and for a few countries in between.

Notice that Switzerland has the highest GNP per capita, at $38,350. The United States ranks fifth in the world, with GNP per capita equal to $30,600. With GNP per capita relatively low, but still much higher than the very poorest countries, are countries such as Brazil and Mexico, with figures of $4,420 and $4,400, respectively. The 10 poorest countries of the world are listed at the bottom. Ethiopia is the world's poorest country with GNP per capita of $100.

As you examine the 10 poorest countries on the list, refer back to Table 8-1 to identify the regional location of each. You will discover that the majority of these countries are located in Africa. Nevertheless, most of the world's poor live in Asia, due to the huge *numbers* of poor people living in Asian countries such as China, India, Indonesia, and Pakistan.

ECONOMIC GROWTH

Economic growth
Growth in GNP per capita over time, usually several years.

Just as economists sometimes look to GNP per capita as a measure of a country's prosperity, they often look at the growth in real GNP (or GDP) per capita as a measure of improvement, or we can say a measure of **economic growth.** Such growth will be discussed in more detail in Chapter Seventeen. For now merely recognize that economic growth is calculated as the difference between average annual growth in GNP (or GDP) over some time period and average annual population growth over the same time period. Economic growth rates for select countries for the period 1990 to 1999 are listed in the last column of Table 8-3. These growth rates are expressed as average annual growth rates, meaning that they are growth rates per year, averaged over the nine years of the time period. The first two columns remind you that economic growth is calculated as the average annual growth rate of GNP (or GDP) minus the average annual population growth rate.

Notice that economic growth rates may be positive, approximately zero, or negative, ranging from highs of almost 10 percent in the table to lows of almost negative 10 percent. The growth rates of China, Vietnam, and Chile are extremely high, due to high GDP growth rates and relatively low population growth rates. The approximately zero economic growth rates for Honduras and Ecuador are due to growth in GDP that is cancelled out almost precisely by growth in population. The negative growth rates for Burundi, Sierra Leone, and Congo are due to negative growth in GDP coupled with rapid population growth. Clearly any discussion of economic growth must encompass the issues of population growth as well as GDP growth.

Negative growth rates sound abominable, and positive growth rates sound so good. And they are! But before we can address the problem of poverty in less-developed countries, we must ask an important question. Economists have traditionally viewed GNP per capita as an indicator of poverty or prosperity, and they

TABLE 8-3 Average Annual Growth Rates, Select Countries, 1990–1999, with Economic Growth Calculated as Column 1 Minus Column 2

COUNTRY	COLUMN 1: AVERAGE ANNUAL GROWTH OF GDP		COLUMN 2: AVERAGE ANNUAL GROWTH OF POPULATION		COLUMN 3: ECONOMIC GROWTH
China	10.7%	–	1.1%	=	9.6%
Vietnam	8.1%	–	1.8%	=	6.3%
Chile	7.2%	–	1.5%	=	5.7%
Honduras	3.2%	–	2.9%	=	0.3%
Ecuador	2.2%	–	2.1%	=	0.1%
Burundi	–2.9%	–	2.4%	=	–5.3%
Sierra Leone	–4.8%	–	2.4%	=	–7.2%
Congo, Democratic Republic of	–5.1%	–	3.2%	=	–8.3%

Source: Data from http://www.wto.org

have viewed economic growth as an indication that matters are improving, but are these GNP-based statistics adequate measures of the economic well-being of people? As we shall see, *they are not!*

Problems in Measuring Well-Being

Composition of GNP
The items of production of which GNP consists.

One problem with the use of GNP data is that it ignores the issue of the **composition of GNP.** That is, of what does gross national product actually consist? Certainly it makes a great deal of difference whether a country produces quality health care, education, housing, and food for its people or whether it produces large amounts of military hardware for regional warfare, nonessential luxury goods for a few, and grandiose skyscrapers and structures that fail to serve the needs of most. Compare Costa Rica and Botswana. The 1999 GNP per capita for Botswana is $3,240, well above the GNP per capita of $2,740 for Costa Rica, yet Botswana has a much lower average life expectancy and a much higher infant mortality rate. **Average life expectancy** is the age to which a baby born in a particular year can be expected to live. **Infant mortality rate** is the number of babies who die within their first year of life, per 1,000 live births. The average life expectancy in Botswana is 46 years, whereas the average life expectancy in Costa Rica is 77 years. The infant mortality rate in Botswana is 62, whereas the infant mortality rate in Costa Rica is only 13. A likely explanation for these differences is that 7 percent of GNP is devoted to health care in Costa Rica, whereas less than 3 percent of GNP is devoted to health care in Botswana. Costa Rica does not have an army and diverts less than 1 percent of GNP to military expense. (Its constitution prohibits any armed forces.) Contrast this military expense with that of Botswana, which devotes more than 5 percent of GNP to the military. Life expectancies and infant mortality rates in Costa Rica are similar to those of much more prosperous countries because Costa Rica chooses to produce more products and services that benefit its people.

Average life expectancy
The age to which a baby born in a particular year can be expected to live.

Infant mortality rate
The number of babies who die within their first year of life, per 1,000 live births.

Distribution of GNP
Distribution of output (or income generated from the production of GNP).

An even more serious problem concerns the **distribution of GNP**—or more to the point, the distribution of the income generated from the production of GNP. Recall that this issue was discussed in the previous chapter on U.S. poverty. Remember that GNP per capita tells us the average GNP (or income) per person, assuming that this income is distributed equally to all. We know, in fact, that neither in prosperous countries, such as the United States, nor in poor countries, such as Ethiopia, is income distributed equally. To the extent that a small, well-to-do elite of any particular country may receive the bulk of the nation's income, the masses of people may live very poorly indeed. A high value of GNP per capita really tells us nothing about the standard of living of most of the country's residents, because it tells us nothing about the distribution of this output and income.

Income Distribution

One way of examining the income distribution is with the Lorenz curve introduced in the appendix to Chapter Seven. You may recall that this curve is based on data showing the share of total income in a country that goes to each fifth of the population. Another measure of income distribution is the share of total income that goes to the poorest 40 percent of the population. We can say that those countries with the largest share of income going to the poorest 40 percent of the people have the greatest equality of income distribution, and those countries with the smallest share going to the poorest 40 percent have the least equality of income distribution. Statistics for selected countries are presented in Table 8-4. Note that many of the lowest income countries—Bangladesh and Laos, for example—have more equitable income distributions than do higher-income countries such as South Africa and Brazil. A comparable statistic for the United States (1999) is 13 (see Chapter Seven).

Brazil provides a good example of a relatively prosperous country with an income distribution severely distorted in favor of the rich. According to Table 8-4, only 8 percent of total income is distributed to the poorest 40 percent of the Brazilian population. Despite a 1999 per capita GNP of $4,420, Brazil has an average life expectancy of 67 and an infant mortality rate of 33. The fact that much poorer countries are superior in these measures attests to the significance of income distribution. Contrast Brazil with China, which has a per capita GNP of only $780, but a life expectancy of 70 and an infant mortality rate of 31. Table 8-4 shows that the poorest 40 percent of people in China receive 16 percent of total income, explaining the higher standards of living in poverty-stricken China than in Brazil.

Mechanisms to improve the equality of the income distribution are almost always controversial, at least in the short run, because some individuals must lose while other individuals gain. Policy measures might include the elimination of price distortions to ensure that certain groups of people receive more adequate incomes. The raising of agricultural prices would lead to higher incomes for low-income farmers, for example. (This measure will be discussed in greater detail shortly.) Higher taxes on the wealth and income of high-income people might also be imposed, and the government might use this revenue to improve basic services to the poor. Government provision of adequate nutrition, health care, and

TABLE 8-4   Share of Total Income Going to the Poorest 40% of the Population, Select Countries*

COUNTRY	SHARE (%)
Brazil	8
South Africa	8
Zimbabwe	10
Mexico	11
Costa Rica	13
China	16
Ethiopia	18
Vietnam	19
Sri Lanka	20
India	20
Ghana	21
Bangladesh	21
Laos	23

*Based on studies in various years in the 1990s. Data may represent distribution of income or distribution of consumption expenditures, depending on availability.
Source: Data from http://www.wto.org

Asset
Property that is owned,
such as land.

education could go a long way to improve the well-being of the poor. Finally, government policies might include a redistribution of **assets** (the most notable of which is land), because greater equality in ownership of income-earning assets is fundamental to ensuring greater equality of incomes.

Indigenous
People who are of native-born ancestry in a country.

One of the problems facing many countries with an **indigenous** population is the loss of ownership of native-owned land. The situation in Chiapas State in Mexico is a case in point. The 1990s brought forth a series of changes designed to move the Mexican economy toward a more market-based economy. One of these changes was a change in the Mexican constitution to allow commercial sales of indigenous land. The native Indian people traditionally maintained communal ownership of their land, and rights to use the land were allocated to individual people and families within the community. As more and more indigenous land is now being sold, Indian farmers are losing their livelihoods, as well as their cultural ties to the land. This and other issues culminated in January 1, 1994, when the people of Chiapas rose up in demonstration against the Mexican government. The Mexican army responded by destroying farms, killing livestock, confiscating property, and taking the lives of many Chiapas residents. The January date of the uprising corresponded with the date that the North American Free Trade Agreement was implemented. This treaty is discussed in Chapter Five.

The issue of land ownership has come to a controversial test in the East Central African nation of Zimbabwe, which is one of the poorest countries and has one of the most unequal income distributions in the world. The cause of the unequal income distribution is the fact that a tiny white minority owns about one third of the productive land in the country, leaving very little remaining for each of the vast majority of black farmers. In February 2000, squatters began occupying white-owned farms with the support of President Robert Mugabe, who called the occupation a legitimate protest against unfair ownership. Legitimate or not, some of the occupations have become violent, and some people have been killed. With government plans to confiscate more than half of white-owned farming land becoming increasingly controversial at the international level, it remains to be seen whether there will be a stable and peaceful reform in Zimbabwe's land distribution.

ECONOMIC DEVELOPMENT AND STANDARDS OF LIVING

Economic development
A multifaceted process that involves improvements in standards of living, reductions in poverty, and growth in GNP per capita.

Largely due to the issue of distribution, we cannot say that growth in GNP per capita is synonymous with economic development. This notion bears repeating: *Economic development is not the same as economic growth.* Indeed, we can define **economic development** as a multifaceted process that improves the living conditions of the masses. It entails improvements in standards of living and reductions in poverty, as well as growth in GNP per capita. Economic development also incorporates the idea of liberation from any economic or political oppression. Although growth in GNP per capita is one element of the definition of economic development, it is clearly not the whole story.

Many economists use measures that directly indicate the actual well-being of people of less-developed countries rather than rely on GNP data alone. Some of the best indicators of living standards are the average life expectancies and infant mortality rates already mentioned. These measures avoid the distribution problem mentioned above with respect to GNP per capita. Although life expectancies tend to be higher for the very elite of a country, they will not differ by multiples of hundreds and thousands as do income levels and GNP. A high-income person may have an income of 1,000 times the income of a low-income person, but the rich person's life expectancy will not be 1,000 times the life expectancy of the poor person.

Moreover, indicators such as life expectancies and mortality rates avoid the measurement problems inherent in GNP statistics. Life expectancies, for example, do not need to be adjusted for inflation, exchange rates, market prices, and so on. These measurement problems sometimes distort comparisons of GNP between different countries.

In addition, life expectancies and mortality rates measure end results of government programs and the state of the economy. Other measures sometimes used to reflect standards of living, such as calories per capita, number of doctors per person, or school enrollment figures actually measure "inputs" into the development process. They do not tell us the quality of calories, health care, or education; and they do not tell us the outcome of these measures. Life expectancies and mortality rates, on the other hand, measure the *impact* of all such policies and programs. Finally, life expectancies and mortality rates are easily conceptualized by policymakers and the populace alike.

Life expectancies range from a low in Sierra Leone of 38 to a high in Japan of 81. The United States has an average life expectancy of 77. It is important to realize that a life expectancy of 38 in Sierra Leone, for example, does not mean that a typical person will die at age 38. What it means is that a very large number of babies and children die, bringing down the average life expectancy for the country as a whole.

Life expectancies and infant mortality rates are shown for select LDCs in Table 8-5. Countries are listed in order of their GNP per capita, from highest to lowest.

TABLE 8-5 Life Expectancies and Infant Mortality Rates for Select Countries, 1998

COUNTRY*	LIFE EXPECTANCY	INFANT MORTALITY RATE**
Brazil	67	33
Mexico	72	30
Botswana	46	62
Costa Rica	77	13
China	70	31
Zimbabwe	51	73
Vietnam	69	34
Laos	54	96
Sierra Leone	38	169
Ethiopia	43	107

*Countries are listed in order of their GNP per capita, from highest to lowest.
**Number of infant deaths per 1,000 live births.
Source: Data from http://www.wto.org

Worldwide statistics for infant mortality rates range from a high of 169 in Sierra Leone (meaning that 169 of every 1,000 babies, or roughly 17 of every 100, will die before their first birthdays) to a low of 4 in Japan and five other countries. The United States has an infant mortality rate of 7.

All of these statistics suggest both enormous divergence of the standards of living in poor countries and those in prosperous countries, and the appallingly miserable conditions in the very poorest countries. With this understanding of standards of living in mind, as well as the definitions of economic growth and development, we need to address the most important question of all: How can economic development and economic growth be achieved to improve the economic well-being of all? The sections that follow will address this issue.

GROWTH AND DEVELOPMENT

Development economists and Third World governments have traditionally favored development theories and practices patterned after the Western industrialized world. This preference has led to policies directed toward the urban and industrial sectors. This strategy has proven successful for countries such as Singapore, South Korea, Taiwan, and Hong Kong (as of 1997, Hong Kong is no longer considered a separate country from China). These countries are classified as **newly industrializing countries,** or **NICs.** They had many characteristics contributing to the success of their industrialization strategies, including a well-educated labor force; a fairly homogeneous, entrepreneurial culture; and international conditions conducive to their success at the time of their early development. Nevertheless, industrialization strategies failed to produce the same results in many other countries. One major reason is that industrialization emphasized **capital-intensive technology** (technology utilizing large amounts of physical capital), as well as mechanisms to squeeze savings for investment from low-income residents. Agriculture was viewed only as a means of acquiring cheap food and tax revenue with which to develop the industrial sector and support the urban population. Only more recently have economists and policymakers begun to see that other policies may be more appropriate for many developing countries. We are discovering that the key to development often lies in the agricultural sector itself. We are recognizing the importance of **labor-intensive technology** (as opposed to capital-intensive technology), which can utilize large numbers of people who would otherwise be unemployed. At the same time, we are beginning to acknowledge the important role of women—indeed, all people—in development.

Newly industrializing countries (NICs)
Singapore, South Korea, Taiwan, and other countries achieving rapid growth through industrialization.

Capital-intensive technology
Technology utilizing large amounts of capital.

Labor-intensive technology
Technology utilizing large amounts of labor.

Agricultural Development

The specter of famine was rising on the horizon. . . . The rice drooped, then wilted, and finally died. . . . He saw tears on his mother's cheeks. His father came and put an arm around his wife's shoulders. "Mother of my sons," he said, "we shall both go without food for ourselves so that the rice lasts longer. The children must not suffer." The summer passed almost without a single downpour and once again it was time for the winter sowing. Without water, however, there would be no winter sowing. . . . It was then that he realized that all the livestock was going to perish. November went by. The departure of the cattle had cut off the peasants' only fuel supply. . . . Gone was the sound of the children's laughter. Their small stomachs swelled up like balloons and several of them died, the victims of worms, diarrhea, and fever—yet in reality victims of hunger. . . . the women wept in silence.[3]

Development of the agricultural sector in most less-developed countries is now recognized as extremely important for several reasons. First, most of the world's poor live in the agricultural sector; hence efforts to benefit this sector will most directly benefit the needy as well. Second, the agricultural sector typically offers the greatest potential for development. In a society with scarce technology and capital, the fruits of investment come most easily from agriculture. Techniques also tend to be far more labor-intensive in agriculture than in modern industry, thereby offering employment for larger numbers of people. And finally, the agricultural sector most directly addresses the most vital need of all people, that of food security. With careful planning and policy, the Indian famine described in the preceding passage needn't occur.

Access to Inputs, Extension, and Markets

For agricultural development to occur and food security to be achieved, both the government of the developing country and the international community must fulfill important roles. The local government must recognize that although appropriate policies can dramatically improve agricultural productivity and the lives of the poor, inappropriate agricultural policy can do far more harm than good. Policies aimed at land reform are often vital. In many countries (especially throughout Asia and Latin America) a select few control large landholdings, resulting in severely distorted income distributions, as well as inefficiencies in agricultural production. Land must be redistributed in a manner that allows more appropriate income distribution and maximum incentives for agricultural production. In addition to land, other agricultural inputs are important. Farmers must have access to the necessary seeds, fertilizer, irrigation, animals, structures, and vehicles. Perhaps the most important input is agricultural credit; unless financing can be arranged for the masses of poor farmers, access to the other inputs will probably also be denied.

Adequate inputs are not enough. Farmers will require extension services if they are to use increasingly complex but more productive farming techniques and inputs. They will also require reliable transport and market facilities. Poor farmers frequently must travel long distances over poor-quality roads, and without any form of transport other than their own labor, to reach areas to market their products. Even when transport vehicles are available, there may be serious problems. Consider this Kenyan farmer's story:

One Friday afternoon, Mwangi Muchai, 50, . . . climbed into his Toyota pick-up bound for Nairobi, 100 kilometers away. He had loaded over a ton of cabbages from his farm onto the pick-up, hoping to sell them in the capital's . . . wholesale market. "I never made it to Nairobi," he says sadly. "I was barely 15 minutes on my way when it started raining and the earth road became slippery.". . . The pick-up skidded into a ditch, and that was the end of his journey. Mr. Muchai says he and some neighbors tried to push the vehicle out of the ditch, but it proved too heavy. . . . In any case, the road was altogether too slippery to drive on even if the pick-up had been rescued. "As I walked back to my house and abandoned the pick-up," Mr. Muchai remembers, "I felt the greatest disappointment of my life and, for a while, regretted ever becoming a farmer. I felt anxious about facing my wives and telling them that a whole season's sweat for the family would go down the drain as the vegetables rotted in that ditch." Before the time the rains ended, Mr. Muchai had lost his entire load of cabbages.[4]

Economists recognize that governments must take responsibility for providing adequate **infrastructure,** such as the extension services, roads, and market facilities just discussed, lest agricultural productivity break down at any of these points. This undertaking is difficult for governments strapped for financial resources.

Infrastructure
Social overhead capital, including facilities for transportation, communication, marketing, and extension services.

Agricultural Prices

Beyond ensuring access to inputs, extension, and markets, government policy must focus on appropriate agricultural prices. Economists and international agencies have recently promoted market-based prices to revitalize the agricultural sector. Far too often LDC governments have administered prices, in this case by creating a **price ceiling,** to maintain low food prices and placate the end consumer, who is typically a resident of an urban area. One goal of price ceilings is to keep prices of basic necessities low for poor consumers. Although many urban people may be poor, urban dwellers tend to have higher incomes than rural residents do. In the process of holding down prices for this better off—but politically more vocal—group, the government also keeps low the agricultural prices received by farmers. This practice results in two serious problems. First, rural incomes fall and poor farmers become poorer. Second, incentives for agricultural production are reduced; those with other options will seek to produce in sectors where the incentives are greater. These problems are illustrated in Figure 8-1, using the market for rice as an example. A similar example, using the market for rental housing, is discussed in Chapter Eleven on housing.

Price ceiling
A legalized maximum price for a good or service.

The demand for rice is indicated by *D*. The supply curve is indicated by *S*. If the market operates freely, an equilibrium will occur at the point at which the price of rice is $2 per bushel and the quantity is 1,000 bushels. If the government places a price ceiling on rice, however, the price may be held down at a level such as $1 per bushel (representing the price ceiling). The rice cannot legally be sold at a price above this price ceiling. The artificially low price causes consumers to move down along their demand curve, as they try to buy larger quantities of rice at the attractive low price. Consumers will wish to purchase 1,500 bushels (quantity demanded). Suppliers, on the other hand, will have less incentive to produce and sell rice. They will move down along their supply curve, reducing the quantity supplied to 500 bushels (they may produce other products instead). Quantity demanded exceeds quantity supplied. A shortage of rice is the result. Consumers have been encouraged to "over consume." Suppliers have been encouraged to "under supply." Despite the lower prices, many consumers have become worse off, particularly those who are unable to buy the rice. Incomes to many poor agricultural workers have fallen as well.

FIGURE 8-1   LDC Price Ceilings on Rice

At the market equilibrium price of $2 per bushel, quantity demanded equals quantity supplied at 1,000 bushels of rice. When a price ceiling of $1 per bushel is imposed, quantity demanded increases to 1,500 bushels, while quantity supplied falls to 500 bushels. A shortage of rice results, and producer incomes fall.

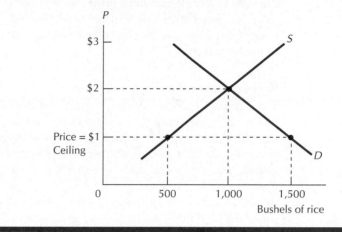

Many less-developed countries have adapted market-determined agricultural prices, including the communist country of Vietnam. As part of the economic reforms designed to move the Vietnamese economy closer to a market-based economy, the government of Vietnam has raised rice prices to market-determined levels. Previously, as in many other countries, the government had kept the price of staple food artificially low to please urban consumers. As a result of the price decontrol, Vietnam's status has changed in just a few short years from a rice importer to one of the world's largest rice exporters. Rising incomes in the rural sector have come far in reducing previously high rural poverty rates.

Although agricultural prices are often found to be too low, care must be taken as governments promote market-based prices. Poor urban residents, who must purchase their food, will suffer from higher prices. We are also becoming aware that even rural residents are often net buyers of food, selling their agricultural produce at harvest and buying food and other agricultural products throughout the year. Rising food prices will hurt these farmers as well. In the face of rising agricultural prices, government assistance must be targeted directly to low-income consumers who purchase their food. In addition, poor farmers will require special assistance to ensure their access to inputs, infrastructure, and markets. The benefits that result from this assistance, productivity improvements and rising incomes, would outweigh the increased prices that farmers would pay for their purchases.

Export cropping
Agricultural production for export, rather than production of food for local consumption.

Export Cropping

In relation to food security, the issue of **export cropping** must also be addressed. Export cropping refers to a pattern of agricultural production for export, rather than production of food for local consumption. Many countries choose to produce products like coffee, tea, rubber, and cocoa to export and thereby obtain foreign currency. Although the theory of international trade tells us that a country should specialize in products it is "good at," as we have seen in Chapter Five, it is also true that export cropping can trigger food insecurity and inequality in the income distribution in low-income countries. We will see in Chapter Seventeen that the international debt crisis has increased LDC dependence on export cropping, as Third World governments are forced to earn foreign currency to pay off their debt. This practice has often been at the expense of the food security needs of local residents.

International Role

The international community must assist low-income countries to meet their agricultural development and food security needs. We must develop systems to ensure that adequate and timely food aid will be available to countries in emergency situations. At the same time, we must be cautious about continuing to provide food aid in nonemergency situations, a practice that can often do more harm than good. As was previously discussed in Chapter Two on agriculture, ongoing food aid leads to dependence by less-developed countries and pushes down food prices, thereby lowering incentives for local food production. Nevertheless, it is vital that food aid be available in emergency situations and other times when it is appropriate.

The international community might also enact measures to ensure the greater stability of world food prices. One suggested measure is the establishment of an international **buffer stock** of cereal grains, whereby managers can buy up grain in years of high production (thereby pushing up low market prices) and sell off grain in years of low production (thereby pushing down high market prices). In this manner, prices are stabilized within a medium range rather than allowed to fluctuate wildly. Greater price stability would ensure that low-income food-importing countries are not left unable to buy when world shortage conditions would normally send prices skyrocketing.

We must also undertake efforts to ensure that the bottlenecks of inadequate transport, shipping, port, and storage facilities are resolved. We can offer technical assistance in terms of better seed varieties, improved production methods, and agricultural extension services. Most important, we must recognize that hunger is caused by poverty. If we assist agricultural development and help alleviate rural poverty, we will go a long way toward reducing the travesty of hunger in a world of plenty.

Buffer stock
A mechanism for stabilizing agricultural prices, whereby an agricultural product is purchased and placed in storage during years of high production and released from storage and sold during years of low production.

Human and Natural Resource Development

Regardless of emphasis on industrial or agricultural development, investment must also be made in each nation's most precious resource: people. Economists sometimes refer to this as an **investment in human capital,** likening it to an investment in physical capital. This concept was discussed in Chapter Seven and will be addressed again in Chapter Ten. Human investment programs have not only an immediate benefit, namely the improved standard of living of the beneficiary, but also a long-term payoff, just as other forms of investment do. The long-term benefit is the development of a more productive labor force and a better-educated citizenry.

Investment in human capital
Spending that is designed to improve the productivity of people.

Human investment programs include those designed to improve health, sanitation, education, and skills. Again, it is important that we abandon some of our Western notions about the form of these programs. Most poor Third World countries can derive far more benefit from village-level health practitioners providing basic health care, immunizations, and prenatal care than from expensive high-tech hospitals located in capital cities, out of reach of the masses of people. Most countries will benefit more from the spread of primary education to school-age children and basic literacy training to adults than from several expensive doctoral universities located in major cities. Just as with income distribution, benefits that spread to large masses of people rather than to an elite few are most likely to foster positive development.

Education probably holds the greatest promise. Numerous studies have linked education (primarily of women) to widespread benefits: reduced infant mortality rates, improved child nutrition, later age of marriage, lower birth rates, and greater likelihood that *their* children will be educated. The cycle is thus self-perpetuating.

Increasingly, development economists are also recognizing the need for a safe and convenient water supply. Many women and children have the task of spending several hours every day walking long distances to retrieve water, carrying it home in the exhausting fashion of head-loading. Often the water carries bacteria and waterborne diseases. Fresh wells located in villages would improve the health of the people and free the time of women and children for other activities.

Women also spend considerable time gathering firewood, especially as wood becomes increasingly scarce. Wood is the primary source of fuel, and cooking is its primary use, especially in Africa. The clearing of forests for expansion of farming and commercial timber operations is causing a serious problem of **deforestation** in many countries. As trees are depleted, soil and wind erosion increase. **Desertification** may follow, as desert areas are left with no natural barriers to their continual encroachment on cropland. The ultimate effect is the depletion of soil fertility. Villages and organizations have begun the search for solutions to this problem, ranging from the production of wood lots for village fuel use to the invention of simple, fuel-efficient cooking stoves. Natural resource development as such should improve the well-being of people and at the same time preserve the environment.

Deforestation
The clearing of forested areas.

Desertification
The encroachment of desert on previously fertile land.

http://www.bread.org
This is the Web site of Bread for the World, a national citizens' lobby on world poverty and hunger issues. It contains information on current U.S. legislation involving world hunger and poverty and the names and addresses of U.S. legislators so that interested citizens can contact them.

Women's Role in Development

In the workplace, women are at the bottom of the pyramid inside the country. They are also the poorest people in the country. They are the people who lose their jobs first. They're the people who are taken off of agricultural farms when these farms are turned into cash crop farms. They ultimately decide whether or not a child is fed. They cry when their boys or husbands are detained, arrested, or made refugees, or die. . . . [6]

As the previous discussion suggests, women play an important role in economic development. And in the words of the South African woman quoted above by lobbying group Bread for the World, we see that women face the greatest obstacles. For a long time, government and international policies alike have neglected women in developing countries. Women have therefore been treated unfairly.

Third World women also have lower standards of living than their male counterparts. Women typically have **literacy rates** far below those of men. In Niger, for example, only 7 percent of women can read and write, whereas 22 percent of men are literate. In Nepal, the literacy rate is 57 percent for men, but only 22 percent for women. The reason for this disparity in many less-developed countries is simply that fewer girls go to school than do boys, often for cultural reasons and because girls are needed to help their mothers on their farms. Furthermore, because families often must pay expensive school fees, they choose to invest in the boy child instead of the girl child. The boy will often remain responsible for his family of origin, whereas the girl will go to live with the family of her husband. Where adult education programs exist, women are frequently unable to participate for the same types of reasons that girls don't participate. Child care, farm work, and homemaking leave little time for the "extravagance" of education.

High maternal mortality rates are another serious problem. The **maternal mortality rate** is the number of deaths of women for pregnancy-related reasons per 100,000 live births. In Eritrea, for example, the rate of 1,000 tells us that 1,000 of every 100,000 or 1 of every 100 live births is associated with the death of the mother. Because women in Eritrea have an average of six children in their lifetime, the average Eritrean woman has a 6 percent chance of dying for pregnancy-related reasons (1×6). This statistic is alarming, especially when we consider the children left behind when their mothers die.

The problems of women in developing countries go far beyond unfairness, however. Although women are primarily responsible for producing most **subsistence food crops** in much of the Third World, and although they produce and market many other agricultural crops and processed items, they are least likely to receive agricultural extension services, agricultural credit, and access to agricultural inputs such as quality land. Women also tend to be primarily responsible for food preparation and homemaking; fuel and water acquisition; safeguarding of the family's nutrition, hygiene, and health care; and oversight of the children's education. As long as policy measures that provide education, credit, agricultural extension, technology, and agricultural inputs are targeted toward men, neither the agricultural productivity of the country nor the well-being of the family will be adequately served.

POPULATION GROWTH

The preceding discussion of the role of women in developing countries returns us to the issue of population growth. Many people believe that high population growth is a problem in many low-income countries because more people means more sharing of already limited resources. Other people, including many in the less-developed countries, do not believe that population growth is a problem. If we consider population to be a problem only relative to resources, then we must consider that the 15 percent of the world's population in the developed world consumes three-fifths of the world's total production of goods and services.[6] The residents of LDCs consume very little. One could argue further that the problem is not so much too many people in the developed world, but rather our highly consumption-oriented lifestyles.

To the extent that rapid population growth is a problem in the Third World, intense controversy attends possible solutions. One thing we know: merely passing out contraceptives to the world's low-income women is ineffective. This simple strategy does not address cultural and religious factors, nor does it get at the issue of the motivation to have children. Clearly, people have important reasons for having the children that they do. In agricultural societies, children are necessary to provide labor on the farm and assist their mothers in gathering water and fuel. Because poor countries lack formal social security systems, having children is usually the only means that parents have to ensure that they will be cared for in their old age. And finally, as long as women expect that a certain number of their children will die (recall the high infant mortality rates), they will have "extra" children to ensure the survival of a certain number. Consider the words of a woman farmer in Africa:

> "My first child died at the age of two," says Hamza Amadou, a farmer in Niger...who wants to have at least eight children. "The second caught malaria and died at the age of seven. At this rate, how can I think of practicing contraception? If I don't have any children, who will help me to produce food and feed my family, and who will take over when I die?[7]

On a more optimistic note, we also know that as development proceeds, population growth rates naturally tend to fall because women become motivated to have fewer children, and they gain a greater sense of control over their lives. As women receive greater income-earning alternatives to the bearing of children, as they have greater expectations that their children will survive, as agricultural productivity improves, and as schools and better futures become available to their children, women naturally tend to have fewer children and are better able to provide for the ones they do have. An important element in all of this change is a sense of empowerment. Once women are able to ensure their children's survival as well as control the economic aspects of their family's well-being, they have a greater sense of control over their entire lives and take a more active role in structuring them. To talk about limiting births to the Nigerian woman whose first two children died is to ignore the root of her problems.

If we view development as a process of liberation from oppression, population policy must not be oppressive. Any policies to limit births must take into account the religious and cultural values of the people involved. In an area of devout Roman Catholics, for example, research on and promotion of effective natural family planning techniques would perhaps be appropriate. Policies that intrude on the morals and human rights of individuals, particularly policies that are coercive, are not elements of true development.

It is also important to keep in mind that real development is necessary for birth rates to fall. That is, a rise in GNP per capita alone may not achieve the desired results. The benefits of economic development must accrue to the masses of people, including women, before a substantial impact on birth rates can be expected. The fundamental problem underlying rapid population growth is poverty. The fundamental solution is economic development. A narrow focus on birth rates alone will not be effective.

The problem of highly concentrated population is particularly evident in many Third World cities. In fact, 7 of the 10 largest metropolitan areas of the world are in developing countries. Five of the 10 cities are in Asia, and 2 are in Latin America. The 2000 projected populations of these metropolitan areas are presented in Table 8-6.

Along with high concentrations of people is the concentration of poverty in many Third World cities. More than one-third of the entire Third World metropolitan population lives in slums or shantytowns. In some cities, such as Mexico City (Mexico), Calcutta (India), and Casablanca (Morocco), the proportion of people dwelling in slums is quite high. Most of these slum dwellers lack adequate water supplies, sewerage, plumbing, electricity, and even shelter. Many inhabitants are forced to live in makeshift shacks of cardboard, tin, or plastic sheeting; many simply live on the sidewalk.

One of the causes of urban poverty is a high level of unemployment and **underemployment.** Underemployment refers to situations in which people work limited hours or with low productivity. Much underemployment occurs in the urban **informal employment sector.** The informal sector consists primarily of service occupations: shoe shining, drug dealing, prostitution, collection of paper and metal scraps for sale, bicycle transportation, and street sales. The latter include the sale of virtually everything: cigarettes, used clothing, charcoal, blood, sticks for starting fires, food, and so on. Low productivity, low incomes, irregular work hours, and no benefits characterize many of these services. They do, however, provide work and income for people who might otherwise remain unemployed. Furthermore, some of these informal occupations provide important services to the community, such as carpentry, brick-laying, and sewing.

Although natural population increases can sometimes explain high urban population density, the other important factor is migration. **Rural–urban migration**

Underemployment
A situation in which people work limited hours or with low productivity.

Informal employment sector
An employment sector consisting primarily of service occupations in an unofficial setting.

Rural–urban migration
The movement of people from the rural sector to the urban sector, often in search of better living conditions.

TABLE 8-6   2000 Projected Population of the World's 10 Largest Cities, in Millions

CITY IN ORDER OF POPULATION SIZE	PROJECTED 2000 POPULATION
1. Tokyo-Yokohama, Japan	28.0
2. Seoul, South Korea	19.1
3. Mexico City, Mexico	18.1
4. Mombai (Bombay), India	18.0
5. São Paulo, Brazil	17.7
6. New York, United States	16.6
7. Shanghai, China	14.2
8. Lagos, Nigeria	13.5
9. Los Angeles, United States	13.1
10. Beijing, China	12.4

Source: Data from Scott Sernau, *Bound: Living in the Globalized World* (Bloomfield, CT: Kumarian Press, 2000), p. 164; U.S. Bureau of the Census 1997; and Lester R. Brown, Nicholas Lenssen, and Hal Kane, *State of the World 1999* (New York: Norton, 1999).

Different economists have different views about how economic development should take place. Conservative economists will prefer a growth-oriented strategy that focuses on increasing GNP per capita. The assumption is that all people will eventually benefit from the growing prosperity of the country. Issues like income distribution and poverty do not receive primary attention because it is assumed that the incomes of all people will rise as economic growth proceeds. Indeed, conservative economists may argue in favor of an unequal income distribution on the grounds that high-income people save more than low-income people do. (Low-income people need to spend all of their income on food and consumer goods.) By placing more income in the hands of the rich, savings will increase, thereby enabling greater investment, and ultimately increased national productivity and growth.

Liberal economists feel that economic growth by itself is not the panacea for underdevelopment. They note that although some people benefit from economic growth, notably the owners of large landholdings and businesses and those able-bodied and fortunate enough to take newly created jobs, many others do not benefit. In particular, workers with few skills and little education, those who are physically disabled, the very young and the very old, and farmers who grow crops on too little land with too few inputs will not be able to take advantage of benefits of economic growth. Strategies must be designed to focus on poverty and income distribution. Otherwise, it is argued, high-income groups will only become richer, while low-income people become poorer.

brings in countless people from the countryside to the cities each day. These people are searching for better jobs, higher incomes, and the "glamour" of the city life. Thousands of migrants arrive daily in the cities listed in Table 8-6. Even on the African continent, several million migrants come to the cities each year.

An interesting problem may emerge when policymakers attempt to reduce the poverty and misery in many Third World cities. As better housing and services are provided, and better employment opportunities are created, even larger numbers of migrants may be attracted to the cities. As migrant numbers swell, even more people may become homeless and unemployed. Efforts to reduce urban problems may turn out to be counterproductive!

This consideration returns us to our earlier focus on agricultural development. Along with any policy efforts to improve urban standards of living must be policy measures to improve the well-being of people in the countryside. Only then can the incentives for rural–urban migration be reduced and the flow of urban migrants tempered. Policy measures must focus on improving agricultural productivity and incomes. Health care, educational programs, infrastructure, and services must be provided in the rural sector as well as the urban sector. Price incentives for agricultural production and opportunities for small-scale, labor-intensive industries in rural areas must exist. Only then will the rural–urban balance be improved and urban problems reduced.

AIDS

One final challenge of many less-developed countries is that of AIDS (Acquired Immune Deficiency Syndrome). AIDS is a serious problem in many countries around the world, but it has reached epidemic proportions in many countries of Africa. According to the United Nations, AIDS has replaced malaria as the leading cause of death in Africa. Of the estimated total of 2.8 million AIDS-related deaths around the world in 1999, 2.2 million were in sub-Saharan Africa. An additional 25 million Africans are currently living with AIDS or are infected with HIV, the virus that leads to the development of AIDS. Women represent more than half of the African adults with AIDS/HIV, and more than 12 million African children have been orphaned from the disease. In many African countries, the share of infected adults is astounding, as high as 24 percent in Lesotho, 25 percent in Swaziland and Zimbabwe, and 36 percent in Botswana.[8] Many children are dying as well, acquiring AIDS from their mothers at birth. Aside from the direct impact of AIDS, the health systems of poor countries are overwhelmed in the face of the epidemic. Efforts to assist AIDS patients reduce the systems' capacity to deal with other important health problems, including preventative and primary care. We are seeing the stark effects of AIDS as life expectancies drop in afflicted countries.

A PEOPLE-ORIENTED STRATEGY

Many issues of development have been addressed. As we consider each issue, as well as any strategy to invoke change, we must be mindful of the needs and participation of Third World people. Empowerment not only of women but of all residents of low-income countries is important. Poverty and lack of opportunity undermine power, preventing people from taking control of their lives, and in the process improving their lives. This consideration suggests that development efforts must ultimately meet the needs of the masses of people themselves if they are to be successful.

SUMMARY

Economists define economic growth as the increase in real gross national product per capita. GNP per capita reflects the value of output, or income, accruing to each individual person, on average. In 1999, GNP per capita ranged from a high in Switzerland of $38,350 to a low in Ethiopia of $100. Other measures, such as infant mortality rates and life expectancies, are usually better indicators of standards of living, particularly because GNP per capita does not address the issues of the composition and distribution of GNP.

Economic development is a multifaceted process involving growth in GNP per capita, improvement in standards of living, and reduction of poverty. Economic development must take into account the needs of agricultural development and food security, human and natural resource development, and the role of women and all residents of low-income countries, as well as the issues of population growth, AIDS, and rural–urban migration. Appropriate policies at the domestic and international levels are vital to the development needs of low-income countries.

NOTES

1. From *Child of the Dark*, by Carolina Maria de Jesus, translated by David St. Clair, translation copyright © 1962 by E. P. Dutton & Co., Inc., New York, and Souvenir Press, Ltd., London. Used by permission of Dutton, a division of Penguin Putnam, Inc. The words are those of a woman (the author) living in a favela (slum) of São Paulo, Brazil.

2. The World Bank, *World Development Report 2000/2001* (New York: Oxford University Press, 2001). Unless otherwise indicated, all data in this chapter are from this source.

3. Dominique Lapierre, *The City of Joy* (New York: Warner Books, 1985), pp. 15–21. These words describe the despair of a family in famine-struck India.

4. John Araka, et al., "Getting Produce to Market," in *African Farmer* (New York: The Hunger Project, December 1989).

5. Sharon Pauling, "She Speaks with Wisdom," in *Bread* (Washington, DC: Bread for the World, Spring 1988).

6. Calculation based on data in World Bank, *World Development Report 2000/2001* (New York: Oxford University Press, 2001).

7. Souleymane Anza, et al., "Farmers and Family Planning," in *African Farmer* (New York: The Hunger Project, December 1989).

8. United Nations AIDS Program, "Report on the Global HIV/AIDS Epidemic," June 2000 (http://www.unaids.org). Adults are defined as age 15–49.

DISCUSSION QUESTIONS

1. *Is GNP per capita an adequate indicator of the well-being of people in less-developed countries? Why or why not? Are there better indicators?*

2. *Consider the countries listed in Table 8-1, and choose one that interests you. Go to the World Bank Web site at http://www.worldbank.org, and chose the country from the country listing. What is the country's current GNP per capita and life expectancy? How do these statistics compare with those of other countries mentioned in this chapter? Is the life expectancy what you would expect, based on the level of GNP per capita?*

3. *Now choose the same or a different country, and look it up on the CIA Web site (http://www.odci.gov/cia/publications/factbook). After locating the country, click on People and find statistics relating to standards of living. What is the infant mortality rate? Compare the statistics that are available for males and females. How do their life expectancies compare? How do their literacy rates compare?*

4. *Refer to the information in Chapter Seven on the U.S. income distribution. How does the United States compare with the countries listed in Table 8-4 with respect to its share of income to the poorest 40 percent of the population? Does the comparison surprise you? Prosperous countries have greater means to ensure equitable income distribution, but this greater capacity does not mean that they choose to do so.*

5. *Why does hunger persist in a world of plenty? Is the problem one of underproduction, overpopulation, distribution of income, overconsumption, or all of the above? Explain.*

6. *How might land reform be achieved in developing countries? What issues are involved? What are the political and ethical implications?*

7. *Agricultural development has garnered much attention. Equally important is the development of "human capital"—that is, improvement in the most important economic resource: people. How can better education,*

housing, health, hygiene, and nutrition develop human capital—and thereby develop the country as well?

8. Why must women be targeted for assistance in the development process? Why is it important that all beneficiaries of development policies and programs be active participants in the design and operation of these programs?

9. What are some of the means used to control population growth in various parts of the world? Are these effective? Are they appropriate? Are they ethical? Do the ends justify the means?

10. How can efforts to reduce unemployment and misery in Third World cities be counterproductive and actually increase urban problems? What are some alternative solutions?

11. What is the role of the developed countries in promoting development policies in the less-developed countries? What are the ways that we as individuals can become involved?

CHAPTER 9

Health Care

Lifesaving drugs are an indispensable part of modern medicine. No one creating a Medicare program today would even think of excluding coverage for prescription drugs. Yet more than three in five of our seniors now lack dependable drug coverage. . . .

William Jefferson Clinton, *State of the Union Address,* 2000

What do you think of the health care that you and your family receive? Do you worry about your grandmother's ability to afford prescription drugs? Do you have good health insurance that is tied to a family member's job? Do you ever worry about losing your health insurance if that person loses that job? Do you have to remain a full-time student to be covered by your parents' medical insurance? Has your insurance plan changed to a health maintenance organization (HMO) from a more traditional plan?

Ask Americans what they think of health care in the United States, and most of them would respond that U.S. health care is probably the best in the world. After some thought, a few might qualify that response by noting that medical care is certainly expensive. Still others might express concern for people who cannot afford health insurance, or who cannot buy health insurance because someone in their family has a preexisting illness. In an era of organ transplants, nuclear medicine, and technological innovations in pharmaceuticals, many of our medical concerns involve the economics of medical care. Our medical delivery system has been characterized by escalating costs, inadequate access to quality medical care, and waste and inefficiency.

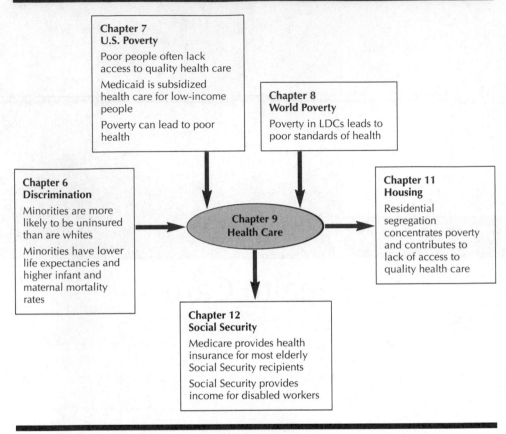

**Chapter 7
U.S. Poverty**

Poor people often lack access to quality health care

Medicaid is subsidized health care for low-income people

Poverty can lead to poor health

**Chapter 8
World Poverty**

Poverty in LDCs leads to poor standards of health

**Chapter 6
Discrimination**

Minorities are more likely to be uninsured than are whites

Minorities have lower life expectancies and higher infant and maternal mortality rates

**Chapter 9
Health Care**

**Chapter 11
Housing**

Residential segregation concentrates poverty and contributes to lack of access to quality health care

**Chapter 12
Social Security**

Medicare provides health insurance for most elderly Social Security recipients

Social Security provides income for disabled workers

In this chapter we will examine data on health care in the United States. We will then look at the unique characteristics of health care that contribute to the problems above. Finally, we will look at proposals for reform of the health care system. Let us begin by looking at health care costs in the United States.

U.S. HEALTH CARE PROBLEMS

Escalating Health Care Costs

Gross domestic product (GDP)
A measure of the total output (and income) produced in a nation in one year.

Total health care expenditures in the United States reached $1,149 billion in 1998, a mind-boggling 13.5 percent[1] of our **gross domestic product (GDP),** or national output, in that year. Our health care expenditures are the product of the amount of health care we consume and the price we pay for health care. Health care prices have increased more rapidly than the prices of most other goods and services. We have also consumed an increasing amount of health care over time. Therefore, our health care expenditures have increased absolutely and as a share of GDP in the last 40 years.

TABLE 9-1	National Health Expenditures, Selected Years, 1960–1997 (dollar amounts in billions)		
YEAR	TOTAL HEALTH EXPENDITURES CURRENT DOLLARS	TOTAL HEALTH EXPENDITURES CONSTANT 1997 DOLLARS	PER CAPITA 1997 DOLLARS
1960	$26.9	$145.6	$806
1965	$41.1	$208.9	$1,075
1970	$73.2	$302.4	$1,475
1975	$130.7	$390.0	$1,816
1980	$247.0	$481.7	$2,115
1985	$428.2	$637.8	$2,675
1990	$697.5	$857.6	$3,431
1997	$1,092.4	$1,092.4	$4,095

Sources: Committee on Ways and Means, U.S. House of Representatives, *1998 Green Book* (Washington, DC: U.S. Government Printing Office, 1999) and http://www.census.gov/statab/freq/99s

Consumer price index (CPI)
A weighted average of the prices of a fixed basket of goods and services purchased by a typical urban household.

Inflation
Increase in the average price level.

Table 9-1 shows our health care expenditures for selected years in current and constant 1997 dollars. The constant dollar figures have been adjusted for the effects of inflation using the **consumer price index (CPI).** This is important because the constant dollar figures are then comparable from year to year, whereas the current dollars for any particular year are not comparable to any other year. The final column shows per capita, or average, health care spending in inflation-adjusted 1997 dollars.

Quite obviously, our health care expenditures have risen substantially in the past four decades. The increase is great even when we have adjusted for **inflation,** as we have in the second column of Table 9-1. Simply put, we are spending much more on health care, as a society and as individuals, than in previous years, and the trend is continuing steadily upward.

Social Significance of Increased Expenditures

Money costs are a claim on the nation's resources. When health care expenditures as a percentage of our national output increase, it means that we are allocating more of our resources to health care. Therefore, we are giving up other goods and services to acquire medical care. Recall the production possibilities curve from Chapter One. Over any given time period, assuming full employment and a fixed quantity and quality of resources and technology, our nation is capable of producing only a limited amount of goods and services. If we choose to have more of one good, such as health care, we must necessarily produce less of something else. Figure 9-1 on page 196 shows a production possibilities curve for medical care and all other goods and services. We have moved from point *A* in 1960 to point *B* today. We have high-quality, high-technology health care, but at the cost of giving up other products.

How do we pay for these billions of dollars in health care? Figure 9-2 on page 196 shows the percentage distribution of our 1995 health care expenditures

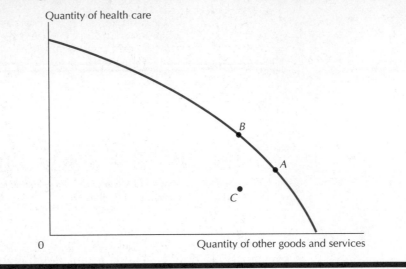

FIGURE 9-1 Production Possibilities Curve for Health Care

As we have moved from point *A* to point *B*, we have obtained more health care, but we have given up other goods and services. At point *C*, we are using our resources inefficiently.

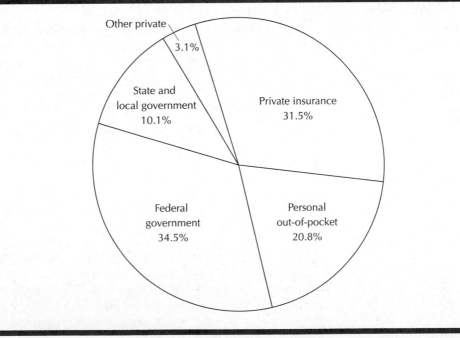

FIGURE 9-2 How We Paid for Health Care, 1995

Source: Committee on Ways and Means, U.S. House of Representatives, *1998 Green Book* (Washington, DC: U.S. Government Printing Office, 1999).

among ourselves, government programs, and private insurance. The federal government, mainly through the Medicare and Medicaid programs, accounts for the greatest proportion of payments, followed closely by private insurance. State and local government payments, largely additional contributions to Medicaid, account for a hefty 10.1 percent. Perhaps the most striking feature of the distribution is the small percentage of health care costs borne directly by patients and their families. Personal out-of-pocket expenditures account for only 21 percent of total spending. The government and private insurance account for more than three-fourths of our health care payments. This **third-party payment** is one of the unique characteristics of health care that we will discuss later.

Third-party payment
Health care payment made by someone other than the patient's family.

International Comparisons

Expenditures

Table 9-2 shows the health care expenditures of various countries as a percent of gross domestic product for 1960 and 1997, as well as per capita spending in U.S.

TABLE 9-2 Health Care Expenditures as a Percent of Gross Domestic Product in 1960 and 1997, Per Capita Health Expenditures in 1997, and Percent of Health Care Expenditures Covered by Public Insurance in 1997

COUNTRY	1960	1997	1997 PER CAPITA	1997 PERCENT PUBLIC
Australia	4.9	8.4	$1,909	66.7
Austria	4.3	8.3	$1,905	73.0
Belgium	3.4	7.6	$1,905	87.6
Canada	5.4	9.2	$1,768	69.8
Denmark	3.6	8.0	$2,042	83.8
Finland	3.9	7.4	$1,525	76.0
France	4.2	9.6	$2,047	74.2
Germany	4.8	10.7	$2,364	77.1
Greece	3.1	8.6	$1,196	57.7
Iceland	3.5	7.9	$1,981	83.8
Ireland	3.8	6.3	$1,293	76.7
Italy	3.6	7.6	$1,613	69.9
Japan	3.0	7.2	$1,760	79.9
Luxembourg	NA	7.0	$2,303	91.8
Netherlands	3.8	8.5	$1,933	72.6
Norway	2.9	7.5	$2,017	82.2
New Zealand	4.3	7.6	$1,357	77.3
Portugal	NA	7.9	$1,148	60.0
Spain	1.5	7.4	$1,183	76.1
Sweden	4.7	8.6	$1,762	83.3
Switzerland	3.1	10.0	$2,611	69.9
Turkey	NA	4.0	$259	72.8
United Kingdom	3.9	6.8	$1,391	84.6
United States	5.2	13.9	$4,095	46.4

Source: Organization for Economic Cooperation and Development, *OECD Health Data 1999*.

dollars for 1997. The table also shows the percentage of these countries' health care expenditures that were paid by the government through some sort of public insurance scheme. The table demonstrates that the United States is certainly not the only nation in which health care expenditures have increased since 1960. Medical care has become both more technologically sophisticated and more expensive throughout the world. Let us look at some other health care indicators by which we might judge the results of our spending.

Note that the United States, Germany, and Switzerland are the only countries with double-digit percentages of GDP taken up by health care expenditures in 1997, and that the percentage of such expenditures in the United States is significantly higher than the percentages in the other two countries. Most nations have experienced an increase in health care payments, but the rate of increase has leveled off for most. Furthermore, the United States is the only country whose per capita expenditures exceed $3,000 (let alone $4,000). Do these facts indicate that health care in the United States is significantly better than that in the rest of the world? Let us look at some health indicators to answer that question.

Health Indicators: Assessing the Results of Our Expenditures

The three most commonly used health care indicators are the infant and maternal mortality rates and life expectancy at birth. The infant mortality rate measures the number of infant deaths (deaths of children under one year old) per 1,000 live births; the maternal mortality rate measures the number of women who die due to pregnancy-related reasons per 100,000 live births. Life expectancy is the average number of years that a child born in a particular year is expected to live. These measures are shown in Table 9-3.

Note that the United States has neither the lowest infant mortality rate nor the lowest maternal mortality rate. Nations that spend less per capita and as a

TABLE 9-3   International Comparison of Infant and Maternal Mortality Rates and Life Expectancy at Birth

COUNTRY	INFANT MORTALITY RATE (PER 1000 LIVE BIRTHS) 1998	MATERNAL MORTALITY RATE (PER 100,000 LIVE BIRTHS) 1990–1998*	LIFE EXPECTANCY 1998
United States	7	8	77
Canada	5	6	79
Australia	5	9	79
France	5	10	79
Italy	5	7	79
Japan	4	8	81
Netherlands	5	7	78
Portugal	8	8	76
Spain	5	6	79
United Kingdom	6	7	78

*Data are for the most recent year available within the period.
Source: Data from http://www.wto.org

percentage of GDP do as well, and some do better, in minimizing infant and maternal deaths. Nor do we have the highest life expectancy. Furthermore, other statistics suggest that the quality of health care in the United States varies enormously among racial groups. Table 9-4 reveals the differences between whites and blacks in the United States with respect to life expectancy, infant mortality, and maternal mortality.

These differences are enormous. African Americans have infant mortality rates more than twice the rate of whites and maternal mortality rates more than three times the rate of whites. Nutrition and other lifestyle characteristics may influence these statistics, and these characteristics depend on income and cultural factors. The overrepresentation of African Americans in poverty statistics may have a consequence that is reflected in the health indicators shown in Table 9-4. Many factors undoubtedly play a role in these statistics, unequal access to health care is certainly an important one. Pregnant women with limited access to quality prenatal care, for example, are more likely to die from complications of pregnancy and delivery, and their babies are more likely to be premature or in poor health.

Health care in the United States is not evenly distributed. A recent World Health Organization study ranked the United States thirty-seventh in the world for the quality of its health care delivery system. Chris Murray, a director of the organization, commented that there are really three Americas. Rich Americans are the healthiest people in the world, but Murray characterizes the health care of middle-income Americans as mediocre, and notes:

> But it's the bottom 5 percent or 10 percent, made up of Native Americans living on reservations, the inner city poor, rural blacks and Appalachia that is a third America. They have health conditions as bad as those in sub-Saharan Africa.[2]

Financial Access to Medical Care

Financial access to medical care depends on health insurance coverage or eligibility for government health programs, such as **Medicare** or **Medicaid.** Medicare is a

Medicare
A government program providing medical coverage largely to elderly people.

Medicaid
A government program providing medical coverage for eligible low-income people.

TABLE 9-4	Comparison of Infant Mortality Rates, Maternal Mortality Rates, and Life Expectancy, by Race			
INDICATOR			BLACK	WHITE
Infant mortality rate, 1998			14.2	6.0
Maternal mortality rate, 1997			20.8	5.8
INDICATOR	BLACK MALES	BLACK FEMALES	WHITE MALES	WHITE FEMALES
Expected life at birth, 1998	66.1	74.2	73.8	79.6

Sources: Data from U.S. Department of Commerce, Bureau of the Census, *Statistical Abstract of the United States: 1999;* Bernard Guyer and Donna Hoyert, "Annual Summary of Vital Statistics—1998," *Pediatrics* (December 1999); and Centers for Disease Control and Prevention, *National Vital Statistics Reports,* vol. 47, no. 19 (June 30, 1999).

system of subsidized health insurance for the aged, whereas Medicaid is subsidized health care for poor people and the medically indigent. U.S. Census figures indicate that about 15.5 percent of Americans, or 42 million people, had no private health insurance in 1999, nor were these people eligible for Medicaid or Medicare. Table 9-5 shows the type of insurance and demographic characteristics of the U.S. population in 1999.

Note the differences in the type of coverage that people of different races and ethnicities were likely to have, as well as the proportion of a group not covered by private or public insurance. Whereas only 11 percent of whites were without coverage, 21 percent of blacks and 33 percent of Hispanics were without coverage of any kind. Furthermore, racial and ethnic minorities are much more likely than whites to be covered by a government program than by private insurance acquired through employment. The members of female-headed families are in much the same position with regard to insurance as are racial and ethnic minorities. (Because these groups were overrepresented in poverty statistics, as was discussed in Chapter Seven, these findings are not surprising.) Medical care prices have increased much faster than prices in general and, without coverage, most of us cannot afford quality medical care. U.S. Census Bureau statistics show that most people who have private insurance acquire it as a fringe benefit from employment. Employees of large firms are much more likely to have such a fringe benefit than are employees of small firms. Only 69 percent of workers in firms with fewer than 10 employees are insured, compared with 91 percent of workers in firms employing more than 1,000 workers.[3]

Medicaid

One of the keys to understanding why large percentages of the poor are without insurance coverage has to do with the way that Medicaid is administered. Medicaid is a program designed to pay for medical services for the nation's poor families and for medically indigent persons. (Medically indigent people have such high medical expenses that, whatever their income, they cannot afford their medical care.)

http://www.hcfa.gov/
This is the home page of the Health Care Financing Administration, the agency that administers Medicaid and Medicare.

TABLE 9-5 Health Insurance Coverage by Race and Ethnicity, 1999*				
	TYPE OF INSURANCE			
	FROM EMPLOYMENT (%)	OTHER PRIVATE (%)	GOVERNMENT (%)	UNINSURED (%)
All persons	62.8	8.2	24.1	15.5
White	64.9	9.0	23.2	11.0
Black	51.7	4.1	31.4	21.2
Hispanic	43.3	3.7	24.0	33.4

*Rows do not add to 100 percent largely because Medicare recipients often also carry private Medigap insurance.
Source: U.S. Department of Commerce, Bureau of the Census, *Health Insurance Historical Table I* (http://www.census.gov/hhes/hlthins/historic/hihistt1.html).

Although Medicaid is national in scope, it is administered by the individual states, and states are free to establish their own eligibility requirements and benefit levels within certain federal guidelines. They also have the option of supplementing federal financing with state revenues. As a result, Medicaid varies considerably by state. In 1995, fewer than half the families with income below the poverty line received medical assistance.[4] In many states the family must not only be poor, it must be extremely poor before it receives health assistance. Typically, an eligible family must also include children. As a result, poor single individuals and couples, including the working poor, are often ineligible for Medicaid. One of the consequences of the recent reform of our welfare laws was that nearly a million poor parents lost Medicaid coverage when they went off welfare and began working at low-wage jobs. Furthermore, eligibility for Medicaid does not guarantee access to quality medical care. Medicaid recipients may find it hard to find physicians who will treat Medicaid patients, because the government reimburses only about one-half the average physician's fee, and doctors are prohibited from passing the remainder on to the Medicaid patient.

More than one-half of Medicaid payments are for nursing home care of people over the age of 65. Medicare (discussed below) does not cover nursing home care. It is quite common for middle-class couples to use up their assets keeping one or the other in a nursing home. When their assets are exhausted, they are considered medically indigent, and Medicaid pays the nursing home.

Medicare

The Medicare program was established in 1965 when it became evident that many aged Americans could not afford the health care that they needed. Medicare is an insurance program sponsored by the federal government. Medicare hospital insurance is financed by required payroll taxes on workers and employers. Optional Medicare medical insurance for physicians' services, medical equipment, certain treatments, and other medical services is financed through monthly premiums paid by the insured person. Because these premiums never cover the full amount of the covered services received by Medicare patients, the federal government finances the difference each year. Almost all elderly persons over the age of 65 are covered, as well as disabled people who are eligible for Medicare benefits. Medicare is not **means-tested**—that is, benefits do not depend on a person's having few assets and low income. Both rich and poor are covered alike.

Means-tested
Benefits depend on low-income status as defined by law.

Due to both rising medical costs and the increasing proportion of elderly people in our population, Medicare has become an increasingly expensive program. As costs have increased, the burden of taxes on workers and employers has increased, until each is now responsible for taxes equaling 1.45 percent of all wages earned. As a result, efforts have been made to cut government costs. Premiums paid by recipients have increased, deductibles have increased, and certain benefits have been cut. The elderly are being encouraged to enroll in managed care health delivery organizations. (These terms will be discussed later.) As a consequence of these austerity measures, Medicare recipients are now paying larger out-of-pocket amounts of their health care costs than formerly.

**Diagnosis-related group
(DRG)**
One of approximately
490 categories into which
a medical diagnosis might
fall. The DRG determines
the prospective payment
by Medicare.

Prospective payment
Flat rate paid a hospital
by Medicare to treat a
particular patient having
a given diagnosis.

Perhaps the greatest change in the Medicare program was the establishment of **diagnosis-related groups (DRGs)** and the system of the **prospective payment** in 1983. This change was made in an attempt to contain runaway program costs. When admitted to a hospital, a Medicare patient is given a diagnosis that will fall into a particular diagnosis-related group. The prospective payment is the total reimbursement to the hospital for treatment of the patient; its amount depends on the diagnosis-related group into which the patient falls. This prospective payment is determined before any provision of health care. No matter the actual cost of the patient's treatment, the hospital is paid the prospective payment. If the hospital can treat the patient for less, it keeps the difference. If the patient's treatment costs the hospital more than the prospective payment, the hospital is out these costs (they cannot be passed along to the patient). Prospective payment provides an incentive for hospitals to curtail lengths of stay in their facilities, to avoid unnecessary treatments, and to generally promote efficiency. Critics argue that Medicare patients may be discharged before they are recovered sufficiently, but there is little evidence that this is so. A Rand Corporation study cited in the *Wall Street Journal*[5] indicated that the prospective payment system had instead reduced average hospital stay by about 3 days and reduced the death rate 30 days after admission by 1 percent.

Medicare does not cover all of older people's medical care. It only covers 80 percent of most hospital bills. Many older Americans therefore carry expensive "Medigap" insurance, which covers the medical expenses not covered by Medicare. Medicare also severely limits covered nursing home care and does not cover prescription drugs.

Many issues with Medicare are similar to the issues of medical care in general in the United States. High and escalating costs, affordability of care, and access to care (because clinics and hospitals do not have to accept Medicare patients) concern the elderly who rely on this program. A particular issue that recently has become a political and an economic issue (as evidenced by the quote from the State of the Union address that introduced this chapter) is expansion of Medicare coverage to include prescription drugs. Many older Americans take a number of expensive pharmaceuticals that did not exist at the time Medicare was created. Whether, or how, to cover these expenses was a major political campaign issue in 2000 and is now being debated in Congress.

Waste and Inefficiency

Consumer advocates maintain that between one-fifth and one-fourth of our health care expenditures are wasted.[6] These wasted dollars represent unnecessary tests and medical procedures, and unnecessary surgeries and drugs. Expensive technologies, such as magnetic resonance imaging (MRI), are overused. In cities, many hospitals each operate extremely expensive equipment instead of sharing identical million-dollar machines. This duplication leads to both higher costs and more unnecessary tests, because use justifies the investment in the machines in the first place. Finally, paperwork costs are tremendous. Every private insurance company and the government have their own forms to be filled out. If you have a friend who works for a physician or hospital, ask about the paper maze. It has been estimated that paperwork adds about $20 to every $100 of health care costs.

Refer again to Figure 9-1. In terms of the production possibilities curve, we are probably neither at point *A* nor at point *B*, but at a point such as point *C*, inside the curve. By cutting some of the waste and inefficiency now present in U.S. medical care, we could move toward the curve and clearly be better off.

CHARACTERISTICS OF THE MARKET FOR MEDICAL CARE

We rely on the market to allocate most health care dollars in our country. And the market for medical care is quite unlike the markets for hamburgers, pajamas, or romance novels. The qualities that set it apart contribute to waste, increased costs, and a resulting lack of access for some citizens. These characteristics are physician sovereignty, third-party payment, rapid technological change, inadequate cost containment, and patients' attitudes toward medical care.

Physician Sovereignty

Physician sovereignty
Medical doctors' control of demand for medical procedures.

Physician sovereignty is concerned with the doctor's control of demand for medical care. We do not shop around for the most appropriate medical care, comparing price and quality characteristics of numerous models, as we would if we went to the hardware store to buy a hammer. Instead, we accept that we need the tests, drugs, and treatments that the doctor prescribes. Medical care requires expert knowledge; we are not capable of making sophisticated diagnoses on our own. Instead, we rely on the physician. The doctor may take cost considerations into account, but they are clearly secondary. Decisions are made on the basis of accepted medical practice and the assurance of good medical care. The normal frugality of a shopper who compares prices carefully and budgets wisely is not present in medical care. Furthermore, under traditional fee-for-service insurance, the more services recommended, the more income the medical clinic receives. This situation may lead to unneeded services with benefits that are not worth their costs. Indeed, there may even be a tendency to overprescribe, overtest, and overservice, especially if this overcare reduces the likelihood of costly medical malpractice suits. Physician sovereignty thus leads to a higher demand for medical care, waste, and higher medical costs.

Third-Party Payment

We discussed third-party payment earlier in the chapter, noting that fully three-fourths of medical expenditures are paid by either government programs or private insurance. This phenomenon makes patients less cost conscious than they would be if they had to pay directly for medical services themselves. The indirect link between insurance premiums and our medical costs is tenuous—our insurance premiums do not appear to be directly linked to the number of visits we make to the doctor's office or to the number of trips we make to the hospital emergency room. When a third party pays for our medical care, so that we do not pay directly for each medical service, we are more willing and able to ask for additional medical services. Like physician sovereignty, third-party payment increases the demand for medical care and therefore its price and the quantity consumed.

Rapid Technological Change

Kidney dialysis machines, magnetic resonance imaging, transplant techniques, nuclear medicine, high-dosage chemotherapy, and Viagra are some medicine-related technological advances in recent years. When hospitals invest in highly specialized equipment, hospital costs, which have been the most rapidly escalating element of health care costs in the past 30 years, must then increase.

Medical experts and their patients judge hospitals by the quality of physicians who are on their staffs. Reputable medical doctors choose to practice at hospitals that have all the latest technology available, so that every hospital competing for first-class medical specialists must have it all. Thus expensive machinery is duplicated in the several hospitals of our cities. Doctors must use it to justify its installation. The number of expensive tests and treatments increases, representing a rise in demand for health care. Many experts believe that expensive and rapidly changing technology is the major force driving hospital costs.

In the last half of the 1990s, one of the fastest-growing elements in health technology spending was prescription drugs. New pharmaceutical products can increase the quality and length of life. Many of these new drugs are very expensive, and they may bring new patients into the health care system. (Experts estimate that a large portion of Viagra sales was to men who had not previously been treated for impotence.) Thus spending on prescription drugs has increased rapidly.

Inadequate Cost Containment

Responsibility for containing the costs of medical treatment is so diffused that keeping these costs down is very difficult. Third-party payment makes the patient and the patient's family less concerned about costs. Hospital administrators find it relatively easy to pass along cost increases for needed treatments. Furthermore, hospitals and physicians routinely engage in **cost shifting,** which is the transfer of the unpaid costs of some patients to well-insured patients through the raising of fees. The hospital reimbursement procedures of Medicaid and Medicare often leave a portion of a patient's costs uncovered, and hospitals treat very urgent cases even if payment is unlikely. They then cover these uncompensated costs by raising their rates and collecting more from insurance companies for the treatment of patients who have good insurance (or from affluent patients with no insurance). Cost shifting distorts decisions made about health care and makes calculation of the costs of a given treatment difficult.

Cost shifting
Practice of recovering the unpaid costs of some patients by charging higher prices to other patients.

Attitudes of Patients

Americans' attitudes toward medical care affect our health care system in several ways. First, we *believe in* our high-tech medical system. We hear on the television and radio about new treatments and studies, and we believe that virtually any treatment should be available to us. We believe that more tests are better than less, that aggressive medical treatment can cure virtually anything, and that we do not need to take much responsibility for our own health. This belief leads us to demand excessive care without much regard for cost.

Second, we are a litigious society; if we suspect a physician of an error, we sue for malpractice. As a result, doctors take out **malpractice insurance** and practice **defensive medicine.** Malpractice insurance pays the settlement if a physician is found guilty of a mistake that harms a patient. As malpractice case settlements have increased over the years, malpractice insurance premiums have increased, and higher insurance costs have driven up medical fees. Doctors have sought to protect themselves by practicing defensive medicine, which also drives up medical costs. Rather than be found guilty of carelessness, doctors prescribe tests that are virtually certain to be unnecessary. It has been estimated that one-half the cesarean-section deliveries performed in the United States each year are unnecessary, but malpractice awards are so large when babies are injured in the birth process that cesareans are done at the first sign of any irregularity, despite their high cost. (Cesarean operations cost about twice what vaginal deliveries cost.) Such defensive medicine also implies an increased demand for medical services.

Defensive medicine distorts medical care markets in other ways also. Many clinics carry obstetric malpractice insurance on only a few physicians, for example, and many family practice doctors therefore no longer deliver babies. Consequently, some areas of our country suffer a shortage of obstetricians.

Malpractice insurance
Insurance carried by health care professionals to protect them from large malpractice damage awards.

Defensive medicine
Ordering of unnecessary tests and services solely to protect oneself from charges of malpractice.

Consequences of These Characteristics

These characteristics of the market for medical care have caused medical costs to skyrocket over time as shown in Figure 9-3. Physician sovereignty, third-party

---

FIGURE 9-3   Increased Demand and Supply of Medical Care

Because demand has increased more than supply since 1960, medical care costs have risen as we have consumed a greater quantity of health care.

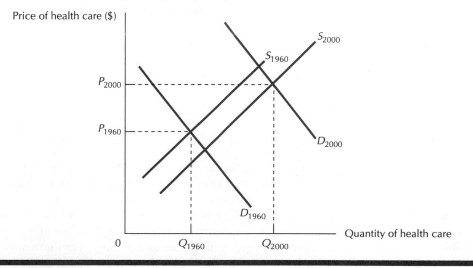

payment, and the increase in tests and treatments due to rapid technological change and defensive medicine all imply increases in the demand for health care. The installation of new technology and the continual replacement of "old" technology, as well as expansion of the number of hospital beds and doctors, represent an increase in the supply of health care. Our attitudes as patients represent larger demands for medical care. Since 1960, therefore, both the demand for and the supply of medical care have increased, but demand has increased by a much greater amount than supply. We now consume more medical care at higher prices.

ALTERNATIVES FOR HEALTH CARE IN THE UNITED STATES

As the production possibilities curve shows, we must make choices between medical care and other goods and services. We must also make choices: Who gets health care? How much health care do they get? What kind of health care? Who provides the health care? Some of these choices are expressed in the market; some are made by the government. Regardless of who makes the decisions, we must realize that they *are* being made. Within our society decisions are made about what share of gross domestic product will be allocated to medical care. Within the field of health care itself, decisions are made about how health care dollars will be distributed to members of society. We tend not to like choices concerning health care. We do not want to choose between treatment of a heart transplant patient or a person on kidney dialysis. We do not like to choose between spending money on prenatal care for poor, pregnant women and lead-poisoning screening for inner-city children.

We don't like to make such choices, but they are being made, in part on the basis of income and ability to pay, and in part on the basis of eligibility for private or public insurance. At times, decisions appear to be made by default. The wisdom of our choices is difficult to assess because of cost shifting, which distorts the market. But many of us are upset by the continually increasing costs of health care, or the problem of access, or simply the waste. If we wish to change the distribution of medical benefits or the types of medical services available, we as a nation certainly have that power. What then are the possible alternatives for health care in the United States?

Privatization and Increased Competition in Health Care

Privatization
Returning government functions to the private sector.

Some economists and political scientists argue that the government has too big an influence on health care in this country. They desire the elimination or a sharp reduction in the government's participation in the health care market, the **privatization** of publicly owned hospitals, and an increase in the competitiveness of the health care industry. Recall that the strength of free markets is their efficiency in equating private demand and supply. This consideration fosters arguments in favor of a return to free markets on both the demand and the supply side of the health care market.

Curtailment or Elimination of Medicare and Medicaid

It has been noted that rising health care costs are at least partly the result of demand that is not tempered by the usual norms of frugality and concern for price. Certainly the existence of Medicare and Medicaid is of prime consideration here. Without these programs, many people who could otherwise not afford medical care presumably would not receive medical care, or at least not the type of care that they now receive. Because a high level of care for these people is reflected in the total demand for medical care, demand would decrease without these programs, and health care prices would go down. This withdrawal of medical care from the poor and the elderly may, however, be deemed unfair by others in society. A fairly significant portion of Americans view basic medical care as an elemental right.

Medical Savings Accounts

Medical savings account
Type of insurance in which the purchaser makes payments into an account that can be drawn against in times of illness.

A related proposal would replace current health insurance replaced with the **medical savings account.** Some proponents of this proposal view it as a possible way to eventually reform Medicare. The medical savings account is a type of insurance. The purchaser—whether employer, government, or insured—makes regular payments into a medical expenses account, which the insured can draw against if he or she becomes ill. Catastrophic-care insurance to take care of really high medical bills is usually included. The insured party controls how the funds in the account are spent: what tests are performed, what procedures are done, and by whom they are done. Monies not spent for medical care are returned to the insured, giving him or her a stake in minimizing the costs of treatment. Proponents of medical savings accounts believe that the accounts would eliminate the perverse incentives built into other third-party payment systems. Critics believe that they would benefit only relatively healthy people, who would save money on health care. Seriously ill people, they argue, would find that their insurance was inadequate for any high level of sophisticated care.

Privatization of the Supply of Medical Services

Elements on the supply side of health care contribute to high medical costs as well. Many argue that a more privatized, competitive supply of health care services would result in lower costs. First, most hospitals are not run on a "for profit" basis; other goals, such as offering quality overall care, utilizing the most advanced technology, or specializing in particular services, are paramount. Critics argue that the way we finance health care allows hospitals to pursue these goals by allowing them to shift uncompensated costs to well-insured patients. The privatization of government-owned and -run hospitals and other reforms to increase competition among hospitals, it is argued, would force them to pay more attention to the bottom line, thus eliminating a great deal of inefficiency. On the other hand, supporters of public hospitals argue that some existing "for profit" hospitals have increasingly come under attack for their "bottom line" mentality: their specialization in high profit services, their neglect of other less profitable but important services, their cost-cutting measures (which dangerously decrease the quality and safety of patient care), and their highly publicized turning away of uninsured and low income patients.

Second, advertising within the health care industry, especially the type of *price* advertising in which we see optical companies engaging, was long considered as unethical. Since optical firms have begun to advertise, we have seen lower prices for glasses and contact lenses. If prices charged by physicians, clinics, and hospitals were advertised, as well as the prices of various services and medication, perhaps competitiveness among suppliers would increase, keeping prices lower. It should be noted, however, that the sort of *nonprice* television and magazine advertising in which the large pharmaceutical firms are now engaging will not make prices lower. Advertising of Zocor and Lipitor is aimed at increasing patient demand, increasing both price and quantity sold. And, of course, the advertising campaigns drive up the drug companies' costs, putting even more upward pressure on prices.

Group Practices and Managed Care

Various forms of group practices may increase efficiency and lower costs. For example, physicians operating in a clinic may have lower costs per service than a doctor in solo practice. Expensive technology and equipment can be more efficiently utilized, and physicians can specialize in various fields. Specific forms of group practices may yield additional efficiencies. **Health maintenance organizations (HMOs)** utilize the services of group physicians either working within or for the organization. The organization itself contracts with insurance companies to care for the insured person's medical need for a given rate. A patient's care is coordinated by a medical clinic, or primary care physician. The patient will need a referral from the primary care physician to be treated by a doctor who is not in the organization. A similar form of group practice is the **preferred provider organization (PPO),** which contracts with health insurance companies to provide health services at a reduced rate. Together these organizations are what is meant by "managed care."

Managed care is rapidly replacing traditional fee-for-service insurance in the United States. The major reason is the high cost of providing fee-for-service coverage. In 1996, 24 percent of insurance coverage was in the form of managed care. Thirteen percent of Medicare patients were in managed care, as were 40 percent of Medicaid recipients.[7] Managed care is simply a less expensive way of obtaining medical care. As medical care costs rise, driving up the cost of standard fee-for-service insurance, many people are electing to become members of managed care organizations, and the organizations are becoming larger. The growth of managed care and evolving competition among managed care organizations are generally credited with slowing the growth of U.S. health care expenditures in the 1990s. It is worth noting that fee-for-service insurance, especially when combined with physician sovereignty, provides an incentive to give more medical care, whereas managed care provides an incentive to give less.

Health maintenance organization (HMO)
A health insurance plan under which the covered care is limited to designated providers and the use of services is coordinated by a patient's primary care physician.

Preferred provider organization (PPO)
A health insurance plan under which a group of medical providers contract to provide the insured patient's medical care at discounted rates.

As with the Medicare program of prospective payment, there is an incentive for the managed care provider to be cost-efficient in its provision of medical services. Services costs that "go over contract" would be costly to an HMO. Costs below the contracted price benefit the HMO. As a result, services that cut costs in the long run, such as health screening, nutrition and exercise classes, and smoking cessation clinics are often provided by HMOs. There is a healthy emphasis on preventive medicine. Still, some people complain that they cannot get a referral for their insurance to pay for a visit to an outside specialist, and others worry about the quality of care when the emphasis is on cost control. There is some evidence that HMOs' pressure on rates for medical reimbursement is slowing the pace at which some geographic areas adopt new technology. Many states, therefore, have passed laws regulating HMOs, while Congress has considered a "Patient's Bill of Rights."

In the late 1990s, many elderly people were encouraged to enroll in HMOs rather than standard fee-for-service Medicare coverage. Those who did so usually gained some prescription drug coverage, as well as some other additional benefits. Some of the HMOs that initially sought out Medicare patients, however, have found them to be unprofitable and are no longer covering them.

Anecdotes about managed care are common, but there has been relatively little research about the quality of that care. A Rand Corporation study compared the outcomes of treatments for patients with hypertension and non-insulin-dependent diabetes who were treated by generalists and subspecialists in three different systems of care. It was the first case-by-case comparison of treatment and costs of HMOs and traditional medical practices. Researchers found no evidence that any one system of care or physician specialty achieved consistently better two-year or four-year outcomes than the others. The HMOs, however, were more cost-effective than the other systems.[8]

National Health Insurance

National health insurance
Government program ensuring universal and comprehensive coverage of the population.

National health insurance represents the opposite alternative to privatized free-market care. National health insurance of one kind or another is common throughout the developed world. Indeed, we are in a minority by having no national health insurance. Of all the industrialized countries of the world, only the United States and South Africa lack such a program. Refer back to the last column of Table 9-2 to see the percentage of each country's health care expenditures that is covered by some public insurance scheme. You will note that the United States covers a lower percentage of its expenditures (through Medicare and Medicaid) than any other country in the list. The goal of national health insurance is universal coverage. Under such coverage, everyone would have health insurance; people would not fall between the cracks and lack coverage, as they do in our present health care delivery system.

Canada has a system of national health insurance. The Canadian system stands midway between the United States' free enterprise system and Britain's socialized medicine, in which doctors are salaried government employees. Like U.S. physicians, Canadian doctors can practice wherever they want and charge whatever they like. Most doctors choose to practice within the Canadian insurance program.

They are paid by the government according to a negotiated schedule of fee-for-service. The tax-supported Canadian program pays all hospital and medical bills. The system is thus an example of a single-payer health insurance system, and the single payer is the government. All people, whether rich or poor, employed or unemployed, have access to medical services.

The system is not perfect, however, and its costs are rising as new technologies are adopted. Although most Canadian citizens and physicians are happy (on balance) with the system, a common criticism is that elective surgeries are often postponed (and sometimes more critical interventions are delayed) due to shortages of funds. Indeed, one way the Canadian system contains costs is purposely to slow down the adoption of new technologies. Many U.S. citizens are uncomfortable with the overt rationing of medical services under the Canadian system.

A single-payer health insurance system is much less expensive to administer than is our health care system. A 1991 General Accounting Office study cited by Baker and Weisbrot estimated that the United States could save about 11 percent of its total health care costs by switching to a single-payer social insurance system.[9] Others have put the savings even higher.

A very different proposal for national health insurance was made by the Clinton Administration in 1993 and defeated in Congress. The proposal would have stressed managed care to contain costs and required employers to purchase health insurance for their employees, while the government would have provided insurance for the unemployed. It was an extremely complex proposal that was opposed by the small business lobby, which argued that the increased costs to businesses would lead to loss of jobs, and by the insurance lobby, which argued that patient choice would be constrained. Discussion of alternative, incremental ways to improve access to and cut costs in U.S. health care continues.

Recent Legislation Affecting U.S. Health Care

The Kennedy–Kasselbaum Health Care Reform Bill, passed in 1996, requires insurers to continue to offer policies to workers who change jobs or lose their jobs. It makes health insurance easier to purchase by workers with preexisting chronic health problems.

In 1997 a federal plan to expand health care coverage for children in low-income working families was passed. Under the State Child Health Insurance Program (SCHIP), states could expand Medicaid or begin a new program to provide health care to children in families whose income was too high for the children to qualify for Medicaid, but too low for the family to afford private insurance. Congress appropriated $40 billion to help the states improve insurance coverage for children during the first 10 years of SCHIP.

Although poor children are more likely to have insurance coverage now than in the early 1990s, their parents often remain uninsured. A particular problem with the 1996 reform of welfare is that many families went off welfare and into very low-paying jobs. When they left welfare, they lost Medicaid, but they did not obtain a job that provides medical insurance and they cannot afford to purchase health insurance. The 1996 welfare reform law did give the states the flexibility to expand Medicaid coverage to people at whatever income level they determine is appropriate. A number of states have extended Medicaid coverage to all families below the poverty line, and a few states now cover families whose income is above the poverty line. In addition, state plans to increase coverage for low-income pregnant women have become more common. Although no national health plan has been adopted, incremental changes have been made to improve access.

Legal Reforms

A few states have capped the amount of damages that can be awarded in a malpractice lawsuit. Juries have made truly huge malpractice awards, which both drive up malpractice insurance premiums and lead physicians to practice defensive medicine. Caps, it is argued, will decrease health care costs by decreasing the unnecessary tests doctors order solely to protect themselves.

Additional Issues within Current Government Programs

In the context of the continuing discussion of health care and solutions to our health care problems, it might be helpful to focus a bit more attention on issues within existing health care programs. These issues must be taken into consideration in any remedy, whether a national health program or privatization. Some of these issues are discussed below.

Who Will Be Covered?

The objectives of extending insurance coverage to the currently uninsured and cutting health care costs obviously conflict. Not all people or not all elderly persons may need to be covered by government programs, whether national health insurance, Medicare, or Medicaid. A national health plan need not be universal in its coverage, but only *ensure* universal coverage for all. That is, high-income and employed individuals might continue to be covered by private insurance, and the national plan might pick up coverage for the rest. In addition, the national plan might pick up catastrophic coverage for individuals with exorbitant medical costs when their private benefits run out.

The benefits of this option are reduced costs to taxpayers. Government financing would cover only those who could not privately finance their health care. One concern, however, is that physicians and other health providers might prefer to treat private patients, especially if government payments are not as high as private ones. The result might be a "two-tiered" system of health care: one for the rich and one for the poor. Another concern is that, as is the case with Medicare and Medicaid now, health care providers would shift uncompensated costs to private insurance companies.

Similar changes could be made in Medicare. Medicare currently covers all elderly retired people, whatever their income or assets. Some have suggested, however, that eligibility should be tied to income. Those who can afford to purchase private insurance should be required to do so, or they would receive lower Medicare benefits. Those with lower incomes should receive full Medicare coverage. As we debate the addition of prescription drug benefits to Medicare, one option to stem the rising tide of Medicare costs would be to extend such benefits only to lower-income elderly people.

How Will the Program be Financed?

In both our current Medicare system and private insurance, the patient pays a portion of the cost through an array of **premiums, deductibles,** and **coinsurance payments.** A premium is a payment (usually made on a monthly basis) to own an insurance policy and to be eligible for its benefits. A deductible is an amount of health care charges that the patient must pay before receiving insurance payments on the remainder of health care charges. It is usually a given amount specified for a time period or on a per-service basis. A coinsurance payment is some percentage of medical care charges over and above the deductible that the subscriber must pay.

If your insurance company requires a $200 deductible annually and 10 percent coinsurance, and your yearly covered medical expenses are $1,000, you will pay the $200 deductible plus 10 percent of the remaining $800 ($80) for a total of $280. The insurance company will pay the remaining $720. Most health care policies have maximum amounts that they will cover as well.

Deductibles and coinsurance keep costs to the insurer down, as well as discourage excessive use of medical services. If subscribers are required to pay some amount per service, they will be less inclined to use unnecessary services frivolously. On the other hand, the expense to the subscribers may actually deter them from seeking important services. Furthermore, the financing, including premiums, becomes **regressive** for subscribers. Even if a low-income and a high-income family pay the same dollar payments of premiums, deductibles, and coinsurance, the low-income family is paying a *larger percentage of its income* in these payments. Thus, the poorer family has a greater burden in paying these expenses. This regressivity could be eliminated if premiums and other payments were tied to income.

Our current Medicare system has the regressivity mentioned above. Some low-income elderly people refrain from using medical services because they cannot afford the deductible. Some cannot afford the optional portion of Medicare, because they cannot afford the monthly premiums. And, as discussed previously, some important medical services and supplies are not covered at all.

What Will Be Covered?

Any system that does not offer comprehensive coverage of virtually all medical expenses must deal with the issue of what medical services will be covered. This issue faces Medicaid, Medicare, private insurance, and any proposed national health program. It has been suggested that because most people can afford to pay for routine care, such as checkups, immunizations, and prenatal visits, programs ought to address themselves to catastrophic coverage for serious and expensive medical conditions. After all, treatment of these conditions is beyond the means of all but the most wealthy Americans. Incurring some of these expenses could wipe out the savings and assets of even middle-income families. Indeed, health care problems are implicated in 50 percent of the consumer bankruptcy filings in the United States.[10]

Premiums
Payments to purchase and keep in force an insurance policy.

Deductibles
Payments on an annual or per-service basis that must be made by the insured person before the insurance company's payments begin.

Coinsurance payments
Percentage of medical expenses remaining after the deductible, which the insured person must pay.

Regressive
Taking a larger percentage of lower incomes than of higher incomes.

On the other hand, others argue that this type of focus is not the most cost-effective, and certainly it ignores the basic needs of the poor. Ensuring that all children are immunized against preventable diseases is cheaper in the long run than treating the illnesses that would otherwise exist. Ensuring that poor women get quality prenatal care is cheaper than treating low-birth-weight premature infants in neonatal intensive-care nurseries. If patients must pay the costs of preventive care themselves, many will be forced to go without that care, and society may bear greater expenses in the long run. Preventive medicine is cost-effective, as well as an issue of equity to many of us.

SUMMARY

The United States leads the world in health care expenditures, both in absolute dollars and as a percent of gross domestic product. Despite these expenditures, the United States does not have the world's lowest infant or maternal mortality rates. Furthermore, the racial and ethnic differences in these statistics are pronounced.

The market for health care is different from other markets in ways that cause demand to be inflated and costs to be poorly constrained. As a result, we face escalating health care costs, inefficiency and waste, and unequal access to health care. Public and private health insurance leave more than 43 million Americans uncovered.

Alternative proposals for health care in the United States include an increase in privatization and competition, expansion of managed care practices, development of national health insurance, the revision of laws governing malpractice suit damages, and the revision of the existing Medicaid and Medicare programs.

NOTES

1. Calculated from information provided by the Health Care Financing Administration (http://www.hcfa.gov/stats/) and the U.S. Bureau of Economic Analysis (http://www.bea.doc.gov/).

2. St. Paul Pioneer Press, June 21, 2000, p. 1A.

3. Committee on Ways and Means, U.S. House of Representatives, *1998 Green Book* (Washington, DC: U.S. Government Printing Office, 1999).

4. U.S. Department of Commerce, Bureau of the Census, *Statistical Abstract of the United States: 1999*.

5. Cited in Ron Winslow, "Medicare Curbs Aren't Harmful to Care Quality," *Wall Street Journal*, October 7, 1990, pp. B1, B6.

6. "Wasted Health Care Dollars," *Consumer Reports* (July 1992), p. 435.

7. Health Care Financing Administration, http://www.hcfa.gov

8. "Research Supports Quality of HMO Healthcare," *Physican's Management* (March 1996).

9. Dan Baker and Mark Weisbrot, *Social Security: The Phony Crisis* (Chicago: The University of Chicago Press, 1999), p. 98.

10. Melissa B. Jacoby, Teresa A. Sullivan, and Elizabeth Warren, "Medical Problems and Bankruptcy Filings," *Norton Bankruptcy Law Adviser* (May 2000), p. 2.

DISCUSSION QUESTIONS

1. *How do the health expenditures of the United States compare with those of other countries?*

2. *How do the infant and maternal death rates in the United States compare with those of other industrialized countries? with the less-developed countries discussed in Chapter Eight?*

3. *Define each of the following terms and explain how each affects the demand for medical care: (1) physician sovereignty, (2) third-party payment, (3) defensive medicine, and (4) attitudes of patients.*

4. *How does cost shifting make calculation of the cost of particular medical treatments difficult?*

5. *Compare and contrast Medicare and Medicaid.*

6. *What features do you think a national health plan should have?*

7. *How does managed care decrease health care expenditures?*

8. *Do you believe that basic medical care is a right of citizenship?*

9. *What is the conservative position on national health insurance? the liberal position?*

10. *Do you agree that it is possible to overallocate resources to health care?*

11. *Go to the Organization for Economic Cooperation and Development site, http://www.oecd.org, and find the latest figures on health care expenditures for industrialized countries. How does the United States compare with other countries in the latest year?*

CHAPTER 10

Education

I have something to say to every family listening to us tonight. Your children can go on to college. If you know a child from a poor family, tell her not to give up—she can go on to college. If you know a young couple struggling with bills, worried they won't be able to send their children to college, tell them not to give up—their children can go on to college. If you know somebody who's caught in a dead-end job and afraid he can't afford the classes necessary to get better jobs for the rest of his life, tell him not to give up—he can go on to college. Because of the things that have been done, we can make college as universal in the 21st century as high school is today. And, my friends, that will change the face and future of America.

William Jefferson Clinton, *State of the Union Address,* 1998

Historically, the United States has valued education highly. The words from the political speech above truly reflect our values. We provide public kindergarten through high school (K–12) education free to the student and the student's family. State colleges and vocational schools are partly financed by tax revenues so that tuition is affordable for the average student. Public education is viewed as the force that levels the playing field and ensures that all Americans have an equal opportunity to succeed in our society. Historically, it has been one of our most important antipoverty policies. Furthermore, our economy reaps the benefits of education in the form of literate, productive workers. Education is the classic example of a good that yields spillover benefits.

In this chapter we will look at the U.S. education system. First we will discuss the spillover benefits of education. Next we will analyze our K–12 public education

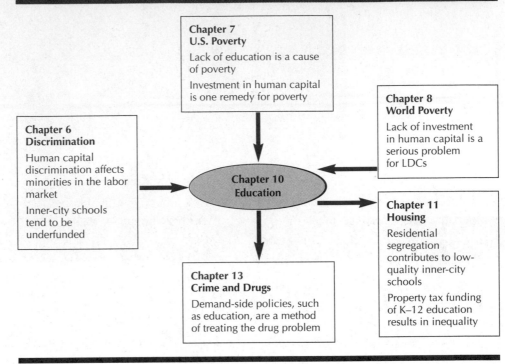

Chapter 7
U.S. Poverty

Lack of education is a cause of poverty

Investment in human capital is one remedy for poverty

Chapter 6
Discrimination

Human capital discrimination affects minorities in the labor market

Inner-city schools tend to be underfunded

Chapter 8
World Poverty

Lack of investment in human capital is a serious problem for LDCs

Chapter 10
Education

Chapter 11
Housing

Residential segregation contributes to low-quality inner-city schools

Property tax funding of K–12 education results in inequality

Chapter 13
Crime and Drugs

Demand-side policies, such as education, are a method of treating the drug problem

---

Public schools

Schools that are financed by tax revenues and operated by the government.

Private schools

Schools that are not operated by the government and are mainly financed by student tuition.

system, paying particular attention to the effects of financing K–12 education by means of the property tax; we will also consider some proposed reforms for our **public schools.** Public schools are those that are financed and operated in large part by government. They are largely financed by taxes. We also have a number of **private schools** at both the K–12 and postsecondary levels. Private schools are not owned and operated by government but by churches, businesses, or other groups in the private sector. They are largely financed by tuition. Next we will discuss higher education in the United States. We will examine the private and public university system. We will discuss higher education as an investment in human capital, which, if you recall from Chapter Seven and Chapter Eight, refers to spending that improves the productivity of people. Finally, we will examine other issues in higher education.

EDUCATION'S SPILLOVER BENEFITS

The provision of education creates private benefits that go to the student and the student's family. The educated, skilled individual is able to earn higher wages than the uneducated, unskilled worker. The educated worker is less likely to be frequently unemployed and is more likely to find a job that is intellectually rewarding. He or she is exposed to a wider variety of aesthetic experiences that enrich life. These are the private benefits of education that the student receives. We imagine that you and your family considered many of these factors while you were deciding whether or not to go on to college.

Spillover benefit
Positive externality in which benefits are shifted from the private market to society.

The provision of education also creates **spillover benefits** to society. Spillover benefits are the positive effects of an economic activity that accrue to society as a whole. Educated citizens are more likely to vote and otherwise participate in public life. They have more productive skills and contribute more to the economy's output. They earn more and therefore pay more income taxes. They are less likely to be chronically unemployed than are uneducated workers. They are less likely to go on welfare and less likely to commit crimes, or at least violent crimes. Therefore society receives spillover benefits from education, and the educated person receives private benefits.

Externalities
Benefits or costs of an economic activity that spill over to the rest of society.

Spillover benefits are examples of economic **externalities.** Externalities are benefits or costs of some economic activity that spill over from the private market to society as a whole. These externalities can be either negative or positive. A positive externality provides a benefit to society and is also called a spillover benefit. A negative externality imposes a cost on society and is also called a **spillover cost.** The classic example of a spillover cost is pollution, which we discussed in detail in Chapter Three. Externalities cause society's resources to be inefficiently allocated. Our economy will produce either too much (overallocate resources) or produce too little (underallocate resources) when externalities occur.

Spillover cost
Negative externality in which costs are shifted from the private market to society.

Figure 10-1 shows the underallocation of resources that results from education's spillover benefits. D_p is the demand for education in the private market. The benefits that students and their families perceive they will receive determine this demand. The supply curve intersects the demand curve at an equilibrium quantity of 5,000. Thus 5,000 students would enroll.

FIGURE 10-1   Effects of the Spillover Benefits of Education

Because the private market does not reflect the spillover benefits of education, the number of students enrolled in college (5,000) is less than the socially optimum number (6,000).

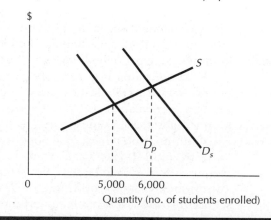

But the private market demand curve is not the socially correct demand curve, because it does not reflect the benefits gained by society from education. If we take the spillover benefits into account, demand would be greater. So the true socially correct demand curve, based on the benefits received by students *and* by society, is D_s. D_s intersects supply at an equilibrium quantity of 6,000, which is the socially optimal amount. Because the private market demand does not reflect the positive externalities, the market will produce too little education. We say that the market *underallocates resources* whenever spillover benefits exist. The market equilibrium is not efficient, or optimum for society, when this occurs.

The spillover benefits justify the government's provision of K–12 education, subsidization of college education through grants and financial aid to students, and establishment of public colleges and universities. These policies correct the underallocation of resources. If the government's contribution toward the student's education is just equal to the spillover benefits that society receives from education, the socially optimum amount of education will be produced and consumed in our economy.

Different levels and types of education yield different amounts of private and spillover benefits. Most people agree that the spillover benefits of K–12 education are tremendous, because basic literacy is developed through such education. The provision of primary and secondary education free to the student is therefore justified by the societal spillover benefits. Some argue, however, that most of the benefits of postsecondary education are private and that spillover benefits from college education are few. They therefore feel that the primary burden of college costs should be borne by the student and the student's family. What do you think?

FINANCING K–12 EDUCATION AND ITS EFFECTS

Primary and secondary education in the United States may be free to the student, but the government incurs great expense for them. In 1996–1997, spending for public K–12 education was $313.1 billion.[1] Local, state, and the federal governments each contributed part of that amount. Figure 10-2 shows the percentages paid by each level of government and others in 1996–1997. Note that the local and state governments bear the principal burden for funding primary and secondary education. Indeed, spending for the local public school system is the largest item in most municipal (city) budgets.

http://www.ed.gov/
The Department of Education home page has excellent links to statistical information.

K–12 education is largely funded by the local property tax. The state's contribution toward public K–12 education is meant to enrich and equalize education within a particular state. There are rich and poor communities in every state, and local property tax revenues vary greatly, so state aid is intended to provide more equal funding and educational opportunities among rich and poor communities.

If we fund K–12 education primarily by means of the property tax, we create inequities too great to be resolved by state aid, especially because state aid distribution formulas often provide aid to all, not only poor, school districts. Some rural school districts are severely underfunded, as are most inner-city school districts. Inner-city school districts are terribly underfunded in comparison with suburban public schools. Spending per student varies widely. Spending more than some

FIGURE 10-2   Financing Public K–12 Education, 1996–1997

The chart below shows the percentages of funds provided by each level of government to public elementary and secondary schools.

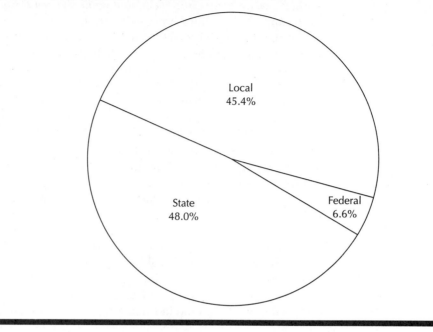

threshold amount on each student may not buy students a better education, but spending well below that threshold means shoddy facilities, inadequate supplies, and understaffed or unstaffed classrooms. In turn, these conditions contribute to high dropout rates and functional illiteracy.

ADVERSE CONDITIONS IN INNER-CITY SCHOOLS

Social critic Jonathan Kozol reported on terrible conditions in six inner-city school systems in the early 1990s in *Savage Inequalities: Children in America's Schools*. In each case the physical facilities were dreadful. He observed schools with holes in their roofs (and no means of repairing them), vocational classes in which young people were being taught typing on old manual typewriters in the age of computers, libraries converted to classrooms because schools housed half again as many students as they were built to house, and classes in which students had to share the few books available. Such basics as working toilets, toilet paper, soap, and chalk were in chronically short supply.

Teachers' salaries were lower in these underfunded school districts than in other school districts. Young teachers tended to burn out and quit, either to find teaching jobs in better-paying, better-supplied suburban districts or to leave teaching altogether. The top salary in one Chicago high school that Kozol visited in

1990 was two-thirds what Chicago suburban school districts paid teachers. To cut costs, the inner-city school districts often hired "permanent subs" at still lower salaries and without benefits. Even that measure was not enough to stretch the budget to cover the entire year, and some classes simply went unstaffed, especially in the spring when funds were exhausted.

Many students observed in Kozol's study were chronic truants by the time they reached eighth grade. In effect they had dropped out before they even reached high school. High school dropout rates, which measure the percentage of freshmen who do not finish high school, were high. Dropout rates were in the neighborhood of 50 to 60 percent in the schools Kozol visited. Nor did graduating mean much. The quality of education was so poor that a high school diploma did not guarantee literacy. Kozol noted that in Chicago 27 percent of high school graduates read at the eighth-grade level or below. At the city's community colleges, which received most of their students from the Chicago public schools, the non-completion rate was 97 percent.

There is, of course, a racial dimension to this phenomenon. The overwhelming majority of the students in the inner-city schools described above were either African American or Latino. Whites have moved to the suburbs, leaving the inner cites to minorities who lack the means to escape. This migration means that our public education system is still largely segregated in fact, if not by law. Minority children receive inferior education because they must attend these poor schools. They emerge inadequately prepared to enter our labor markets or to go on to college. This is the discrimination in human capital phenomenon referred to in Chapter Six.

Property-Tax Financing

Tax base
Value of income, earnings, property, sales, or other variables to which a tax rate is applied.

Tax rate
Percentage of the tax base that must be paid to the government as tax.

Kozol argues that financing public schools by means of the local property tax lies at the base of this problem. The amount of property taxes that can be collected to support the schools depends on the **tax base** and the **tax rate.** The tax base is the value of taxable property (land and buildings) in the school district, whereas the tax rate is the percentage of the tax base that will be collected as property tax. Property in the suburbs has a high value. Industrial plants, stylish shopping centers, and $400,000 homes add up to a large tax base. But decaying inner-city slums have little value. Moreover, a large percentage of inner-city property is exempt from the property tax. Tax is not collected on municipal buildings, colleges, hospitals, and art museums. The tax base to support the city schools is thus relatively small compared with tax bases in the suburbs. If the tax rate is the same, the suburbs will collect many more tax dollars per student. In fact, tax *rates* are usually higher in the cities, but due to their inadequate tax *bases,* inner cities cannot come close to matching the suburbs in educational spending per student.

In 1989, the school funding system of the state of Texas was found to be unconstitutional by its supreme court. Spending per pupil ranged from $2,112 in the poorest district to $19,333 in the richest. The property tax base in the poorest district was only $20,000 per pupil, whereas in the richest district it was $14,000,000. Although the spending figures include property taxes plus the state and federal contributions, it is obvious that the citizens of Texas inner cities taxed themselves by much higher rates to finance their schools than the suburbs. The problem was their extremely low tax bases.[2]

Other areas of the country also have significant differences in property tax bases and spending per student. For example, the tax base per student in Camden, New Jersey, is only 10 percent of the state average. In 1989–1990, the property tax base per pupil ranged from $39,000 to more than $340,000 in Kentucky. In Kentucky, however, some of the poorest districts were rural.[3] These discrepancies have led to numerous court cases in which low-property-value school districts have challenged their state's school financing system. Several of these cases, such as one in Kentucky, have resulted in changes in the way states finance K–12 education. Many states have revised the formulas by which they distribute funds to equalize spending per student. Federal funds have been designated to improve education in our poorest school districts. Although some terribly underfunded inner-city school districts remain, the picture is somewhat brighter than it was in the early 1990s.

Despite new financing measures, which resulted in greater spending per student in inner-city schools, students in such schools continue to perform poorly on standardized tests. In 1999 about two-thirds of New York City eighth graders failed the language arts test and three-fourths failed the math test.[4] A national debate on our inner-city schools has ensued. Some have argued that the level of spending per student doesn't matter, because research has shown that increased spending per student does not immediately *by itself* improve average student performance (or doesn't improve it much). We have discovered that the best predictor of a school's student performance is that school's poverty rate. Simply put, students from schools with high poverty rates do not, on average, perform as well on standardized tests as students from schools in more affluent areas. As we will discuss in Chapter Eleven, residential segregation creates inner-city ghettoes, concentrates poverty, and contributes to the creation of an underclass. The poor performance of students from these areas reflect a host of economic and cultural factors outside of school. Increasing spending on schools is one step toward greater educational opportunity for ghetto students, but many researchers now believe that programs to alleviate poverty and the social dysfunction that accompanies poverty are also needed to improve the academic performance of inner-city students.[5]

As a nation, we pride ourselves on the equal opportunity we offer our citizens. One of the most important means of ensuring equal opportunity is through our public school system. The public schools are meant to give all students the tools to survive and compete in our highly technological economy. If differences in spending per student are vast because of the way we finance our public schools, we do not have equal educational opportunities. If we do nothing about the underlying poverty that affects student performance in our inner cities, we do not have equal educational opportunities.

PROPOSALS TO IMPROVE OUR PUBLIC SCHOOLS

Many of us are dissatisfied with the performance of our public K–12 school system. We see the system as characterized by high dropout rates, inequality, and average student scores on achievement tests that have declined over time and now lag behind some other countries with which we compete economically. A number of experiments and proposals to improve our schools have been made recently. The two most common types of policy proposals would either increase the competition among schools or reform the tax system through which we support our public schools.

Policies to Increase Competition among Schools

Advocates of policies designed to increase competition among schools note that competition in product markets results in greater efficiency in production and allocation of resources. They argue, therefore, that measures to increase the competition among a city's schools can be expected to improve performance and simultaneously cut costs. Competition presupposes that consumers can choose among various suppliers. However, public education has traditionally operated on a take-it-or-leave-it basis: a student could either attend the public school in his or her school district or attend a private or parochial school. Traditionally, there have not been choices of public schools for students. Proposals to increase competition therefore aim to increase choice.

One means through which cities have increased the choices of students and their families is the establishment of so-called magnet schools. Magnet schools focus on some particular type of curriculum in an attempt to excel in that aspect of education. The city of St. Paul, Minnesota, offers magnet schools that focus on international business, the sciences, and the fine arts. Parents and students can choose any one of them, regardless of the school district in which they reside.

The major argument in favor of magnet schools is that if a school's specialty is desired by families and it does a good job of providing an education, the school's enrollment will grow; conversely, if a magnet school's specialization is in low demand or it does a poor job of educating, its enrollment will decline. Money to run the schools will depend on enrollment. The school with increasing enrollment will be allocated more resources. The budget of the school with decreasing enrollment will decrease. The net effect will be better performance of the educational system.

Opponents of magnet schools argue that some equalization of funding is needed before the concept is workable. Our poorest school districts, such as those cited in the Kozol case study, simply cannot compete. Furthermore, opponents point out that in cities that have experimented with magnet schools, the more popular schools close enrollment early because they run out of space, so students who want to enroll in them often cannot do so.

Another popular proposal to increase consumer choice is the tuition voucher. Each student would be given a voucher for some particular amount of money to apply toward tuition in qualified public *or* private schools. The student's family would choose the school it likes best. If parents were satisfied with their child's public school, they would use their voucher to keep their child in that school. Parents who are dissatisfied with the local public schools could enroll their children in private schools, and tuition could be paid with the voucher. Proponents of vouchers argue that the increased competition would be healthy for our educational system. We would tear down the financial barriers between public and private schools. Good schools should prosper, and really bad schools should go out of

WEB LINK

http://www.cato.org
This is the home page of the conservative think tank, the Cato Institute. It presents arguments for conservative positions on home schooling, school vouchers, and so on.

business. Opponents of vouchers, however, argue that voucher schemes endanger the existing public education system. Poor public schools would receive fewer resources and become poorer. Even bad schools in urban ghettos, they argue, are preferable to none. They fear that ghetto schools would close and either not be replaced or be replaced by bad private schools. Convincing middle-class taxpayers to allocate funds to rebuild the public schools would then be difficult. Finally, opponents argue that the consumers of education (students and their parents) are not sufficiently well-informed about educational options for a voucher system to result in an efficient market. School vouchers were an important issue in the 2000 presidential campaign. Support of vouchers was part of the Republican Party platform advocated by George W. Bush. Vouchers were opposed by the Democratic candidate, Al Gore, who argued that vouchers would endanger public education by siphoning off money from public schools.

Tax Reform: The Michigan Experiment

As we noted in our discussion of inner-city schools, property-tax financing of public education results in unequal spending per student and unequal tax burdens throughout states. Redistributing funds through state equalization measures and federal grants to poor school districts is one way to alleviate this problem. Tax reform is another.

In 1993, the state of Michigan changed the way it finances education, and the rest of the country is watching the results. If the Michigan experiment works, other states may follow. Here's how the Michigan experiment evolved.

Although Michigan was a national leader in economic growth and high living standards in the 1960s, it became an economic laggard in the decades thereafter. The primary reasons were the restructuring of the U.S. economy and profound changes in the automobile industry, on which Detroit's economy is based. High-paying jobs in manufacturing have disappeared, while lower-paying service-sector jobs have been created. It was argued that Michigan's high average property tax rate caused businesses to locate in other states.[6]

Michigan's average property tax rate was about 30 percent above the national average, but the property tax rates of school districts in the state varied. Businesses tended to locate in districts with low property tax rates, because lower taxes meant lower costs of doing business. These districts spent considerable sums per pupil on education, but their large tax bases enabled them to do so at low tax rates. At the same time Detroit, which in 1990 had a high property tax rate of 4.40 percent (compared with the national average rate of 1.67 percent), could not attract new business investment and was forced to postpone government expenditures of all types. Local spending per Michigan student ranged from $3,000 in property-poor districts, such as Detroit, to $11,000 in property-rich districts. The state needed to reform its tax laws to encourage economic development as well as to provide more equality in educational opportunity throughout the state.

Michigan's new tax plan replaces the property tax with a blend of tax sources to finance education. More specifically, the new law raises the state sales tax by 2 percent, increases the tax on cigarettes by 50 cents, and levies a new real estate transfer tax and a new 6 percent tax on out-of-state telephone calls.

This new tax scheme involves some redistribution of funds from rich to poor districts. Revenues raised from local property taxes are pooled and distributed to the schools by the state. Minimum per-student funding was increased from $3,000 to $4,200 the first year. High-spending districts may increase their spending per pupil only by a local referendum in which the citizens of the district vote to increase spending.

Property taxes to finance education were not fully eliminated, but locally determined rates were replaced by statewide tax rates that vary for different types of property. The new rates are, on average, lower than the property tax rate on businesses. Because the rates are the same throughout the state, businesses' locational decisions should not be distorted.

Critics of the Michigan plan argue that it threatens local autonomy. Local school boards have traditionally controlled public education. Critics fear that state funding will inhibit local choice. Proponents argue that something had to be done to attract business and equalize education throughout the state. Because the property tax burden is high and educational opportunities are unequal in many other states, these same arguments are heard elsewhere. If the Michigan experiment is a success, other states are likely to revise their tax systems.

POSTSECONDARY EDUCATION

U.S. postsecondary (higher) education consists of colleges, universities, community (junior) colleges, and technical-vocational schools. Some are private schools, not operated by the government. Many others are run by the states, and a few are operated by municipalities. These are our public schools. Virtually none of these schools, private or public, is free to the student as is K–12 education. Costs to the students and their families vary widely, however. The estimated average tuition plus room and board paid by a student in 1998–1999 at a four-year private institution was $19,970; the estimated tuition plus room and board at a similar public institution that year was only $8,018.[7] There is considerable variation around both averages.

Why are the costs of public institutions and those of private institutions so different? Is it because the cost to deliver education in private colleges is greater by a factor of more than two? The answer is no. Expenses of similar types of private and public schools are not that different. Table 10-1 shows educational and other expenses of public and private four-year colleges in 1995–1996.

Note that both types of colleges spend about the same per student on instruction, whereas public institutions spend more on research and less on student services than do private schools. Private schools spend more on administration and far more on scholarships to partially offset their higher tuition. But on average, total spending per student varies far less than tuition. What, then, is the explanation for the great difference in average tuition?

The answer to this question lies in the funding of the two types of colleges and universities. Private schools receive a large proportion of their income from tuition, whereas public schools receive a large proportion from state governments. Figure 10-3 shows funding sources for public institutions of higher education. In contrast,

TABLE 10-1 Educational and General Expenditures of Public and Private (Nonprofit) Four-Year Colleges, 1993–1994, per Student

EXPENDITURE	PUBLIC	PRIVATE
Instruction	$5,486	$5,593
Administration	$2,638	$3,481
Student services	$780	$1,512
Research	$1,351	$713
Libraries	$389	$475
Public service	$619	$655
Maintenance, etc.	$1,170	$1,395
Scholarships, etc.	$727	$3,032
Mandatory transfers	$242	$321
Total	$13,403	$17,177

Source: U.S. Department of Education, National Center for Education Statistics, *Digest of Education Statistics 1999,* Table 339 and Table 342, pp. 350 and 353.

FIGURE 10-3 Sources of Revenue for Public Institutions of Higher Education, 1995–1996

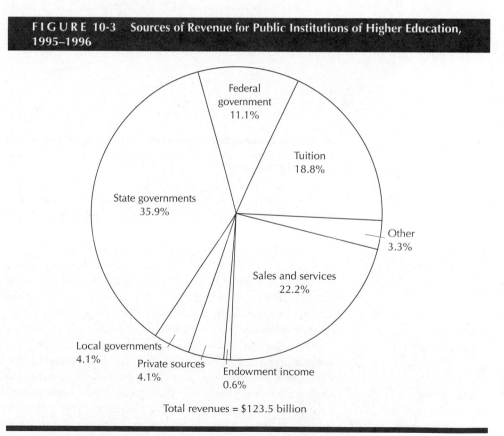

Federal government 11.1%

Tuition 18.8%

State governments 35.9%

Other 3.3%

Sales and services 22.2%

Local governments 4.1%

Private sources 4.1%

Endowment income 0.6%

Total revenues = $123.5 billion

Source: U.S. Department of Education, National Center for Education Statistics, *Digest of Education Statistics 1999,* Figure 18.

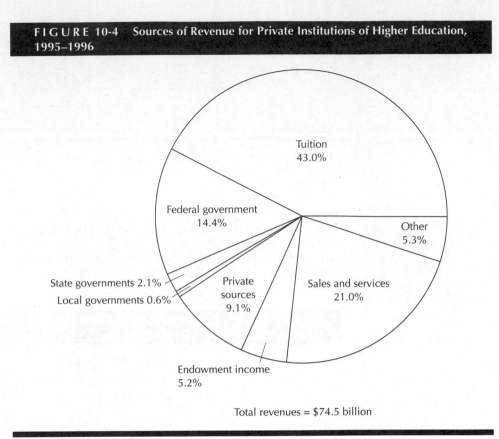

Tuition
43.0%

Federal government
14.4%

Other
5.3%

State governments 2.1%
Local governments 0.6%

Private
sources
9.1%

Sales and services
21.0%

Endowment income
5.2%

Total revenues = $74.5 billion

Source: U.S. Department of Education, National Center for Education Statistics, *Digest of Education Statistics 1999*, Figure 19.

Figure 10-4 shows funding sources for private institutions. The figures are for all types of institutions: vocational-technical schools and community colleges, four-year colleges and universities, and doctoral-granting research-intensive schools.

Note that the single biggest source of revenue for public postsecondary schools was state governments, which contributed about 36 percent of revenue. Tuition contributed only about 19 percent of the income of the public higher education system. Clearly, tuition does not cover the full cost of education in the public institutions, and states contribute a large share of those costs from tax revenues. Thus the states heavily **subsidize** public education. We will look at who receives subsidies later.

On the other hand, tuition is the major source of revenue for private schools, accounting for 43 percent of their income. These schools also receive some subsidies from government, but these payments account for a much smaller share of their revenues. Moreover, they have larger **endowments** than do public schools. Endowments are investments owned by the school that earn income for the school. Income from endowments accounts for more than 5 percent of revenues of private schools, but less than 1 percent of revenues of public schools. Private schools also receive greater income from private gifts, contracts, and grants than do public schools.

Subsidize
Pay part of the cost.

Endowments
Income-earning investments of a school.

The single most striking difference in the funding of public and private schools is the share of costs covered by tuition. Given that education is highly subsidized by the states in public universities, it is not surprising that 78 percent of the students enrolled in U.S. higher education in 1997 attended public institutions.[8]

EDUCATION, AN INVESTMENT IN HUMAN CAPITAL

Investment-in-human-capital theory
The theory that people invest in education in the same way that businesses invest in machines, by calculating the investment's return, or profit rate.

What we call **investment-in-human-capital theory** is the theory of many economists that spending on education can be explained as an investment made by the student (and the student's family) to increase skills and productivity and therefore income. Average income increases with more education whatever the worker's race, ethnic group, or gender, although disparities in incomes among these groups persist, as we discussed in Chapter Six. Table 10-2 shows median annual incomes for men and women who worked full-time, year-round in 1998. Note the systematic increase in median income for both groups as the level of education rises, as well as the lower incomes of women at all levels of education.

Obtaining an education costs money, as you know. But having an education and the increased skills and knowledge acquired in the process of getting that education makes you a more valuable worker. Therefore wages will increase as your level of education increases. The decision to bear the costs of obtaining your education is a decision to invest in your own skills and future as a worker, at least to some extent. Furthermore, students and their families consider many of the same variables that a business would consider if deciding whether or not to invest in new machinery or equipment.

In considering an educational investment we analyze the expected benefits and costs. The benefits are increased earnings throughout our working life subsequent to our graduation. The costs are both direct and indirect. Direct costs include tuition and fee payments, books and supplies, and all the other expenditures we

TABLE 10-2 Median Annual Income of Year-Round, Full-Time Workers 25 Years Old and Older, by Highest Level of School Completed and Gender, 1998

EDUCATIONAL ATTAINMENT	MEN	WOMEN
Total population, 25 and older	$37,906	$27,956
Less than ninth-grade education	$19,380	$14,467
Ninth through twelfth grade (no diploma)	$23,958	$16,482
High school or GED	$31,477	$22,780
Some college, no degree	$36,934	$27,420
Associate's degree	$40,274	$29,924
Bachelor's degree or more	$56,524	$39,786
Bachelor's degree	$51,405	$36,559
Master's degree	$62,244	$45,283
Professional degree	$94,737	$57,565
Doctor's degree	$75,078	$57,796

Source: U.S. Department of Education, National Center for Education Statistics, *Digest of Education Statistics 1999,* Table 386.

make to obtain a degree. Indirect cost is the opportunity cost of forgone earnings. (Recall from Chapter One that opportunity costs are forgone alternatives.) Because we are in school, we do not work—at least not full-time—so we give up earnings. Like our tuition payments, these forgone earnings are a cost. We will make the investment only if the expected increased earnings justify the total direct and indirect costs.

Figure 10-5 describes the decision variables. Pretend you are the decision maker. The horizontal axis represents your expected working life if you graduate from high school at the age of 18 and can expect to work until retirement at 65 years. We have assumed that you will attend college full-time until the age of 22 and then graduate, or not attend college at all. We further assume that you will not work while you are a college student, which is not the case for many students but which simplifies the discussion greatly. If you do not attend college, you will go to work in a relatively low-wage job after graduating from high school. Therefore annual earnings will be relatively low and increase only modestly as you gain job experience throughout your working life. Some income will be earned, however, during the four years subsequent to high school graduation.

If you attend college instead of working, those first four years' earnings will be given up, so they are part of your opportunity costs of obtaining a college education. The income given up to attend college is labeled "Indirect cost" in Figure 10-5. Direct costs will also be incurred. You must pay tuition and fees, buy supplies and

FIGURE 10-5   The Decision to Invest in College Education

The investment will be made only if the increase in lifetime earnings justifies the direct and indirect costs of education.

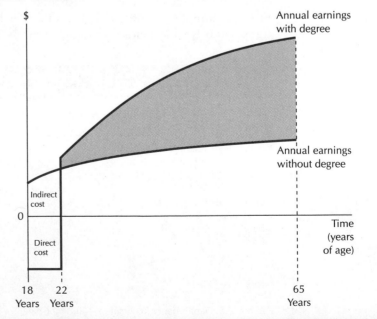

books, and pay board and room, which may be more expensive than living at home. The increase in living expenses is also a part of your costs as a student. The direct costs are shown by the area below the horizontal axis, because they are negative amounts, or money paid out.

After you graduate, you may go to work for only slightly higher earnings than you would receive had you simply worked since high school. But because you obtained your education, you will be more promotable. Employers put more educated employees into positions of greater responsibility. Furthermore, employers invest in more on-the-job training for educated workers than they do for uneducated workers. On-the-job training makes you a more valuable employee. You can reasonably expect your earnings to increase substantially as you establish yourself in your field. The *possibilities* are much greater if you graduate from college than if you do not. Therefore your annual earnings will be greater and the difference between what you earn and what you would have earned without the degree will increase over time. The total increased earnings over your working life are represented in the shaded area in Figure 10-5.

You compare the expected increased earnings to the costs of your college education. Alternatively, you may compare the increased earnings to other earnings that you might have accrued if you had invested your college costs in some other way, such as in an apprenticeship program or a vocational school. If you are a very sophisticated decision maker, you compute a **rate of return** on your investment, which is the cost of your college education. Then you compare the rate of return on your college education to the rates of return on other investments you could have made.

Rate of return
Profit rate computed by dividing profit by investment.

The preceding discussion is based on the assumption that you are a traditional student who entered college right after high school. In fact you may be a nontraditional, older student, and you may be a part-time rather than a full-time student. About 43 percent of students were 25 years old or older in 1997, and 42 percent attended college part-time.[9] U.S. colleges have diverse populations. For those of you over 25, the decision may be more complex because you probably have greater responsibilities and greater indirect costs, but it will be made on much the same basis.

Investment-in-human-capital theory has been criticized for being overly simplistic and for its implicit assumption that the only reason we obtain an education is to increase our lifetime earnings. Many of us obtain an education because we simply like to learn. We know that our life will be fuller and more intellectually rewarding if we are educated. In some disciplines we may not necessarily expect to earn a great deal more money with our degree, but we do hope to have a job that is more rewarding in its nonmonetary aspects. In short, our decisions have more dimensions than the theory incorporates.

Investment-in-human-capital theory does have considerable explanatory power, however. It offers an explanation for the young age of most people in college. First, young people have many years to earn the higher salaries that result from their education. The increased earnings over their lifetimes is therefore greater. Second, young people will have smaller indirect costs than older workers who have some labor market skills and who probably earn at least slightly higher wages.

This theory also helps us explain the effects of financial aid to students on enrollment in our colleges and universities. Financial aid decreases the students' direct costs, which makes the investment (and enrollment) more likely.

OTHER ISSUES IN HIGHER EDUCATION

At the present time, higher education is plagued by many economic problems. Costs have risen. State government support of public higher education has decreased, and as a result tuition in public institutions has increased greatly. Financial aid rules have changed, and Pell grants' values have been diluted. Colleges and universities have adopted various policies to cope with these problems, and students (especially, but not exclusively, students from low-income families) have had to cope with problems of access to our nation's public colleges.

Let's look at some issues related to state funding in higher education. First, we will look at who benefits from the state governments' tax support of public universities. Second, we will examine the trend toward decreasing government support of higher education. Third, we will analyze the possible use of different tuition for different programs to increase the efficiency of our colleges. Finally, we will look at financial aid programs, including the Pell grants intended to extend educational opportunity to poor students.

Who Benefits from the States' Tax Support of Public Postsecondary Education?

In most states, the public postsecondary education system consists of one major research institution (the flagship), a number of comprehensive universities, and a number of community (junior) colleges. The flagship institution is a major, doctoral degree-granting institution, whereas the comprehensive schools are principally four-year teaching institutions that may offer a few master's degree programs. The two-year community colleges offer associate's degree programs and serve as feeder institutions to the comprehensive schools. These two-year schools also offer remedial programs, and their cost is significantly lower than the cost of four-year schools. In most states vocational and technical schools are financed separately and are governed by a different board than is the university and community college system.

As you will recall from Figure 10-3, state taxes are the major source of income for these public school systems. Because the states contribute to the cost of operating these schools, tuition is lower than the full cost of educating a student. In other words, education is subsidized by the state government. Historically, the subsidy has been justified by the spillover benefits to the state of having an educated citizenry and by the concept of equal access to education. Americans believe in equal opportunity to earn a college education, and the state subsidy decreases the cost to students from low-income families.

The questions we now want to investigate are: Who are the students that attend our public postsecondary schools? Are they from low- and middle-income families? Do high-income students attend private schools? Financial aid records answer these questions.

In 1993, a study was done to determine the family income of freshmen in our public and private schools.[10] Financial aid regulations in that year established that students from families whose income was below $22,000 were classified as full-need students, entitled to aid for the entire college budget of the school they attended. Students from families with income above $67,000 were classified as no-need students, eligible for no aid. Students from families with incomes between these two extremes were entitled to partial aid.

Examination of the distribution of freshmen in public research universities (the flagships) revealed that only 12.2 percent were full-need students, and that 37.5 percent were no-need students. Only 17.4 percent of the public four-year college (comprehensive universities) freshmen were full-need students, and 28.3 percent were no-need students. More of the two-year community college freshmen were from low-income families (28.8 percent), and fewer (27.4 percent) were no-need students. These figures indicate that most of the students in public universities and colleges come from high- or middle-income families and that more low-income students attend our community colleges. We may still justify the government subsidy of education by its social spillover benefits, but *most of the students we are subsidizing are not from poor families.*

Decreasing State Government Support for Public Higher Education

As we noted above, state support of public higher education has decreased. Indeed, the proportion of state spending that goes to postsecondary education has decreased almost every year since 1982. Furthermore, until 1999, state appropriations for higher education have declined as a percent of the personal income of the states.[11] These changes represent a change in social values and spending priorities. At the state level, higher education has been squeezed out by increased spending on Medicaid and prisons, which are discussed further in Chapter Nine and Chapter Thirteen, respectively.

As state spending on higher education has decreased, U.S. public universities and colleges have reacted in various ways. One of the most common reactions has been to cap enrollments. Furthermore, virtually all of our states have increased tuition significantly. Let's look at each of these policies.

Enrollment Caps

Enrollment caps

A maximum limit on the number of students allowed to enroll in a school.

An **enrollment cap** is a maximum limit on the number of students allowed to enroll in a school. In order to maintain relatively low faculty/student ratios, reasonably small class sizes, and other widely accepted measures of quality in a time of declining state education budgets, many state college systems have instituted enrollment caps.

Once established, enrollment caps will generally decrease enrollment to some specified level over time, necessitating rationing of openings. A common way to accomplish this task is to increase admission standards. Raising the cutoff score on the ACT or the PSAT college entry tests or increasing the minimum high school class rank for entry into the college system will eliminate a number of students who would have been admitted in the past. This measure has the advantage of eliminating students who might have been poor risks for completion of college, rather than simply excluding students at random. On the other hand, it might eliminate "late bloomers," who achieve mature study habits in college instead of in high school. At any rate, enrollment caps serve to reduce access of the general public to publicly supported education.

As more students graduate from high schools and seek to enter the public university system, there is pressure on the system to become more efficient and to move students speedily through the educational pipeline, so that a backlog of those desiring entrance does not build up. There is pressure on the system and especially on specific popular programs. After a certain level of class overcrowding in these programs is reached, schools tend also to limit entry into these particular programs, because they simply do not have the resources to allow students into them. There is pressure on students to graduate in the minimum amount of time, or with the minimum number of credits, so that their places will be open to entering freshmen.

Raising Tuition

When state tax funds decrease, an obvious reaction is to increase tuition to make up the missing funds. Over time, tuition revenues must cover a larger share of the costs of the public institutions. As a result, tuition has increased substantially. Average public four-year in-state tuition rose by 105 percent between 1989 and 1999.[12]

Quite obviously, tuition levels affect access to the university system. Some students simply cannot afford the higher tuition unless they can obtain greater financial aid to offset their higher educational costs. Equally obviously, the students who feel the negative effects most are from low- and middle-income families.

Different Fees for Different Programs

There are tremendous pressures on U.S. universities and colleges to become more efficient. Greater efficiency would enable schools to meet student needs at lower cost and therefore hold down tuition to an affordable level. One suggestion has been to charge different tuition for different programs to increase efficiency.

One problem that universities face is that they are slow to react to changing demands for programs. To attract quality faculty to the university, the institution has made a commitment to tenured faculty in particular disciplines. The school has acquired physical facilities that are needed for a particular program and may be inappropriate for most other uses. Yet demand for particular programs varies over time. Schools' adjustments to these changes in demand take time, and while the adjustment is taking place efficiency decreases. There may be either surpluses or shortages of class sections in particular majors.

A number of years ago, there was a great deal of discussion in higher education about charging higher tuition for very popular, growing majors and lower tuition for declining majors. You will probably recognize this discussion as an exercise in demand and supply analysis, and you are right. Consider the following situation. A school has a pre-law program, which is growing rapidly. Influenced by the popular television show "The Practice," many freshmen are declaring pre-law majors. At the same time, interest in the school's philosophy major is declining. Tuition and fees are the same whether you major in pre-law or philosophy. Figure 10-6 illustrates this situation.

Assume that the school's tuition is $3,000 and that the school would supply classes for 300 majors in either program at that tuition (price). But the number of students demanding the pre-law major (quantity demanded) at that tuition is 600. So there is a shortage of 300 slots for pre-law majors at the $3,000 tuition. In fact, the shortage is not so obvious, but it is felt in greatly increased class size in the pre-law major. It is observed in closed classes and bottlenecks in students' programs. Students cannot graduate in four years, because they cannot get the classes they need. The demand is simply beyond the school's capacity to meet it.

Now look at the graph for the philosophy program. Here again, the school will supply classes for 300 students at the uniform $3,000 tuition. But demand is so low that only 100 philosophy students enroll. There is a surplus of philosophy classes available. This surplus will be felt in very small classes and inefficient use of university resources. To help alleviate the problem, some philosophy professors may become part-time administrators or participate in a program to advise students who have not yet decided on majors.

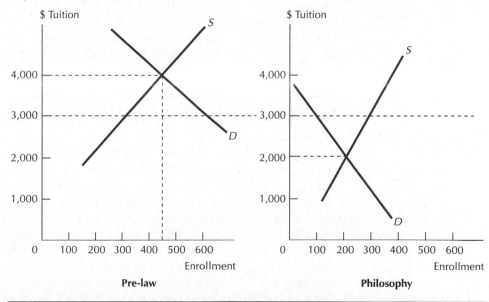

FIGURE 10-6 Improving Resource Allocation by Charging Different Tuition for Different Programs

At uniform tuition ($3,000), there will be a shortage for pre-law students and a surplus for philosophy students. Different tuition ($4,000 and $2,000) eliminates the shortage and surplus and improves resource allocation.

Now assume that the school increases the tuition in the pre-law program to $4,000, the equilibrium price. The shortage will be eliminated, and the school will have an equilibrium number of 450 pre-law majors. Because the school receives extra tuition, it can hire part-time faculty to teach more sections of pre-law courses, and pre-law students will encounter fewer bottlenecks.

Simultaneously, the school lowers the tuition to $2,000 for philosophy majors. At $2,000, philosophy attracts 200 majors (quantity demanded), and the surplus is eliminated. Classes are a reasonable size, and resources are used more efficiently. Differential tuition has greatly decreased the school's resource allocation problems.

You may be somewhat skeptical. You might wonder why a student would change majors just because the tuition was lower. Or you might think it is unfair to charge different tuition for different programs. You might not believe that schools could adjust tuition precisely enough to achieve a really efficient allocation of resources. And indeed the educational community has had the same reservations, so there has been little experimentation with different tuition for different programs.

There has been some experimentation with user fees, however. As state funding has decreased, schools have instituted various fees in an attempt to increase their revenues. Some fees are, in fact, surcharges designed to discourage students from entering overcrowded majors or to cover the costs of providing majors that require expensive supplies and equipment.

Now for the good news! The economy's healthy condition at the end of the millennium resulted in significantly increased state support of higher education for the first time in many years. Fiscal year 1999 state **appropriations** to higher education were $52.8 billion, which amounted to 12 percent of the states' total spending.[13] This increase represented an increase of 6.5 percent over 1998, and it was also the largest amount ever budgeted by the states for higher education. Furthermore, this increase represented a small (12.09 percent to 12.11 percent) increase in the percentage of the states' budgets that went to higher education. If this reversal of the long-term trend toward decreased state appropriations continues, students can expect smaller tuition increases in the future.

Appropriations
Monies authorized by a legislative body to be spent for certain purposes.

Financial Aid: Does It Give Us Equal Access to Higher Education?

Financial aid is available through many sources to help low- and middle-income students bear the costs of education. For most students, aid comes from a combination of programs, including grants and loans. According to the Bureau of the Census, in 1993–1994 about 61 percent of postsecondary students received some kind of financial assistance to help them pay for schooling. They received, on average, about three-fourths of their expenses, though in many cases the aid was in the form of loans that must be repaid. The proportion of students receiving aid declined as family incomes rose, with 72 percent of students from low-income families receiving aid and only 49 percent of students from high-income families receiving aid.[14] Black students were more likely than either white or Hispanic students to receive aid, but white students received larger amounts of aid than either Hispanics or blacks.

Conservatives favor policies to increase competition in our public K–12 system, whereas liberals emphasize tax reform and the redistribution of tax dollars from rich to poor districts to equalize educational opportunities. Therefore conservatives favor school voucher systems to give parents and students more choices of schools and curricula. Liberals, on the other hand, fear that widespread use of school vouchers would endanger our public school system by transferring funds from the poor schools that need them most.

Both liberals and conservatives usually believe that providing universal education through the high school level is a legitimate government role, given basic education's demonstrated spillover benefits to society. Conservatives do not in general favor extensive tuition subsidies or financial aid, however, unless spillover benefits can be shown to result from postsecondary education. Liberals are more likely to favor expanded financial aid to low-income students, as well as tax credits for educational purposes. Conservatives are more likely to favor general tax cuts instead of tax credits for specific purposes.

Aid comes in many forms: scholarships and fellowships, employer assistance, veterans' assistance, college work study, loans, and Pell grants. The program in this list that is the foundation of the financial aid package for students from low-income families is the Pell grant. Targeted to poor students, this grant is not received by high- and middle-income students. Although the Pell grant program was targeted to students from the lowest-income families when the first grants were awarded in 1974, eligibility criteria have been liberalized over the years, so now students from less-poor families receive some grants. The Pell grant has never covered all costs for poor students. Other forms of aid have been added to financial aid packages to help the neediest students meet educational costs. Now the most common aid package for those students is a Pell grant and a loan. More important, the Pell grant has lost considerable purchasing power in the last 20 years. In 1979 the maximum possible Pell grant was $1,800, which covered 77 percent of the average costs at a public four-year college. In 1998 the maximum Pell grant had risen to $2,700, but that $2,700 covered less than 40 percent of costs at such a school.[15] To meet the remainder of the costs, students must take out correspondingly larger loans. The Pell grant program appears to have veered from its original focus. It is available to a wider range of students than originally intended, but its value to these students is significantly less.

A new element in aid for higher education is the Clinton Administration's Hope and Lifetime Learning Tax Credits program. Families with incomes as high as $100,000 qualify for the credits, which are not refundable. That means that families so poor that they do not pay income taxes will receive no tax credit. Thus, these tax credits are not a vehicle for financing the education of very-low-income students.

Tuition subsidies of our state universities and financial aid packages help students meet the direct costs of higher education. But these policies do not address the indirect cost of education in the form of forgone earnings from work. Low- to middle-income students may not be able to afford the opportunity cost of these forgone earnings, because they and their families count on this income for survival.

All students do not have equal access to our institutions of higher education. First, you need to graduate from high school before attending college, and we have seen that all Americans do not have an equal chance to graduate from high school. Income is the major factor in determining who goes to a good high school with a high graduation rate, and low-income students are more likely to attend poor high schools with high dropout rates. Second, the state subsidizes tuition by financing a large share of the construction and operation of public postsecondary schools, but this support benefits all students who attend public postsecondary schools, most of whom are not students from low-income families. Third, the value of Pell grants to really poor students has declined over time, and financial aid is not adequate to enable students from very-low-income families to afford college. Finally, the opportunity cost of education in the form of forgone earnings while attending school prevents many low-income persons from obtaining higher education.

SUMMARY

Funding our public elementary and high schools primarily from local property taxes results in extremely unequal spending per student. As a result, underfunded schools have inadequate facilities, high student/teacher ratios, unstaffed classrooms, and various other inadequacies. Underfunded high schools have very high dropout rates, and their graduates receive a poor education. State tax revenues somewhat alleviate this inequality, but many experts feel that we need to move away from property-tax financing to some other form of funding. Simply increasing funding to schools in areas of concentrated high poverty appears to be ineffective in improving student outcomes. In these areas we also need programs to alleviate poverty.

Our postsecondary school system consists of vocational-technical schools, community colleges, four-year colleges, and universities, both public and private. Public schools have lower tuition than private schools, because the states subsidize them. Nearly 80 percent of American postsecondary students attend public institutions. Our public higher education system benefits mainly upper- and middle-income families, not low-income families. Decreasing state support, rising tuition, and the decreasing value of Pell grants have worsened problems of access to higher education for both low- and middle-income students.

NOTES

1. U.S. Department of Education, National Center for Education Statistics, *Digest of Education Statistics 1999*, Table 33,

2. Much of this discussion is taken from Jonathan Kozol, *Savage Inequalities: Children in America's Schools* (New York: Harper-Collins, 1992). See specifically pages 58–59, 69, and 225.

3. Margaret E. Goertz, "The Finances of Poor School Districts," *Clearing House* (November–December 1994), pp. 74–77.

4. James Traub, "What No School Can Do," *The New York Times* (January 16, 2000, late edition).

5. See Traub, "What No School Can Do," and Denise C. Morgan, "The Less Polite Questions: Race,

Place, Poverty and Public Education," in *Annual Survey of American Law* (New York: New York University School of Law, 1998).

6. The principal source for the material in this section is the *Chicago Fed Letter* (Chicago: Federal Reserve Bank of Chicago, May 1994).

7. U.S. Department of Education, *Digest of Education Statistics 1999*, Table 317.

8. U.S. Department of Education, *Digest of Education Statistics 1999*, calculated from data in Table 170.

9. U.S. Department of Education, *Digest of Education Statistics 1999*, calculated from data in Table 177.

10. Thomas G. Mortenson (ed.), *Postsecondary Education Opportunity*, March 1994, pp. 3–8.

11. Mary McKeown-Moak, *Financing Higher Education: An Annual Report from the States* (http://www.sheeo.org/Other/finance99.htm).

12. Mary McKeown-Moak, *Financing Higher Education: An Annual Report from the States.*

13. Mary McKeown-Moak, *Financing Higher Education: An Annual Report from the States.*

14. Jennifer Cheeseman Day and Kristine Witkowski, *Financing the Future: Postsecondary Students, Costs, and Financial Aid,* U.S. Census Bureau Current Population Report P70-60, November 1999, pp. 5–6.

15. Thomas G. Mortenson (ed.), *Postsecondary Education Opportunity,* January 1998, p. 11.

DISCUSSION QUESTIONS

1. *How do spillover benefits distort the allocation of resources to education? Can you think of other examples of goods with spillover benefits?*

2. *Draw a graph indicating how negative externalities or spillover costs would (1) result in a lower price of a good when its production creates the spillovers, and (2) cause overallocation of resources. (Hint: refer to Figure 3-1.)*

3. *How does property-tax funding of K–12 education create inequality? Consider your response in terms of both the tax rate and the tax base. What can be done to create greater equality?*

4. *What could be done to help inner-city schools other than providing them with more funding?*

5. *How would charging different tuition for different majors improve the allocation of a school's resources? Do you think this measure would be a good one?*

6. *Who benefits from public higher education? Why do middle- and low-income students encounter problems as they seek access to higher education?*

7. *Consider the following. Joe is deciding whether or not to go to college full-time. If he does not attend college, he will continue to work at his present job. Joe earns $14,000 annually. He estimates that tuition and fees at the local public college will be about $10,000 per year and that he can graduate in four years if he does not work. The starting salary in the field he hopes to enter is about $30,000, and he estimates that he will earn about $600,000 more in his working lifetime with a college degree than without one. What will be Joe's opportunity cost of four years of college? What will be his net benefits (benefits minus costs)? Should he make the investment in education?*

8. *Go to the Census Bureau Web site (http://www.census.gov). Click on E for education. Find the latest data for the percent of the population that has a high school degree and the percent of the population with a bachelor's degree.*

CHAPTER 11

Housing

I have to make the choice of whether to have a house with no gas or light, or have gas and lights . . . with no home to live in.

From *In Our Own Words: Mothers' Perspectives on Welfare Reform*[1]

Housing, like food, is a commodity that has special connotations for many of us. Shelter from the elements is a basic biological need, and most of us see adequate housing (however defined) as a basic right. We are concerned, and often confused, about the homeless. We worry that low-income families (such as the family headed by the woman quoted above) cannot afford to rent houses or apartments in our cities. We realize that the single largest investment most U.S. families make is the purchase of their home. And we regard home ownership as an essential part of the American dream. We wonder if young families just starting out will be able to afford to buy a home. We know that the federal and many state governments have developed policies to promote home ownership and access to adequate housing, but we often do not know details about these policies. In this chapter, we will look at the housing market in the United States.

We will begin by looking at issues involving home ownership, affordability, and government policy with regard to ownership. We will then turn our attention to low-income housing and measures that are intended to ensure that poor families have access to adequate housing. We will look at the economic consequences of housing segregation. Finally, we will discuss the problem of the homeless among us.

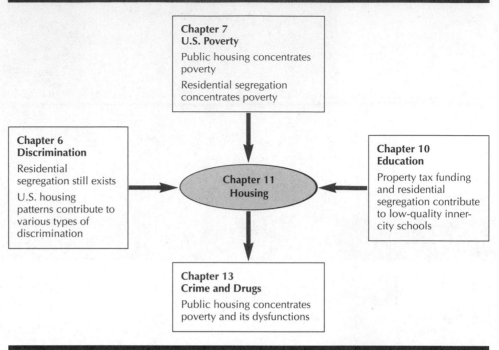

Chapter 7
U.S. Poverty

Public housing concentrates poverty

Residential segregation concentrates poverty

Chapter 6
Discrimination

Residential segregation still exists

U.S. housing patterns contribute to various types of discrimination

Chapter 11
Housing

Chapter 10
Education

Property tax funding and residential segregation contribute to low-quality inner-city schools

Chapter 13
Crime and Drugs

Public housing concentrates poverty and its dysfunctions

HOUSING MARKETS: IS HOME OWNERSHIP WITHIN OUR REACH?

http://nar.realtor.com/ research/home.htm This site presents data on housing values in various regions and cities.

Although we tend to speak of *the* housing market in the United States, there exist a great many markets for housing within our country. There are markets for single-family dwellings, duplexes, and multifamily dwellings such as cooperatives and condominiums. If you live in a college dormitory, that building is part of the broader housing market. Market conditions vary greatly with geography and the socioeconomic characteristics of different locations. These markets are subject to the forces of supply and demand, as are other markets. Thus the price of the average residence, as well as its size and other characteristics, varies with the location of the house. Homes in areas with healthy economies and growing populations tend to gain in value over time, whereas the value of houses in depressed regions with declining populations goes down.

Figure 11-1 illustrates this concept. Assume that the two graphs are for houses with the same size and quality characteristics in two cities, Detroit and Atlanta. Detroit, part of the so-called Rust Belt, is a city in decline. Factories and jobs have moved out of Detroit to other cities and other countries. Unemployment is high, and many workers have left the area. Atlanta, on the other hand, is enjoying a boom. Companies are locating in this Sun Belt city, and workers are moving in as jobs are created. The declining population in Detroit results in a decreasing

FIGURE 11-1   Regional Differences in the Price of Housing

The decreased demand for housing over time in Detroit will cause the price of housing to fall, whereas the increased demand in Atlanta will cause housing prices to rise.

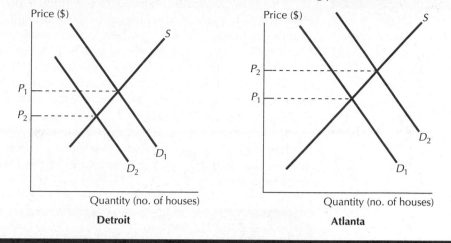

Detroit   Atlanta

demand for housing, whereas the growing population in Atlanta results in an increasing demand for housing. Thus the two cities will be subject to opposite shifts in the demand for housing. In each graph demand will shift from D_1 to D_2. This change amounts to a decrease in demand in the Detroit area and an increase in demand in the area around Atlanta. As a result of the demand shifts, the equilibrium market price of housing will change to P_2 in each of the diagrams. The price of similar housing in Detroit will be lower than in Atlanta.

Really large differentials in housing prices can occur as the result of long-term growth trends in particular areas. The economy and the population of the southern California region grew rapidly in the period following World War II. Housing prices escalated until, in the 1980s, houses in southern California cost three or four times as much as similar houses in the Midwest. With the post–Cold War defense cuts of the early 1990s, which threw the California economy into a severe recession, the regional housing demand slackened and housing prices began to decline. With the current economic recovery, these prices have risen again.

Trends in Housing

When the U.S. Bureau of the Census first surveyed housing in the United States in 1940, the median (middle) value of nonfarm owner-occupied homes was $2,938 and the median rent was $27.28 per month. A majority of Americans (56.4 percent) were renters.[2] In 1999 the median value of existing U.S. housing units was $133,100, and the median rent was $785 monthly, and 67 percent of us were homeowners.[3] Obviously the 1940 and the 1999 figures are not directly comparable. If, however, we adjust the 1940 figures to account for inflation between 1940 and 1999 by using the consumer price index, we will have comparable figures. In

1999 dollars, the median value of homes was $35,319 and the median rent was $327.94 in 1940. In real terms, the value of the average U.S. home has increased fourfold, and rent has more than doubled.

The U.S. Census Bureau has noted that in the 50 years between 1940 and 1990, the U.S. housing inventory grew from 37 million units to 107 million units. The major housing problem in 1940 was the poor condition of our housing stock: 31 percent of units had no running water; 18 percent needed major repairs; 44 percent had neither a bathtub nor a shower; and 35 percent had no flush toilet in the structure. These deficiencies no longer exist; in 1990, 99 percent of all housing units had hot and cold running water, toilets, and a bathtub or shower. Our major concern now is the affordability of housing.[4]

If we focus only on the past quarter-century, we see that the cost of new housing has risen more rapidly than household income. Table 11-1 contains data on the median (average) price of new houses in the United States, as well as median household income.

TABLE 11-1 Median Sales Price of New Housing Units and Median Household Income, 1970 and 1998			
YEAR	MEDIAN SALES PRICE OF NEW HOUSING UNIT	MEDIAN HOUSEHOLD INCOME	HOUSING PRICE/ INCOME RATIO
1970	$ 23,400	$8,734	2.68
1998	151,300	38,885	3.89

Source: U.S. Department of Commerce, Bureau of the Census, *New One-Family Houses Sold,* 1999 (www.census.gov/cgi-bin/briefroom/BriefRm).

The last column of the table shows the ratio of the housing sales price to household income. In 1970 the median price of new housing units was only 2.68 times the median household income, whereas in 1998 it was 3.89 times the median household income. On average, households must spend almost an entire year's additional income to buy a new house now than they did 30 years ago. This statistic leads us to question whether the average American family can now afford a single-family home.

It should be noted, however, that houses being built now are not only larger than those built in 1970 but also different in other ways. They are nearly three times as likely to have two stories as the homes built in 1970. They are more than twice as likely to be air-conditioned and nearly twice as likely to have fireplaces. Table 11-2 on page 243 summarizes these changes.

Indeed, quality changes between the houses built in 1970 and those being built today are significant. Many of these new structures may have been built for middle-aged baby boomers who are "stepping up" to larger, more prestigious dwellings, selling their former residences to younger, less-affluent families.

Factors Influencing the Affordability of Housing

Will you be able to afford a house when you are ready to buy one? What factors determine families' monthly house payments if they do buy a house? The elements

TABLE 11-2 Characteristics of New Privately Owned One-Family Homes Completed, 1970 and 1998 (all figures in percentages)

	1970	1998
Size (floor area)		
<1,200 square feet	36	7
>2,100 square feet	21	50
Average square feet	1,500	2,190
Number of stories		
One	74	48
Two or more	17	50
Split-level	10	2
With central air conditioning	34	83
With one or more fireplaces	35	61

Source: U.S. Department of Commerce, Bureau of the Census, www.census.gov/ftp/pub/const/C22

that must be considered in analyzing the affordability of home ownership are (1) the down payment, (2) monthly mortgage payments, and (3) the buyer's income and debt. Let us look at each of these elements.

The Down Payment and Other Expenses at the Time of Purchase

Down payment

Amount of home buyer's own money required by the lender for the purchase of a home.

Mortgage insurance

Insurance that pays off a mortgage if the borrower defaults.

Points

Fees charged by a lender at the time it grants a mortgage.

Usury laws

Laws establishing a maximum legal interest rate.

Closing costs

Expenses paid at the time that a loan is finalized and the title is conveyed to the buyer.

The **down payment** is the amount of the buyer's own money that must be paid at the time of the purchase. A standard mortgage usually requires a 20 percent down payment, which means that the buyer must "put down" 20 percent of the purchase price at the time of the purchase. For those eligible, a housing loan from the Federal Housing Administration requires only a 10 percent down payment. Finally, some new houses are sold with only 5 percent down payments. These homes are seen as good investments, and the lender assumes that they can easily be resold if it is necessary to foreclose on the loan. Older housing usually is sold with traditional mortgages that require the higher down payments. As a general rule, lenders require buyers who pay less than 20 percent down to purchase **mortgage insurance.** Mortgage insurance protects the lender if the buyer defaults on the loan.

In addition to the down payment, the buyer must make other payments at the time of purchase. These payments include mortgage **points,** which are fees charged by lenders at the time they grant mortgages. Points are like interest in that they are a charge for borrowing money. One point equals one percent of the amount borrowed, so if you were to pay one point on $100,000, you would pay $1,000.

Lenders typically use both the interest rate and points to establish the charges for lending you money. Lenders might be willing to give you a lower interest rate if you pay more points, or they might charge more points if you make a smaller down payment. In some localities, laws have been passed that establish a legal maximum interest rate. These laws are called **usury laws.** In these localities, points are often used to offset the low interest rates that can be legally charged.

Closing costs refer to the total expenses, including points, that buyers pay at the time that the loan is finalized and the title to the property is conveyed to them.

The closing cost is money you must come up with if you are to buy a house. Closing costs include loan application fees, points, title search fees and title insurance, attorneys' fees, appraisal fees, and other miscellaneous charges.

Monthly Mortgage Payments

The monthly mortgage payment is made up of payments on the principal (unpaid balance) of the loan plus interest payments. For most of the life of the loan, more of the monthly payment goes to pay interest charges than to repay principal. The amount of interest paid over the life of the loan is extremely sensitive to the length of the loan. Table 11-3 illustrates this fact. The table shows the monthly payments for an 8 percent conventional mortgage loan of $50,000 to be paid over 10 years, 15 years, 20 years, and 30 years. The borrower will pay 8 percent annually on the unpaid balance of the loan, and the amounts by which the unpaid balance is reduced is much smaller if the payments are stretched out over a longer period of time. The monthly payment is the amount that the buyer must pay if the $50,000, plus 8 percent interest, is to be paid in the stated number of years. The total paid is the monthly payment times the number of payments, and the interest paid is the difference between the total payments and the $50,000. Note that a 30-year conventional mortgage involves the payment of nearly four times as much interest as a 10-year conventional mortgage.

The mortgage payment will increase with the amount borrowed and with the interest rate charged by the lender. Therefore an increase in the average price of housing units or in the interest rates charged by lenders will increase the homebuyer's monthly payments.

In the late 1970s we experienced an extremely high rate of inflation, or increase in the average level of prices. Both housing prices and the interest rates charged by lenders for long-term loans increased markedly. The housing market was stifled by the high interest rates. Many potential buyers could not afford the monthly payments at the high rates of interest. Lenders did not want to tie up funds for 30 years because the interest rate they could receive on other loans or investments might increase significantly in that time period. Lenders therefore began issuing **variable rate mortgages,** which are still used quite widely. On a variable rate mortgage loan, a rate is established for a period of time, such as two or four years. When the time is up, the buyer can either renew the mortgage at the current market interest rate or pay the remainder of the loan off.

Variable rate mortgages
Mortgage loans on which interest rates are periodically adjusted.

TABLE 11-3 Monthly Payments on a $50,000 Mortgage, Various Lengths of Loan				
	10 YEARS	15 YEARS	20 YEARS	30 YEARS
Monthly payment	$606.65	$472.85	$418.25	$384.50
Number of payments	120	180	240	360
Total paid	$72,798	$86,013	$100,380	$138,420
Principal	50,000	50,000	50,000	50,000
Interest paid	$22,798	$36,013	$ 50,380	$ 88,420

Property taxes and homeowner's insurance are sometimes part of the monthly payment of the borrower. **Property taxes** are levied by local governments to fund services such as education and police protection. These taxes are generally a given percentage of the approximate market value of real property (land and buildings) within the community, so more expensive houses will bear more property taxes. **Homeowner's insurance,** which covers the replacement cost of the house and its contents, may be required by the lender to protect itself in the event of natural disaster. Monthly payments toward insurance and property taxes are sometimes required by the lender. These payments are placed in a temporary escrow account from which insurance and taxes are paid when due.

The Income and Debt of the Buyer

Most lenders require that prospective borrowers satisfy affordability guidelines. The most common affordability criterion is that monthly mortgage payments not exceed 25 to 30 percent of the borrower's before-tax income; total monthly installment payments—for example, auto loans and charge card payments—cannot exceed 33 to 38 percent of before-tax income. The prospective homebuyer's monthly income is therefore an important factor in determining whether the family can afford to buy a particular home.

In addition to income, debt is an important factor in a family's ability to purchase a house. Credit cards "maxed out" or other consumer debts may prevent a buyer from meeting mortgage lenders' guidelines.

Who Can Afford to Buy a House?

The Bureau of the Census periodically issues reports on the affordability of homes in the United States. It considers that three factors may prevent a household's affording a home: (1) insufficient cash for the down payment and closing costs, (2) insufficient income to afford the monthly mortgage payments, or (3) too much debt to qualify for a mortgage.

A 1995 Census Bureau report revealed that 44 percent of American households could not afford to buy a modestly priced home (defined as a house priced higher than 25 percent but lower than 75 percent of the houses in the same area). The most common reason that current homeowners could not qualify for a mortgage on a modestly priced home was that their debt was too high. Renters usually did not qualify due to more than one of the three reasons above. The report found that houses are most affordable in the Midwest and least affordable in the West. Far more whites can afford the modestly priced home than can racial and ethnic minorities. More than 75 percent of single-parent families with children under 18 cannot afford to buy the modestly priced home.[5] Not surprisingly, the same groups that are overrepresented in the poverty statistics discussed in Chapter Seven are less likely to be able to afford home ownership than other groups. The Census study implies that it is not a foregone conclusion that American families can afford the single-family dwelling that is part of the American dream.

It should be noted that neither the material discussed here nor the Census Bureau study considers alternative types of housing such as mobile homes and condominiums, which have both increased as a percentage of our housing stock.

In 1990, 7 percent of all U.S. housing units were mobile homes. Both the average income and the average age of mobile home owners was lower than the average income and average age of the population at large.[6] The obvious inference is that some young families are buying mobile homes as starter homes.

Government Policy toward Home Ownership

A number of state and federal policies promote home ownership. The Federal Housing Administration (FHA) insures home loans that allow mortgage applicants to spend a higher percentage of their income on housing and debt payments than conventional mortgage guidelines require. In addition, applicants can finance part of the closing costs, including points and the mortgage insurance premium. Use of FHA-insured loan guidelines rather than conventional mortgage guidelines reduces the percentage of Americans who cannot afford to buy a house. These mortgages, therefore, benefit lower-income applicants. In practice, however, a smaller percentage of new homes are now financed with FHA-insured mortgages than in the past. In 1970, 30 percent of new homes were financed by FHA-insured loans. In 1998 the figure had decreased to 8 percent.[7] In part this change is due to the FHA's raising of standards for homes of acceptable quality. Realtors now describe the agency as "nitpicking," and many realtors steer buyers away if possible.

Far more important, the federal income tax code promotes home ownership by permitting the deduction of mortgage interest payments from income before personal income taxes are calculated. This deduction benefits mainly middle- and higher-income households, however, because higher-income households, on average, buy more expensive homes and also pay personal income taxes at higher tax rates. On the other hand, low-income households buy less expensive homes and are far more likely to rent than to own, in which case they will receive no interest deduction on their federal income taxes.

The income tax deduction is a housing subsidy for middle- and upper-income classes, not for the poor. The value of the mortgage interest deduction was $51.7 billion in 1998. To put this figure into some sort of perspective, the government spent $28.7 billion on housing assistance for low-income families that same year.[8]

HOUSING LOW-INCOME FAMILIES

Some families cannot afford, or may not want, to buy a house. The availability of low-cost, adequate quality rental housing for low-income families is therefore important. Since 1970 the percentage of income that renters spend on housing has increased, as rental prices have increased far more rapidly than wages and other income. A recent report by the Department of Housing and Urban Development (HUD) indicates that in 1997 and 1998, rents increased at twice the rate of general inflation, while the number of affordable rental units decreased by 372,000 units between 1991 and 1997.[9]

The high price of rental housing results from the interaction of demand and supply. Figure 11-2 shows the changes that have taken place over time in the market for relatively low-cost rental housing. The shift of supply from S_1 to S_2 is a

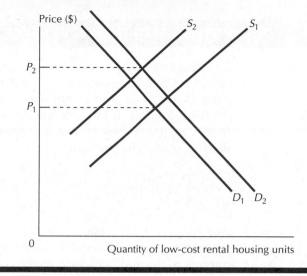

FIGURE 11-2 Trends in the Market for Low-Cost Housing Units

The reduced supply of low-cost housing and increased demand for it have resulted in higher-priced and less-affordable housing for low-income families.

Gentrification
Conversion of low-cost apartments into middle- and upper-middle-class housing.

decrease in supply. Some people trace the decrease in the supply of affordable housing units to the development of superhighways and urban renewal in the 1950s. Both of these programs destroyed thousands of low- and moderate-rental units in the name of urban development. Indeed, some pundits renamed the phenomenon of urban renewal "urban removal," because the poor tenants who had formerly lived in the "renewed" areas could no longer afford to live there. More recently, the process of **gentrification** has further reduced the supply of low-cost housing as traditional low-cost rental units have been restored and converted into middle- and upper-middle-class properties. The conversion of apartment buildings into condominiums throughout our cities has further decreased the supply of rental housing. In addition, some of our cities are experiencing a process of disintegration. Housing units have been abandoned and vandalized. Public housing stands vacant due to a lack of funds for upkeep and modernization. All of these factors have reduced the supply of adequate, low-cost housing.

The demand for low-cost rental housing has also increased over time. Part of the increase is the result of population growth. Part results from the growth in the number of poor and near-poor families as the income distribution has become more unequal, as we discussed in Chapter Seven. Both the increase in demand and the decrease in supply have caused the price of so-called low-cost housing to increase, as is shown in Figure 11-2. The final result is a housing affordability crisis for poor families—a crisis that is worse in some regions than in others.

The search for affordable rental housing has become more difficult for poor families. The high rental prices obviously harm the well-being of low-income families, because when families spend a large percentage of their incomes on housing, little remains for food, clothing, and other necessities. One result is that low-income families are often crowded into older housing units that have physical problems. Another result is an increase in homelessness.

PROGRAMS DESIGNED TO HOUSE THE POOR

Rental ceiling (rent control)
A legally set maximum rent on an apartment.

One measure used to assist low-income households is **rental ceilings** or **rent controls,** by which the government establishes a maximum rent for certain housing units. Other programs to help the poor obtain affordable rental housing can be divided into programs to increase the supply of low-cost housing and programs to enable the poor tenant to acquire (demand) higher-quality housing. Let us look at all three options individually.

Rental Ceilings

During World War II, we had a national system of rental ceilings. After the war, only New York City retained its rental ceilings, but during the 1970s a number of other cities, many of them "university towns," adopted such measures. Some cities considered, but did not adopt, rental ceilings.

Suppose that your school is located in College Town, which has adopted rental ceilings. Most college students are low-income people, and there is often a great demand in college towns for reasonably priced off-campus student housing of acceptable quality. At the same time, towns dominated by colleges often have landlords who buy up old houses and rent them to groups of college students, charging exorbitant rents. Therefore you might initially be much in favor of controlling the rents that landlords could charge you. But let us consider the consequences of rental ceilings.

Administered prices
Prices regulated by the government.

Rental ceilings are examples of **administered prices,** which are prices regulated by the government rather than set by supply and demand in the market. Rental ceilings are just one example of a broader category of administered prices called price ceilings. Price ceilings were discussed in Chapter Eight in the context of food price ceilings in less-developed countries. (Other examples of price ceilings are discussed in the appendix to this chapter.) To be effective (which means to matter in the market), price ceilings must be below market equilibrium prices. Because prices are not free to rise above some specified maximum, price ceilings interfere with the rationing function of price. As we discussed in Chapter One, markets tend to clear at an equilibrium price and quantity, and in the process shortages and surpluses are rationed away. This is the rationing function of price in a competitive market. Because rent prices cannot rise above the rental ceiling to the equilibrium price, they cannot perform a rationing function. Therefore they actually create a shortage.

Figure 11-3 shows the effects of the rental ceiling on the hypothetical rental market in College Town. Before the rent controls are imposed, the equilibrium rental market price is $500 per month and the equilibrium quantity of apartments is 100. The local government establishes a rental ceiling of $400 to help poor tenants, including struggling students. Initially, nothing much happens except that

FIGURE 11-3   Market Effects of Rental Ceilings in College Town

The rental ceiling of $400 creates a shortage of 40 apartments in College Town.

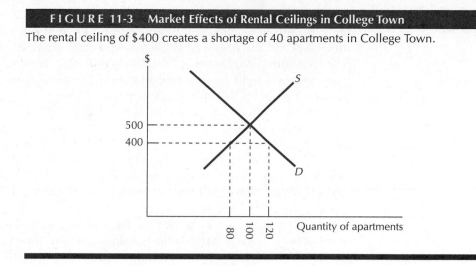

tenants pay lower rents and landlords receive lower rents. But as time passes, both prospective tenants and landlords adjust to the rental ceiling. Because they are receiving lower rents, landlords have less incentive to provide rental housing, and they move down their supply curve until they are supplying only 80 units at the rental rate of $400. They do this by abandoning units that need repairs, demolishing some units so the land can be used for commercial purposes, and converting some units to other uses such as condominiums. Meanwhile, the quantity demanded of these apartments increases to 120, because at the low rent, more people desire to live in rental housing. Young adults may move out of their parents' houses, students may move off campus, and people living with roommates may seek their own apartments. There is a shortage of 40 rental units in College Town. And it is a shortage that the market cannot ration away, because the rental price cannot rise above $400 to reach the market equilibrium.

Rental ceilings produce some gainers and some losers. Obviously the original tenants in the rent-controlled units gain. They stay there and pay lower rents. Those who move into rent-controlled units also gain, because their rents are lower than they would be without the controls. But households that cannot find an apartment in College Town because the controls exist lose. And the landlords lose in two ways. They receive lower-than-market equilibrium rents; and if they sell their buildings, they will receive lower prices, reflecting the lower income generated by the properties.

Over time, rental ceilings have other effects. Landlords do less routine maintenance, and the properties deteriorate more rapidly. In effect, landlords let the apartments deteriorate until they are worth only the lower rent. Because of the housing shortage, landlords also can afford to be choosy about who they accept as tenants. Therefore they may refuse to rent to college students, pet owners, families with children, or racial minorities.

The rent-controlled units that are in good repair are a real bargain, encouraging development of illegal markets. Units might be subleased at rates higher than the rental ceilings. Alternatively, landlords may require large payments, perhaps in the form of huge damage deposits, before they rent out their property. Both the subleasers and the prospective tenants who make up-front payments to obtain the rent-controlled apartments are usually middle-class families, rather than the poor. A program to help low-income households afford decent rental housing has become a program that subsidizes the middle class.

Rental ceilings are generally intended to help the poor, which certainly include many college students. In the end, however, the poor are probably the group harmed the most by rent controls. They have fewer choices. They cannot afford to buy homes. They cannot afford to move out to the suburbs. They cannot afford the huge security deposits needed to move into a rent-controlled apartment in good repair. They are likely to continue to be crowded into substandard, over-priced housing or to become part of our nation's homeless.

Rental ceilings are attractive on the surface, but they cause shortages and a deteriorating stock of affordable housing. Because they benefit the poor house-holds for which they were intended less than they benefit higher-income house-holds, rental ceilings are an inefficient method for providing affordable rental housing to low-income families.

Programs to Increase Supply

Public Housing

The oldest and perhaps best-known program to supply low-income housing is **public housing,** which began in 1937. Constructing public housing was justified initially as a means to create employment during the Great Depression of the 1930s. Public housing units are owned and operated by a local public housing authority, but the units are federally subsidized and often federally regulated. The federal government establishes the eligibility requirements for tenants and the ratio of rent relative to income that will determine what the individual tenant will pay for housing. The current rent/income ratio is .30, which means that the tenant will pay 30 percent of his or her monthly income as rent.

Currently about 1.3 million Americans live in public housing, but the public housing program is criticized because it tends to concentrate poor and distressed populations in particular areas. It may also segregate people both racially and by income level. Thus life in the "projects" has become synonymous with poverty, social dysfunction, and high crime rates.

Much of the political support for public housing over the years has come from the construction industry. Indeed, the whole program was terminated under President Nixon's administration in 1973, which was a boom year in the construction industry. The program was then reactivated in 1976, when the bottom had fallen out of the construction market. Moreover, several studies have shown that public housing is an expensive method to house the poor. Public housing units cost more than either new private housing units or used low-income housing. Therefore the availability of public housing is limited. Many eligible families remain on waiting lists for years. Furthermore, some economists argue that public housing displaces private housing, causing the latter to be abandoned or converted to other purposes because the supply of public housing units causes the market price of available private housing units to fall. The private landlords then either retire some of their units or use them for other purposes. Public housing is an increasingly controversial policy, so let us look at other methods to house the poor.

Subsidies to Developers

Subsidies to developers
Government payments to landlords who build housing for the poor.

One alternative method is the provision of **subsidies to developers** to encourage them to build, or convert other property to, low-income housing units. The major federal program of this type is the Section 8 project-based program that began in 1975. This program pays landlords the difference between the rental payments received from tenants and the market rent that the landlord would otherwise receive. A **fair market rent** for each unit is established and guaranteed to the landlord. The fair market rent is an amount determined by the Department of Housing and Urban Development to be a reasonable rent for low-income housing in a given area. The eligible tenant's rent is then set at 30 percent of the tenant's income. The government pays a subsidy equal to the difference between the fair market rent and the actual rent paid by the tenant to the landlord. Thus if an eligible low-income family has income of $600 per month, it could rent an apartment in the Section 8 building at $180 per month (30 percent of $600). If the fair market rent for the apartment is $500, the government will pay an additional $320 to the landlord as a subsidy. Initially, landlords were required to sign 20-year contracts to provide Section 8 housing. Now many of the original contracts are expiring, and HUD is signing contracts for a shorter duration. A current concern is that many of the original 20-year contracts will not be renewed and that these nonrenewals will decrease the supply of affordable housing for the poor. The Section 8 program has led to the construction of moderately priced housing. Studies of both public housing and subsidies to developers, however, indicate that one of the biggest gainers is the construction industry, rather than the poor. As with public housing, waiting lists for these housing units are often long.

Fair market rent
Amount determined by HUD to be reasonable rent for low-income housing.

Programs That Affect Demand

Supply-side policies help the poor by providing more low-income housing in the rental market. Another way to help low-income households would be to give them subsidies and to let them choose their own housing. These subsidies increase the poor families' ability to express their demand for housing in the private housing market.

Housing (Rent) Vouchers

Housing voucher
Housing subsidy in the amount of the difference between fair market rent and 30 percent of a poor family's income.

The principal demand-side housing program is the **housing vouchers** program, which is also part of the Section 8 housing program. Most housing vouchers go to very poor families. Recipients must occupy a dwelling that meets minimum government standards. The housing vouchers are based on the difference between the fair market rent for the locality and 30 percent of the tenant's income. If the fair market rent for an apartment is $450 and the family's income is $700, the voucher will be in the amount of $240 ($450 – 30 percent of $700). The family will receive this housing voucher based on its income even if it rents an apartment with a lower actual rent. If the family moves, it takes the voucher with it. The number of Section 8 housing vouchers was frozen between 1995 and 1998 but recently has begun to increase again.

These demand-side housing subsidies initially cause the price of low-cost housing to increase, but over time landlords supply more units. They increase maintenance on their dwellings and upgrade lower-quality housing to participate in this housing submarket.

Many economists prefer demand-side subsidies to the supply-side methods of aiding low-income families to obtain housing. Demand-side subsidies actually increase the private supply of low-cost housing units, whereas public housing appears to decrease that supply. The demand-side subsidies are paid directly to low-income households rather than to developers or construction firms, and some argue that the benefits thus are more certain to go to the intended group, our low-income families.

Adequacy of Current Programs and New Directions for Policy

Although 3 million U.S. families are helped by one or the other Section 8 program, housing activists maintain, and government officials acknowledge, that there is simply not enough money available to provide adequate housing for all our ill-housed poor and near-poor families. Many families eligible for housing assistance receive no aid, because budget constraints do not permit assistance for all qualifying families. Fiscal appropriations for assisted housing decreased throughout most of the 1990s as we strove to balance the budget, and appropriations only began to increase again after 1998.

Henry Cisneros, HUD secretary in the first Clinton Administration, vowed to replace money, which is simply not available, with innovation. He therefore initiated many small and inexpensive programs, most on an experimental basis. One of the more promising is the conversion of some of the hundreds of thousands of housing units owned by the government to low-income housing. The government acquired many of these units as the result of foreclosures in federal insurance and loan programs such as the Federal Housing Administration's. HUD's goal is to make these units available to families of low and modest means.

HUD also expanded a program to sell property obtained by the government in the savings-and-loan crises of the late 1980s. Since 1990, HUD has sold more than 20,000 single-family homes obtained from the Resolution Trust Corporation (RTC) to families of modest means. The Resolution Trust Corporation is the agency responsible for selling off the assets of failed savings and loan institutions. Approximately 600 apartment buildings from the RTC have been sold to public agencies, nonprofit organizations, and other owners that agree to rent at least 35 percent of the units to low- and very-low-income families.

The problem with these creative attempts to provide affordable housing to the poor is that the RTC and other government-owned housing units are often not located where the need for such housing is greatest. Furthermore, even though rents on RTC apartments are usually set quite low, they are still too expensive for the very poor in high-cost municipalities such as New York, Boston, and San Francisco.

Many regard the RTC program as a model program, but HUD is also guilty of great waste and inefficiency. Probably the most obvious example was its role in promoting so-called welfare hotels for the homeless, which we will discuss shortly in the section on homelessness.

HOUSING SEGREGATION

The problem of racial segregation in housing in the United States is serious. Fifty-five percent of blacks and 48 percent of Hispanics live in our central cities. Blacks make up 23 percent of the central-city population in the United States but only about 8 percent of the population in the suburban areas surrounding these cities. Hispanics represent 18 percent of the central-city population but only 10 percent of the population of the suburban ring.[10] A relatively recent study indicates that areas that have countywide desegregation plans, mainly in the South, have slowly become more racially integrated. But inner cities heavily populated by minorities and surrounded by a ring of white suburbs experience persistent racial segregation, especially those cities with a history of racial antagonism.[11]

Index of dissimilarity
Measure of segregation.

Segregation occurs not only between the central city and its suburbs, but within central cities as well. Several indexes have been developed to measure the extent of segregation within central cities. The one most commonly used is the **index of dissimilarity.** This index is calculated by adding together the differences between the percentage of blacks and the percentage of whites living within each district of the city and dividing this sum by two. The reason we divide by two is that if segregation were to be reduced, a two-way move would have to take place. A white person would have to move into a black area, replacing a black person who would move into a white district.

To illustrate the calculation of the index of dissimilarity, assume that a city consists of two equal-size districts. In District 1 live 80 percent of all blacks and 20 percent of all whites. The difference in the district is 60 percent, or 60. In District 2 live 20 percent of all blacks and 80 percent of all whites. Again the difference is 60. To calculate the index, add together the differences and divide by two, as follows:

Difference in District 1	60
Difference in District 2	60
Sum	120
120 divided by 2	60

If there were no segregation, 50 percent of both blacks and whites would live in District 1, so its difference would be 0. The same would be true of District 2, in which the remaining 50 percent of each race would live. The index of dissimilarity would therefore be 0. On the other hand, if we had total segregation, with 100 percent of blacks in District 1 and 100 percent of whites in District 2, the index would be 100. The index of dissimilarity will vary between 0 and 100, and the higher it is, the greater is residential segregation.

In 1990, cities with particularly high values included Detroit (88), Milwaukee (83), and Cleveland (85).[12] In some other cities, the index of dissimilarity has declined as blacks have moved to the suburbs and whites have moved back into the cities. Researchers Douglas S. Massey and Nancy A. Denton note, however, that the index of dissimilarity is a measure that understates residential segregation. They note that blacks who move from central cities usually go to segregated suburbs. Their moving to the black suburb therefore would decrease the index of dissimilarity for the central city without decreasing segregation. Furthermore, they note that black residential areas that are contiguous with other black residential areas represent greater segregation than black residential areas that touch on white residential areas. When the dissimilarity indexes are adjusted for these factors, Massey and Denton argue that a third of U.S. blacks live under conditions of intense residential segregation.[13]

Housing segregation, in combination with the labor market discrimination discussed in Chapter Six, serves to isolate minorities, especially African Americans, who are the most strictly segregated of all minorities. Isolation puts blacks at an economic disadvantage. They live in the ghetto, and the jobs are usually in the suburbs. They have neither information about who is hiring nor easy access to work sites by means of public transportation. African American poverty rates are significantly higher than the poverty rates of whites. Therefore poverty is concentrated in the ghetto. These circumstances guarantee that poor blacks have a markedly inferior economic environment than do poor whites. Concentrated poverty leads to family instability, crime, welfare dependency, housing abandonment, and low educational attainment. The housing stock of the inner cities deteriorates. The public schools are seriously underfunded, and the quality of public education is exceedingly poor. (This issue was discussed in Chapter Ten.) In short, segregation contributes to the isolation and impoverishment of U.S. minorities. An underclass is created.

HOMELESSNESS IN THE UNITED STATES

http://4homeless.
hypermart.net
This site provides links to information on homelessness and programs for the homeless.

By the very nature of homelessness, the homeless are difficult to count, so estimates of their number vary widely. The National Law Center on Homelessness and Poverty, an advocacy group for the homeless, estimated in 1999 that as many as 2 million people are homeless in a year in the United States.[14] Homeless people live on the street, in abandoned buildings, in homeless shelters, and in welfare hotels. The homeless population is diverse. Some homeless people are women and children fleeing abusive relationships. Some homeless people are teenagers running away from dysfunctional families. But the fastest-growing group of people without homes is families with children, who are now thought to represent about 40 percent of the homeless. The homeless include entire families, single parents with children, single men and women, and children (usually teenagers) living alone.

The most common stereotypes suggest that many homeless persons are alcoholics, drug addicts, or the mentally ill. Some of the homeless do fit into these categories, but many others are people very much like us, only poorer. Many of our families are just one or two paychecks away from homelessness. If an emergency (such as the loss of a job, death or desertion of a spouse, or serious illness) occurs, our savings may not be adequate to pay the rent or the mortgage.

Our government policy since the 1970s has been to deinstitutionalize mental health care. So we have released many mentally ill patients from public mental hospitals. At the same time, government has not allocated the funds needed to support community-based mental health services such as halfway houses. Many deinstitutionalized patients have joined the ranks of the homeless. Others come to be homeless because their substance abuse is so severe that they simply cannot hold a job or pay rent on an apartment.

Still others are homeless simply because they cannot afford housing in the area in which they live. As low-quality housing is renovated to rent to middle-class tenants, the very poor are often displaced. Their former residence may have been substandard housing and a blight on the city, but it was housing they could afford. Its renovation decreases the housing stock available to the poor.

Unemployment may be a consequence of homelessness. Holding down a job when you are primarily concerned about where you and your family will sleep is difficult. Homelessness may also be a consequence of unemployment. Losing a job and the income it represents can cause a poverty-level family to lose housing because it can no longer pay the rent.

Probably the most desirable way of leaving the ranks of the homeless is to find a job that pays enough for rent on a housing unit. But searching for employment is difficult, if not impossible, for homeless people. It is hard to present yourself well if you do not have bathroom facilities available to you, let alone washing machines and ironing boards. The homeless also have neither an address nor a phone by which prospective employers can contact them.

Homelessness compounds the problems of poverty. Homeless children often do not attend school, or attend school sporadically. Homeless parents have difficulty keeping their children clean and appropriately dressed for school. The children are often malnourished as well as homeless, and malnourishment leads to difficulty in learning. Studying and doing homework while homeless are obviously far more difficult than studying and doing homework in a supportive environment. Thus homeless children face great burdens that keep many from succeeding in school, a prerequisite to rising out of poverty as an adult.

Government Policy Concerning the Homeless

Homeless advocates argue that we have no coherent, long-run policy concerning the homeless. Instead, we react in an ad hoc way to perceived emergencies. When the temperature drops in our northern cities, we worry that the homeless will die of exposure. If a tragedy occurs, such as the 1993 death of a homeless woman in a bus-stop shelter across the street from the Washington headquarters of HUD, we initiate emergency programs designed to put the homeless in shelters run mainly by private charities or into controversial and expensive welfare hotels.

Welfare hotels are hotels that have seen better days. They no longer are attractive to travelers or middle-class renters, but local departments of Health and Human Services use them to temporarily house the homeless under emergency conditions. Under the discontinued Aid to Families with Dependent Children (AFDC) program, the Department of Housing and Urban Development reimbursed local human services departments for 50 percent of the cost of such housing. HUD

Housing policy is one area in which the conservative and liberal viewpoints are quite clearly delineated. The conservative position is that government participation in housing markets should be eliminated, or at least minimized. Thus conservatives would encourage the transfer of public housing units to the private sector (private tenants or landlords) and eliminate subsidies to the construction industry. Consistently conservative economists would also eliminate the mortgage interest deduction, although many conservative politicians regard this deduction as the equivalent of a sacred cow. (Politicians who argue for the repeal of cherished middle- and upper-class tax breaks seldom get reelected.) If it is necessary to aid poor families to obtain shelter, conservatives favor such measures as rent vouchers, which allow poor families to afford housing in the private sector. Their principal argument is that the market is more efficient in solving housing problems than is the government.

Like conservatives, many liberals favor rent certificates and rent vouchers to help the poor. Unlike conservatives, however, liberals are more likely to stress government's role in solving housing problems. They see homelessness as a problem that government should treat by building public housing and temporary shelters. Liberals are not unconcerned with efficiency, but they stress that government's involvement in housing markets may be necessary to increase poor people's access to housing.

therefore contributed to the growth of the so-called welfare hotel strategy. HUD and the local agencies both concede that conditions in the hotels are deplorable, but welfare agencies may pay as much as $3,000 a month to house a family in decrepit hotel rooms. The "temporary" housing may stretch into a stay of more than six months. To the extent possible, most localities use alternative shelters.

Housing advocates, and some economists, argue that the country needs a comprehensive housing policy that includes both emergency shelters and permanent low-cost housing. They argue that our reactive policies, such as the welfare hotel strategy, are both inadequate and wasteful. They believe that we must devise policies to prevent homelessness, rather than using so-called Band-Aid treatments once the problem occurs.

SUMMARY

The housing market is in fact many markets, which differ by region, type of housing, and other characteristics. The cost of the median single-family dwelling has increased more rapidly than average family income over the past 25 years, leading to concern about housing's affordability. Census data indicate that many American households cannot afford the modestly priced single-family home in their area. Whites and two-parent families are more likely to be able to afford the median-priced home than are minorities and single-parent families.

Policies to aid low-income households in obtaining shelter included rental ceilings, supply-side policies such as public housing and subsidies to developers, and demand-side policies such as rent certificates and housing vouchers. Rental ceilings create shortages of housing. Supply-side policies benefit both the construction industry and low-income households. Demand-side policies appear to benefit low-income families and to encourage the provision of low-cost and moderate-cost housing units by the private sector.

Residential segregation remains a problem in the United States. It leads to a disadvantaged economic environment for minorities in this country.

The problem of homelessness is complex and only partially related to a scarcity of low-cost housing. Housing advocates argue that we need a cohesive, long-run strategy to attack the problem, instead of the reactive strategies we now have.

NOTES

1. These words, and the words of other women throughout the text, are actual quotations of women who were involved in a project of the Women and Poverty Public Education Initiative, funded by the Charles Stewart Mott Foundation. The source is *In Our Own Words: Mothers' Perspectives on Welfare Reform,* The Women and Poverty Public Education Initiative, 1997. Major portions of the report were prepared by Laura Wittmann, Anne Statham, and Katherine Rhoades as well as Loretta Williams, Jean Verber, Julie Elliott, Selina Vasquez, Kathe Johnson, Nancy Bayne, Ethel Quisler, May Kay Schleiter, Diana Garcia, Iredia Seiler, Mary Ellen Lemke, Michelle Graf, Bets Reedy, Jean Radtke, Kim Noyd, Susan Taylor-Campbell, and Davida Alperin. (Quotations may contain slight grammatical alterations made by the authors.)

2. Nancy E. Schwenk, "Trends in Housing," *Family Economics Review,* March 1991, p. 14.

3. U.S. Department of Commerce, Bureau of the Census, http://www.census.gov/hhes/housing/hvs/annual99/ann99t12.html and http://www.census.gov/hhes/www/housing/soms/qtr100t2.html

4. U.S. Department of Commerce, Bureau of the Census, *Tracking the American Dream—Fifty Years of Housing Changes,* SB94–8.

5. Howard A. Savage, *Who Can Afford to Buy a House in 1995?,* U.S. Bureau of the Census, Current Housing Reports, H121/93–3 (Washington, DC: U.S. Government Printing Office, 1995).

6. U.S. Department of Commerce, Bureau of the Census, *Mobile Homes,* SB 94–10.

7. U.S. Department of Commerce, Bureau of the Census, *Statistical Abstract of the United States, 1999,* Table 1201.

8. U.S. Department of Commerce, Bureau of the Census, *Statistical Abstract of the United States, 1999,* Table 548 and Table 549.

9. Department of Housing and Urban Development, *The Widening Gap: New Findings on Housing Affordability in America* (http://www.hud.gov/pressrl/afford/afford.html).

10. Calculated from Congressional Information Service, U.S. Department of Commerce, Bureau of the Census, "Mobility and Region of Residence, by Race and Hispanic Origin," *Current Population Reports,* 2000.

11. "News Roundup: Nation: Housing Segregation Declining in U.S. Cities, Study Shows" *Education Week,* March 2, 1994, p. 4.

12. David Rusk, *Cities Without Suburbs* (Washington, DC: Woodrow Wilson Center Press, 1993), p. 28.

13. Douglas S. Massey, and Nancy A. Denton, *American Apartheid* (Cambridge, Mass.: Harvard University Press, 1993), p. 77.

14. National Coalition for the Homeless, NCH Fact Sheet #2, February 1999 (http://nch.ari.net).

1. *What are the factors that affect a family's ability to afford housing? According to the Census Bureau study cited in this chapter, what was the major factor that made American households unable to afford the modestly priced home in their area in 1995?*

2. *Describe the effects of rental ceilings. Who benefits from rental ceilings? What are the long-run effects of rental ceilings? How can landlords and tenants cheat on rental ceilings? Do you think that rental ceilings might lead to more discrimination against certain groups?*

3. *What two groups are the primary beneficiaries of public housing and subsidies to developers?*

4. *How are rent certificates and rent vouchers different? If we had only so much money for housing assistance, would we be able to help more families under rent certificates or under vouchers?*

5. *Should we subsidize housing for each of the following groups?*

    a. *homeless families*
    b. *low-income families*
    c. *middle- and upper-income families*

Do we subsidize these groups? How?

6. *Do you take the conservative or the liberal position on the issue of housing?*

7. *How many paychecks away from homelessness is your family? What would you do if disaster struck and you (or your family) lost your income? Would you rely on savings, relatives, or friends? What if none of these resources were available to you?*

8. *Go to the Web site of the National Association of Realtors (http://nar.realtor.com). Click on the data bank and find the most recent value of the average existing home.*

Chapter Eleven Appendix:
Price Ceilings

Y ou may never have lived in rent-controlled housing, but some real-world examples of price ceilings have almost certainly affected you and your family. Let's consider some of these price ceilings.

THE PRICE OF FOOTBALL TICKETS

Your school probably has a football (or basketball, hockey, or baseball) team that you, your fellow students, and even college alumni follow. Imagine that your team is having an exceptional year. All seating is filled to capacity. In fact, many fans who want to attend games cannot get tickets. To obtain tickets, you either have to stand in line for hours or have some "connection" allowing you to receive preferential treatment.

Such a situation is shown in Figure 11-4. Note first that the supply curve is vertical (perfectly inelastic). There are 20,000 seats in the football stadium, so whatever the price of football tickets is, there will be 20,000 tickets available. Quantity will not change, no matter what happens to price. The demand curve for tickets, however, has the usual downward slope, implying that more people are willing and able to buy tickets if the price is lower. If the market were allowed to operate by itself, an equilibrium would occur at a price of $9 and the quantity 20,000. There would be no shortage of football tickets.

But let's assume that the school administration sets a price for football tickets of $5, which administrators believe to be a fair and appropriate price for sports tickets. After all, the administrators do not want to unduly burden students and

FIGURE 11-4   The Market for Football Tickets

The $5 price ceiling for football tickets results in a shortage of 10,000 tickets.

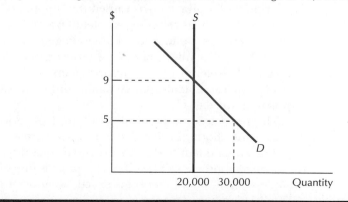

alumni with high ticket prices. They want only to bring in enough ticket revenue to cover the team's costs.

The $5 price operates like a price ceiling, because the price is set below the equilibrium level. Thirty thousand fans demand the $5 tickets. But there are only 20,000 seats available, so only 20,000 fans will be able to obtain tickets. There is a shortage of 10,000 tickets in the market.

Without intending to do so, the school administration created an inefficient market. Fans were given an over-incentive to buy a football ticket, and a shortage was the natural result. In addition people wasted hours standing in line, and those with "connections" became angry. If the price of tickets were allowed to rise to the $9 level, these conditions could have been avoided.

GASOLINE PRICE CEILINGS

If you did not drive in the 1970s, ask your parents about the gasoline shortage that occurred. They will undoubtedly tell you about long lines of cars trying to reach gas pumps and about gas stations closing early because they had sold all their gasoline. Some gas stations sold only to their established customers and turned away strangers. Many customers were unable to purchase gasoline. Other customers continually "topped off" their almost-full tanks whenever they had a chance. We got up early to wait in line, spent a lot of time looking for gas, worried about shortages of gas, and were extremely frustrated by the situation. If ever a market were inefficient, it was the 1970s U.S. gasoline market.

Problems in the gasoline market were closely related to problems in the market for petroleum. In the early 1970s, many Arab governments initiated a boycott on petroleum products sold to the United States. This was known as the Arab Oil Embargo. It effectively reduced oil supplies headed toward the United States. At almost the same time, the 13-member Organization of Petroleum Exporting Countries flexed its economic muscles by reducing the world supply of crude oil. The natural result of these actions was a dramatic increase in the price of crude oil. Prices went from $2.50 per barrel in the fall of 1973 to $10 per barrel in the spring of 1974. Consequently, prices of petroleum products, including gasoline, also skyrocketed. Because oil-based inputs are central to many production processes, the higher prices for oil products caused the supplies of virtually all manufactured and agricultural products that use petroleum products in their production to decrease. These declining supplies caused prices in general to rise, resulting in inflation.

Again in 1979, oil supplies were reduced as Iran cut off its supplies to the United States. Petroleum prices jumped again, and gasoline prices rose as well. Gas shortages became acute. Once again, inflation was the political and economic problem of the day.

The restricted supplies and resulting high prices of petroleum did not *cause* the gasoline shortages. If price is free to increase, equilibrium will occur at the point at which quantity demanded equals quantity supplied, and there will be no shortage. A shortage will result only if price is prevented from rising to the equilibrium level. This phenomenon is exactly what occurred in 1973–1974 and again in 1979. Price ceilings on petroleum and petroleum products existed throughout this

FIGURE 11-5   The Effect of a Gasoline Price Ceiling

The effective price ceiling on gasoline results in a shortage of gasoline.

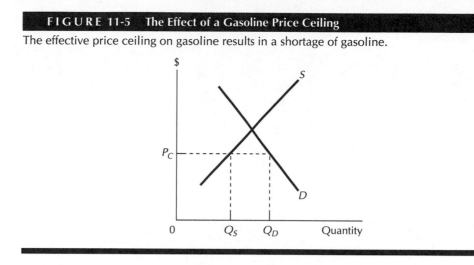

period. These ceilings became effective (that is, had an effect on the market), however, only when the market prices of petroleum products rose above them. (As long as the market price remains below a price ceiling, the government prohibition against charging prices too high cannot have an impact. Price simply remains at the equilibrium level.) When gasoline prices skyrocketed in 1973–1974 and again in 1979, the price ceilings became effective and encouraged suppliers to under-supply at the same time they encouraged consumers to over-demand. The shortage depicted in Figure 11-5 was the result.

Would it have been better to simply allow the higher gasoline prices to exist? Certainly the market would have been more efficient; quantity demanded would have equaled quantity supplied, and no shortages would have been created. But the high gasoline prices might have created problems for low-income consumers. Gasoline is a necessity to those who must drive to work. Can you think of any better ways to ensure that low-income commuters had the necessary gasoline?

YOUR SOCIAL
SECURITY CARD
WHAT TO DO WITH YOUR CA

DEPARTM
HEALTH, EDUCATION, AND WE
SOCIAL SECURITY ADMINISTRATION

CHAPTER 12

Social Security

Let us say to all Americans watching tonight—whether you're seventy or fifty, or whether you just started paying into the system—Social Security will be there for you.

William Jefferson Clinton, *State of the Union Address,* 1998

The United States Social Security system, and the associated Medicare health insurance system, affect us all. If we work, we pay Social Security and Medicare taxes. If we become disabled, we will be able to collect benefits from the Social Security Administration. If our spouse dies, we may be able to receive benefits for ourselves and our surviving children from the Social Security Administration. When we retire, we will collect retirement benefits from Social Security. Retirement probably seems impossibly far away for most of you, but you undoubtedly have relatives who are retired, and they receive Social Security checks on the third of each month (unless their Social Security is automatically deposited to their bank account). You may sometimes worry about the future of the Social Security system, and you may worry whether it will be there for you when you finally retire.

Entitlement
Payment to which eligible citizens have a right by law

A Social Security payment is an **entitlement,** or a payment to which eligible citizens are given a right by U.S. law. Entitlements are a huge share of the federal budget, and because these payments are mandated by law, they are outside the discretionary control of Congress. The only way payments can be decreased is to change the law that entitles citizens to them. In the current political atmosphere, in which cutting federal government expenditures appears to be of paramount

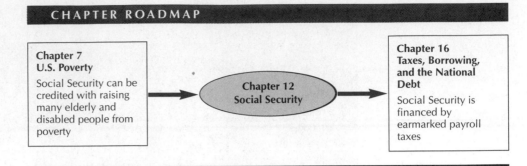

Chapter 7
U.S. Poverty
Social Security can be credited with raising many elderly and disabled people from poverty

Chapter 12
Social Security

Chapter 16
Taxes, Borrowing, and the National Debt
Social Security is financed by earmarked payroll taxes

importance, discussion of entitlements and the laws that govern entitlements is both loud and emotional. Social Security and Medicare are therefore controversial. Because Social Security receives so much media coverage, it is one of those programs about which most of us have an opinion but little knowledge to back it up.

In this chapter we will describe the Social Security program as it now exists and look at some of the problems and controversial issues that surround it. We will also discuss the probable future for the program.

SOCIAL SECURITY: A SOCIAL INSURANCE PROGRAM

The Social Security Act of 1935 established the Social Security program. Widespread unemployment, hunger, poverty, and wasted human resources during the Great Depression of the 1930s had focused the nation's attention on the economic insecurity that resulted. The Social Security Act was seen as a solution to these problems. The original law provided only retirement benefits at age 65 for most workers in industry and commerce. Since then the law has been amended many times. Social Security now has provisions for disabled workers and their dependents and for survivors of deceased workers. It covers virtually the entire working population, including the self-employed, and benefits are tied to the consumer price index so that they increase automatically with inflation in the economy. Therefore the purchasing power of retirees' benefits remains the same even when the average price level goes up. Medicare, which provides highly subsidized medical insurance for aged and disabled Social Security beneficiaries, was established in 1965.

Social insurance
Government program funded by earmarked payroll taxes of employers, employees, or both. Its purpose is the pooling of risk of losses.

Social Security is a good example of **social insurance.** Like private insurance programs, such as your life or health insurance, the purpose of social insurance programs is to pool risk of losses from such occurrences as death or illness. This means that combining high-risk and low-risk individuals enables us to manage the consequences better. Social insurance benefits are paid for by contributions of employees, employers, or both, to special funds, rather than from general government revenues. The Social Security and Medicare taxes deducted from your paycheck are examples of such contributions. Because the concept of social insurance is sophisticated and difficult to explain by itself, we are going to contrast

TABLE 12-1	Characteristics of Social Insurance and Private Insurance

SOCIAL INSURANCE	PRIVATE INSURANCE
1. Purpose is pooling of risk	1. Purpose is pooling of risk
2. Compulsory	2. Voluntary
3. Government monopoly	3. Competition of private insurers
4. Tax payments	4. Insurance premiums
5. Pay as you go	5. Fully funded
6. Statutory right	6. Contractual right
7. Social adequacy and individual equity	7. Individual equity

Private insurance
Program provided by for-profit insurance companies and funded by premiums. Its purpose is the pooling of risk of losses.

Social (public) assistance
Any government program that is targeted to aid low-income people.

Payroll taxes
Taxes based on earnings from work, usually deducted directly from the paycheck.

Fully funded
Having sufficient reserves to pay all expected liabilities; legal requirement of private insurance.

Pay-as-you-go program
Program in which current taxes pay current benefits.

social insurance to two other types of programs that contribute to the economic security of the population. These are **private insurance** and **social (public) assistance.** Private insurance is provided by for-profit insurance companies, not the government, and its purpose, like that of social insurance, is the pooling of risk of losses. Social—or public—assistance programs are needs-based welfare programs of the government. Table 12-1 compares social insurance with private insurance programs.

Although the basic purpose of the two kinds of insurance is the same, they differ in most other characteristics. Social insurance is compulsory, whereas private insurance is voluntary. If you are a covered worker, you *must* pay Social Security taxes and participate in the program; no one requires that you purchase a private insurance policy. The reason that social insurance is compulsory is obvious. Many people might choose to postpone participation until they neared retirement or choose not to participate at all if the decision were left up to them. Then the cost per covered worker would increase.

The private insurance industry is composed of a large number of competing firms, although it is dominated by a much smaller number of large firms. The Social Security Administration is the sole provider of this social insurance, and it is therefore a government monopoly.

Revenue for social insurance programs is provided by **payroll taxes** that are earmarked for providing benefits to those qualifying for benefits. In the case of Social Security and Medicare, the payroll tax is a matching tax with equal amounts paid by employees and their employers. This financing mechanism contrasts with private insurance, in which benefits are financed from premium payments made by policyholders.

By law private insurers must operate on a **fully funded** basis—that is, they must have reserves sufficient to pay all the claims likely to be made on them. Social insurance, such as Social Security, is not fully funded. Instead it is a pay-as-you-go system. The taxes collected from current workers and employers are used to pay benefits to current retirees and other current beneficiaries. The decision to make Social Security a **pay-as-you-go program,** rather than a fully funded one, came about in the 1930s. It was reasoned that there would always be new workers coming into the compulsory program to pay taxes to support beneficiaries, so a fully funded program was unnecessary. Contingency funds intended to cover six

TABLE 12-2	Characteristics of Social Insurance and Public Assistance

SOCIAL INSURANCE	PUBLIC ASSISTANCE
1. Covers entire population	1. Covers needy
2. Financed by earmarked payroll taxes	2. Financed from general revenues
3. Social adequacy and individual equity	3. Social adequacy
4. No stigma attached to receipt of benefits	4. Stigma attached to receipt of benefits

Statutory right
Right specified by law.

Contractual right
Right specified in contract between parties.

Individual equity
Principle that benefits received are proportional to amounts paid in.

Social adequacy
Principle that benefits are sufficient to provide a minimum level of economic security to the population as a whole.

months' to one year's benefits were established, but the program's current taxes were intended to pay current benefits.

Your right to benefits under Social Security is a **statutory right**—that is, this right is defined by the current Social Security law. If Congress changes the law to make benefits either more or less generous, your right to benefits will change with the law. On the other hand, you have a **contractual right** to payments as specified in a policy purchased from a private insurer. The company cannot unilaterally change the terms of your policy.

Finally, private insurance is based on the principle of **individual equity.** You get back benefits proportional to what you paid in. If you purchased a larger policy, paying more premiums to do so, you will get back larger payments (or your heirs will). Social insurance is based on the principles of individual equity and **social adequacy,** or the need to provide a minimum floor of economic security to the population as a whole. Furthermore, the emphasis of the program is more on social adequacy than individual equity. Low-wage workers will therefore receive benefits that are proportionately larger in comparison to the taxes they paid in than will high-wage workers.

Social insurance shares some characteristics with private insurance, but it shares other characteristics with social assistance. Table 12-2 contrasts social insurance with public assistance programs.

Public assistance programs are needs-based. To receive benefits from these welfare programs, a person must demonstrate that he or she is poor or that assets and income are below a certain level. Benefits are paid not from earmarked taxes, but from the government's general revenues. There is no relationship between taxes paid in, currently or in the past, and the benefits received by beneficiaries. Public assistance programs are pure welfare programs. Because every worker is eligible for Social Security and Medicare, but only the poor receive welfare, a stigma is attached to welfare that is not present for social insurance programs.

SOCIAL SECURITY TAXES AND BENEFITS

Social Security taxes and benefits are a significant part of the federal budget. In December 1998, 44.2 million beneficiaries received monthly payments totaling $31.2 billion.[1] Social Security and Medicare taxes account for more than one-third of federal taxes collected. Moreover, Social Security's share of the budget has increased greatly over time. Let's first discuss taxes and benefits separately; then we will look at the total program.

Social Security Taxes

Tax base

Maximum amount of earnings subject to payroll taxes.

Tax rate

Percent of taxable earnings that will be collected as tax for payroll taxes.

The Social Security tax paid is determined by the **tax base** and the **tax rate.** The tax base is the maximum amount of an individual worker's earnings that is subject to the tax. The tax rate is the percentage of the tax base that will be collected for Social Security.

The tax rate is 6.2 percent for Social Security and 1.45 percent for Medicare, so we often speak of a total payroll tax rate of 7.65 percent. Because employees and employers pay equal amounts of these payroll taxes, the combined tax rate of both workers and employers for both taxes is 15.3 percent. Self-employed persons pay the entire 15.3 percent after some adjustments have been made to their earned income. The Social Security and Medicare tax bases are also different. As of 2000, the Social Security tax base was only the first $76,200 of each worker's annual earnings, whereas all of the worker's earnings were taxable for Medicare.

Let's examine how the tax has increased during the life of the Social Security program. In 1937 the tax base was $3,000, and the tax rate was 1 percent. (Of course, the program only covered retirement benefits for those over 65 years of age.) Even if we adjust for inflation, the average worker pays a much larger share of his or her earnings in Social Security taxes now than at the inception of the program.

The Social Security tax is often criticized because it is regressive. Taxes may be either regressive, proportional, or progressive. **Regressive taxes** take a larger percentage of income from low-income people than from high-income people, whereas **progressive taxes** take a larger percentage of income from high-income people than from low-income people. **Proportional taxes** take the same percentage of income from all people. There is certainly room for discussion about whether proportional or progressive taxes are fairer, but few would argue that regressive taxes are equitable. This issue is discussed in greater detail in Chapter Sixteen.

Regressive tax

Tax that takes a larger percentage of lower incomes than of higher incomes.

Progressive tax

Tax that takes a larger percentage of higher incomes than of lower incomes.

Proportional tax

Tax that takes the same percentage of income from people at all income levels.

The Social Security tax is regressive for two reasons. First, only the tax base is taxed in any given year. So in 2000, only the first $76,200 earned by each worker was taxable. Therefore, the entire wages and salaries of most workers were subject to the tax, but only a portion of the earnings of workers who earned more than $76,200 was taxable. So low-earning workers paid Social Security taxes equal to 6.2 percent of their total earnings, and high-earnings workers paid a lower percent of taxes on their *total* earnings. (Think how much of Julia Robert's earnings was exempt from the Social Security tax!)

Second, only earnings from working are taxable for Social Security and Medicare. Other forms of income, such as rents, interest, capital gains, and stock dividends, are not subject to these taxes. Because higher-income people have more income from sources other than wages and salaries, they also have more income that is not taxable for these social insurance programs. Thus Social Security and Medicare taxes are rightly characterized as regressive. We shall see shortly, however, that the progressivity of benefits offsets the regressiveness of taxes.

http://www.ssa.gov
This Social Security Administration home page has links to reports and some statistical data.

Social Security Benefits

Social Security benefits are mainly in the form of checks mailed by the U.S. Treasury to beneficiaries on the first of each month. Most recipients receive their

TABLE 12-3   Preretirement Earnings, Social Security Benefits, and the Replacement Rate for Workers Retiring in 1999

	EARNINGS	BENEFITS	REPLACEMENT RATE
Low earner	$13,100	$ 6,943	53%
Average earner	46,663	14,932	32%
Maximum earner	72,600	17,424	24%

Source: Social Security Administration Office of Policy, "Is Social Security All I Need for Retirement Income," April 8, 1999.

checks on the third of the month, if the benefits are not automatically deposited in their bank account. Medicare benefits are in the form of payments to hospitals and doctors for medical care. Medicare's effects on our health care system were discussed in Chapter Nine. Here we will concentrate on the discussion of Social Security retirement benefits.

To qualify for Social Security benefits, the recipient must be a fully insured worker or the dependent of a fully insured worker. That is, the worker must have paid Social Security taxes on a minimum amount of earnings for forty quarters (10 years).

Benefit amounts are based on the retired worker's prior Social Security tax contributions. A complex formula that takes into account the worker's entire earnings and Social Security tax history, rather than a small number of years, such as private pensions often use, determines the amount of the worker's monthly check. The benefits are progressive in the sense that low-earnings workers will receive a higher **replacement rate** than high-earnings workers do. The replacement rate is the percentage of the final working year's earnings that is replaced by Social Security benefits. Table 12-3 contains data from a 1999 Social Security Administration study showing the relationship between earnings, benefits, and the replacement rate.

Replacement rate
Percentage of worker's last working year's earnings that is replaced by Social Security retirement benefits.

Under law current in 1999, low-earner workers who retire in 2000 at 65 years of age, and who earned $13,100 in the previous year, would receive $6,943 in Social Security benefits, which would replace 53 percent of the previous year's earnings. On the other hand, maximum-earner workers, whose 1999 earnings were the 1999 tax base of $72,600, would receive a larger benefit ($17,424), but only 24 percent of their previous year's earnings would be replaced.

The progressivity of Social Security benefits offsets the regressive effects of Social Security taxes. The entire Social Security program is therefore somewhat progressive and involves a transfer of income from high-earnings workers to low-earnings workers.

PROBLEMS AND ISSUES

Let us discuss some of the many problems and issues connected with this social insurance program. First, we will examine the U.S. demographics and the system's long-run problem as the nation ages. Second, we will discuss the issue of making the Social Security system voluntary rather than compulsory. Third, we will analyze whether Social Security is a "bad buy" for younger workers. Fourth, we will look at the system's treatment of women workers. Finally, we will discuss the controversy over Social Security's effect on private savings.

The Long-Run Problem: An Aging Population

The long-term problem of Social Security is demographics. The average age of the U.S. population is increasing, which implies that we have fewer workers paying taxes and more retirees receiving benefits. In addition, more workers are retiring at earlier ages, and early retirements imply longer periods of retirement during which workers do not pay Social Security taxes but do receive benefits. Moreover, the baby boomers, that post–World War II demographic bubble, are expected to begin retiring in the first decade of the twenty-first century. This group will swell the ranks of the retired still more.

Because Social Security is a pay-as-you-go system, it is sensitive to such demographic changes. In 1960, 5.1 workers paid taxes for every Social Security beneficiary. In 1980 only 3.2 workers paid taxes for every beneficiary, and the Social Security Administration predicts that by 2020 the ratio of workers to beneficiaries will fall to 2.4.[2] The implications of these numbers for taxpayers, retirees, and the financial viability of the system are substantial. Let us look at these implications.

First, if fewer taxpayers are going to provide the same benefits to Social Security retirees on a pay-as-you-go basis, then these taxpayers individually must pay higher taxes. On the other hand, if more taxes are not collected per worker, benefits must be cut, or a source of funding other than the payroll tax must be found. If nothing is done, the financial viability of the system is in doubt.

Congress first wrestled with this problem in the early 1980s, and the result was an amendment to the Social Security Act in 1983. Major provisions of the amendment were (1) to raise the **normal retirement age,** (2) to begin building up **trust fund** accounts to take care of the increase in benefits expected when the baby boomers retire, and (3) to begin to tax a portion of Social Security retirement benefits for income tax purposes.

Increasing the Normal Retirement Age

The normal retirement age is the minimum age at which covered workers can retire and still receive full benefits from Social Security. For the first 60 years of the program, the normal retirement age was 65. Workers can also retire at 62 years of age, but their retirement benefits are proportionally reduced if they do so. At the present time, many workers choose to retire earlier and receive smaller benefits.

Life expectancy in the United States has increased since the beginning of the Social Security program. In 1940 the life expectancy at birth of a male was 61 years; in 2000 it was 74 years. The increase in life expectancy for females during this period was even more pronounced. In 1940 a female's life expectancy at birth was 66 years; in 2000 it was 80 years.[3] The percentage of the population that is over 65 years of age is increasing. Increased life expectancy means that there will be more older people collecting retirement benefits.

Normal retirement age
Minimum age at which workers can retire with full Social Security benefits.

Trust fund
Taxes invested to pay future Social Security benefits.

Note that life expectancies represent average life spans for males and females. But keep in mind that the increase in male and female life expectancies of 13 and 14 years, respectively, does not mean that men and women will live 13 and 14 years longer on average. Instead, it means that child and infant deaths are falling, thereby raising the average life expectancy for the population as a whole. Thus beneficiaries will receive benefits for somewhat longer periods of time, but they will not receive benefits for the full 13 to 14 years longer that is indicated by the changes in life expectancies. A larger fraction of infants now born will live to collect Social Security benefits, however.

However we interpret it, the increase in life expectancy is one factor that has decreased the worker/beneficiary ratio. Some way had to be found to offset the effects of this change. The 1983 amendment to the Social Security Act gradually raises the normal retirement age to 67 by the year 2022. Workers will still be able to retire at age 62, if they are willing to accept lower monthly benefits for the remainder of their lives. The closer to the normal retirement age that they are when they retire, the smaller the reduction in benefits that they will incur.

The increase in the normal retirement age means that many workers will pay taxes for two years longer, and they will collect retirement benefits for two years fewer. Because we are living longer on average, working longer on average may make sense.

Building Up Trust Fund Balances for Baby Boomer Benefits

The other change begun in 1983 was a partial departure from the pay-as-you-go philosophy of Social Security. Tax levels were set to increase trust fund balances to pay benefits to baby boomers. The baby boomers were born after World War II and before about 1965, a period during which the economy was booming and the birth rate increased. As this exceptionally large cohort of Americans has advanced through life, they have made a difference. When they began school, they overcrowded the nation's schools and put stress on our public education system. When they reached maturity, they began families of their own and strained the nation's housing resources. They will begin retiring in about 2010, stressing the Social Security system.

To accommodate the baby boomers, trust fund balances are being built up. That is, the government is now collecting more taxes than are needed to pay benefits to current retirees. The surplus taxes are invested in U.S. government securities and therefore earn interest that is also credited to the trust funds. The intention is to have the funds available to pay benefits to baby boomers. As more and more baby boomers retire, the trust fund balances will be drawn down, because more benefits will be paid out than will be collected in taxes. Eventually the trust fund balances will be virtually exhausted, and the system will revert to a strictly pay-as-you-go system.

Taxing Social Security Retirement Benefits

Originally, Social Security retirement benefits were exempt from income taxation. In 1984, retirees first began to pay federal income tax on a part of their Social Security benefits. The taxes paid are credited to Social Security trust funds and invested in U.S. securities. By 1992, more than six billion dollars, or 2.2 percent of total benefits paid,[4] had been collected in income taxes on Social Security benefits. This taxation is somewhat controversial and will be discussed in more detail later, but let us point out here that the taxation of benefits has resulted in substantial revenues and contributed to the financial viability of the system.

Long-Run Financial Viability of Social Security

The board of trustees of the Social Security program must file periodic reports about the long-range (75-year) financial outlook of the program. In preparing these reports analysts make assumptions about growth in the economy, growth in the workforce, number of retirees, and the length of time that retirees collect benefits, as well as other economic variables. They use different sets of assumptions, ranging from rosy to bleak outlooks about projected variables affecting the program in the future. In 1999 the intermediate projection was that the trust funds would continue to be built up over the next 20 years and then begin to be drawn down but that they would not be exhausted until 2037.[5] After the trust funds are exhausted, the system will return to a pay-as-you-go system. Given the increasing proportion of older people in the population, this change could lead to either higher Social Security taxes or decreased retirement benefits. If no changes are made to the program, the Social Security Administration estimates that retirees after 2037 will receive benefits equal to 72 percent of the benefits of today's retirees. In the short term, the program is solvent, but in the long run the program is not expected to be financially sound. Although more steps will be needed to ensure the financial viability of the Social Security retirement system in the future, it is currently not in any danger of collapsing.

The same cannot be said of Medicare. This social health insurance system reflects the problems of all health care in the United States. Outlays on a per-patient basis are rising rapidly. The outlays on current beneficiaries are increasing more rapidly than are payroll taxes collected to fund Part A, the compulsory portion of the Medicare program. Part B, voluntary supplemental Medicare coverage, is financed by premiums paid by beneficiaries *and* by the general revenues of the federal government. Each year premiums are inadequate to cover increasing costs, and the government contributes from its revenues to cover the program's shortfall.

Should Social Security Be Made Voluntary?

U.S. citizens are independent souls, and they tend to dislike being forced to do anything. The compulsory nature of Social Security therefore has been controversial since the program's beginnings. Many conservatives argue that Social Security should be made voluntary, rather than compulsory. Their arguments are based on principles of greater economic freedom and limitation of the role of government in our lives. A related question concerns the fairness of the Social Security system to younger workers (a complex issue we examine in detail in the next section).

A voluntary system implies that individuals would have the option of participating or not participating in Social Security. If they choose not to participate, they could buy private insurance to satisfy their needs for economic security, or they could choose to provide for their needs through other means.

The arguments for a compulsory Social Security program are (1) that a voluntary program would make provision of a minimum level of economic security to the entire population more difficult, (2) that a voluntary system would be subject to greater adverse selection, and (3) that the poor could not afford to purchase private insurance or save to provide for their own economic security. Let us look at these arguments more closely.

First, social insurance is intended to provide a minimum level of income to the entire population. Carrying out this intention through a voluntary program would be far more difficult. Some people simply would choose not to provide for themselves by saving money, buying private insurance, or participating in Social Security. Others might purchase retirement income insurance through private firms but let the insurance lapse if they encountered hard times. Because letting people starve or go homeless is repugnant to us, we might find ourselves taking care of these individuals through welfare programs instead of social insurance.

Adverse selection
Process by which insured people's choices lead to higher-than-average loss levels.

Second, a voluntary system would increase the probability of **adverse selection.** Adverse selection is a problem for both social and private insurance. Adverse selection is any process by which the choices made by insured persons lead to higher-than-average loss levels for the program. (If healthy people do not purchase health insurance but sick people do, for example, the insurance companies will have higher average loss ratios and receive fewer premium payments.) Remember that the benefits of social insurance are based more on social adequacy than on individual equity. Therefore, some workers receive a higher return on their tax contributions than do others. If the program were made voluntary, the workers receiving the lower returns (younger workers, healthier workers, and workers with fewer dependents) might well decide to withdraw from the program and purchase private insurance in which the returns are based only on the principle of individual equity. If they were to withdraw from the Social Security program, the program would cover a greater proportion of high-risk people (workers slated to retire soon and workers likely to become disabled) and a smaller proportion of low-risk people. Loss levels and the cost per covered worker of the program would rise. Taxes for those who chose to participate would need to be increased, and more workers would find private insurance a desirable option. Social Security might eventually be reduced to an expensive program covering mainly those who are poor risks.

Finally, low-income workers who work at or near the minimum wage simply could not afford to buy private insurance. Because their replacement rate (benefits as a percentage of earnings) is higher than that of high-income workers, lower-income workers have higher returns on their tax contributions to the present compulsory program than do higher-income workers. Premiums necessary to purchase similar coverage from private insurers would be beyond the financial capability of this group. Nor would these low-earning workers be able to save enough to provide for their family's economic security.

During the congressional debate that led to the passage of the Social Security Act of 1935, an alternative proposal for a voluntary system was made. It was not adopted, because the arguments for a compulsory system were more compelling. As we have seen, the issue is controversial to this day.

The "Bad Buy" Issue: Is Social Security Unfair to Younger Workers?

One of the concerns you may have about Social Security is its fairness to you and your generation. Social Security is quite generous to current retirees. But will it be as generous to you? Would you be able to provide better for your old age if you could just use your current Social Security taxes to invest any way you want? Is Social Security a "bad buy" for young workers?

One of the most complex issues involved in the Social Security program is whether young workers will receive their money's worth from Social Security. These workers pay Social Security taxes to support retired persons, survivors, and the disabled. The value of the taxes paid by younger workers *and their employers* exceeds the value of the benefits that they can expect to receive. Thus some critics of Social Security argue that younger workers are being cheated and that they should be allowed to opt out of Social Security and purchase private insurance protection. They argue that young people will get a fairer deal from buying private insurance than they get from Social Security. This is, of course, an argument for a voluntary Social Security program. Let us look at the "bad buy" argument carefully.

Most of the studies indicating that the young worker is cheated under Social Security make the assumption that the individual employee is entitled to all of his or her employer's tax contribution. This assumption is based on the belief that firms pay lower wages to their workers because the employers must pay Social Security taxes to the government. To the extent that workers may receive lower wages because employers must pay taxes on the workers' wages, this belief may be justified. But this belief foreordains the results of the studies. If we look only at the individual worker's contributions, we will come to a different conclusion.

The employer's matching half of the Social Security tax was never intended to be credited to an individual worker's account. Its purpose is to benefit all covered persons rather than a specific person. At the beginning of the program it was necessary to provide benefits to many workers who worked a relatively few years in employment covered by Social Security before retiring and collecting Social Security benefits. The employer's portion of the tax was intended to make that possible. Moreover, the employer's tax contributions make redistribution of income from high-income to low-income workers possible. The employer's share of the tax provides for social adequacy, not individual equity.

If we were to use only the employee's taxes, excluding the employer's half, we would arrive at a vastly different conclusion. All workers, including high earners and young people, receive benefits well in excess of the tax contributions they make.[6]

In addition, many of the studies supporting the "bad buy" argument consider only survivor and retirement benefits. Researchers make the assumption that if the individual worker were given the taxes paid by both the employer and the employee, the worker could purchase life insurance and a retirement annuity more cheaply than he or she could acquire the same coverage through the Social Security program. This assumption does not account for all the benefits provided by Social Security. Social Security is a unique social insurance program that also provides disability coverage and medical insurance through Medicare. If we adjust for these benefits by removing taxes paid to support them, the results of the studies change greatly. It is far less clear that Social Security is a "bad buy" for younger workers when these benefits are taken into consideration.

Social Security's Treatment of Women

Social Security is meant to be gender-neutral; it is supposed to treat men and woman equally. But, largely because our society and culture do not treat the sexes equally, men and women are not treated equally under Social Security. We will discuss two of the women's issues in Social Security. They are the widow's income gap and the possibly unfair treatment of working wives under the program.

The Widow's Income Gap

Widows (or widowers) of covered workers can collect monthly survivorship benefits based on the earnings record of the deceased spouse. Surviving children are also entitled to benefits until they reach the age of 18. The surviving spouse's benefits are paid only until the youngest child reaches the age of 16. Then at the age of 60, the surviving spouse can again collect benefits on the earnings record of the deceased worker. The benefits will be lost if the surviving spouse remarries before reaching the age of 60.

Consider the following case. Tom and Mandy are a young couple with three small children. Mandy worked before their second child was born but hasn't worked outside the home since that time. Tom suddenly dies. Mandy is 28 years old. Her youngest child is three years old. Mandy can receive survivorship benefits, as can the three children. Her benefits will end, however, when the three-year-old reaches 16 years of age. Mandy will be only 41. She cannot again collect benefits on Tom's earnings record until she reaches the age of 60. If she has stayed home with the children, she will probably have few marketable skills with which to support herself

Mandy will face a gap in survivor's benefits of 19 years. So will many middle-aged widows who are under 60 years of age but have grown children when their husbands die. It should be noted that widowers face the same problem as widows. If the wife was the primary (or even an equal) wage earner in the marriage, a surviving widower will face the same situation. Given, however, that there are still a great many so-called traditional marriages in the United States and that men on average earn more than women, the coverage gap is primarily a women's issue.

Unfair Treatment of Working Wives

A wife can receive retirement benefits based on her own earnings record, or she can receive retirement benefits based on her husband's record as his spouse. As a matter of course the Social Security Administration will pay her the highest retirement benefits after calculating the benefits using her own record and her husband's. Usually her spousal benefits will be one-half of what her husband receives. Wives who have never worked outside the home, or who did not work enough to be fully covered for retirement benefits, are entitled to the same spousal benefits as are wives who worked throughout their married life.

Many wives, on applying for Social Security retirement benefits, discover that they are entitled to larger spousal benefits than they would be entitled to if they were to receive benefits based on their own earnings record. It therefore appears as if their tax contributions are lost, and, at least for Social Security retirement purposes, that their years of working do not matter.

Why is this the case? Remember from Chapter Six that women make significantly less on average than do men. If the couple is typical in this way, the man will have compiled a larger earnings record. Furthermore, women are in and out of the labor market due to family responsibilities more than men are. This too will contribute to a lower earnings record. Thus the one-half of her husband's retirement benefit is more than the benefits based on her own earnings. It appears as if her years of working and paying payroll taxes are wasted.

It should be noted that husbands might find themselves in the same situation if their earnings record is much smaller than their wives'. They might find that their spousal benefits are larger than benefits paid on their own records. The Social Security law treats spouses of either gender the same. But the labor market institutions of the United States treat men and women differently, and this differential treatment is reflected in treatment for Social Security.

Does Social Security Decrease Savings?

Critics of the Social Security program argue that it has decreased private saving in the United States. They argue that the need to save for retirement privately is decreased because the Social Security program exists. This phenomenon is called the **Social Security wealth effect.** The wealth effect causes us to spend more during our working years on consumer goods, because we do not feel the need to save. Indeed, the United States has one of the developed world's lowest private savings rates.

Social Security wealth effect
Tendency of the population to substitute Social Security for private saving, thus decreasing private saving.

Others argue that Social Security actually increases private savings by encouraging earlier retirements. This effect is called the **early retirement effect.** Workers who retire earlier must provide for a longer period of retirement and therefore must save more during their working years. If the wealth effect is greater than the early retirement effect, Social Security decreases private savings. But Social Security increases private savings if the early retirement effect exceeds the wealth effect.

Early retirement effect
Social Security's effect of increasing private savings by encouraging earlier retirements.

Social Security's effect on private savings is an issue for empirical research, and many studies have been done on the issue. Measuring savings affected by Social Security as opposed to savings not affected by Social Security is difficult, however, and the results of the studies are inconclusive. Most of the studies do not take into account that workers may save for purposes other than retirement. If many workers save for vacations, down payments on houses, or other purposes, these studies understate the extent to which Social Security decreases savings. Nor do the studies consider that children might have to support their aged parents if Social Security did not exist. They might therefore save less due to their expenditures on their parents. They might also save less if, in the absence of social insurance, we had to support a much greater public assistance program from tax revenues. Then we would have less discretionary income after taxes to save. The question is truly complex, and we simply do not know the effect of Social Security on savings.

COMMON MISCONCEPTIONS ABOUT SOCIAL SECURITY

Let's examine some common misconceptions about the system and its finances. Some people argue that the trust funds are fictitious, because the government securities held by the trust funds are merely IOUs owed by one branch of the government to another. This conception is incorrect. The trust funds are real. The collected taxes are invested in U.S. securities so that the money earns interest instead of just sitting in a non-interest-bearing account. The government securities, also called government bonds, are issued by government agencies to borrow money from the public. They are similar to the government savings bonds you may have received from your Aunt Gertrude. The government bonds held by the trust pay the Social Security program interest and can be redeemed whenever the trust fund managers decide to redeem them. Government bonds are one of the safest possible investments that the trust funds could make, because the bonds are backed by the full faith and credit of the United States.

Others argue that the trust funds increase the national debt when Social Security taxes are invested in government securities. This conception also is incorrect. The national debt increases when the government spends more than it collects in tax revenues in a year. This action is called running a deficit, and it is discussed in more detail in Chapter Sixteen. When the government runs a deficit, it sells newly issued securities—in reality, it borrows from the purchasers of the securities. The government decides, on the basis of its desire to borrow, how many government securities to issue. It doesn't matter whether a government agency, a bank, or a private citizen buys these securities. The purchase of new securities by the Social Security trust funds has the same effect on the national debt as your Aunt Gertrude's purchasing a new Series EE savings bond. In fact, the two transactions are alike from the perspective of financing the government.

WHAT DOES THE FUTURE HOLD FOR THE SOCIAL SECURITY SYSTEM?

When we talk to our students, they express doubt that Social Security will be there for them. You probably have the same worries. If you are working, you know that a chunk of your earnings is taken for Social Security taxes. You know you must continue to pay Social Security taxes—but what, if any, benefits can you expect to receive?

Americans have long been skeptical about the promise of Social Security. Each generation has applauded the system's support of their parents and grandparents but has doubted that Social Security will "be there for them." Each generation fears the collapse of the system before it reaches retirement. In opinion poll after opinion poll, Americans express their uneasiness. This skepticism was only briefly allayed by the changes made by Congress in 1983.

In part, workers' renewed doubts are the result of Social Security's worsening financial position. It is now obvious that trust fund balances will be drawn down more rapidly than was predicted in the early 1980s. But part of the skepticism aris-es because most Americans simply do not understand the system. And inaccurate reporting in the media contributes to both their uneasiness and their lack of understanding. When, for example, the Social Security board of trustees reported in 1999 that the retirement trust fund balances were to be exhausted by 2037, newspaper headlines throughout the country read "Social Security Bankrupt by 2037." Although the exhaustion of trust fund balances is not exactly good news, the return to a pay-as-you-go system is not the same as bankruptcy. After 2037 the system will continue to pay benefits of about 72 percent of today's benefit level, even without our making changes to increase its financial stability. But benefits will have to be paid from current tax collections after that date.

Nevertheless, financing and financial soundness issues remain. Trust fund bal-ances are now predicted to be drawn down more rapidly than previously expected. The Medicare hospital insurance trust fund is in really poor condition. There is some cause for concern, and proposals to amend the system have been made in the past few years. Without doubt, changes will be made to the Social Security sys-tem. Because the system offers a measure of economic security to us all, we should be concerned that these changes reflect the underlying principles and values of the social insurance system. If we allow the system to deteriorate until it reaches a crisis situation, changes made at that point may not be consistent with these val-ues. Let's look at some of the changes that might be made in the future.

Cutting Current Social Security Benefits

Various proposals have been made to cut current Social Security benefits, either across the board or for high-income recipients. Some proposals would tinker with the benefits formula to decrease the benefits of particular earnings classes. Others would eliminate adjustments for inflation, either temporarily or permanently. Eliminating such cost-of-living adjustments are, in fact, a form of benefits reduc-tion. Obviously, cutting current benefits would make the trust funds last longer.

A proposal introduced in Congress in 1999 would have cut current benefits. The proposal was to revise the Cost of Living Adjustment (COLA) of current social security recipients. Social Security benefits are adjusted each January to cover the inflation that occurred in the preceding year. The inflation is measured using the consumer price index (CPI). Economists generally agree that the CPI somewhat overstates inflation but disagree about how much. (This issue is discussed in Chap-ter Fourteen.) The legislative proposal would have adjusted the COLA and de-creased the annual increase in benefits of current beneficiaries. The proposal was defeated in Congress.

Proponents of cutting the benefits of high-earner retirees point out that not all Social Security recipients are poor. People who earned more while working were also likely to have enjoyed more fringe benefits. They are more likely to receive private pensions and have investment income than low earners. In other words, they do not need the Social Security check as much as low earners. Elimi-nating or cutting their benefits would make the system more progressive, keep a minimum floor of income under the lower and average earners, and cut the costs of the Social Security program.

On the other hand, cutting the benefits of high earners might threaten the individual equity principle that makes Social Security a social insurance program instead of a welfare program. As a social insurance program, Social Security has enjoyed widespread acceptance and a lack of stigma. As a wise person once said, "Programs for the poor tend to be poor programs." Social Security has always been perceived as a program for everyone. Eliminating the benefits of high earners might lead people to view Social Security as a welfare program, and welfare programs are more vulnerable to political maneuvering than are social insurance programs.

Taxing All Social Security Benefits

A proposal that is highly likely to be adopted in the future is taxation of all Social Security benefits as though they are any other sort of income. This proposal does not mean that income taxes would be paid on every dollar of Social Security benefits. Our income tax system is progressive, and people with very little income pay little or no taxes. So the individual who was paid at near the minimum wage for all the years he or she worked, and whose total income is in the form of Social Security, would probably not pay tax on those benefits. But people with other sources of income or very high Social Security benefits would pay taxes on Social Security benefits just as they do on income from investments.

Increasing Retirement Ages

As we mentioned previously, the so-called normal retirement age will increase over time to 67 under our current law. But the earliest age at which workers can retire with reduced benefits remains at 62 under current law. Another suggestion to strengthen the system is to raise both the normal retirement age and the early retirement age.

Proponents of an additional increase in the normal retirement age point out that the U.S. economy is evolving from a manufacturing economy to a service and information economy. Jobs are therefore less physically demanding, on average. Furthermore, advances in health care have made U.S. workers healthier in their fifties and sixties. Therefore, they argue, it will not be a disservice to increase the normal retirement age further.

Over time U.S. workers have retired at younger ages. Many argue that Social Security has contributed to this trend. Currently, a worker can retire at age 62 and receive 80 percent of the monthly Social Security benefits that he or she would have received at age 65. When the normal retirement age increases to 67, the worker will still be able to retire at age 62 and receive 70 percent of the monthly benefits that he or she would have received at the normal retirement age. Those who propose an increase in the earliest age that a worker can retire and still receive Social Security benefits argue that workers who choose early retirement at reduced benefits often do so without realizing how long they will need to provide for themselves in retirement. As their other assets are exhausted, their reduced Social Security benefits may not be adequate to provide for their needs, or certainly not enough to keep them comfortably. Raising the early retirement age would encourage workers to continue working—and paying Social Security taxes—

longer. Because their monthly benefits would be greater when they retire, they would be better off, and so would the Social Security system.

Investing Social Security Taxes in the Stock Market

Recall that the Social Security trust funds are invested to earn interest until they are needed to pay benefits. The trust funds must, by law, be invested only in government securities, which are the safest possible investment because the full faith and credit of the federal government stands behind them. But stocks in America's corporations pay investors far higher rates of return, on average, than do government bonds. Many critics of the system argue that allowing the managers of the Social Security trust funds to invest a portion of the taxes collected in the stock market would greatly increase the investment earnings of the funds. Others point out that investment in the stock market is also more risky than investing in government securities. A portion of the trust funds will probably be invested in stocks at some point in the future.

Partial Privatization

http://www.cato.org
The home page of the Cato Institute, a conservative think tank, has links to papers arguing for privatization of Social Security.

http://userdata.acd.net/ demarco.chris/sspriv.htm This page, maintained by Chris Demarco, has links to papers opposing the privatization of Social Security.

During the 2000 campaign for the presidency, the partial privatization of Social Security became an issue when candidate George W. Bush proposed that 2 percent of the worker's earnings be put into investment accounts selected by the worker. The Social Security tax rate would be reduced by the same amount. Instead of the Social Security Administration investing all taxes in government securities, the individual worker could direct that part of his or her tax contribution be invested in stocks or mutual funds. The worker would then retain control over this portion of his or her retirement funds. Allowing workers to direct the investment of tax contributions is quite different from simply allowing the managers of the Social Security trust funds to invest in corporate stocks. Critics argue that high-wage earners will receive more sophisticated investment advice than will low-income workers. Thus, they argue, the proposal would increase the retirement income of high earners and decrease the retirement income of low-income earners.

On the other hand, candidate Al Gore campaigned on the promise to leave the current system alone, but to add to it an optional investment feature whereby the individual worker could make investments in various types of retirement accounts. The government would match the individual's contribution, and the amount of the government's contribution would vary with the income of the individual worker. The government's match for low-income workers would be greater than the workers' contributions, whereas the match for high-income workers would be only 30 percent of the high-income workers' contributions. The Gore proposal would have been expensive, and the government's contributions would have come from general tax revenues rather than from the Social Security payroll tax. What will be done to the Social Security program after President Bush's election is still unknown as we write this.

Social Security has been called the "third rail" of American politics. It represents economic security to some people and an undue tax burden to others. One thing is certain: Social Security will change over time. And it is highly unlikely that the system will be as generous to us as it is to today's retirees. What does this mean to you as you begin your careers? It means that you should save and invest for your retirement to maintain your living standard. Social Security may supplement your savings, but you should not expect to be able to retire comfortably on Social Security benefits alone.

SUMMARY

Social Security is a social insurance system. Although Social Security taxes are regressive, benefits are progressive, and the system as a whole is mildly progressive. The purpose of the system is to provide a minimum floor of economic security to U.S. workers. The size and tax burden of the system has increased over time.

Social Security is controversial. Its long-run problem is that fewer workers pay taxes to support each recipient as time passes. Trust fund balances

are now being built up to pay benefits to the baby boomers. Other issues include the system's fairness to women and to younger workers, the effect of Social Security on private savings, the desirability of making the system voluntary, and the long-run financial viability of the system. Changes likely in the future are a decrease in benefits, an increase in the normal and early retirement age, and full income taxation of benefits.

NOTES

1. Social Security Administration, *Social Security Bulletin: Annual Statistical Supplement—1999.*
2. Committee on Ways and Means, U.S. House of Representatives, *1993 Green Book* (Washington, DC: U.S. Government Printing Office, July 7, 1993), p. 109.
3. Central Intelligence Agency, *World Factbook,* 2000 (http://www.odci.gov/cia/publications/fact book/geos/u.s.html#people).
4. *1993 Green Book,* p. 31.
5. Social Security Administration, *2000 OASDI Trustees Report* (http://www.ssa.gov/oact/tr/trod).
6. Robert J. Myers, *Social Security,* 3d ed. (Homewood, Ill.: Richard D. Irwin, 1985), pp. 481–482.

DISCUSSION QUESTIONS

1. *Do you believe that Social Security is unfair to women? to younger workers? Why or why not? If you think that Social Security is unfair, what could be done to make it more fair? What other problems might these measures cause?*

2. *Explain how Social Security taxes are regressive, but the Social Security system is progressive.*

3. *Compare and contrast social insurance with public assistance and with private insurance.*

4. *Do you believe that Social Security should be made fully funded? What would the advantages and disadvantages be?*

5. *What changes do you feel are likely to be made in Social Security in the next 20 years? Why?*

6. *What is the long-run problem with Social Security? Do you feel that steps taken in 1983 to solve the problem were adequate?*

7. *Go to the Social Security Administration Web site (http://www.ssa.gov), click on Publications, then click on fact sheets, and find the average social security retirement benefit.*

CHAPTER 13

Crime and Drugs

Bobby's got a gun that he keeps beneath his pillow
Out on the street your chances are zero
Take a look around you (come on now)
It ain't too complicated
You're messin' with Murder Incorporated
Now you check over your shoulder everywhere that you go
Walkin' down the street there's eyes in every shadow
You better take a look around you (come on now)
That equipment you got's so outdated
You can't compete with Murder Incorporated
Everywhere you look now, Murder Incorporated.

Crime, broadly defined, imposes huge costs in the United States each year. These costs include both the damage to property and people from criminal activity and the cost of policies undertaken by government to prevent and punish criminal activity. Not all these costs can easily be assigned a monetary value. We can calculate the replacement cost of a building destroyed by arson, but what is the cost of an assault victim's trauma and pain? One element of these costs that is relatively easy to measure is the cost of administering the criminal justice system, which consists of police, courts, and prisons. This system, intended to prevent and

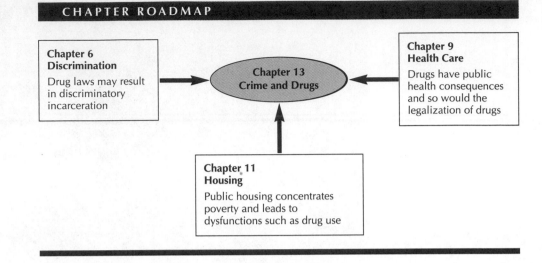

CHAPTER ROADMAP

Chapter 6
Discrimination

Drug laws may result in discriminatory incarceration

Chapter 13
Crime and Drugs

Chapter 9
Health Care

Drugs have public health consequences and so would the legalization of drugs

Chapter 11
Housing

Public housing concentrates poverty and leads to dysfunctions such as drug use

punish crime, was responsible for expenditures of $120 billion by federal, state, and local governments in 1996.[1] Indeed, expenditures for the criminal justice system are an increasingly important item in state government budgets over time. Resources absorbed by the criminal justice system cannot be used for tax relief, education, housing, health care, or any other worthwhile purpose, so it is important that these resources be used wisely. Economics may help us to analyze the effectiveness of our policies to combat crime.

When we think of crime, we usually think of violent crimes such as murder, rape, robbery, and assault. Perhaps we also include various offenses against property, such as arson and theft. However, a crime is any action that is forbidden by law and carries criminal penalties, which often include imprisonment. Among other crimes in the United States are gambling, prostitution, possession and trafficking in drugs, and sales of pornography. These are crimes because society, or a significant portion of society, thinks they are bad and has prohibited them by law.

The Federal Bureau of Investigation reports the number of crimes that occur per hundred thousand people in the country. These crime rates indicate that crimes decreased about 7 percent in 1999. The rate of the violent crimes rape, robbery, and assault decreased by 7 percent during the same year. This was the eighth straight year in which crime rates decreased.[2] Despite these data, people indicate in opinion surveys that they do not feel safer. The Bruce Springsteen lyrics quoted at the start of the chapter resonate for many of us.

In this chapter we will look at several issues involving crime and economics. We will begin by examining the economic characteristics of crime prevention and the proper focus for evaluation of our criminal justice system. Then we will analyze the controversy over legalization of so-called victimless crimes, using drugs as an example.

Crime Prevention as a Public Good

Public goods
Goods often provided by the government because their unique characteristics make it unlikely that the private market will provide them in sufficient quantity.

Indivisible
Characteristic of public goods in that they are impossible to divide into units sufficiently small to be sold in private markets.

Nonrivalrous
Characteristic of public goods in that use by one person does not prevent use by others.

Nonexcludable
Characteristic of public goods in that their benefits cannot be kept from persons who do not pay for the goods' provision in a private market.

Free rider problem
Situation in which individuals who do not pay their share for a good or service nevertheless enjoy its benefits.

Cost-benefit analysis
Study that compares the costs and benefits of a policy or program.

Police activity and other crime prevention measures are examples of **public goods.** These goods and services, first discussed under market failures in Chapter One, have characteristics that make private market production of them inefficient. First of all, public goods are **indivisible,** which means that they cannot be divided into rational and small enough units to be sold on a market to individual consumers. Second, up to a point they are **nonrivalrous.** The protection afforded to one citizen by a police officer on patrol, for example, does not "use up" the benefits of police protection and prevent other citizens from receiving the same benefits. (Most goods are rivalrous. Consider a hamburger: if you eat it, no one else can.) Finally, public goods are **nonexcludable** in that we cannot prevent specific citizens from deriving benefits from police crime prevention activity. Thus public goods are subject to the **free rider problem**—for example, if police protection were provided by the private market, we could not withhold from nonbuyers the benefits of safer streets that result from police activity. (Most goods, on the other hand, are excludable, so no free rider problem exists. A good example is a theater seat; you can't get one if you don't have a ticket.)

The private market is extremely efficient in providing hamburgers and theater seats and many other goods that are divisible, rivalrous, and excludable. The intersection of demand and supply at the equilibrium price results in neither shortages nor surpluses, and both buyers and sellers agree that the value of the product is the equilibrium price. But the private market is not efficient in providing public goods. Therefore we usually have the government provide public goods and finance them with tax revenues.

Crime Prevention Measures

Crime prevention measures are undertaken by the police, the criminal courts, and our prison system. Police cars patrolling our neighborhoods, police-sponsored activities for young people, the support of neighborhood watch programs, and the investigation of crimes are among the duties of the police. The courts are responsible for bringing to trial those who have been accused of violating criminal law and who have been apprehended by the police. The prison system exists to incarcerate, punish, and sometimes rehabilitate those convicted of crimes. Some practices, such as the operation of programs for disadvantaged youth, are preventive in that they may keep crime from occurring. Other activities involving the investigation of crimes, trial of suspects, and sentencing of those found guilty are crime prevention measures because they have a deterrent effect.

Evaluation by Cost-Benefit Analysis

The appropriate method to evaluate government policy is **cost-benefit analysis.** Using this method we would add up the benefits from a particular course of action and compare them to the costs. The activity is justified only if the benefits are greater than the costs. Furthermore, if two policies both have greater benefits to society than their costs, the one with the larger **net benefits,** or excess of benefits over cost, should be adopted. Cost-benefit analysis was discussed in the context of environmental protection policies in Chapter Three.

Net benefits
The excess of benefits over costs.

Benefits and Costs of Crime Prevention Activities

In the context of anticrime policy, the benefits of prevention activities include the value of property damage that is prevented as well as the medical expenses, psychological trauma, loss of income, and other expenses not incurred when assaults are prevented. Finally, any social **spillover benefits** that adhere to society at large are benefits of crime prevention activities. An example of a spillover benefit of crime prevention might be increased business activity because people feel safer on the streets in the downtown area; another might be the increased feeling of community pride and increased community activity that result from orderly neighborhoods. You probably can think of many other spillover benefits of crime prevention activity.

Spillover benefits
Benefits of private market activity shifted to society at large.

Costs of anticrime activity include the costs of equipment, such as squad cars and prison cells; the salaries and fringe benefits of police, court, and corrections personnel; and the costs of administering the system. Can you think of other costs?

Our direct expenditures on the criminal justice system have increased markedly during the past three decades. For the period between 1982 and 1996, for example, spending on police protection increased by 179 percent, expenditures on our judicial system increased by 237 percent, and expenditures on corrections increased by 353 percent when measured in current dollars. If our criminal justice expenditures are adjusted for inflation, these increases are 87 percent, 126 percent, and 273 percent, respectively.[2] The latter figures are directly comparable. The increase in expenditures mean that more resources are allocated to the criminal justice system. In terms of the production possibilities curve introduced in Chapter One, resources spent on the criminal justice system are not available for other uses. Figure 13-1 shows a production possibilities curve with crime prevention on the vertical axis. The curve illustrates that resources used for crime prevention are not available for other uses such as education. Furthermore, we have moved from a point such as *A* to one such as *B*, which indicates increased criminal justice activity relative to other goods and services over the past quarter-century.

http://www.albany.edu/ sourcebook
This is the site for the *Sourcebook of Criminal Justice Statistics*. It contains great amounts of relevant data.

Increased Costs of Our Prison System

The greatest percentage increase in spending on the criminal justice system is for corrections activities. The increase in resources devoted to our prison system mainly reflects a change in the thrust of our crime control policies. We now lock up in prison, or incarcerate, far more people than we did in the past. In 1999 we had nearly five times as many prison inmates as we had in 1970. The United States' incarceration rate of 682 inmates per 100,000 people is the second highest incarceration rate ever reported by any country. It is second only to Russia's 1998 rate of 685.[4] Higher levels of incarceration and longer prison sentences are supposed to reduce crime in two ways. They deter would-be offenders from committing crimes

FIGURE 13-1   Crime Prevention and the Production Possibilities Curve

Resources used for crime prevention are not available for other uses. Over time, the United States has moved from a point such as *A* to a point such as *B* on the curve.

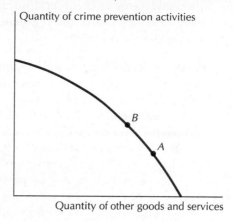

because of the increased likelihood of a prison sentence. And they physically prevent convicts from committing new crimes while they are in prison. This movement toward prison expansion and greater incarceration is perhaps the most controversial of our current crime prevention activities. As a result, there has been significant effort to rationally evaluate this policy by cost-benefit analysis. The results of the studies, however, are not conclusive. Let us see why.

Empirical Studies of the Trend toward Higher Incarceration Rates

The discussion of our imprisonment policy is usually couched in terms of (1) decreasing violent crimes against persons or (2) prison overcrowding and the nature of the prison population. We all agree that we want to prevent rapes, murders, and muggings. Whether harsher sentences and more prisons prevent them is the question.

Decreasing Violent Crimes against Persons.   Some researchers have indicated that the violent crime rate has indeed gone down as a result of our tougher policy; others have disagreed. These conflicting conclusions are the result of differences in research methods. Specifically, some studies control for age in the raw data, whereas others do not.

Lack of age adjustment results in smaller crime rates in recent years. The ages 15 to 29 are violence-prone years in our society. As people mature, they are less likely to commit violent acts. The average age of the U.S. population is increasing, which in itself should cause a decrease in our violent crime rate. Age adjustment of data takes into account the changing demographic characteristics of the population in an attempt to rid the data of age bias. When the data are adjusted for the age distribution of the population, data indicate a much smaller decrease in violent crime t⟨ ⟩ an be attributed to "get tough" policies.

How do higher incarceration rates and increased expenditures on prisons correlate with violent crime rates? Studies without age adjustment show greatly decreased violent crime rates, leading researchers to conclude that the benefits of increased rates of incarceration greatly exceed the costs. Studies that use age-adjusted data tend to find few benefits and great costs. Thus conflicting data lead to uncertain conclusions.

Prison Overcrowding and the Nature of the Prison Population. The second aspect of our incarceration policy concerns prison overcrowding and the need to continually build more prisons to accommodate the increased number of prisoners. This need will, of course, lead to a still greater allocation of resources to corrections. Although crime rates fell throughout the 1990s, the prison population soared. A number of factors contributed to this increase. (1) Mandatory minimum sentences have been established for drug violations, and now one in four prisoners is a drug offender. Research by the Department of Justice and other agencies has documented that many of these prisoners are low-level offenders whose continued incarceration is extremely costly and wasteful of prison space. (2) In 1994, the federal crime bill contained a "Truth in Sentencing" provision. Under this law, half the states have qualified for federal prison funding by changing their sentencing laws to require that certain offenders serve at least 85 percent of their prison sentence before being considered for parole. (3) The federal government and nearly half the states have passed "three strikes and you're out" laws that require sentences of life without parole for a third conviction of certain serious crimes. As a result of these policies, the national prison population is expected to exceed two million in 2001.[5] States have built new and larger prisons, but the prison population has been increasing as rapidly as has prison capacity.

http://www.ojp.usdoj.
gov/bjs
This Bureau of Justice Statistics site has data on U.S. prisons and prisoners.

SHOULD DRUGS BE LEGALIZED?

One of the most controversial topics in the field of crime and criminology today is legalization or decriminalization of now-illegal drugs. If we were to legalize drugs, we would simply repeal the laws that make possessing and selling drugs a crime. If we were to decriminalize the possession or selling of drugs, we would reduce the severity of the laws against these offenses, making them misdemeanors punishable by modest fines. Economic theory can add another dimension to the discussion of this emotionally charged subject. Furthermore, the economic analysis we use here can be extended to other related topics. Let us begin by discussing the possibility of legalizing drugs.

Background on the Legal Status of Drugs

The United States has a history of prohibiting or regulating the use of "mind-altering" substances. Laws and public policy concerning these substances do, however, change over time. Opiates have been illegal since 1914 and marijuana since 1937. Alcohol was entirely prohibited between 1920 and 1933. Currently alcohol and tobacco are legal, but legally cannot be sold to minors. All of these substances are at least somewhat addictive, and our dominant attitude is that, at a minimum, they should be regulated. Legalization is therefore unlikely, but at least partial decriminalization might be politically feasible.

The War on Drugs: U.S. Antidrug Policy

In the last half of the twentieth century two U.S. presidents have declared war on drugs: Richard Nixon in 1971 and Ronald Reagan in 1982. The drug war has been one of the most popular of our recent conflicts. The majority of the populace supports the concept. In economic terms, the so-called War on Drugs involves measures to decrease both the supply of and the demand for drugs.

Decreasing the Supply of Drugs

Among the measures designed to decrease the supply of drugs have been (1) efforts to prevent drugs from entering the country and (2) increases in the severity of the punishment for selling drugs. We have hired more personnel: federal agents for the FBI and Drug Enforcement Agency, U.S. attorneys to prosecute drug cases, and clerical staff. We have given drug enforcement agencies more money with which to operate, and we have redirected dollars formerly allocated to drug treatment programs and research into law enforcement programs. We have built more prison cells to accommodate more people with drug-related convictions. We have passed stricter laws and cut through bureaucracy in the attempt to decrease the supply of illegal drugs on the streets of our cities.

Since the 1980s, efforts to stem the supply of drugs coming into this country from abroad have involved the U.S. military. The century-old Posse Comitatus Act, which prohibited the military from enforcing civil laws, was amended in 1982 to permit the war chest of the U.S. military to be used for drug enforcement. As a result the military is now involved in drug enforcement training, intelligence gathering, and detection. Military personnel operate Navy, Army, and Marine Corps equipment for these purposes under the direction of civilian agencies.

Decreasing the Demand for Drugs

To decrease demand, we have instituted drug awareness and education programs for our youth. To deter our citizens from experimenting with drugs, we have increased the penalties for the possession of illegal drugs. Our prisons have drug treatment programs for offenders. Any education or treatment program is designed to act on the demand side of the drug market.

In 1988 the White House policy of "zero tolerance" of drug use was announced. This policy appears to be based on the belief that drug abuse starts with a willful act on the part of the drug user, and that without users there would be no drug problem. The underlying idea is that the market is created not only by the supply of drugs but also by the demand for them. The public perception that drug addicts are unable to control their drug habits is presumed to be wrong, and it is held that users could stop their drug use and must be held accountable if they do not. Therefore the public tolerance for drug use has been reduced to zero. From this position come more severe penalties for drug users in an attempt to reduce the demand side for drugs.

Although these policies were initiated under Republican presidents, the War on Drugs is bipartisan. The Clinton Administration's "drug czars" Lee Brown and Barry McAffrey have overseen one of the world's strictest drug prohibition programs. About 70 percent of the money spent on the War on Drugs has been directed toward activities designed to decrease supply; the remainder has targeted programs to decrease demand.

The Argument against Legalization of Drugs

The argument against the legalization of drugs is based mainly on (1) the adverse public health consequences of drugs, (2) the uncertain link between drug use and criminal behavior, (3) the expected increase in drug-related social problems if drugs were to be legalized, and (4) the successes of the War on Drugs.

Public Health Consequences

Proponents of continued drug prohibition argue that there is solid evidence that the legalization of drugs would have great public health consequences. Some studies indicate that marijuana is at least as harmful to the lungs as tobacco—maybe more harmful—because it delivers more concentrated tar than do filter-tipped cigarettes. Moreover, the potency of marijuana has increased in recent years, so its effects persist longer. Marijuana is thought to inhibit personal growth and effective coping with personal problems. Furthermore, marijuana may serve as a "gateway drug" from which the inexperienced user advances to more harmful substances. Marijuana may not be physically addictive, but many of the other drugs available are addictive. Opponents of legalization believe that drug use would soar if we were to legalize drugs.

Criminal Behavior and Drug Use

The link between criminal behavior and drug use is uncertain. Proponents of legalization argue that the high cost of illegal drugs leads to criminal behavior by drug users who finance their drug habits through criminal activity, but recent research casts doubt on this relationship. It's obvious, however, that some crimes are committed by individuals under the influence of drugs. Opponents of legalization are concerned about this fact but allege that although many criminals have a history of drug use, the high cost of illegal drugs cannot be shown to cause the crime. Instead, they argue, the drugs may be merely a symptom of an established pattern of antisocial behavior: these drug-using criminals would be crooks whether drugs were legalized or remained illegal.

Drug-Related Social Problems

Opponents of legalization also argue that because more people would use drugs if they were legal, we would have more drug-related problems. Like alcohol use, drug use contributes to higher worker absenteeism and lower productivity. Driving under the influence of alcohol contributes to car wrecks, injuries, and loss of life, and so would driving under the influence of legal drugs. And like alcohol, drug use may contribute to birth defects or miscarriages. Alcohol currently contributes to many antisocial behavior patterns; legal drugs would contribute to such patterns as well.

Successes of the War on Drugs

The War on Drugs is certainly not an unqualified success, but it assuredly has had some limited victories. Use of marijuana and cocaine in the United States fell during the 1980s, as did the use of most other drugs. Opponents of drug legalization argue that we certainly should not adopt any policies that would conflict with this trend. Because most people in the United States oppose legalization anyway, legalization would be politically impractical.

Other Arguments against Legalization

Proponents of drug legalization argue that our current drug laws infringe on our individual liberties and our right to make our own choices, even if these choices are self-destructive. Opponents of drug legalization argue that society has always regulated our choices to protect itself and individuals from harm. Allowing us access to addictive, harmful substances would really be a perversion of liberty. Note that virtually no one who provides treatment to crack cocaine addicts recommends the legalization of currently illegal drugs.

Instead of legalizing drugs, opponents of legalization argue that we should strengthen supply-side programs that keep heroin and cocaine from crossing our borders. Furthermore, they believe that we should commit more resources to drug education and treatment programs. The emphasis on supply-side programs instead of demand-side programs has been largely political, as arrests and seizures of drug shipments are widely publicized measures of success used to justify the resources devoted to drug control. Data on addicts in treatment are less compelling justifications for continued or increased expenditures.

The Argument for Legalization of Drugs

Proponents of drug legalization argue that the War on Drugs has been lost and that our current antidrug policies have had disastrous side effects. They maintain that efforts to restrict supply have largely failed.

The Failure of International Drug Control

Many U.S. experts on drug control have emphasized international drug control efforts, because domestic efforts to control supply have been virtually futile. The problems encountered in such efforts, however, doom them to failure. Marijuana and opium can be grown almost anywhere, and the coca plant, from which cocaine is derived, is now grown in environments that were once thought inhospitable to it. Whenever supply from one area of the globe is disrupted, other areas rush to fill the void. It has been likened to pushing in on a balloon. For example, successful eradication of marijuana from Mexico in the 1970s led to greater importation of marijuana from Colombia and expanded marijuana production in the United States.

Controlling drug supply at the source faces many other obstacles. In some of the Third World countries that export drugs, political parties are involved in the production and sale of these commodities. In others, drug cartels have power rivaling that of the government. Low-income peasants producing raw drugs cannot switch to legal crops and make nearly as high a profit. In some cases growing and using the products is cultural: some Andean natives, for example, grow and chew coca leaves. These producers do not perceive themselves as criminals who hurt the U.S. people through their endeavors. So long as Americans demand drugs, there will be producers who try to meet that demand. It has been estimated that we have managed to stop only about 10 percent of drug shipments that originate from abroad.

The Costs of Prohibition

Proponents of drug legalization argue that our current drug laws not only are ineffective in controlling supply but also have unintended and huge costs. First, because drugs are illegal, they are provided by an illegal, or underground, economy. Therefore the major beneficiary of drug prohibition is organized crime. Organized crime is the major source of illegal drugs, and it has been estimated that sales of illegal drugs account for half the revenues of organized crime in the United States. Drugs command a high price on the street, but this price is not based on high costs of manufacture. Instead, the price is largely attributable to the risks traffickers take, risks for which they charge a high premium. These risk premiums are like an illegality tax that swells the coffers of organized crime.

Second, drug prohibition may contribute to crime in other ways. Because the street price of illegal drugs is so high, addicts may commit crimes to buy their drugs. And much violent crime results from turf wars among drug dealers. A real victim of drug prohibition may be the law-abiding citizen hurt in the crossfire of a drug turf war.

Third, the taxpayers bear the burden of the criminal justice system. The War on Drugs has increased both the absolute dollar expenditures on this system and the percentage of our resources devoted to drug violations. About 25 percent of the convicts in state and federal prisons are there for drug law violations. The more effective our current drug laws, the more prison cells we will need. The burden on taxpayers will escalate as we build and equip more prisons to accommodate drug violators. Furthermore, drug laws may result in discriminatory incarceration. The mandatory sentence for possession of crack cocaine, often used by blacks, is higher than the mandatory sentence for powdered cocaine, which is more often used by whites. Finally, resources used by the police to arrest pushers cannot be used to investigate violent crimes and crimes against property. There is a conflict here. In some localities, law enforcement has come to mean drug law enforcement.

Fourth, proponents of legalization argue that another cost of drug prohibition is its contribution to the corruption of the police and others in the criminal justice system. All vice-control efforts are particularly susceptible to bribes, and bribes are difficult to detect because there is no victim of bribery to file a complaint. Police may be disillusioned by the widespread use of illegal drugs. The financial temptations are enormous and understandable, given the difficulty involved in enforcing our laws concerned with drug prohibition.

Fifth, another cost of drug prohibition may be the violation of our constitutional rights. Proponents of legalization argue that roadblocks and random searches of automobiles, exclusionary rule exceptions that allow authorities to use illegally seized evidence in court, and random drug testing all are violations of constitutional rights. These actions are, however, accepted by society because public opinion so greatly favors drug-law enforcement.

Finally, proponents of legalization argue that although drugs themselves may have adverse public health consequences, so does drug prohibition. Because drugs are illegal, we cannot regulate their safety. Users cannot tell if they are pure or adulterated or what their strength is. Marijuana may have been sprayed with the dangerous herbicide paraquat or grown with dangerous fertilizers that are more hazardous to the user than is the marijuana. Some argue that drug prohibition also keeps us from adopting sane policies to combat the spread of AIDS through the use of shared needles. Although some governments have instituted policies to exchange needles as an AIDS control measure, ours has not. The prevailing belief is that to support needle exchange programs is to support, or at least to condone, the use of illegal substances.

The Benefits of Legalization

Proponents of legalization argue that repealing drug prohibition laws would provide many advantages. First, net financial benefits to the government from legalization would be considerable. We could tax the producers of the formerly illegal substances, generating many tax dollars for the government. Enforcement expenditures could be cut, or redirected toward more serious crime. And we would be able to halt the constant expansion of the prison system at the expense of other social programs. Second, drugs would be safer if they were legal. We could regulate quality and institute needle exchange programs in good conscience. Third, the risk premium that stems from the illegality of drugs would disappear. As a result, drugs would not be such a profitable business for organized crime. We could expect that organized crime syndicates would exit the drug industry and be supplanted by legal pharmaceutical firms. Fourth, we would expect less criminal activity on the part of users who engaged in crime to finance their expensive drug habits when drugs were illegal. Finally, some of the resources saved could be directed toward education and treatment programs. This emphasis on the demand side of the drug market may well be more effective than the historical emphasis on supply-side programs.

The Economics of Prohibition or Legalization

Having laid out the cases for and against legalization, let us now add careful economic analysis to this discussion. The tool we will use will be supply and demand analysis. Note that because drugs are illegal, both sellers and buyers are, by definition, criminals. Therefore, both supply and demand will be less than they would be if drugs were legalized. Let us look at the effects of legalization on supply and demand separately, and then put supply and demand together. Figure 13-2 on page 294 analyzes the effect of legalization on the supply of drugs. The graph

FIGURE 13-2   Effect of the Legalization of Drugs on the Supply of Drugs

Legalization of drugs would increase supply from S_1 to S_2 and decrease the price of drugs to P_2; quantity would increase to Q_2.

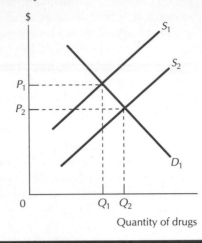

shows supply and demand in a market for a particular drug. D_1 and S_1 are the demand and supply curves if drugs are illegal. The supply curve S_1 incorporates a risk premium to the drug traffickers and the high costs of bribing the local police. The demand curve D_1 shows demand after some potential users have been deterred from using the drug by the penalties prescribed by our legal system.

Now assume that we legalize this particular drug. Supply would expand to S_2, because the corruption costs (such as bribery) of the illegal sellers and the risk premium would no longer exist. The price of the drug would decrease. This price decrease might indeed cut into profits enough to cause organized crime syndicates to look elsewhere for profits. But the equilibrium quantity would increase; we cannot ignore the fact that use would increase with legalization.

How much use of the drug would increase depends on whether the demand for the drug is inelastic or elastic. If the demand for drugs is inelastic, use will not increase much. Recall from Chapter Two and its appendix that an **inelastic demand** means that consumers are relatively unresponsive to changes in price: when prices go either up or down, quantity demanded doesn't change much. Therefore we represent an inelastic demand with a relatively steep demand curve. Figure 13-3 shows both an inelastic demand curve and a flatter (more elastic) demand curve. **Elastic demand** simply means that buyers are more responsive to changes in price. Thus quantity demanded changes more as price changes, and we would graph this as a flatter demand curve. Note the increase in equilibrium quantity (use) that would result from the same increase in supply in each case. Equilibrium quantity (drug use) will increase significantly if demand

Inelastic demand
Demand in which buyers are relatively unresponsive to changes in price.

Elastic demand
Demand in which buyers are relatively responsive to changes in price.

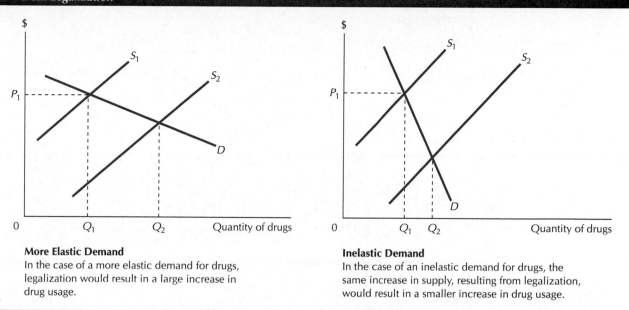

More Elastic Demand
In the case of a more elastic demand for drugs, legalization would result in a large increase in drug usage.

Inelastic Demand
In the case of an inelastic demand for drugs, the same increase in supply, resulting from legalization, would result in a smaller increase in drug usage.

is elastic, but use will not increase very much in the case of an inelastic demand for the drug.

The fact of the matter is that we do not know whether the demand for most drugs is inelastic or elastic. Because drug markets are illegal, we lack information about price–quantity combinations in the real world. Although we would expect those addicted to a narcotic to have a highly inelastic demand, we do not know much about the responsiveness of casual users to changes in the price of controlled substances. What little experimental knowledge we have comes from the decriminalization of marijuana by several U.S. states and the legalization of drugs by the Netherlands. The states that decriminalized marijuana in the 1970s experienced the same use patterns as neighboring states that continued to prohibit it. And the Netherlands' legalization was not accompanied by greatly increased drug use, if we adjust for the international movement of addicts from more restrictive countries into the Netherlands. Assuming that drug prices fell in both of these cases, the findings that drug use did not greatly increase in either case is somewhat reassuring and indicative of inelastic demands.

Now let's consider the effect of legalization on the demand for drugs. When drugs are prohibited by law, some potential users are deterred from using the drugs by drug law penalties. In addition to the increase in supply, demand would also increase if drugs were legalized. Those formerly deterred only by legal penalties would enter the market. We might well see more people experimenting with drugs

FIGURE 13-4 Effect of Legalization of Drugs on the Demand for Drugs

Legalization would increase demand from D_1 to D_2, which would increase price to P_2 and quantity to Q_2.

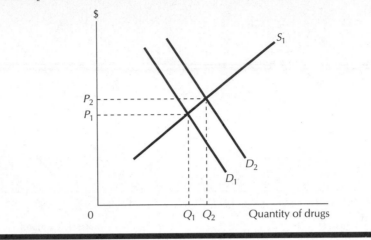

than we do now. The increase in demand is shown in Figure 13-4. When demand increases from D_1 to D_2, price and quantity increase to P_2 and Q_2, respectively.

Note that the increase in supply decreases the price of drugs and that the increase in demand increases their equilibrium price. The changes are offsetting, so the effect on equilibrium price is really quite difficult to predict. Most experts, however, predict that the price of drugs would go down at least somewhat with legalization. But note also that both the change in demand and the change in supply would increase equilibrium quantity; it is quite clear that use would increase with legalization.

Regulation through Economic Policies

Economists who favor drug legalization or decriminalization often also suggest economic means of influencing the legal markets for drugs. First, they argue that a much greater percentage of the government's expenditures on drug-related programs should be directed toward demand-side treatment and education programs. As we have already noted, only 30 percent of drug-related expenditures are directed to demand-side policies. By decreasing demand we can decrease use. Second, a system of excise taxes can be levied on the legal drugs. The level of the tax on each substance should be correlated with the drug's harmful public health effects. If the clinical evidence indicates that the consequences of using cocaine are more severe than the consequences of using marijuana, the tax levied on cocaine should be higher. The effect of these excise taxes would be similar to the pollution taxes discussed in Chapter Three, in that they would decrease supply as the producers' costs increased. This phenomenon occurs because it is the supplier of the drug who pays the tax dollars to the government. We can view this tax payment as just another increase in the cost of producing or supplying drugs. Remember that an increase in

FIGURE 13-5   How Excise Taxes Could Decrease the Use of Legal Drugs

Assuming that cocaine constitutes a greater public health risk than marijuana, a higher excise tax would be imposed on cocaine. In either case the tax would cause a backward shift in supply, which would result in higher prices and lower use.

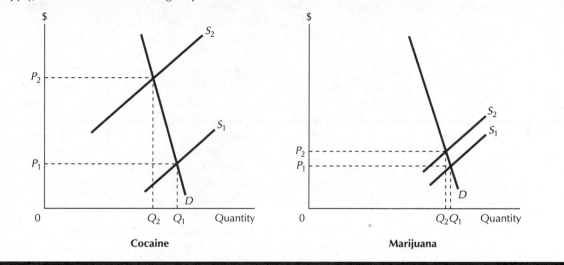

the costs of production will shift the supply curve backward. This decrease in supply will cause an increase in the drug's price and a decrease in its use.

Figure 13-5 shows hypothetical markets for cocaine and marijuana with public health taxes levied on producers. Ideally, the amount of the tax would be just equal to the public health costs in each case. The vertical distance between the two supply curves in each graph is the amount of the tax per unit. Thus the larger public health tax on cocaine results in a greater decrease in supply, increase in price, and decrease in usage than the smaller tax on marijuana.

Furthermore, revenues from the taxes could be earmarked for treatment and education programs. In addition to the excise taxes, the substances would be regulated and kept out of the hands of minors, as we currently attempt to keep both alcohol and tobacco from being purchased by teenagers. So legalization and the imposition of the taxes would not eliminate the need for policing the market for drugs entirely. The policing burden would, however, be far lighter than it is under prohibition.

THE LEGALIZATION OF OTHER VICTIMLESS CRIMES

The economic analysis (and many of the noneconomic arguments) we have used to examine the controversy over the legalization of drugs can also be applied to arguments about the legal status of other so-called victimless crimes such as pornography and prostitution. These are crimes not because of violence against persons or property, but because of public censure and disapproval. It can be

When discussing emotionally charged social issues such as the control of drugs, pornography, and prostitution, it is especially important to apply care in the way we use the terms liberal and conservative. The terms often have opposite meanings when we are considering government involvement in our daily lives versus government involvement in the economy. Let's try to understand the distinction.

Economic conservatives support less government involvement in economic realms. They favor a market-oriented approach to most situations. Thus economic conservatives would support the legalization of drugs and other victimless crimes. (Note that social conservatives would not support such legalization.) The economic conservative would value the efficiencies attained when market forces shift demand and supply curves if legalization occurs. Furthermore, they would prefer excise taxes and other market approaches to account for the harmful community effects of drugs and other victimless crimes, instead of the prohibition of the activity itself.

Economic liberals, on the other hand, favor greater government intervention in the marketplace. They would favor the criminalization and prohibition of drug use and other victimless crimes. They might especially favor efforts to reduce the supply of drugs and support the law enforcement expenditures needed to increase the effectiveness of the war on drugs. (Note that social liberals are more likely to support legalization of drugs.) We should point out, however, that economists, like the rest of our society, usually hold opinions about the legalization of drugs and other victimless crimes that are not based solely on economic principles.

argued that, like drug use, the purchase of pornography or the services of a prostitute is a consensual transaction. That is, both buyer and seller consent to the trade. Thus there is no victim. Policing by the vice squad for these victimless crimes is difficult because there is no victim to file a complaint. Corruption of police working the vice squad is thought to be higher than of police working details such as robbery. The same arguments for legalization, regulation, and taxation therefore can be made for these offenses. As with drugs, the equilibrium quantity would undoubtedly increase with legalization, but regulation and taxation for regulatory purposes might well be more efficient than prohibition. But as with drugs, social issues related to legalization may outweigh the economic issues.

SUMMARY

A crime is any activity forbidden by law and punishable by criminal penalty. Our expenditures on our criminal justice system, which includes police, courts, and prisons, have increased greatly in inflation-adjusted dollars in the past 20 years. The greatest increase has occurred in the prison system.

The appropriate methodology to evaluate crime prevention measures is cost-benefit analysis. A policy should be adopted or kept only if its benefits are greater than its costs. The results of cost-benefit studies on our prison expansion are contradictory and inconclusive.

Some crimes are victimless because they are the result of consensual transactions between two parties. These crimes are illegal only because society, or a significant group in society, disapproves of them on moral, health, or ethical grounds, so we have passed laws prohibiting them. Legalizing these victimless crimes arguably may be more efficient than prohibiting them. Both demand and supply would increase, price would decrease at least slightly, and equilibrium quantity would increase. Although use would increase, the goods and services involved would be provided legally and earn lower profits, so their provision would be less attractive to organized crime. If these victimless crimes were made legal, we could regulate them, in part through taxation.

NOTES

1. U.S. Department of Justice, Bureau of Justice Statistics, *Expenditure and Employment Statistics 1996* (http://www.ojp.usdoj.gov/bjs/cande.htm).

2. U.S. Department of Justice, Federal Bureau of Investigation, *Preliminary Annual Unified Crime Report* (http://www.fbi.gov/ucr.prelim99).

3. Calculated from U.S. Department of Justice, Bureau of Justice Statistics, *Sourcebook of Criminal Justice Statistics*, Table 1.1 (http://www.albany.edu/sourcebook). The figures were deflated using the GDP deflator.

4. The Sentencing Project, *Facts about Prisons and Prisoners* (http://www.Sentencingproject.org).

5. The Sentencing Project, *National Inmate Population of Two Million Projected for 2001* (http://www.Sentencingproject.org).

DISCUSSION QUESTIONS

1. *What are the characteristics of a public good? Name some other public goods in addition to crime prevention.*

2. *What is the free rider problem? Why does it exist?*

3. *What is meant when we say that a public good is indivisible, nonrivalrous, and nonexcludable?*

4. *Discuss cost-benefit analysis. What are the benefits of crime prevention? What are the costs? Are all the benefits and costs easily measurable? Are there situations in which cost-benefit analysis is inappropriate?*

5. *Of what significance is the elasticity of demand for drugs in the debate about legalization of presently illegal substances?*

6. *How could taxes be used to regulate legal drug markets?*

7. *Is it possible to be a social liberal and an economic conservative (or vice versa) with regard to victimless crimes?*

8. *Go to the Federal Bureau of Investigation Web site (http://www.fbi.gov), click on Uniform Crime Report, and find the latest statistics on violent crime.*

CHAPTER 14

Unemployment and Inflation

We are fortunate to be alive at this moment in history. Never before has our nation enjoyed, at once, so much prosperity and social progress with so little internal crisis. . . .

William Jefferson Clinton, *State of the Union Address,* 2000

The year was 2000. We had entered the new millennium in a position of macroeconomic health. The 1990s were a period of economic growth and expansion. Unemployment and inflation rates were the lowest in decades. How long can this state of affairs last?

The words from the speech that began this chapter echo the vibrant economy of the new millennium. If you are a traditional student in your late teens or early twenties, you are only familiar with a healthy economy. The stories of job layoffs and unemployment lines are just that—stories from years gone by. Perhaps your grandparents lived during the Great Depression of the 1930s. Ask them to tell you about the one of four people who couldn't find work, the bread lines, and the frugality of the era. Perhaps your grandparents still won't throw anything away, despite being comfortably well off. The lessons of hard times are difficult to erase.

Maybe your parents remember the inflation of the 1970s with skyrocketing energy prices and long lines for gasoline, or the recession of 1981–1982, when President Reagan and the Federal Reserve brought inflation under control but ushered in the highest unemployment rates since the Great Depression. Perhaps you even remember talk of higher-than-normal unemployment at the beginning of the 1990s, when jobs were more scarce and the job search more lengthy.

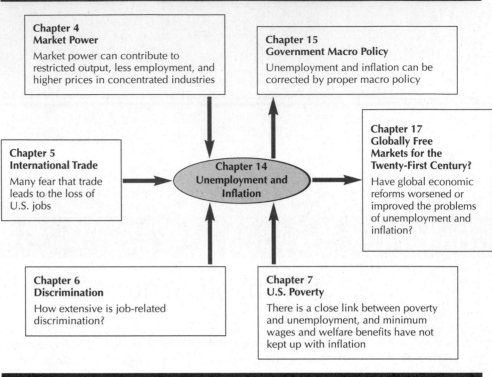

Chapter 4
Market Power
Market power can contribute to restricted output, less employment, and higher prices in concentrated industries

Chapter 15
Government Macro Policy
Unemployment and inflation can be corrected by proper macro policy

Chapter 5
International Trade
Many fear that trade leads to the loss of U.S. jobs

Chapter 14
Unemployment and Inflation

Chapter 17
Globally Free Markets for the Twenty-First Century?
Have global economic reforms worsened or improved the problems of unemployment and inflation?

Chapter 6
Discrimination
How extensive is job-related discrimination?

Chapter 7
U.S. Poverty
There is a close link between poverty and unemployment, and minimum wages and welfare benefits have not kept up with inflation

These days are behind us now, and the economic picture is rosy. As indicated above, we are experiencing macroeconomic health. What does this health mean for us? What does it mean for you as you look to your job horizon and to your spending habits as an American consumer? And more importantly, will it last long enough for you to prosper from it?

THE MACROECONOMY

Macroeconomy
The total economy.

Macroeconomics
The study of the total economy.

Microeconomics
The study of individual aspects within the total economy.

As you recall from Chapter One, when we study unemployment and inflation and the policies designed to control them, we are focusing on the **macroeconomy.** Indeed, **macroeconomics** is the study of the overall economy. In previous chapters we've considered individual markets such as the markets for health care, housing, and agricultural products. The study of individual markets within the economy is part of the study of **microeconomics.** Some economists refer to microeconomics as the study of the trees, whereas macroeconomics is the study of the forest. We're looking at the same economy, but contrasting the individual parts with the overall picture.

Recall our study of agricultural markets in Chapter Two. We were interested in the output of corn or wheat and how the prices of these agricultural goods were

Gross domestic product (GDP)
Total output in an economy.

changing. In macroeconomics, we are concerned instead with the quantity of *total* output in our economy (which we call **gross domestic product,** or GDP) and how the average price level for all of this output is changing. An increase in the average price level is what we mean by inflation. And although employment within any individual market is closely related to output in that market, in macroeconomics we are more concerned with employment for the country as a whole, which is closely related to *total* production.

UNEMPLOYMENT

We begin the new century with over 20 million new jobs; the fastest economic growth in more than 30 years; the lowest unemployment rates in 30 years; . . . the lowest African American and Hispanic unemployment rates on record. . . . We have built a new economy.

President Clinton, *State of the Union Address,* 2000

Clearly the prosperity of this moment in history is highlighted by our success in reducing unemployment rates. So let's begin our study of macroeconomics with topics related to unemployment. To do so, we need to understand what is meant by the concepts of the labor force and the labor force participation rate.

The Labor Force Participation Rate

Labor force
All people age 16 and over who are working for pay or actively seeking employment.

The **labor force** refers to all people aged 16 and over who are working for pay *plus* all people in this age range who are actively seeking employment. Think about this definition for a moment. Clearly the concept of the labor force goes beyond just those people who are working. It also includes those who would like to be working and who are looking for a job. We sometimes refer to the labor force as the work force. It refers to those actively interested in working.

Who is *not* included in the labor force? Obviously, not children. But neither are retired people, full-time homemakers who do not desire a job outside of the home, full-time students who do not wish to work for pay along with their studies, people in institutions such as prisons and mental hospitals, nor anyone else who is *not* actively seeking a job. The labor force is clearly a subset of the entire population.

Why is this concept of the labor force important? First, it demonstrates the quantity of our labor resource available for the production of national output. It also reflects societal trends and attitudes. In the 1950s and 1960s, for example, many women did not work outside of the home. Indeed, many in society believed that women's place was in the home, and not in the labor force. This attitude was not prevalent during earlier war times or in recent years. Attitudes have changed about the work habits of teenagers, single mothers, and even fathers of newborns; and financial necessity has increased the likelihood that many college students support themselves with part-time work.

The phenomenon of working mothers is very interesting. In the early 1960s, only about one-fourth of married mothers worked outside the home, whereas more than one-half of single mothers did. Over the next few decades, the share of

TABLE 14-1 U.S. Labor Force Participation Rate for Men and Women, Individually and Combined, 1964 and 2000

	MEN	WOMEN	MEN AND WOMEN
1964	81.0%	38.7%	58.7%
2000	74.7%	60.2%	67.2%

Source: U.S. Department of Commerce, Bureau of Labor Statistics.

Labor force participation rate
The ratio of the number of people in the labor force to the number of people age 16 or over in the population.

working married mothers increased dramatically, but the share of working single mothers remained stable. By the mid-1980s, the share of working married mothers exceeded that of single mothers, and by the late 1990s, almost two-thirds of married mothers worked.[1] What do you think are the reasons for these trends?

The **labor force participation rate** is the share of the population aged 16 and over that is in the labor force. It is calculated as the number of people in the labor force divided by the total number of people aged 16 and over. We can think of the labor force participation rate as the percentage of all adults who are actively interested in working. Table 14-1 shows the U.S. labor force participation rate for males and females, individually and combined, in 1964 and 2000. Overall, the labor force participation rate has increased somewhat since 1964. Notice, however, that the participation rate of men has decreased, whereas the participation rate of women has increased dramatically. The rate remains much higher for men than women though.

To compare the labor force participation rate of one country with that of another country, we must adjust our definition of that rate. Because child labor is much more extensive in other countries, particularly in less developed ones, we need to take a broader view of the labor force. World Bank data indicate, for example, that more than 52 percent and 47 percent of children aged 10 through 14 are part of the labor force in the West African countries of Mali and Burkina Faso, respectively. In other parts of the world, 43 percent of children in this age group in Nepal and 29 percent in Bangladesh belong to the labor force. In the United States, of course, the official percentage is zero.

We can use complete population data and statistics on all people in the labor force, regardless of age, to calculate an adjusted labor force participation rate. A sampling of countries is shown in Table 14-2. Because the countries chosen are not necessarily representative of the various regions of the world, we cannot use this sample to make generalizations about the regions. In addition, we must be cautious about our interpretation of the data, because many people in less-developed countries work in informal labor markets and are not always counted as among the officially employed. We do see a wide variation in the participation rates, however, ranging from 39 percent in Argentina to 60 percent in China.

The Unemployment Rate

Ask your friends how they think the unemployment rate is calculated. Unless they've had an economics course, they will probably stammer a little and then

TABLE 14-2 Adjusted Labor Force Participation Rate (inclusive of children) for Select Countries, 1999*

	COUNTRY 1	COUNTRY 2	COUNTRY 3
Africa	Mali	Ethiopia	Nigeria
	46%	43%	40%
Asia	China	Japan	Bangladesh
	60%	54%	52%
Latin America	Brazil	Argentina	Colombia
	46%	39%	44%
Western Europe	France	Britain	Italy
	44%	51%	43%
Eastern Europe	Russia	Poland	Ukraine
	53%	51%	50%
North America	United States	Canada	Mexico
	51%	55%	40%

*The calculations are made by dividing the entire labor force, inclusive of children, by the entire population in each country.
Source: Data from World Bank, *World Development Report 2000/2001* (New York: Oxford University Press, 2001).

make some vague statements about people without jobs. Unfortunately, this answer will not be adequate for economic analysis.

The **unemployment rate** is defined as the percentage of the labor force that is unemployed. The unemployment rate is calculated as follows:

Unemployment rate
The percentage of the labor force that is unemployed.

$$\text{Unemployment rate} = \frac{\text{Number of unemployed people}}{\text{Number of people in the labor force}}$$

Unemployed person
A person aged 16 or over who is actively seeking employment but who is unable to find a job.

To qualify as an **unemployed person,** a person must be in the labor force. As you already know, the U.S. concept of the labor force refers to all people aged 16 and over who are working for pay plus all people aged 16 and over who are not employed but are actively seeking employment. The latter are considered unemployed.

Think about this definition for a moment. Some people are not counted in either the numerator or the denominator. The only people who are classified as unemployed are those who are actively looking for jobs. That is, they must be answering want ads, sending out vitae, engaging in job interviews, or doing whatever is necessary to find a job. Therefore, full-time homemakers and students who are not seeking employment for pay are not categorized as unemployed. (Neither are children, retired people, volunteer workers, people in prison or mental hospitals, or those who would simply rather not work.)

Because the labor force consists of people who are either employed or unemployed, it may sound as though the labor force and the total population are the same. This is not the case! Remember that all of the homemakers, students, retired people, children, and so on that were excluded from the numerator of the

TABLE 14-3 U.S. Unemployment Rates, in Percent, Selected Years from 1960 to 2000

YEAR	UNEMPLOYMENT RATE	YEAR	UNEMPLOYMENT RATE
1960	5.5	1991	6.7
1965	4.5	1992	7.4
1970	4.9	1993	6.8
1975	8.5	1994	6.1
1980	7.1	1995	5.6
1981	7.6	1996	5.4
1982	9.7	1997	4.9
1983	9.6	1998	4.5
1985	7.2	1999	4.2
		2000	4.0

Source: U.S. Department of Commerce, Bureau of Labor Statistics.

unemployment rate are excluded from the denominator as well. They are not actively interested in working for pay.

The Data

What is the national unemployment rate? We already know that the current rate is very low. Just what is considered low and what is high? How do current rates compare with those of the recent past? Do all groups of people within our economy face the same probability of becoming unemployed? What are your chances of becoming unemployed?

The National Unemployment Rate

Let us begin to answer these questions by looking at the annual unemployment rates for our nation in recent years. Table 14-3 displays these data.

Notice that the year 2000 unemployment rate is extremely low by historical standards. This all-time recent low is lower than imaginable even in the prosperous years of the 1960s, not to mention the economic slowdowns of 1975, 1981–83, and 1992. The current low rates have a lot to do with the steady expansion of our economy since 1992. We will discuss these situations more carefully in the next chapter.

The unemployment rates since 1992 are shown more visibly in Figure 14-1. Notice the precipitous decline!

Unemployment Rates for Selected Groups of People

Like the national unemployment rates indicated in Table 14-3, the relative unemployment rates of certain groups of people are important for national policy. Table 14-4 displays these data for the month of May 2000. The national average unemployment rate for this month was 4.1 percent. We can use this number as a benchmark for comparing the unemployment rates of individual groups of people.

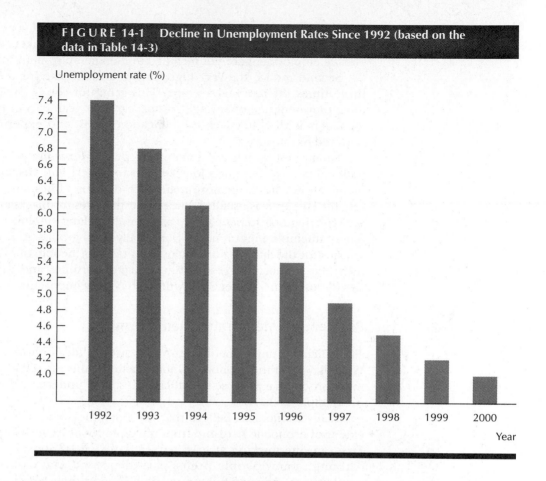

FIGURE 14-1 Decline in Unemployment Rates Since 1992 (based on the data in Table 14-3)

Notice first of all that the unemployment rate for men is slightly lower than that for women. This is not always the case. In fact, unemployment rates for women and men have been similar in recent years. In one year the rate may be a little higher for men, whereas the next year the rate may be a little higher for

TABLE 14-4 U.S. Unemployment Rates for Selected Groups, in Percent, May 2000

GROUP	UNEMPLOYMENT RATE
Nation	4.1%
Men	3.9%
Women	4.3%
Youth aged 16–19	12.5%
White	3.5%
Black	8.0%
Hispanic	5.8%

Source: U.S. Department of Commerce, Bureau of Labor Statistics.

women. Keep in mind that to be classified as unemployed, a person must be actively seeking employment. Therefore any full-time homemakers who are not seeking outside employment are not included in the unemployment statistics.

Second, notice the very high unemployment rate for teenagers, more than three times the national average. This group of young people has the highest unemployment rate of any age group, year after year. Part of the difficulty for our teenagers is that they lack the education, skills, and experience that are often required by employers.

Finally, notice that the unemployment rate for white people is well below the national average and far below the rates for blacks and Hispanics. The unemployment rate for blacks is more than twice that for whites, and the unemployment rate for Hispanics is usually between that the rates for blacks and whites. Again, we are referring only to people who are actively seeking employment. Clearly, the burden of unemployment is not borne equally by all groups. Although there are many reasons for the differing unemployment rates for people of differing race and ethnicity, the numbers suggest that the equal opportunity and affirmative action policies discussed in Chapter Six continue to be very important.

Problems in Measuring Unemployment

The official unemployment rate gives us a rough idea of how the economy is doing. We believe that the economy is doing better if this rate falls. But various measurement problems may cause the official statistics to understate the economic hardship of unemployment.

Many economists believe that the unemployment rate understates the true extent of economic hardship from unemployment in our country for two reasons. First, anyone working at least part-time for pay is considered to be employed. Although many people prefer part-time work, many others prefer full-time employment and need full-time work to support their families. When these people can find only part-time jobs, they experience economic hardship even though they are officially classified as being employed.

Second, some people who would like to work and who have actively sought employment have become so discouraged in their search that they have given up looking for jobs. In many ways, these **discouraged workers** are perhaps the ones most severely affected by unemployment, yet they cease to be tallied in the unemployment statistics as soon as they cease their active job search. When the economy is depressed, the number of discouraged workers increases, and the understating of unemployment becomes more severe. During the Great Depression of the 1930s, the official unemployment rate rose to 24.9 percent. Most economists believe that if all the discouraged workers had been counted, the unemployment rate would have been much higher.

Economists believe that mismeasurement of the unemployment rate can have serious ramifications. First, many of our macroeconomic policies are based on the unemployment rate, and if unemployment is understated, policymakers may not take the problem seriously enough. Second, changes in our economy can have a misleading impact on official unemployment rates. When the economy is in a

Discouraged workers
People who would like to work, but have become so discouraged in the job search that they have stopped actively seeking employment.

downturn, for example, many people who are unable to find employment give up their job search. At that point, they fall out of the unemployment statistics entirely, as they are no longer classified as being unemployed. Thus simply because these workers are now ignored in the statistics, the official unemployment rate may be decreasing as the economy is worsening!

The Effects of Unemployment

Personal Effects

The effects of unemployment on individual workers and their families are obvious. Clearly the income of the family will fall when the breadwinner loses a job. Many people are unaware that most unemployed people do not receive unemployment compensation. Unemployment compensation is an income transfer from the government to the eligible unemployed person. To be eligible, one must first have had a job, and then must have lost the job for clearly defined reasons that vary from state to state. Even when eligible, unemployed people receive benefits well below their former income and for only a limited period of time.

Beyond the income loss, the unemployed person suffers other tangible losses. One such loss might be employment-related health benefits, thereby harming the health of the family. Another loss is on-the-job experience, which might reduce the unemployed person's productivity and marketability. (How does the unemployed person explain the period of unemployment to another potential employer?)

Unemployment causes a variety of problems, not just strictly economic ones. Researchers at Johns Hopkins University and other organizations have noted a high correlation between unemployment rates and a variety of social ills. When unemployment rates go up, we typically see an increase in domestic violence, divorce, alcoholism, child abuse, and suicide.

Macroeconomic Effects

The problem posed by unemployment to the macroeconomy is quite different from the problems it posed to individuals. Recall the production possibilities curve of Chapter One. This graph is repeated in Figure 14-2 on page 310.

Recall that when we use society's resources and technology to their fullest, the economy is represented somewhere along the production possibilities curve. The economy may choose to produce at a point such as point C, with production of 105 tons of bread and 40 tons of roses. However, if some of our resources sit idle, we will not be able to produce to our full potential. With unemployed workers, we may instead be at a point such as point U, perhaps producing only 25 tons of bread and 40 tons of roses. The macroeconomic problem of unemployment is the reduction in our nation's output that it causes. As long as there is scarcity in our world, we must be concerned when we are not producing to our full potential.

Types of Unemployment

There are three basic types of unemployment: frictional, structural, and cyclical unemployment.

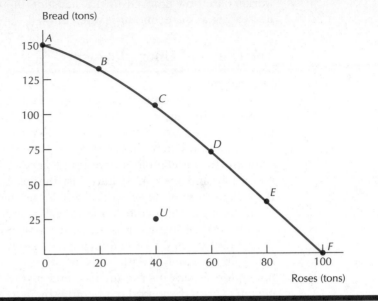

FIGURE 14-2   Production Possibilities Curve

Points *A* through *F* show alternative combinations of bread and roses that the economy can produce over a particular time period; point *U* represents unemployed resources.

Frictional Unemployment

Do you remember looking for your first part-time job? Did you expect to apply, interview, be hired, and begin work the moment you began your job search? Of course not! Similarly, when you graduate from college with your degree in hand, you should not be surprised when it takes time to find that long-awaited "real" job. There is a normal time delay before finding a job—or, for that matter, when changing jobs or reentering the labor force after a period of absence. This is an expected situation and is referred to as **frictional unemployment.** The name reflects the "friction" present in the labor market—that is, our imperfect information about job vacancies and business firms' imperfect information about job seekers. It takes time for employer and employee to get together, to discover their compatibility, and to move through the red tape that is necessary before the job vacancy is filled.

> **Frictional unemployment**
> Temporary unemployment due to a normal time delay when a person seeks a first job, changes jobs, or reenters the labor force after an absence.

Because frictional unemployment is very normal and is assumed, by definition, to be temporary, it is not generally considered to be a serious form of unemployment. In fact, many consider some frictional unemployment to be necessary for a healthy economy. We need to have people move to better jobs to maintain an efficient economy. Of course, the longer the job search, the more serious the situation becomes. Hence we are interested in programs that can improve job information for employers and job seekers. Your college career services office, state job service office, and local employment agency provide this type of service. At the national level, computerized job searches can minimize the time spent seeking information and ultimately bring together employer and employee.

Structural Unemployment

Now consider a more serious problem than the time delay in finding your first postcollege job. Suppose you are majoring in elementary education, with the hope of teaching at the primary level. Perhaps the demand for elementary teachers was very high at the time you planned your career and you have been intently preparing yourself since then. Now, suppose a shift is taking place in our economy. The number of school children may be decreasing, thereby reducing the overall demand for elementary teachers. At the same time, the demand for more specialized schoolteachers may be increasing, as more school districts seek to meet the needs of emotionally or learning-disabled children. There may be unfilled vacancies for specialized teachers at the same time that many nonspecialized teachers remain unemployed. This situation is an example of structural unemployment.

Structural unemployment
Unemployment that results from structural changes in our economy, such as changes in demand or technology.

As the name suggests, **structural unemployment** is caused by structural shifts within our economy. Consider, for example, how the structure of demand has changed within our economy over the last several decades. Consumer demand is on the increase for a variety of services such as health care and child care, whereas in previous years demand was higher for manufactured goods. As a result, job opportunities have opened up in the health and child care fields, whereas jobs have been lost in the manufacturing sector.

Technological advance is another example of structural change within our economy. Robotics in the auto industry has enabled machines to replace welders, creating job loss in the auto industry, at least in the short run. At the same time, jobs have opened up as a result of other forms of technological advance—in the computer industry, for example. The welders who lost their jobs in the auto plant, however, probably do not have the skills to take the jobs in the computer industry.

The point is that with structural unemployment, a job vacancy may exist for each unemployed worker, but due to structural circumstances within the economy, the unemployed worker is not suited to the particular job. The laid-off welder is available, but lacks the skills for the computer industry. The laid-off steelworker lacks the education necessary for a job in the health care field.

Other structural factors that prevent people from taking available jobs may be present. Some workers may lack necessary child care facilities, or face discrimination, or live in an inner city or a part of the country where jobs are scarce. The fact that jobs are available in California's Silicon Valley means very little to the unemployed person on the Minnesota Iron Range, who is unable to participate in that job market.

Many people believe that structural unemployment is serious enough for the government to take action. Job training and education programs are obviously important. So too are the provision of child care facilities and the enforcement of anti-discrimination policies. Mass transit may be helpful to inner-city commuters, and relocation assistance may be needed for workers who must move to find jobs. And finally, the unemployed schoolteacher may need help to return to school to learn specializations that make him or her more employable. These interventions represent microeconomic policies by nature.

Cyclical Unemployment

Cyclical unemployment is the type of unemployment most closely linked to the macroeconomy and to macroeconomic policy. Hence it is the type of unemployment with which we are primarily concerned in this chapter and the two chapters that follow.

Cyclical unemployment is defined as unemployment that results from a drop in economic activity in our economy as a whole. Whereas structural unemployment has to do with changes in sectors *within* the economy, cyclical unemployment has to do with the macroeconomy *in total*. When our economy is expanding and producing larger levels of output, the number of jobs will expand as well, for we need workers to produce higher levels of output. On the other hand, when our economy contracts and produces lower levels of output, the number of jobs will contract as well. Many people lose their jobs in a downturn of the economy, and many are unable to find first-time jobs.

Notice that only with cyclical unemployment do we assume that the economy has an insufficient number of jobs. With frictional unemployment, a job is available for the job seeker. He or she simply hasn't found it yet! With structural unemployment, there are job losses in one sector or geographical area of the economy, but there are job vacancies in others. There is simply a mismatch between available jobs and workers, who lack the skills, education, location, or other forms of access to these jobs. *Only* with cyclical unemployment is the number of jobs insufficient. Macroeconomic policy is necessary to expand the economy and create new employment opportunities.

Full Employment

Have you ever heard the term *full employment*? It's natural to assume that full employment means a job for everyone who wants one, but this is *not* the definition of full employment. **Full employment** is defined as a situation in which there is no cyclical unemployment; that is, jobs are available for all who want to work. It doesn't mean that everyone is suited to a job that exists, or that everyone has actually found a job. What it means is that any unemployment that exists will be structural or frictional, not cyclical. An unemployment rate of 4 to 6 percent is often considered by economists to represent full employment.

Although it appears deliberately misleading, the full employment concept is in fact useful. When the economy achieves full employment, there may be a need to provide better information, training, education, or other services; but there is *no* need for macroeconomic policy to correct the economy. On the other hand, when the economy does not experience full employment, macro policies must come into play. These policies will be discussed in the next chapter.

Employment Effects of Immigration

In the United States and abroad, immigration is a controversial issue. Some of the animosity toward immigrants stems from bigotry, and much stems from fear—fear that large-scale immigration will increase unemployment and cause wage rates to fall. The fact that significant numbers of immigrants enter the United States illegally only increases this fear.

Cyclical unemployment
Unemployment that results from a drop in economic activity in our economy as a whole.

Full employment
A situation in which there is no cyclical unemployment; all unemployment is frictional or structural.

The polar attitudes in the United States toward immigrant workers can be expressed by the following statements: (1) immigrants work for next to nothing and take jobs away from native-born Americans, or (2) immigrants work hard and only take jobs that native-born workers wouldn't want anyway. The truth, as is often the case, is somewhere between these two extremes.

Evidence of animosity toward immigrants permeates our public policy. Proposition 187 was a referendum, approved by California voters by a 3-to-2 margin, preventing illegal immigrants from receiving state education, welfare, and nonemergency medical benefits. *Legal* immigrants in the United States have seen their eligibility for welfare benefits cut and have faced requirements that recipients of welfare and applicants for citizenship use English on their forms and exams. This requirement is especially onerous for elderly immigrants who have difficulty learning a new language. And although activists for economic justice have attempted to restore benefits and permit citizenship exams to be offered in foreign languages, the economic fears that foster the anti-immigration sentiment persist. Therefore, let's consider the economic implications of immigration for U.S. labor markets.

In the short run, large-scale immigration increases the supply of low-skilled workers, lowering the wage rate for these workers. The graph of the low-skill labor market is shown in Figure 14-3. This graph is similar to all of the demand and supply graphs we have considered for various goods and services. But instead of the

FIGURE 14-3   A U.S. Labor Market for Low-Skilled Workers with and without Immigration

The quantity of labor (the number of workers) is shown along the horizontal axis and the price of labor (the wage rate) is shown along the vertical axis. The demand curve D is the demand for low-skilled workers and S_1 is the supply of native-born U.S. workers who offer their labor services to the low-skill labor market. The equilibrium wage rate is $6 per hour and the equilibrium number of U.S. workers is 100,000. The immigration of low-skilled workers increases the supply of labor to S_2, thereby lowering the wage rate to $4 per hour. As a result, the number of native-born workers is just 50,000 workers, while the total number of workers is 200,000.

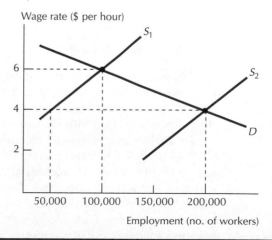

quantity of a product (such as bushels of corn), we have the quantity of labor (such as the number of workers) on the horizontal axis. The vertical axis represents the price of labor, which is the wage rate. The demand curve D is the demand for low-skilled workers by business firms (and anyone else who hires low-skilled workers). S_1 is the supply of native-born U.S. workers who offer their labor services to the low-skill labor market. The equilibrium wage rate is $6 per hour, and the equilibrium number of U.S. workers is 100,000.

Now let's show the effects of large-scale immigration. With such immigration, the supply of low-skilled workers increases to S_2, which includes both U.S.-born and immigrant workers. The increase in supply causes the equilibrium wage rate to fall to $4 per hour. Employment increases to 200,000 workers. But notice that the number of hours supplied by U.S. workers is now only 50,000. The remaining hours are worked by immigrant workers. So we could summarize the labor-market effects of large-scale immigration by saying that large-scale immigration increases the supply of low-skilled labor, thereby decreasing the wage rate. *At the lower wage rate,* fewer U.S. workers will take the low-skill jobs, and immigrants will fill more of these jobs. Other specific low-skill labor markets, such as the markets for domestic workers and for seasonal agricultural labor, are also affected in this way by large-scale immigration.

In the longer run the effects of immigration are less clear. Lower wages decrease business firms' costs of production, thereby increasing their profits. This situation may encourage businesses to expand. American consumers can purchase a larger array of consumer goods and services at lower prices. A larger labor force encourages expanded productivity and economic growth. In addition, research shows that immigrants, as a group, are entrepreneurial and that they are more likely to start up businesses than are native-born citizens.

Lastly, we must keep in mind that many immigrants to the United States are indeed highly skilled and educated. Because of our immigration law, they are often permitted to immigrate to meet the needs of U.S. businesses that cannot find adequate numbers of U.S. workers with the same qualifications. And from a noneconomic perspective, we benefit from greater cultural diversity. After all, we *are* a nation of immigrants.

The Minimum Wage

Minimum wage
A legally imposed minimum price (wage) for labor.

Another issue concerning unemployment and labor markets is the implications of the **minimum wage.** As of the year 2000, the federal minimum wage rate was, with a few exceptions, $5.15 per hour. Several proposals to increase the minimum wage, which has not kept up with the rate of inflation, have been made.

To analyze the effects of the minimum wage, we can return to the type of graph of the low-skill labor market that we examined in the discussion of immigration. In Figure 14-4, the horizontal axis shows the quantity of labor (number of workers), the vertical axis shows the wage rate, D represents the demand for low-skilled labor, and S represents the supply of low-skilled labor. In this example, we'll assume that the equilibrium wage rate is $4.50 per hour and that the equilibrium quantity of labor is 100,000 workers.

FIGURE 14-4   The Minimum Wage in a Market for Low-Skilled Workers

The quantity of labor (the number of workers) is shown along the horizontal axis and the price of labor (the wage rate) is shown along the vertical axis. The demand curve *D* is the demand for low-skilled labor and the supply curve *S* is the supply of low-skilled labor. The equilibrium wage rate is $4.50 per hour, and the number of workers is 100,000. A minimum wage of $5.15 results in a quantity of labor supplied of 110,000 workers and a quantity of labor demanded of 90,000 workers. The result is a surplus of 20,000 workers.

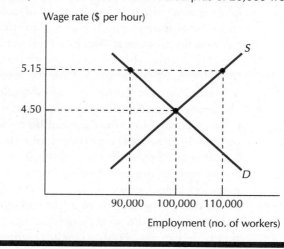

Price floor

A legally imposed minimum price for a good or service.

Suppose that the government decides that a wage rate of $4.50 per hour is too low. People may argue that this wage is a poverty wage, and that it doesn't compensate the worker for the value of a hard day's work. The wage is considered to be inequitable. As a result, the government decides to establish a minimum wage at $5.15 per hour. A minimum wage is a form of administered price, as was discussed in Chapter Two on agriculture, Chapter Eight on world poverty, and Chapter Eleven on housing. In particular, the minimum wage is an example of a **price floor,** such as the price supports discussed with respect to U.S. agricultural products. A price floor is intended to help the supplier, whether it is a supplier of corn or a supplier of labor. The price floor makes it illegal to pay a price (wage) below the established price floor. Therefore it represents a minimum price (or wage).

The minimum wage of $5.15 is indicated in Figure 14-4. Notice that the minimum wage is above the equilibrium wage in this market for low-skilled labor. If the minimum wage is not set above the equilibrium wage, it will have absolutely no effect on the market. Recall that the minimum wage merely prohibits payment of a wage rate below the minimum. It doesn't prevent payment of wages above the minimum. If the minimum wage is below the market equilibrium, the normal equilibrium wage rate will take over.

We can see the effects of the minimum wage in the graph by extending this wage rate to the demand and supply curves for low-skilled labor. We hit the demand for labor curve at a relatively low point on the demand curve, a point corresponding to a quantity of labor demanded of 90,000 workers. This quantity demanded is reasonable, because business firms will try to cut back on the quantity of labor they hire when labor becomes more expensive. We hit the supply of labor curve at a relatively high point on the curve, a point corresponding to a quantity of labor supplied by 110,000 workers. This quantity supplied is also reasonable, because more people may be willing to work when wages are higher. The result is a disequilibrium situation in which the quantity of labor supplied (110,000 workers) is greater than the quantity of labor demanded (90,000 workers). A surplus of labor exists, which is another way of saying that the minimum wage has created some unemployment. While the minimum wage has benefited some workers (those who are able to find jobs and receive the higher wage), it has harmed other workers (those who become unemployed). Business firms also lose as they are forced to pay higher wages. Thus the results are mixed.

Although our graphical representation of the minimum wage may be appropriate for many low-skilled professions, it is not appropriate for most occupations in our country. Certainly the minimum wage is below the equilibrium wage rates in these higher-wage-paying professions, and therefore the minimum wage becomes ineffective in these professions. It does not raise wages, and it does not create unemployment. The analysis is valid therefore for *only* the low-skill occupations we've discussed.

Is there a better way to ensure adequate incomes for hard-working individuals than the minimum wage, since the minimum wage creates problems (unemployment) as well as benefits (higher wages)? Most economists dislike administered prices, whether they be price ceilings or price floors. They oppose these measures because they create disequilibrium situations (shortages and surpluses) and distort incentives in markets. Therefore, direct assistance to targeted groups of people is often preferable. If our concern is for workers who receive poverty wages, a direct solution would be for the government to simply pay the worker the difference between his or her market wage and the wage necessary for an adequate income. Many people are averse to this type of solution because it appears to amount to a "hand out," but it avoids the market distortions caused by the minimum wage. Indeed, we do have an example of the alternative solution in the form of the earned income tax credit, which was discussed in detail in Chapter Seven on U.S. poverty. This **earned income tax credit (EITC)** reduces the taxes owed by (or provides a payment to) workers with incomes below a certain level. It has certainly helped low-income working people, and expansions of the tax credit have been proposed.

Earned income tax credit (EITC)
A federal income tax credit for low-income workers and families.

INFLATION

We must double our fight against the persistent inflation that has wracked our country for more than a decade. We know that inflation is a burden for all Americans, but it's a disaster for the poor, the sick, and the old. No American family should be forced to choose among food, warmth, health care, or decent housing because the cost of any of these basic necessities has climbed out of reach.

President Carter, *State of the Union Address,* 1979

Inflation threatens to put an end to everything we believe in and to our dreams for the future.

President Reagan, *State of the Union Address,* 1981

Inflation, that thief. . . .

President G. H. W. Bush, *State of the Union Address,* 1992

Just like unemployment, it would seem "that thief" inflation threatens the American dream, at least if the words of the three U.S. presidents in office before Clinton provide a clue. But note that finding the word *inflation* in any of the speeches by President Clinton during his eight years of office is virtually impossible. Does the recent lack of reference to inflation mean that this phenomenon is no longer perceived as an economic threat? Or has the recent state of our economy eliminated, for the time being, the problem of inflation?

We have mentioned elsewhere in this text that **inflation** is a rise in the average price level. As you might expect, therefore, **deflation** is a decrease in the average price level. Most of our recent experience is with inflation, so this is the topic that will concern us. To learn how economists calculate the inflation rate, we need to review the consumer price index (CPI).

The **consumer price index** is what we usually mean when referring to the cost of living. It is defined as a weighted average of the prices of a fixed basket of goods and services purchased by a typical urban household. In the early 1980s, studies were done to determine which goods and services, and which quantities of these items, were purchased by American households. The average, or typical, urban household was then determined. The basket of goods and services purchased by this typical household was assumed to remain fixed over time, until a new survey is done. The prices of items within this fixed basket are based on prices in a variety of urban stores; a "weighted average" of these prices is calculated by weighting the prices of large-quantity items more heavily than low-quantity items in the basket. That is, if the typical household purchases ten pairs of jeans and one movie video, the price of jeans receives a weight ten times the weight of the video when calculating the average price of this basket.

Because the CPI is an index, the weighted-average price of this basket of consumer goods and services is manipulated further. We will leave the actual construction of the consumer price index for the appendix to this chapter. Keep in mind though that the resulting CPI does not actually tell us the prices that exist in a particular year. It only tells us how prices in one year *compare* with those in another year.

Using the consumer price index to calculate the inflation rate is easy. We subtract the CPI for one year from the CPI for the prior year, then divide the answer by the CPI for the earlier year. For example, if the CPI is 220 in 2001 and the CPI is 200 in 2000, we can calculate the 2001 inflation rate as follows:

$$2001 \text{ inflation rate } = \frac{2001 \text{ CPI} - 2000 \text{ CPI}}{2000 \text{ CPI}}$$

$$= \frac{220 - 200}{200}$$

$$= \frac{20}{200}$$

$$= 0.10 \text{ or } 10\%$$

Inflation

A rise in the average price level.

Deflation

A decrease in the average price level.

Consumer price index (CPI)

A weighted average of the prices of a fixed basket of goods and services purchased by a typical urban household.

In this example, the 2001 rate of inflation is 10 percent. (Notice that a decimal, such as 0.10 here, can be translated into a percentage by moving the decimal point to the right by two spaces, and adding a percentage sign. That is, 0.10 becomes 10%.)

Inaccuracy of the Inflation Rate

We noted earlier that the unemployment rate tends to understate the true problem of unemployment. We will see that the consumer price index tends to systematically overstate the true problem of inflation for two reasons, both of which have to do with the notion of the fixed basket of consumer goods and services.

The basket of goods and services purchased by a typical household is deliberately assumed to remain fixed for several years so that changes in the prices of the basket reflect changes in prices only, not changes in the quantities of the goods and services themselves. When we ignore quantity changes, we are ignoring the fact that consumers tend to conserve on items for which price is increasing. During a period of rising energy prices, for example, such as we began experiencing in 2000 and 2001, consumers may reduce the amount of energy they consume. They may insulate their homes, drive more fuel-efficient cars, turn down their thermostats and air conditioners, and so on. When we assume a fixed basket of consumer goods, we ignore the fact that consumers are reducing the amount of energy they consume, thereby reducing the price of their *actual* basket of consumer items below the price of the *fixed* basket. Hence the inflation rate, based on the assumption of a fixed basket, is overstated.

Similarly, some quality changes within the basket of consumer items are taken into account, but many other quality changes go unrecorded. A price increase may be recorded for a particular item, such as a personal computer, without taking into account some of the quality improvements of this computer. We think of an increase in price as an indicator of inflation, whereas at least some of the price increase may be due to a change in the nature of the product (its quality). In this fashion, the consumer price index again overstates the problem of inflation.

The issue of the accuracy of the inflation rate is not entirely academic. Certainly if policymakers are to design appropriate policy, they must know with accuracy how serious the problem is. If the problem of inflation is overstated, policies designed to reduce inflation may at times be inappropriate. Other practical issues involve the **cost of living adjustment (COLA)** that is made in wage contracts, Social Security benefits, and other payments that are adjusted for inflation. As was mentioned in the Social Security chapter, politicians have sought to reduce Social Security benefits by offering a revised (lower) estimate of inflation than that provided by the consumer price index, thereby making a more modest inflation adjustment for Social Security benefits. This unpopular measure was never enacted.

Cost of living adjustment (COLA)
An adjustment that automatically increases incomes or benefits when the average price level rises.

The Data

Despite problems with the consumer price index, economists and policymakers continue to use it. Table 14-5 shows inflation rates based on the consumer price index for select years between 1970 and 2000. We can see the reason for the lack of concern regarding inflation during the 1993–2000 Clinton Administration.

TABLE 14-5 U.S. Inflation Rates, in Percent, Selected Years 1970–2000, Based on the CPI with Base Year 1982–84

YEAR	INFLATION RATE	YEAR	INFLATION RATE
1970	5.8	1994	2.6
1980	13.5	1995	2.8
1990	5.4	1996	3.0
1991	4.2	1997	2.3
1992	3.0	1998	1.6
1993	3.0	1999	2.2
		2000	3.4

Source: U.S. Department of Commerce, Bureau of the Census.

Hyperinflation

We in the United States consider any inflation rate above 10 percent to be very high. But many countries of the world experience inflation rates far above this. Many Latin American countries, for example, commonly experience annual inflation rates in the range of several hundred, or even several thousand percent. Recent examples include Brazil (2,739 percent), Argentina (3,080 percent), Peru (7,650 percent), and Nicaragua (14,316 percent). Many Eastern European countries are experiencing extremely high inflation rates during their transition to market-based economies with market-based prices. The inflation rate in Russia, for example, was 1,353 percent for the year 1992.[2] In the context of these extremely high inflation rates, money becomes almost worthless. No one is willing to save, because the value of savings decreases rapidly as the average price level rises. The smart course of action appears to be to spend your money as soon as you get it, because things hold value, whereas money does not! On a recent trip to an African country, your author changed a $10 bill to buy souvenirs. Because of inflation, she ended up carrying a bag full of 20,000 small units of the African currency. In other countries, people literally go shopping with wheelbarrows or baby buggies filled with money.

Even with wheelbarrows and armloads of money, the prices of groceries in an economy hit by severe inflation may be rising before the customer can leave the store. Theater prices may increase while you're watching the movie! Motel prices may double while you are sleeping! (Indeed, your same author had this experience while peacefully sleeping in a motel in Russia!) In any of these cases, even a cart full of money may not be enough to pay the bill. In such situations, people may resort to **barter,** because their money is worth nothing. Inflation this severe is what we mean by **hyperinflation.**

Many people fear inflation because they believe it will lead to hyperinflation, but hyperinflation almost always occurs in countries experiencing war, revolution, or other severe disruptions of their economies. Hyperinflation should not be a concern for the United States—even if severe economic disruptions were to occur, the policies of the Federal Reserve system and the government could mitigate their impact on inflation rates. We will examine these policies in the next chapter.

Barter
The direct exchange of goods and services for other goods and services rather than for money.

Hyperinflation
Extremely high inflation, whereby money becomes almost worthless.

The Effects of Inflation

Purchasing power
The ability to buy goods and services.

Inflation is generally not as serious a problem as you might think, at least not in the ways you might expect. Most people assume that a rise in the average price level means that we as a nation cannot afford to buy as many goods and services—that is, inflation harms our **purchasing power.** In fact, a period of inflation in and of itself does not have that effect because our purchasing power depends on both the price level and our incomes. If the average price level rises by 10 percent at the same time that our incomes rise by 10 percent, our purchasing power is not altered. Unless some other factors are present, the income for the country as a whole does rise along with the price level during a period of inflation. Therefore the purchasing power of our nation is not harmed.

There are, however, other problems associated with inflation. They can be categorized as problems of redistribution, uncertainty, menu costs, and international effects.

Redistribution

Even though the purchasing power of the nation is not harmed by inflation, certainly some people in the country will gain and some people will lose. The economic situation of others will remain unchanged.

Consider Social Security recipients as an example. Because the Social Security program has an automatic cost of living adjuster built into it, Social Security benefits will rise at the rate of inflation. If the rate of inflation in any given year is 4 percent, for example, Social Security benefits will also rise by 4 percent. In this way, the purchasing power of Social Security recipients is unchanged during a period of inflation.

On the other hand, the purchasing power of other people will suffer if their incomes do not increase as rapidly as the price level. Retirees receiving private pensions (not Social Security), workers who have signed a long-term labor contract, and welfare recipients may all experience a decrease in their purchasing power. Civil servants, including professors at public colleges and universities, may also experience such a decrease! The negative effects of inflation on these people will be offset by the positive effects on others who see their incomes rise more rapidly than the average price level (such as workers protected by powerful unions). Although these various groups of people will offset one another so that the purchasing power of the nation is unchanged, it is clear that some people within the country benefit while others lose during a period of inflation. This redistribution of purchasing power means that President Carter (in his statement quoted earlier in this chapter) was wrong, both about old people and about *all* Americans!

Borrowers are said to gain during a period of inflation, whereas lenders are said to lose. Imagine that you lend $100 to your best friend and agree to charge an interest rate of 3 percent. One year from now, you expect to receive your $100 back, plus $3 to compensate yourself for the year you went without your $100. Imagine, however, that the rate of inflation over the year is 7 percent. Your $103 at the end of the year will not buy as much as the $100 when you lent it to your friend. You lose, but your best friend (still your best friend?) gains.

Realize, however, that most lenders will recognize the significance of inflation when entering into a lending contract. If a bank wishes to charge an interest rate of 10 percent and anticipates an inflation rate of 5 percent, it will charge an interest rate of 15 percent (10 percent plus 5 percent) when it makes a loan. In this way, the bank will protect itself from the harmful effects of inflation. Borrowers gain and lenders lose during inflation only if inflation is unanticipated. When inflation is highly variable, borrowers and lenders may be less willing to engage in loan contracts due to uncertainty, resulting in slowdowns in economic activity.

Uncertainty: Inefficiency and Risk Aversion

Another problem with inflation is the inefficiency that may result from uncertainty about prices. Suppose that the rate of inflation has been 3 percent per year for the past 20 years. In this case we have good reliable information on which to base our economic decisions. But suppose instead that the inflation rate has varied considerably from year to year, and no one can reliably predict what the rate of inflation will be over the next few years. You will not know now whether you can afford your tuition four years from now. Others will not know whether it's to their advantage to buy a car or a house in a few years when their finances are in better shape, or whether to buy it now before the prices go up too much. Business people will not be able to predict their costs of production, or their revenues, or their rates of return over the next few years, and will not know whether they should pursue a particular investment project. Our collective decisions may be incorrect in the face of uncertainty about inflation. Furthermore, if we are all risk-averse, meaning that we prefer not to undertake risks, we may all choose to do nothing rather than risk doing the wrong thing. You may decide not to go to college, others may decide not to buy the house or the car, and the business may decide to forgo productive investment. As we slow down our economic activities, we slow the growth of our economy. People and businesses are unwilling to engage in long-term contracts and activities. The uncertainty effects of inflation are most severe when inflation rates are extremely high or volatile.

Menu Costs

Menu costs

The costs associated with reprinting menus, revising cost schedules, adjusting telephones and vending machines, and so on, when inflation occurs.

When inflation is 2 percent per year, the owner of a restaurant will likely reprint its menu with higher prices at the end of the year. If inflation is 15 percent per year, however, the restaurant owner will likely redo its menu every month or two. The costs associated with making adjustments to inflation are what is meant by the **menu costs** of inflation. However, these menu costs are not restricted to the restaurant example. They apply whenever the prices on gasoline pumps must be raised, whenever airlines and bus lines must revise their price schedules, and whenever vending machines and pay phones must have their prices and coin slots altered. These costs are not usually considered too serious, but they (like the uncertainty effects of inflation) tend to be more problematic when inflation rates are high or fluctuating rapidly. Pay telephones in Russia are the greatest bargain around simply because officials have not been able to change the sizes of the coin slots as rapidly as inflation has made this procedure necessary!

International Effects

Finally, another problem of inflation in any country is that it makes the prices in that country higher than those in other countries. If the United States has an inflation rate of 4 percent and Japan has an inflation rate of 1 percent, the prices of Ford vehicles are probably rising more rapidly than the prices of Toyotas. American and Japanese consumers alike will be encouraged to buy Toyotas rather than Fords, thus increasing our imports while reducing our exports. However, as the world becomes increasingly interdependent, inflation in one industrialized country can sometimes occur in other industrialized countries as well. It may therefore become less likely that only the United States will experience inflation and not our trade and financial partners.

Types of Inflation

Different types of inflation are identified according to the conditions that lead to them. We introduce these types now so that they will be familiar to you in the next chapter, in which we will see how inflation is caused in the context of the macroeconomy. First, **demand-pull inflation** is caused when any sectors of the economy (consumers, businesses, or government) increase their demand for goods and services. **Cost-push inflation** occurs when there are increases in costs of production, such as rising energy prices or wages. (Cost-push inflation is the type of inflation that occurred when energy prices were increasing in the 1970s. Rising energy prices again threaten to create the same problem, though of a smaller magnitude.) Finally, **profit-push inflation** occurs when, as a result of market power, business firms deliberately restrict output to drive up prices and profits.

Demand-pull inflation
Inflation that occurs when any sectors of the economy increase their demand for goods and services.

Cost-push inflation
Inflation that occurs as a result of increases in the costs of production.

Profit-push inflation
Inflation that occurs when businesses use market power to restrict output in order to push up prices and profits.

WHICH PROBLEM IS MORE SERIOUS: UNEMPLOYMENT OR INFLATION?

Policymakers are often faced with the question: which is more serious, unemployment or inflation? It's an important question. As we shall see in the next chapter, policy designed to cure one of the two problems will often trigger the other problem. The answer to the question depends largely on whom has been asked the question. An unemployed person will naturally feel that unemployment is the more serious problem. Yet the effects of unemployment on the individual can be alleviated somewhat with government transfers. Thus unemployment in a country such as the United States will be less problematic for the individual than will unemployment in a country like Mexico, for example, which lacks an adequate safety net for its unemployed. Unemployment will nevertheless be very serious for most people in the United States. Furthermore, the effects of unemployment on our nation's output cannot be modified. Output that is forgone today as a result of resources sitting idle will never be available for consumption tomorrow.

A person living on a fixed income will consider inflation the more serious problem. It is indeed a serious problem for individuals whose incomes do not rise as rapidly as the price level. Many have suggested that incorporating a cost of living adjuster into all economic contracts can minimize this problem. Thus all wage

It is difficult to place the issues of unemployment and inflation into the traditional framework of conservative versus liberal. Certainly both conservatives and liberals alike will prefer to see lower rates of unemployment and inflation. Some specific policy actions may correspond more with one philosophical viewpoint than the other, however. For example, the federal government could become more involved in offering computerized national job search programs in an effort to minimize frictional unemployment. More important, liberals may wish to see the government heavily involved in reducing certain types of structural unemployment. For example, they may want to see government provision or financial support for child care services and greater government enforcement of affirmative action and equal opportunity legislation. Both efforts would remove some constraints that prevent groups of people from obtaining available jobs. Another government role could be in expanding training and education opportunities, thereby qualifying more people for available jobs. The government might offer retraining, relocating, and retooling assistance to people laid off and businesses shut down as a result of technological change or international trade. All of these government efforts may be viewed cautiously by those conservatives who are reluctant to see an expanded role of government in the economy and have more confidence in the private sector to solve our economic problems. More often than not, however, both liberals and conservatives will see the value of programs such as these.

As we look at macro policies designed to reduce cyclical unemployment and inflation in the next chapter, we will see that conservatives as well as liberals are concerned with these problems. But they will support very different types of macro policies, depending on their general view toward government involvement in our economy.

contracts, pension plans, lending and rental agreements, welfare programs, and the minimum wage would provide incomes or benefits that rise along with the average price level, just as Social Security benefits do. Although this measure would eliminate some inequity, uncertainty, and inefficiency, it would not rectify the problems of menu costs and international effects.

Policymakers must face the world as it is and make difficult decisions about the outcomes of policy on unemployment and inflation. As we will see in the next chapter, there is often a trade-off in the sense that one policy will reduce unemployment while increasing inflation, and vice versa. If we are combating unemployment, we will want to stimulate the economy, which may cause inflation. If we are concerned about inflation, we will try to contract the economy, which will increase unemployment.

Lastly, recall that we questioned whether the prosperity of our economy would persist long enough for you to take advantage of it. As we've looked at the data, we've noted that while our economy is prosperous today, our recent history is dotted with serious problems of unemployment and inflation. While our policymakers today have the wherewithal to prevent Great Depression types of situations, certainly less serious levels of unemployment could resume at any time. Nevertheless, you, as an aspiring college graduate, are at much less risk than the overall population!

SUMMARY

Unemployment and inflation are two important topics in the context of the macroeconomy. A person is considered to be unemployed when he or she is actively seeking employment but is unable to find a job. Inflation is defined as a rise in the average price level. The national unemployment rate has recently been extremely low, though certain age groups and racial and ethnic groups are more likely than others to experience unemployment. The inflation rate has recently been very low, hovering around 3 percent.

Unemployment is categorized as frictional, structural, or cyclical. Inflation is classified as either demand pull, cost push, or profit push. Both unemployment and inflation can cause serious problems in our economy. Unemployment creates both monetary and nonmonetary problems for the unemployed person and reduces output for our nation as a whole. Inflation, especially when severe, creates problems of redistribution, uncertainty and inefficiency, menu costs, and international effects. Policies to correct these problems are an important consideration in the next chapter on government macro policy.

NOTES

1. David T. Ellwood, "Anti-Poverty Policy for Families in the Next Century: From Welfare to Work—and Worries," *Journal of Economic Perspectives,* vol. 14, no. 1 (Winter 2000).
2. International Monetary Fund, *World Economic Outlook* (Washington DC: International Monetary Fund, May 1995). The years for the inflation rates are 1992 for Russia, 1990 for Brazil, 1989 for Argentina, 1990 for Peru, and 1988 for Nicaragua.

DISCUSSION QUESTIONS

1. *What does it mean when we say that macroeconomics is the forest, whereas microeconomics is the trees? What topics are important in macroeconomics? What topics are important in microeconomics?*

2. *Why do you think the labor force participation rate of men is higher than that of women in the United States? Why has the labor force participation rate of women been increasing so dramatically? What are some of the reasons for variation in labor force participation rates of different countries?*

3. *Have you ever been unemployed? (Remember the technical definition of unemployment!) If so, which type of unemployment did you experience?*

4. *Ask your friends or family how the unemployment rate is calculated. Are they able to give the proper technical procedure?*

5. *Check the Bureau of Labor Statistics Web site (http://bls.gov) to find out the current unemployment rate. Would you say that our economy is currently experiencing full employment?*

6. *Can you explain why it is sometimes the case that as additional jobs are being created in our economy, unemployment rates actually rise? And why is it sometimes the case that while jobs are being lost, unemployment rates may actually fall? (Hint: think in terms of discouraged workers.)*

7. *What are the effects of unemployment on the individual unemployed person? What are the effects on the economy? Which effects are more serious?*

8. *What are some policies that can be used to reduce structural unemployment? Try to come up with some of your own ideas.*

9. *In June 2000, 58 illegal Chinese immigrants were found dead in a sealed area of a truck, smothered by heat and lack of air during a five-hour journey to Britain. It was said that the victims had died "a most terrible death." Similar situations occur frequently as illegal Mexicans cross the U.S. border and as Cubans traverse stormy waters in poorly equipped boats. Who do you think is to blame for these situations? desperate immigrants? crime*

syndicates providing the transportation? a rigid immigration system? a public attitude of hostility toward immigration? a global economic system that permits poverty in one country alongside prosperity in another?

10. *Why is understatement of the problem of unemployment by unemployment statistics a problem? Why is overstatement of the problem of unemployment by inflation statistics a problem?*

11. *Look up the Census Bureau Web site (http://www.*

census.gov) and click on Prices to find the current and last year's consumer price index. Use these numbers to calculate the current inflation rate.

12. *How are you affected by inflation? Think carefully about the effects discussed in this chapter. Are you a gainer or a loser?*

13. *Which problem do you believe is more serious: unemployment or inflation? Why?*

Chapter Fourteen Appendix:
Construction of the Consumer Price Index

An index is constructed first by choosing a base year, such as 1984.[1] We then calculate the 1984 consumer price index by dividing the actual weighted-average price of the fixed basket of consumer goods and services by the same value, and multiplying the result by 100.

Let's calculate the consumer price index for a small hypothetical country. If the 1984 weighted average of prices of the basket of consumer items is $4,000, we calculate the 1984 index as follows:

$$1984 \text{ consumer price index} = \frac{\$4,000}{\$4,000} \times 100$$
$$= 1 \times 100$$
$$= 100$$

The consumer price index for the base year will always be 100.

Now suppose that we want to calculate the consumer price index for the year 2001. Suppose the weighted-average price of the fixed basket of consumer items is $8,000 in 2001. We calculate the 2001 consumer price index by dividing the $8,000 by the weighted-average price for base year 1984, then multiplying by 100. That is, we calculate the 2001 price index as follows:

$$2001 \text{ consumer price index} = \frac{\$8,000}{\$4,000} \times 100$$
$$= 2 \times 100$$
$$= 200$$

Again, a consumer price index of 200 means nothing to us by itself. An index is not an average price of anything. We can use the CPI to compare prices in one year with those in another year. In our example, we can say that prices have doubled between 1984 (with a CPI of 100) and 2001 (with a CPI of 200).

NOTE

1. The base year currently used for the CPI is an average over the 1982–1984 period.

CHAPTER 15

Government Macro Policy

In the long run, we are all dead.

John Maynard Keynes

Now it is time to jump into a complete discussion of the macroeconomy. In doing so, you will find that you can more easily understand the issues of unemployment and inflation, as well as other important economic issues facing our nation today. You will also discover the meaning of government macro policies such as fiscal policy and monetary policy, terms that everyone has heard before but few people really understand. Because you already understand demand and supply, you will have no difficulty understanding these macroeconomic topics.

GRAPHING THE MACROECONOMY

You undoubtedly remember that we promised to present only two basic types of graphs for most of the book. But also remember that we told you we could get a lot of mileage out of these graphs. In particular, we can revise our thinking about the demand and supply graphs of Chapter One and use the graphs to represent our economy as a whole.

Recall that each demand and supply graph in Chapter One was used to represent the market for a particular good or service, such as tutoring services. The

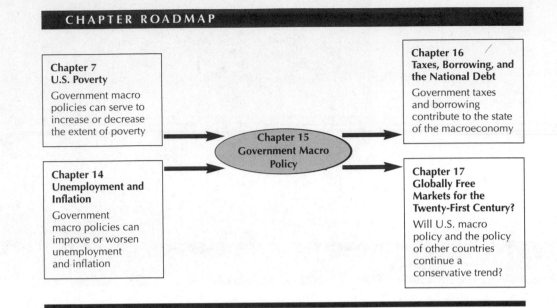

**Chapter 7
U.S. Poverty**

Government macro policies can serve to increase or decrease the extent of poverty

**Chapter 14
Unemployment and Inflation**

Government macro policies can improve or worsen unemployment and inflation

**Chapter 15
Government Macro Policy**

**Chapter 16
Taxes, Borrowing, and the National Debt**

Government taxes and borrowing contribute to the state of the macroeconomy

**Chapter 17
Globally Free Markets for the Twenty-First Century?**

Will U.S. macro policy and the policy of other countries continue a conservative trend?

graph representing the market for tutoring services is repeated in Figure 15-1. Now let's transform this graph into one representing our economy as a whole. Let the *P* on the vertical axis no longer represent the price of tutoring services, but the average price level for the economy as a whole. That is, *P* in Figure 15-2 will now represent the average price of all output produced in our economy. (For example, *P* could be measured by the consumer price index discussed in Chapter Fourteen.)

Instead of the *Q* on the horizontal axis representing the quantity of tutoring services, let's use the symbol GDP to represent total output of all goods and services

FIGURE 15-1   The Market for Tutoring Services, One Week

The market will clear at point *E*. At the price of $3 per hour, quantity demanded equals the quantity supplied (60 hours) of tutoring services.

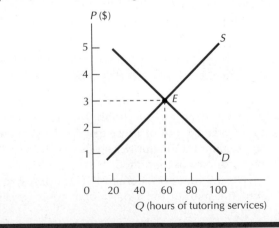

in our economy. Note that GDP stands for gross domestic product, which was introduced in Chapter One and is defined as our nation's total output. We will discuss GDP in greater detail and define it more precisely shortly.

Now let's redefine the downward-sloping demand curve as *AD* rather than *D*, where *AD* stands for **aggregate demand** and is defined as the quantity of total output (GDP) demanded (purchased) at alternative price levels. This definition sounds very similar to the definition of demand, except that now we are looking at the total demand for GDP by all sectors of the economy. Keep in mind that aggregate demand refers to the "purchasing" side of our economy—that is, the quantity of GDP that will be purchased at various price levels. It represents all people in the world who purchase U.S. GDP.

Aggregate demand
The quantity of total output (GDP) demanded (purchased) at alternative average price levels.

Similarly, we will use the symbol AS for the supply curve, where *AS* stands for aggregate supply. **Aggregate supply** is defined as the quantity of total output (GDP) supplied (produced) at alternative price levels. Here we are looking at the total supply of GDP by all producers in our economy. Keep in mind that aggregate supply refers to the "production" side of our economy—that is, the quantity of GDP that is produced. Aggregate supply represents all the people who produce U.S. GDP.

Aggregate supply
The quantity of total output (GDP) supplied (produced) at alternative average price levels.

Notice in Figure 15-2 that aggregate demand is downward sloping (just like a normal demand curve), whereas aggregate supply is upward sloping (just like a normal supply curve). The reasons for the upward slope of aggregate supply are very similar to the reasons for the upward slope of a supply curve in an individual market. Higher prices for products give producers greater incentive to produce their products; hence the quantity of output supplied increases when the prices of output increase.

FIGURE 15-2   The Macroeconomy

In the graph of the macroeconomy, *P* represents the average price level, GDP is total output, *AD* is aggregate demand, and *AS* is aggregate supply. At equilibrium *E*, the average price level is equal to P_0, and GDP is equal to GDP_0.

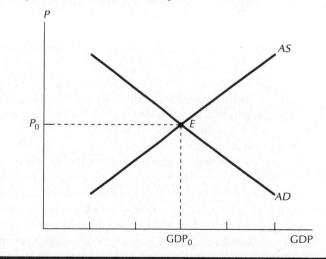

The reasons for the downward-sloping aggregate demand curve are very different from the reasons for the downward-sloping demand curve in an individual market, however. In considering the market for oranges, for example, people are willing to buy more oranges when the price falls because they can more easily afford them. They also might substitute oranges for other types of fruit such as apples and bananas. This kind of substitution is not possible when we are considering aggregate demand, because we are looking at the total demand for all output, and substituting all output with something else is impossible. Similarly, realize that a decline in the average price level does not make GDP more affordable because our purchasing power depends on both incomes and prices, and we generally assume that overall income in the economy declines as the average price level declines, unless other factors are at work. This concept was discussed in more detail in Chapter Fourteen on inflation. These considerations suggest that there must be other reasons why the quantity of GDP demanded increases when the average price level falls. These reasons have to do with trade, assets, and interest rates and are discussed in detail in Appendix 1 to this chapter.

Finally, notice that aggregate demand and aggregate supply intersect at point E in Figure 15-2. At this equilibrium point, we can see that the average price level is designated as P_0 and gross domestic product is equal to GDP_0.

GROSS DOMESTIC PRODUCT

A Definition of GDP

Gross Domestic Product (GDP)
The market value of all final goods and services produced *in* the economy in a given time period (usually one year).

Gross domestic product (GDP) is defined as the market value of all final goods and services produced in the economy in a given time period, usually one year. We need to think about this definition in detail. First, realize that final goods and services include all products (for example, cars and dishwashers) as well as all services (for example, education and health care) that are purchased as final products. Suppose you buy a bag of flour from the supermarket. This bag of flour is a final product, because it will not be processed and resold later. (You may bake a cake and eat it, but you will not sell the cake.) However, suppose the bakery downtown purchases large bags of flour and uses the flour to produce doughnuts and cookies for sale. In this case the flour is an intermediate product, and the doughnuts and cookies are the final products. Only the purchased product at the final stage of production is included in gross domestic product to avoid double counting. The value of the flour is incorporated into the price of the bakery's products; we do not want to count the flour twice.

Second, realize that all of the goods comprising GDP must be *produced* during the particular year. If, for example, you sell your 10-year-old home this year, the value of your home does not constitute part of this year's GDP. However, if you employ the current services of a realtor, the value of the realtor's services is included in this year's GDP because they are current services. Similarly, if a car is produced in one year but is held over as an inventory to be sold in the following year, it is counted as part of GDP in the year that it is produced. We consider the car to have been "purchased," for the time being, by the producer, who holds it in the form of an inventory.

Third, realize that it is necessary to define gross domestic product in value terms, specifically dollars in the United States. We could not add up all the apples, oranges, refrigerators, and television sets produced in our economy, nor could we determine whether GDP was higher in one year in which we produced lots of refrigerators than in another year in which we produced lots of television sets, because we can't compare refrigerators with televisions. And we could not compare the GDP of the United States—let's say it produces plenty of baseball cards, beer, and hot dogs—with that of Russia—let's say it produces large amounts of potatoes, vodka, and caviar—because we can't compare the quantities of these countries' respective products. We think you are getting the picture: we cannot add apples and oranges, nor can we compare them.

For these reasons, we must first attach value to the physical quantities of output produced; then we can add them up to tabulate total domestic product. We use **market prices** to value the physical quantities of output. Market price includes the retail price of the product plus any sales and excise taxes paid by the consumer. Once output is valued in dollars, we can simply add up the dollar values of output to tabulate total GDP. Money serves as a common denominator.

Finally, notice that the definition of gross domestic product refers to goods and services produced *in* the economy. This little word "in" is significant, because it distinguishes gross domestic product from gross national product.

Because some statistics rely on data for gross national product, abbreviated GNP, it is useful to define GNP as well. **Gross national product (GNP)** is defined as the market value of all final goods and services produced *by* the economy over a particular time period. The only difference between the two definitions are the words "in" and "by"!

When we refer to goods and services produced *in* the economy, we mean they are produced within the physical boundaries of the United States. If, for example, a Mexican citizen comes up to the United States during the summer to pick tomatoes, the value of these tomatoes would be included in U.S. gross domestic product, because they are produced within the physical boundaries of the United States. If, however, a U.S. citizen spends the summer making earrings in Mexico, the value of the earrings would not be part of U.S. GDP, because they are not produced within the physical boundaries of the United States.

On the other hand, when we refer to goods and services produced *by* the economy, we mean by U.S.-owned factors of production (that is, by U.S. workers, business owners, and so on). Now, for example, if a U.S. citizen makes earrings in Mexico, the value of the earrings is counted as part of U.S. gross national product. It doesn't matter where the earrings are produced, as long as a U.S. citizen produces them. Handbags produced by a Canadian citizen in the United States would not be tabulated as part of U.S. GNP (because the producer is a foreign citizen), but would count as part of U.S. GDP (because they are produced in the United States).

Gross domestic product is the concept generally used by the U.S. government and generally used in this textbook. However, data for GDP are occasionally not available, and GNP is used instead. In either case, the concepts can be viewed as roughly identical for our purposes, both depicting our national production.

Market price
The retail price of a product plus any sales and excise taxes paid by the consumer.

Gross national product (GNP)
The market value of all final goods and services produced *by* the economy in a given time period (usually one year).

Real vs. Nominal GDP

Real GDP
GDP calculated at constant prices.

Constant prices
Prices that exist in a base year.

Nominal GDP
GDP calculated at current prices.

Current prices
Actual prices of a particular year.

Whenever we use any variable expressed in value terms, including gross domestic product, we must be careful about comparing different time periods. Suppose GDP doubles over the time period 1990 to the year 2000. Does this increase mean that actual output doubles, that just the prices of this output double, or that both output and prices have risen? If we are interested only in whether actual output increases, we need to think in terms of real GDP, rather than nominal GDP.

Real GDP is defined as GDP calculated at constant prices. **Constant prices** refer to the prices that exist in a particular base year. If 1982 is the base year, for example, real GDP in 1990 is calculated by valuing the 1990 production of apples and oranges (and everything else) at the prices that existed in 1982. Similarly, real GDP in the year 2000 is calculated by valuing the year 2000's production of apples and oranges (and everything else) in the prices that existed in 1982. Then when we compare real GDP in the year 2000 with that in the year 1990, any increase in real GDP will be due to increased output, and not rising prices (because the prices are kept constant).

Nominal GDP is defined as GDP calculated at **current prices,** which are actual prices during a particular year. Nominal GDP for the year 2000 would include the production of all those apples, oranges, and everything else, valued at prices that exist in the year 2000; 1990 nominal GDP is valued at 1990 prices. Nominal GDP is the number we want to consider when we are trying to make sense of information for one year only. Real GDP is the number we want to use when we are comparing information over different time periods. Real GDP is adjusted for inflation; nominal GDP is not.

Flaws of GDP

Gross domestic product is typically used as an indicator of economic activity, as well as a measure of standards of living. When GDP is high, the assumption is that the economy is doing well and that standards of living are high. When GDP is growing over time, the assumption is that economic activity and standards of living are increasing. There are some flaws in these assumptions, however. Nonmarket activities, the underground economy, and the distribution and composition of national output make GDP an imperfect measure of economic activity and our standards of living.

Nonmarket Activities

Remember that GDP is defined as the market value of all goods and services produced in the economy. What if a good or service is produced but not marketed? What if you paint your own apartment, eat food from your own garden, or volunteer your services at the local hospital? Or perhaps more important, what if you provide homemaking services in your own home, preparing meals, caring for children, and cleaning the house? All of these activities are productive, but because they are not bought and sold in the marketplace, no market value is attached to them, and they are excluded from GDP statistics.

The exclusion of nonmarketed goods and services serves to understate the full value of productive activity in our economy. Many would argue it also undermines the value of homemaking services, traditionally the domain of women. Failure to fully value these important services may translate into failure to fully appreciate the contributions of women (and an increasing number of men) in our economy.

Exclusion of nonmarketed goods and services also distorts comparisons. During the 1950s most women stayed home as full-time homemakers. By the 1990s, many women had entered the formal labor market, paying out money for services that they had previously provided themselves. As soon as a baby-sitter is hired, a housekeeper is paid, and fast food is purchased on the way home from work, these goods and services enter into GDP statistics. GDP is artificially higher in the 1990s than it was in the 1950s in part because people are now being paid to provide the homemaking services that went unrecorded in the 1950s.

Comparisons of countries' GDP are distorted as well. In many Third World countries, many families grow their own food, build their own homes, and gather their own water and fuel, and GDP statistics are very low in part because many of these nonmarketed activities go unreported. Once again, the services of many women (who perform many of these activities) go unrecorded and undervalued.

Underground Activities

The underground economy involves economic activity that is never reported to the government, either because the activity is illegal or the participants wish to evade taxes. Such underground activity causes GDP to understate actual economic activity.

Suppose you are engaged in illegal activity such as gambling, prostitution, or the drug trade (we hope not!). You will naturally report your income from this activity to the government—NOT! For obvious reasons, illegal economic activity goes unrecorded in gross domestic product statistics. Although we do not know how much underground activity exists, we do know that for many countries it is sizable. In some Latin American countries, for example, a very large share of economic activity consists of illegal drug sales.

Similarly, any time a person engages in under-the-table exchange, usually to avoid payment of personal income taxes, the activity is not recorded and therefore doesn't enter GDP statistics. This type of exchange might include legal activity, such as haircuts or baby-sitting, but if payment for the service is unreported, it never enters the GDP statistics. People who underreport their tips distort the GDP statistics in a similar fashion. Again, the magnitude of such underground activity is unknown, but it is thought to be significant in the United States.

Composition and Distribution

There are two more important reasons why gross domestic product is not an adequate indicator of people's standards of living. These reasons were discussed at length in Chapter Eight on world poverty. For now, let it suffice to mention that the **composition of GDP** is as important as the total value of GDP. If a small country primarily produces armaments and other military hardware, for example, its people may not be achieving the same quality of life as those of another country

Composition of GDP
The goods and services of which GDP consists.

that has a similar level of GDP but primarily produces health care, educational services, and other goods and services directly meeting the needs of people.

Distribution of income
How national income is distributed within an economy.

Also very important is the distribution of GDP, or more technically, the **distribution of income** generated from the production of GDP. It makes a great deal of difference whether a nation's income flows primarily to a small, select, elite group of people or is distributed more equally within the country. The masses of people will live much better in the latter situation. For this reason, standards of living are not adequately measured by the total value of gross domestic product.

One final note: suppose that the GDP of a country is growing very rapidly over time, but at the same time the country experiences more and more pollution, congestion, and depletion of natural resources. Or what if the people of the country must work more and more hours each week in order to produce the high levels of output? Or what if the *Exxon Valdez* disaster, Midwest floods, and Hurricane Andrew all were associated with increased GDP in the clean-up phase? Can we really say that standards of living are improving? Even though we focus a great deal of attention on gross domestic product, be sure to tuck away in your mind somewhere that high GDP is not necessarily synonymous with high standards of living.

AGGREGATE DEMAND AND SUPPLY

Because aggregate demand refers to the quantities of U.S. gross domestic product demanded at alternative price levels, it is useful for us to think of the various sectors that purchase this GDP and that are represented along the aggregate demand curve. In doing so, we can also think through the factors that will shift aggregate demand. For simplicity, let's just think in terms of the factors that might increase aggregate demand. Aggregate demand will increase whenever any sectors of the economy increase their purchases. Let's consider each of these sectors in turn.

What Sectors Are Represented by Aggregate Demand?

Consumers

Durable goods
Products with a life of longer than one year.

Nondurable goods
Products with a life of less than one year.

Individual consumers such as you and I purchase U.S. durable and nondurable goods and services. **Durable goods** are products with a life of longer than one year, whereas **nondurable goods** are those that usually last less than one year. Durable goods include items such as appliances, furniture, and automobiles; food is a good example of a nondurable good. Household purchases of services such as haircuts and doctor visits are included in the consumer category as well. Indeed, consumer purchases represent the largest component of aggregate demand. It is a relatively stable component as well, particularly the portion consisting of nondurable goods. Regardless of whether the economy is doing well or poorly, people tend to purchase products such as food on a steady basis. Durable goods are less stable; when the economy is doing poorly, many people are forced to reduce their purchases of large-ticket items like automobiles and home entertainment centers. When the economy picks up, purchases of these items pick up as well.

Consumers will increase their purchases of goods and services as a result of a variety of factors. When consumer incomes rise, consumer purchases go up. When consumer expectations of the future improve, consumer purchases also go up. (If you expect a promotion in the near future, you may well go out and start celebrating now!)

Consumer incomes can be directly affected by government policies. Policies to reduce personal income taxes, for example, will serve to increase consumer incomes because what is left after paying their taxes will be higher. Similarly, government policies that increase government income transfers (welfare payments, social security payments, and so on) will also increase consumer incomes.

Consumers are also responsive to changes in interest rates. When interest rates fall, the cost of borrowing money declines. As a result, consumers are more willing to purchase expensive items that they must buy with borrowed money (houses, cars, and appliances.) Finally, note that although U.S. consumers make purchases of foreign-produced goods (such as Toyotas and Acer computers), these purchases are *not* part of U.S. GDP. Therefore, these purchases of imports are not represented along the aggregate demand curve for U.S. GDP.

Businesses

Private business firms in our economy also purchase U.S. GDP. They buy a variety of equipment such as machinery, tools, and computers. They also purchase structures such as factories, office buildings, retail outlets, and restaurant buildings. Finally, businesses "purchase" changes in **inventories,** which was referred to earlier. A business normally holds a variety of inventories, which are unsold goods and materials. These inventories include the final product, the product in intermediate stages of production, and raw materials and component parts.

Inventories
Unsold goods and materials.

Business inventories may be held for a variety of reasons. An automobile company, for example, may hold huge inventories of finished cars because the managers anticipate a large demand for the cars in the near future, or because demand for the cars has currently fallen off and the product remains unsold. Whatever the reason, increases or decreases in inventories are included in aggregate demand as business purchases. We can envision these inventories as though they are purchased by business firms, even though manufacturers do not actually purchase their unsold inventories.

Business purchases are a relatively small component of aggregate demand, but they tend to fluctuate a lot. When the economy is in a downturn, owners of businesses are reluctant to expand by purchasing new factories and equipment. When the economy improves, they are willing to increase factory and equipment purchases.

Business purchases are influenced by a variety of factors. Expectations of the future are an important factor. If the economy is improving and businesses expect their sales to boom, they may begin purchasing new factories and equipment now to meet the future consumer demand. Furthermore, businesses, like consumers, are influenced by interest rates. A decline in interest rates means that new factories and equipment are cheaper and easier for businesses to buy. Lastly, as with the consumer sector, we are including only business purchases of U.S. GDP, and not foreign-produced imports.

Government

Government purchases of goods and services represent the third component of aggregate demand. The government purchases a variety of items, including food for government nutrition programs, office supplies for government administrators, and the university computer with which we are writing this book. The government also purchases services, including the services of police officers, firefighters, military personnel, and public teachers (including your authors!). Lastly, the government purchases structures, such as prisons and school buildings. Again, only government purchases of U.S. GDP are represented along the aggregate demand curve.

Income transfer

A cash transfer from the government to an individual for which no good or service is provided to the government in return.

Note that income transfers are not included in the category of government purchases of goods and services. An **income transfer,** as you may recall from Chapter Seven on U.S. poverty, is a cash transfer from the government to an individual for which no good or service is provided in return. Examples of income transfers include Social Security benefits, unemployment compensation, and veterans' cash benefits. These items are not included in the government purchases component of aggregate demand. (When the income transfers are eventually spent by the recipients, their expenditures are then included in the consumption component of aggregate demand.)

The decisions of government can have important impacts on aggregate demand. Because government purchases of goods and services are included as part of aggregate demand, an increase in government spending on national health care, the space program, public education, or any other program will directly increase aggregate demand. It doesn't matter whether the policy is deliberate or not, any increase in government purchases will increase aggregate demand. Thus if the country goes to war, and the government purchases military hardware and the services of the armed forces, aggregate demand will increase just as if the government chose to expand any other program.

Keep in mind that government policies can also indirectly affect aggregate demand. The decrease in taxes or increase in income transfers mentioned previously will increase the incomes of consumers, which will cause their purchases to go up. These government policies influence the consumption component of aggregate demand. We will examine these more carefully shortly.

Foreign Purchasers

As the final component of aggregate demand, we must recognize that foreigners purchase approximately 12 percent of U.S. GDP. These foreigners include individual people, businesses, and governments of other countries, and we refer to their purchases as U.S. exports.

Anything that causes our exports to increase will result in an increase in aggregate demand. The size of our exports is largely determined by factors out of the control of the United States. Because foreigners are purchasing our exports, their purchases depend on variables such as foreign incomes.

FIGURE 15-3   An Increase in Aggregate Demand

When aggregate demand increases, it shifts forward from *AD* to *AD'*.

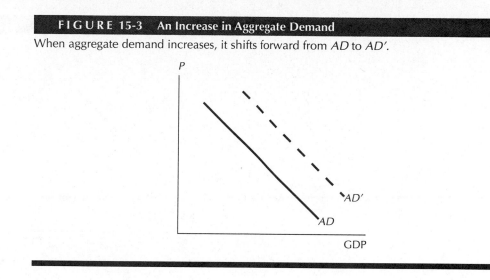

Shifts in Aggregate Demand

An increase in aggregate demand due to an increase in purchases by consumers, businesses, government, or foreigners will be represented as a forward shift in aggregate demand. This shift is shown in Figure 15-3. Similarly, a decrease in purchases by any of the four sectors will cause a backward shift in aggregate demand.

Shifts in Aggregate Supply

Aggregate supply can shift for the same kinds of reasons that the supply of tutors in Chapter One could shift. An increase in aggregate supply would occur if the costs of production (such as energy prices or wage costs) decrease. Aggregate supply would also increase if technological advance makes production of our nation's output cheaper and easier. In the case of agricultural production, aggregate supply would increase if the weather is good. Some economists and politicians believe that the government can use policies to influence a shift in the aggregate supply curve; this issue will be discussed shortly.

An increase in aggregate supply for any of these reasons will cause the aggregate supply to shift forward to the right, as shown in Figure 15-4 on page 338.

We are now ready to translate this analysis into a discussion of inflation, unemployment, and government macro policy.

INFLATION REVISITED

In Chapter Fourteen, we defined the three types of inflation and noted that these could be more easily understood in the context of the macroeconomy. Let's consider each type in terms of the graph of aggregate demand and aggregate supply, focusing on different periods of time in the U.S. economy.

FIGURE 15-4 An Increase in Aggregate Supply

When aggregate supply increases, it shifts forward from *AS* to *AS'*.

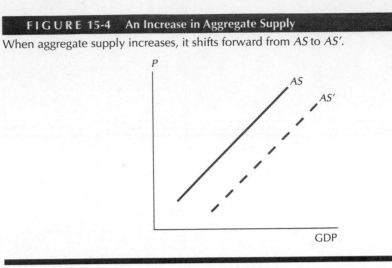

Demand-Pull Inflation

Recall that demand-pull inflation is caused by an increase in aggregate demand. Consider the graph in Figure 15-5. Initial gross domestic product is GDP_0, corresponding to an average price level of P_0. Now imagine some of the conditions that existed during the early 1960s. President John Kennedy had initiated a variety of social programs, which were expanded during the Great Society years of President Lyndon Johnson. All of these programs represented increases in government purchases of goods and services, as well as increases in government income transfers to low-income people. Personal income taxes were also cut in 1963, resulting in higher after-tax income, and consumers increased their purchases of goods and

FIGURE 15-5 Demand-Pull Inflation

An increase in aggregate demand from *AD* to *AD'* results in a higher average price level (*P'*) and a higher level of gross domestic product (*GDP'*).

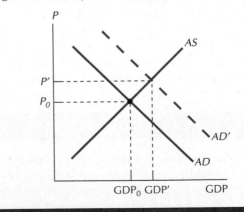

services as a result. Finally, the war in Vietnam consisted of a demand by the U.S. government for armaments and other military supplies, as well as the services of armed service personnel.

All of these factors caused an increase in aggregate demand. The aggregate demand curve shifted forward, as in Figure 15-5, resulting in an increase in gross domestic product to GDP′, as well as an increase in the average price level from P_0 to $P′$. This rise in the average price level is what we mean by inflation; and in this case, it represents demand-pull inflation.

Cost-Push Inflation

Cost-push inflation was earlier defined as inflation caused by an increase in the costs of production. Recall that inflation rates were very high in the mid- and late 1970s. These rising prices can be explained as cost-push inflation.

In 1973–1974, oil supplies were cut off to the United States by the Arab countries in response to U.S. support for Israel during the Arab–Israeli wars. Oil prices rose as a result. And in 1979, the Shah of Iran was overthrown, and Iranian oil was once again cut off to the United States. This time oil prices soared. All these events occurred in the context of increasing market power by OPEC, the Organization of Petroleum Exporting Countries. OPEC used its market power to initiate overall increases in the price of oil. Because oil and related energy products are important components of our overall purchases, the rise in oil prices directly caused an increase in the average price level. But beyond this, realize that energy is an important input in the production of most goods and services. Thus rising energy prices represent an increased cost of production. An increase in the costs of production causes the aggregate supply curve to shift to the left, as shown in Figure 15-6.

In Figure 15-6, the backward shift in aggregate supply results in a decrease in gross domestic product to GDP′, as well as an increase in the average price level to

FIGURE 15-6   Cost-Push Inflation

A decrease in aggregate supply from *AS* to *AS′* results in a higher average price level (*P′*) and a lower level of gross domestic product (GDP′).

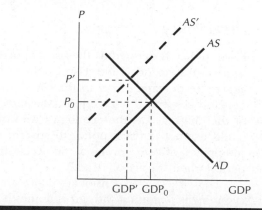

Recession
Decline in a nation's gross domestic product (output) associated with a rise in unemployment.

Stagflation
Simultaneous inflation and recession.

P'. The rise in the average price level is the problem of inflation, whereas the decline in GDP is what we mean by **recession,** as defined in Chapter Seven. During a recession, total production declines, and employment falls off as well. (Fewer workers are needed to produce lower levels of output.) Thus the United States experienced the double whammy of simultaneous inflation and recession. This situation is referred to as **stagflation.** Despite the fact that these problems in the macroeconomy were caused by oil price increases, President Jimmy Carter was largely held accountable for them. Many believe that these problems are the reason that President Carter was voted out of office and President Ronald Reagan was voted in during the 1980 presidential election.

Profit-Push Inflation

This form of inflation results from the market power of various industries within the U.S. economy. When business firms use their market power, discussed in Chapter Four as the ability to influence market prices, output is deliberately restricted to drive up prices and profits. If market power is extensive, these conditions show up as a backward shift in the aggregate supply curve. The graph would look identical to Figure 15-6. Although many fail to recognize it, U.S. market power restricts output and employment in the United States and raises the prices of manufactured items, harming workers and consumers alike. The rising prices of manufactured products have also had negative implications for Third World countries that import these products, as will be discussed in Chapter Seventeen.

GOVERNMENT MACRO POLICY

Fiscal policy
The use of government spending and tax policy to shift the aggregate demand curve.

Expansionary fiscal policy
Fiscal policy that increases aggregate demand, thereby expanding GDP.

Contractionary fiscal policy
Fiscal policy that decreases aggregate demand, thereby contracting GDP.

We are now in a position to analyze the policies available to the government to deal with the problems of unemployment and inflation. You have probably heard the terms fiscal policy and monetary policy. And beginning with President Reagan's first term of office, the nation became familiar with the term supply-side policy. Despite our familiarity with these terms, most Americans do not understand exactly what they mean. We will consider each of them in turn.

Fiscal Policy

Fiscal policy is defined as the use of government spending and taxes to shift the aggregate demand curve. Fiscal policy can be either **expansionary** (shifting the aggregate demand curve to the right) or **contractionary** (shifting the aggregate demand curve to the left). John Maynard Keynes, who is quoted at the beginning of the chapter, was the economist who developed the idea that the government could use active fiscal policy to correct the economy. He felt that government should act while the problem was occurring, rather than wait for the long-run time period when "we are all dead."

The effects of expansionary policy are shown in Figure 15-7. Suppose that the economy is operating with gross domestic product at GDP_0, and the average price

FIGURE 15-7　Expansionary Fiscal Policy

Expansionary fiscal policy shifts the aggregate demand curve forward, resulting in a higher level of gross domestic product (GDP$_F$) and a higher average price level (P')

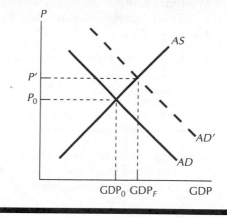

level at P_0. Let's assume that full employment GDP occurs at GDP$_F$. Define full-employment GDP as the level of gross domestic product associated with full employment of the labor force. At full-employment GDP, cyclical unemployment is zero.

If the government can successfully use fiscal policy, the aggregate demand curve will shift forward. Gross domestic product will rise to GDP$_F$, increasing employment in the country. The average price level will increase as well.

You already understand the tools that can be used by the government to cause the shifts in aggregate demand. They are government purchases of goods and services, government taxes, and government income transfers. Recall that government purchases of goods and services represents a component of aggregate demand. Thus whenever the government increases its purchases, aggregate demand will shift forward. Alternatively, the government can reduce personal income taxes. The higher after-tax income of consumers encourages them to increase their purchases, thereby increasing the consumer component of aggregate demand. This higher after-tax income will also cause the aggregate demand curve to shift forward. Finally, an increase in government income transfers will serve to raise consumer incomes, again causing the aggregate demand curve to increase.

Any or all of these policy tools can be used independently. The government may increase its purchases while lowering taxes, for example, because there are other ways it can finance its purchases besides raising tax dollars. Therefore, when one of these policy tools is used, do not necessarily assume that another tool is used simultaneously.

When President Bill Clinton took office in 1993, the nation had been experiencing some difficulty with recession. Unemployment rates were higher than normal, and President Clinton was seeking ways to increase gross domestic product. That is, he was seeking some form of expansionary fiscal policy. Many of his proposals, including expanded highway construction and college-age work programs,

http://www.bls.gov
This is the home page for the U.S. Bureau of Labor Statistics. It presents all data related to employment, including unemployment rates.

were designed to do just that. The difficulty President Clinton ran into was a reluctant Congress. Congress (and much of the American public) was more concerned with reducing government spending than expanding the macroeconomy, and President Clinton was unable to maintain the expanded programs as he desired.

To summarize, expansionary fiscal policy consists of one or more of the following tools:

- an increase in government purchases of goods and services,
- a reduction in taxes, or
- an increase in income transfers.

Similarly, contractionary fiscal policy consists of one or more of the following tools:

- a decrease in government purchases of goods and services,
- an increase in taxes, or
- a decrease in income transfers.

Monetary Policy

Monetary policy
Changes made in the nation's money supply to shift the aggregate demand curve.

Monetary policy is defined as changes that are made in the nation's money supply in order to shift aggregate demand. Whereas fiscal policy is under the control of the government (the president and Congress), monetary policy is under the control of the Federal Reserve. The **Federal Reserve** is our nation's central banking system. The seven members of the board of governors of the Federal Reserve are appointed by the president and approved by Congress. They serve staggered 14-year terms, such that a member is generally appointed every 2 years. Thus although the membership of the board of governors is determined by the government, the role of any one presidential administration is limited. Therefore, the Federal Reserve is somewhat immune to politics.

Federal Reserve
The U.S. central banking system.

Among other things under the control of the Federal Reserve is our nation's money supply. Changes in the nation's money supply will affect the interest rate. (Although economists refer to *the* interest rate, in fact there are many interest rates, depending on the type of loan or financial investment. These rates do tend to move up and down together, however.) Think of the interest rate as the price of money. An increase in the supply of money will cause a reduction in the interest rate (just as an increase in the supply of corn will cause a reduction in the price of corn). A decrease in the nation's money supply will cause an increase in the interest rate.

Contractionary monetary policy
Monetary policy that decreases aggregate demand, thereby contracting GDP.

Monetary policy affects the economy through its effects on interest rates. A rise in the interest rate will cause a reduction in business purchases of factories and equipment, as well as a decrease in consumer purchases of cars, houses, appliances, and other expensive items. Businesses and consumers must borrow money to finance these major purchases, and rising interest rates raise the cost of borrowing. Many business firms and consumers decide that they cannot afford to purchase the items due to the high cost of borrowing money. Thus a reduction in the nation's money supply will cause a rise in interest rates, causing a decrease in consumer and business purchases, and therefore a decrease in aggregate demand. A decrease in the nation's money supply reflects **contractionary monetary policy** (monetary policy that reduces aggregate demand, thereby contracting GDP). An increase in the nation's money supply will increase aggregate demand, and is therefore called **expansionary monetary policy.** It will expand GDP.

Expansionary monetary policy
Monetary policy that increases aggregate demand, thereby expanding GDP.

Thus monetary policy, just like fiscal policy, is an aggregate demand-side policy. Students sometimes get confused when they think of the term money supply and assume it affects the supply side of the economy. Rather, monetary policy, just like fiscal policy, is designed to influence aggregate demand.

The Federal Reserve may choose either expansionary or contractionary monetary policy, depending on the state of the economy. A good case in point is the situation encountered by newly elected President Reagan in 1981. As a result of the rise in oil prices already described, the president faced a serious problem of inflation. Although the president has no direct control over monetary policy, President Reagan did make a national plea to the Federal Reserve to engage in contractionary monetary policy to reduce aggregate demand. The Federal Reserve complied; the results are indicated in Figure 15-8.

As the Federal Reserve reduced the nation's money supply, interest rates soared. The construction industry and the automobile industry were particularly hard hit, as businesses and consumers were unable or unwilling to borrow at such high interest rates and were therefore unable to finance purchases of factories, houses, and automobiles. The reduction in aggregate demand reduced gross domestic product to the level depicted as GDP′ in Figure 15-8. The consequent recession resulted in the high unemployment rates of the early 1980s. Inflation was controlled, but at the serious cost of recession and unemployment. A similar monetary contraction occurred in the early 1990s, resulting in similar, though less intense, recession and unemployment.

These examples of fiscal and monetary policy demonstrate a shortcoming of policy that operates on the aggregate demand side of the economy. An increase in aggregate demand, as in the case of the expansionary fiscal policy in the early

FIGURE 15-8   Contractionary Monetary Policy

Contractionary monetary policy shifts the aggregate demand curve backward, resulting in a lower level of gross domestic product (GDP′) and a lower average price level (P′).

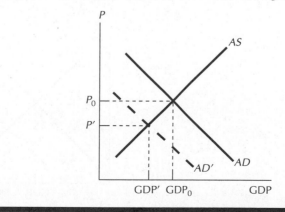

1960s, results in an increase in GDP and employment, but at the cost of creating inflation (the rise in the average price level). A decrease in aggregate demand, as in the case of the contractionary monetary policy in the early 1980s, reduces the problem of inflation, but at the cost of creating recession and unemployment. Thus aggregate demand-side policy creates a trade-off between the problems of unemployment and inflation, at least in the short run. (This trade-off is modified somewhat in Appendix 2 with a bit more realistic view of the aggregate supply curve.)

Wouldn't it be nice to come up with a policy that would simultaneously reduce inflation and unemployment? This objective underlies **supply-side policy** and was the reason for its widespread welcome during the Reagan administration of 1981–1984.

Supply-side policy
The use of various tools to shift the aggregate supply curve to the right.

Supply-Side Policy

Supply-side economics was a revolution in thought. Adopting a general philosophy that promoted less involvement of government in the economy, President Reagan undertook supply-side policies with the stated objective of increasing aggregate supply. The idea behind supply-side policy is that by increasing aggregate supply rather than aggregate demand, GDP and employment will rise, and the average price level will fall. This phenomenon is illustrated in Figure 15-9.

The supply-side tools of President Reagan included cuts in personal income tax rates, cuts in government transfer programs, and cuts in government regulations. These policies are relevant today, because they are the same policies that economic conservatives are proposing. Each policy is considered in turn below.

Cuts in Personal Income Tax Rates
This policy tool is a little confusing, because fiscal policy as well as supply-side policy can utilize cuts in taxes. Recall that in terms of fiscal policy, a tax cut will place

---

FIGURE 15-9 Supply-Side Policy

Supply-side policy shifts the aggregate supply curve forward, resulting in a higher level of gross domestic product (GDP′) and a lower average price level (P′).

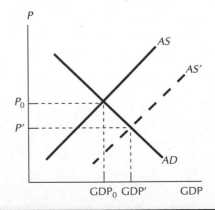

more income in the hands of consumers, who will increase their consumption purchases. This phenomenon is reflected in an increase in aggregate demand. The effects of the tax cut are very different from the perspective of a supply-side theorist, however. From this perspective, the tax cut must take the form of a reduction in tax rates, because it is assumed that tax rates influence our decisions about work effort. A reduction in tax rates is considered tantamount to an increase in hourly wages, and it is assumed that people will respond to the incentive of higher after-tax wages by increasing their work effort. That is, some people will take second jobs, others will accept overtime hours, and still others will take a job that they previously were unwilling to take. Supply-side policies typically center on incentives, and here the incentive is to increase work effort. If the nation's workers respond as desired, the increased work effort will result in expanded production, which will increase the supply side of the economy. Aggregate supply will shift forward, as in Figure 15-9, resulting in expanded GDP and a decreased price level.

In 1981, President Reagan proposed a series of large, three-year tax rate cuts. Although Congress scaled back the magnitude of the cuts somewhat, they remained the largest tax cuts in our nation's history. The tax cuts were subsequently criticized, because high-income households received by far the largest tax reductions, whereas low-income households received very small reductions. President George W. Bush pledged similar cuts in the federal income tax during the election campaign of 2000. While stating that everyone who pays income taxes deserves a tax cut, these proposed tax cuts would primarily benefit higher-income earners. The same conservative agenda of low taxes and less money in the hands of the government motivated this campaign pledge.

Cuts in Income Transfers
Like cuts in taxes, cuts in income transfers can be construed as part of fiscal policy and supply-side policy. In terms of fiscal policy, the cuts in income transfers would lower recipients' incomes, causing their consumption purchases to fall. This outcome would be reflected in a decrease in aggregate demand. In terms of supply-side policy, incentives again become important. Many conservatives argue that transfer programs provide incentives for people to be lazy, seeking handouts from government instead of going to work. By reducing transfers, people are forced to seek employment. With more people working, production expands and aggregate supply increases.

President Reagan enacted large cuts in government income transfers, primarily Aid to Families with Dependent Children, as well as other programs for the poor. As discussed in Chapter Seven, our recent welfare reform has gone beyond work incentives, requiring instead that participants work. Whether the issue is incentives or requirements, the intention is to increase work, thereby increasing production and increasing aggregate supply.

Deregulation

Deregulation
The reduction of government regulations.

A third supply-side tool used by President Reagan was that of **deregulation**—reductions in government regulations affecting American business. The largest cuts were made in the areas of environmental protection and worker safety. The Reagan

Administration argued that these regulations tie the hands of business and increase the costs of production. By reducing these regulations, President Reagan argued that businesses would expand production, thereby increasing the aggregate supply side of the economy. The current conservative agenda is really no different. Reducing government regulations not only creates an incentive for businesses to expand production, but also restricts the role of government in the economy.

Effects of Supply-Side Policy

Were the supply-side tools of the early 1980s successful in increasing GDP? Are the more recent conservative policies effective in expanding our economy? Answering these questions is difficult because supply-side policies do not operate in a vacuum. Implemented simultaneously with the supply-side policies of the early 1980s was the contractionary monetary policy already described. The effects of the monetary contraction by far dwarfed any supply-side effects that may have occurred. Contractionary monetary policy also restrained the growth of the economy in the late 1990s and early 2000s, as the Federal Reserve struggled to prevent inflation from occurring. Monetary expansion after the beginning of the year 2001 sought the opposite in an effort to prevent any downturn of the economy. Furthermore, the effects of supply-side policy in the 1990s and 2000s are probably much smaller than other forces that have served to increase aggregate supply. These forces include technological advances and improved labor productivity. These forces will be discussed further in Chapter Seventeen, as we look at economic conditions in the twenty-first century.

We have reasons to question supply-side effectiveness. Cuts in tax rates have a limited effect, if any, on work effort. Most people are unable to alter the number of hours they work each week, so increased incentives for work effort will not change the number of hours worked. Others may increase their work hours when their after-tax wages go up because the incentive to do so is now greater. Still others may decide to cut their work hours because tax-rate cuts allow them to maintain their desired level of income while working fewer hours. Labor economists believe that the overall impact of changes in after-tax wages is close to zero, meaning that overall work effort remains unchanged.

Many have argued that just like tax rate cuts, cuts in government transfers do not result in expanded work effort. After all, transfer programs such as Aid to Families with Dependent Children in the early 1980s were meant for women with small children and others who were unable to work. Furthermore, many participants in our current welfare system will not be able to work unless child care, transportation, job training, and education are made available. Finally, given the possibility of recession at any time, jobs may simply be unavailable (as was the case in the early 1980s). Just because a person has an incentive to work does not mean that he or she will find a job. Clearly, jobs must exist if the incentives are to be effective in increasing aggregate supply.

Keep in mind that the supply-side policies of the early 1980s, as well as the conservative proposals of the 1990s and 2000s, all have as their objective a reduced role for government in the economy. Supply-siders would reduce government spending and involvement in social programs, they would reduce taxes to increase the spending ability of the private sector, and they would reduce government

Any one of the tools of fiscal policy or the use of monetary policy can successfully expand the economy. Theoretically, the use of supply-side policy can do the same. Even if all these expansionary policies are equally effective, people will disagree about the type of policy to be used. Liberals, you should note, would be in favor of fiscal policy that increases government purchases and transfers. Conservatives would prefer to see fiscal policy that reduces taxes and places more purchasing power in the private sector of the economy.

Conservatives would also prefer the use of monetary policy, which, by lowering interest rates, enables private consumers and businesses to increase their purchases. And, of course, conservatives are the ones who favor the use of supply-side policy.

Thus, although the various policies may be similar in terms of their impact on the macroeconomy, the philosophies underlying them will vary greatly.

regulatory control over business. The conservative objective of reducing the government role in the economy is at the root of supply-side policies.

Trickle-Down

Does President Reagan's willingness to reduce taxes largely for the rich and to reduce government spending largely for the poor mean that supply siders are interested in benefiting the rich and hurting the poor? Does President George W. Bush's support for further reductions in taxes for the rich and for welfare reform that emphasizes work mean that he discards his father's notion of a kinder, gentler America? Supply-side economists and politicians would answer with a resounding no! Instead, they argue that these policies are necessary to generate economic growth (that is, a forward shift in aggregate supply that persists over time). They argue that economic growth will improve the prosperity of the nation, and eventually the benefits of this prosperity will trickle down to everyone, rich and poor alike. No wonder this approach to economics has been dubbed **trickle-down philosophy!** We'll leave it to you, the reader, to decide if this conservative approach to economics will indeed provide benefits to all, or whether the poor will continue to be left out of the prosperity of the nation. This issue is important because the conservative Republican agenda incorporates trickle-down philosophy today.

Trickle-down philosophy
The view that supply-side policy will generate economic growth and prosperity, the benefits of which will eventually "trickle down" to all.

Economic Policy for the New Century

George W. Bush was elected to the nation's highest office in 2000, ending eight years of a Democratic presidency. Bush campaigned as a moderate conservative against the moderate liberal Al Gore. With a margin of just a few thousand votes separating the two candidates and the popular vote going to Gore, the American public was clearly divided. Congress was similarly divided. The unemployment rate was extremely low at 4.0 percent, and the inflation rate was relatively low at 3.4 percent.

The government budget was in surplus, a conservative welfare system was in effect, and an eight-year stretch of economic growth had still continued unmitigated. And President Bush left no doubt about his intentions to reign in government spending, reduce government taxes, and privatize portions of Social Security, health insurance for the poor, and educational opportunities.

The current conservative Republican agenda is in many ways a repeat of the conservative supply-side philosophy of the early 1980s. The objective is once again to reduce the role of government in the economy.

SUMMARY

We can analyze the macroeconomy with a graph of aggregate demand and supply. Aggregate demand is the quantity of total output demanded at alternative price levels, whereas aggregate supply is the quantity of output produced at alternative price levels. The intersection of aggregate demand and supply determines the country's average price level and level of gross domestic product. Gross domestic product refers to the market value of all final goods and services produced in the economy, usually within a one-year time period. Aggregate demand consists of the purchases of consumers, businesses, government, and foreigners.

The government and the Federal Reserve can use policies to shift aggregate demand and supply in an effort to reduce inflation or unemployment. The two types of policies used to shift aggregate demand are fiscal policy and monetary policy. Fiscal policy includes changes in government spending and taxes, whereas monetary policy works by changing the nation's money supply to affect interest rates. Supply-side policies may be used in an effort to increase aggregate supply.

At the root of supply-side policies is the desire to reduce the government's role in the economy. In the process, the goal of these policies is to achieve economic prosperity, the benefits of which are to trickle down to all. Critics of supply-side policies maintain that these policies are ineffective and harm the poor.

DISCUSSION QUESTIONS

1. *Many have argued that the government should attach a value to homemaking services and include this value in gross domestic product statistics. Do you agree? Why?*

2. *Is gross domestic product an accurate measure of standards of living? Why or why not?*

3. *Describe the effect on gross domestic product, employment, and inflation of each of the following: (a) war, (b) passage of a national health care plan, and (c) cuts in welfare cash benefits.*

4. *Look up the current level of GDP at the Census Bureau's Web site (http://www.census.gov). What is the value of nominal GDP? What is the value of real GDP? What is the base year for real GDP?*

5. *Look up the current unemployment rate at the Bureau of Labor Statistics' Web site (http://www.bls.gov). Would you say we currently have full employment?*

6. *Conservatives favor a lesser role for government in the economy, whereas liberals favor a greater role. How would each of these groups feel about a fiscal policy that increases government purchases and income transfers? fiscal policy that reduces taxes? monetary policy that reduces interest rates?*

7. *What is your opinion about the role that government should play in the economy?*

8. *Do you believe in the trickle-down philosophy?*

Chapter Fifteen Appendix:
The Slope of the Aggregate Demand Curve

It was noted earlier that the aggregate demand curve slopes downward, as shown in Figure 15-10. The downward slope indicates that the quantity of gross domestic product demanded increases when the average price level falls, and that it decreases when the average price level rises. The relationship between the quantity of GDP demanded and the average price level is negative for three reasons.

First, let's consider the international trade effect of a rise in the average price level. If the average price level in the United States rises relative to the price levels in other countries, then American consumers will tend to buy more foreign goods and fewer American goods. The price of a Ford vehicle may rise, for example, in comparison with the price of a Toyota. U.S. consumers (as well as the consumers of other countries) will probably buy more Toyotas and fewer Fords. This reduction in U.S. GDP demanded occurs as a result of the rise in the U.S. average price level.

Second, a rise in the average price level reduces the value, or purchasing power, of assets. The money you have tucked away in a savings account (or under your mattress, for that matter), for example, is no longer worth as much when the average price level rises. That is, a fixed amount of money loses its purchasing power when the prices of purchased items increase. Less wealth means that people cut back their purchases (because they feel less wealthy). Thus the quantity of GDP demanded falls when the average price level rises.

Third, a rise in the average price level has implications for interest rates. When people experience a loss in the value of their assets, as we have described, they need to borrow more money from their banks. This increase in the demand for credit pushes up the price of credit—in other words, the interest rate. As interest rates rise, people and businesses reduce their purchases of big-ticket items like

---

FIGURE 15-10   A Downward-Sloping Aggregate Demand Curve

A downward-sloping aggregate demand curve means that the quantity of gross domestic product demanded increases when the average price level falls and decreases when the average price level rises.

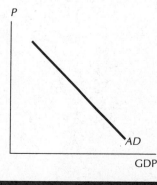

cars, homes, and factories. Thus the quantity of GDP demanded decreases as the average price level rises.

In all of these examples, we have considered why a rise in the average price level causes a reduction in the quantity of GDP demanded. Realize that a decrease in the average price level will cause the opposite effect: that is, an increase in the quantity of GDP demanded.

Keep in mind the difference between factors that cause a *movement along* the aggregate demand curve and factors that cause a *shift in* the aggregate demand curve. Because the average price level is on the vertical axis of the graph of aggregate demand, any change in the average price level that causes changes in the quantity of GDP demanded is reflected as a movement along the demand curve, according to the curve's downward slope. On the other hand, changes not precipitated by a change in the average price level—such as changes in population size, consumer incomes, or government fiscal or monetary policy—will cause a shift in the entire aggregate demand curve.

The Slope of the Aggregate Supply Curve

The actual slope of the aggregate supply curve is important when it comes to policy prescription. Throughout the chapter, we've used a simplified version of the aggregate supply curve, one with a straight-line upward-sloping shape, as is shown in Figure 15-11. This shape is responsible for one of our conclusions in this chapter: that aggregate demand-side policy creates a trade-off between unemployment and inflation. This trade-off is not quite so clear-cut if we look at the aggregate supply curve more carefully.

Economists have come to various conclusions about the shape of the aggregate supply curve, depending on whether they consider the long run or the short

---

FIGURE 15-11   A Straight-Line Upward-Sloping Aggregate Supply Curve

A straight-line upward-sloping aggregate supply curve means that the quantity of gross domestic product supplied rises when the average price level rises and falls when the average price level falls.

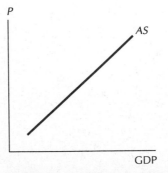

run, as well as other assumptions. We can simplify, however, and draw an aggregate supply curve that incorporates many of these views. This supply curve is depicted in Figure 15-12.

Notice that the aggregate supply curve in Figure 15-12 has a flat range (Range A), an upward-sloping range (Range B), and a vertical range (Range C). The upward-sloping range corresponds to the aggregate supply in Figure 15-11 and can be viewed as reflecting a typical state of the economy—that is, one with moderate levels of GDP and employment. Any shift of aggregate demand within this range will create the trade-off between unemployment and inflation. (See the shift from AD_2 to AD_3 in Figure 15-13 on page 352. GDP increases from GDP_2 to GDP_3, and the average price level increases from P_2 to P_3.)

The flat range of the aggregate supply curve is sometimes called the Keynesian range, because it is typical of the depression era when John Maynard Keynes developed his theory of the economy. Specifically, GDP was low and unemployment rates were extremely high, and workers were willing to work for whatever low wages were being offered at the time. Capital equipment (factories and machinery) was underutilized, operating perhaps only one shift per day instead of two or three. In this context, firms can easily expand production to meet expanded demand. Production costs per unit of output (per car, for example) will not rise because wages and capital prices will not be pushed upward. Without rising costs of production, firms have no reason to raise their prices to consumers. This means that within the flat, Keynesian range of aggregate supply, any increase in aggregate demand will increase output and employment, without causing any attendant inflation. This situation is shown in Figure 15-13 on page 352, where the shift in aggregate demand from AD_1 to AD_2 increases GDP from GDP_1 to GDP_2, but P_2 is equal to P_1.

FIGURE 15-12   An Aggregate Supply Curve with Three Distinct Ranges

The flat region (Range A) represents low output and employment, the upward-sloping region (Range B) represents a moderate level of output and employment, and the vertical region (Range C) represents high output and full employment.

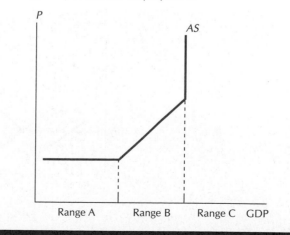

Finally, the vertical range of aggregate supply corresponds to a situation of high GDP and a fully employed economy. Keeping in mind the definition of full employment in Chapter Fourteen, expanding production beyond this level is very difficult. If aggregate demand increases, for example, and the manager of an automobile company wishes to expand production to match additional demand, the only way to hire additional workers will be to offer higher wages. Similarly, if capital is fully utilized, any expansion of car production will require additional capital. Both of these situations will create rising costs of production, which firms will try to pass on to consumers in the form of higher prices. Despite the inflation, however, overall GDP will not expand, because the only way to hire additional resources in a fully employed economy is to bid them away from other firms. The automobile company may be able to expand car production, but a refrigerator company, for example, may lose employees and end up reducing output. An increase in aggregate demand in this context will only create inflation, without creating any additional output or employment. This outcome is shown in Figure 15-13, where aggregate demand increases from AD_3 to AD_4. The average price level rises from P_3 to P_4, but GDP does not increase.

Although the economy is generally not in a state as extreme as Range A or Range C, we can understand that an increase in aggregate demand when employment is low will fairly easily result in expanded output and employment, without triggering much inflation. On the other hand, an increase in aggregate demand when employment is high will largely create inflation, without triggering much of an increase in production or employment.

FIGURE 15-13   Shifting Aggregate Demand in the Three Ranges of the Aggregate Supply Curve

An increase in aggregate demand in Range A increases output and employment without creating inflation; an increase in aggregate demand in Range B increases output and employment and also creates some inflation; and an increase in aggregate demand in Range C results in no increase in output and employment, but merely creates inflation.

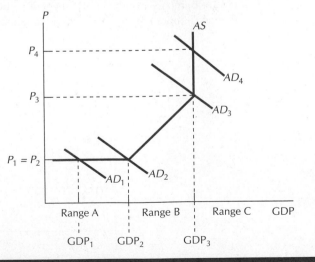

CHAPTER 16

Taxes, Borrowing, and the National Debt

In this world nothing can be said to be certain, except death and taxes.

Benjamin Franklin (1706–1790)

So far we have considered a variety of government expenditures, including spending on social and poverty programs, expenditures to control pollution and big business, spending to ensure equal opportunity, expenditures on agriculture and the control of crime, and government spending to increase aggregate demand and stabilize the economy. We have not yet carefully addressed a critical question: How does the government come up with the money to finance these programs and policies?

One of the most obvious ways that the government acquires revenue is through taxes. By taxing the public (including individual income earners, property owners, businesses, and consumers), the government acquires a large portion of the expenditure dollars that it needs. The other means of financing is borrowing. The government borrows when it issues **government securities,** which include government bonds, treasury notes, and treasury bills. A government security is really just an IOU: it is a piece of paper saying that the government has borrowed money and promises to repay it, plus interest, at some future point in time. The government sells these pieces of paper to banks, corporations, some foreigners, and a

Government securities
Government bonds and treasury bills.

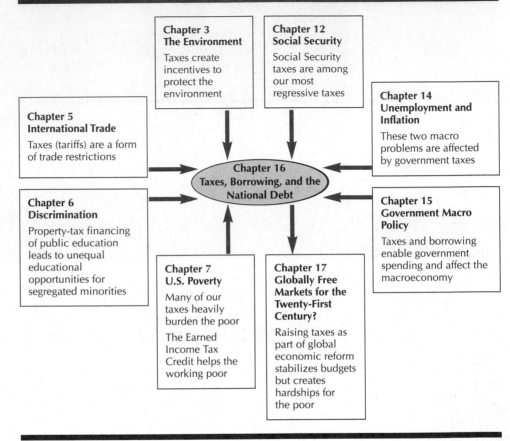

Chapter 3
The Environment

Taxes create incentives to protect the environment

Chapter 12
Social Security

Social Security taxes are among our most regressive taxes

Chapter 14
Unemployment and Inflation

These two macro problems are affected by government taxes

Chapter 5
International Trade

Taxes (tariffs) are a form of trade restrictions

Chapter 16
Taxes, Borrowing, and the National Debt

Chapter 6
Discrimination

Property-tax financing of public education leads to unequal educational opportunities for segregated minorities

Chapter 7
U.S. Poverty

Many of our taxes heavily burden the poor

The Earned Income Tax Credit helps the working poor

Chapter 17
Globally Free Markets for the Twenty-First Century?

Raising taxes as part of global economic reform stabilizes budgets but creates hardships for the poor

Chapter 15
Government Macro Policy

Taxes and borrowing enable government spending and affect the macroeconomy

large number of ordinary American citizens. You may own some government savings bonds; if so, you are lending your money to the government. We will consider these two basic means of financing government spending in the sections that follow.

GOVERNMENT TAXES

As the quote opening this chapter states, "In this world nothing can be said to be certain, except death and taxes." Those who are civic-minded recognize that government programs will require government revenue, but they want these taxes to be fair and reasonable.

Government taxes come in various forms and are imposed by the federal government as well as by state and local governments. We will consider these various taxes and then analyze their impact on the macroeconomy, the distribution of income, and individual markets within the United States.

Federal Taxes

Figure 16-1 displays the principal federal taxes and the proportion of 1999 federal tax revenue accounted for by each type of tax.

We can see from Figure 16-1 that the federal income tax is the most important of the taxes levied by the federal government. The personal income tax brings in roughly 48 percent of total federal tax revenue. This tax is placed on most forms of individual income. A **tax rate** is applied to different increments of income (the **tax base**). That is, a portion of your income is covered by one tax bracket and a corresponding tax rate, the next portion of your income is in the next bracket and covered by a higher rate, and so on. Until 1986, there existed 14 different tax brackets. The portion of the income of highest-income individuals was in the very highest bracket and was taxed at the highest rate. This maximum tax rate was 90 percent until 1964, when it underwent the first of several reductions until reaching a low of 28 percent by 1991. Since 1991, the maximum tax rate has increased to 39.6 percent for a few Americans. There are currently five tax brackets with corresponding tax rates of 39.6 percent, 36 percent, 31 percent, 28 percent, and 15 percent. As a result of successive tax rate cuts, the tax rates for high-income Americans are now

Tax rate

The percentage of the tax base that must be paid to the government as tax.

Tax base

Income, earnings, sales, property, or other valued item that has a tax rate applied to it. In the case of the personal income tax, the tax base is incremental income.

http://www.census.gov
This is the Web site for the U.S. Census Bureau, Department of Commerce. It presents a great deal of information about the U.S. economy, including taxes and spending, and provides links to several statistical publications.

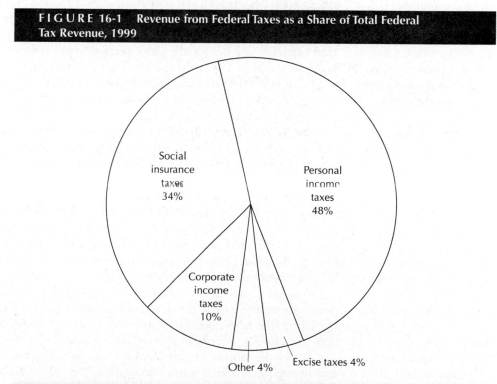

FIGURE 16-1   Revenue from Federal Taxes as a Share of Total Federal Tax Revenue, 1999

Social insurance taxes 34%

Personal income taxes 48%

Corporate income taxes 10%

Other 4%

Excise taxes 4%

Source: U.S. Department of Commerce, Bureau of the Census, *Statistical Abstract of the U.S.: 1999* (http://www.census.gov/statab).

among the *lowest* of all tax rates in Western industrialized countries. Taxpayers with extremely low incomes are not required to pay federal income taxes.

Americans can take advantage of several tax breaks in the federal personal income tax. Households can claim **exemptions** for each family member and deduct various expenditures from their taxable income (or take the **standard deduction**). They might *also* be eligible for various **tax credits** that directly reduce their tax amount payable to the government.

Aside from reducing the number of tax brackets and reducing tax rates, the 1986 tax code eliminated many deductions, increased the standard deduction, and increased the earned income tax credit. The **earned income tax credit (EITC)** has increased in size over time and is available to eligible low-income workers. It is **refundable,** meaning that it provides a refund to eligible workers whose earnings are too low to be taxed.

The federal personal income tax was the target of controversy during President Clinton's administration, and both Al Gore and President George W. Bush promised changes in the tax code during the 2000 campaigns. President Bush has pledged to cut taxes by $1.6 trillion by reducing the number of tax brackets to four and cutting the tax rates to 33 percent, 25 percent, 15 percent, and 10 percent, respectively. Gore and other Democrats had proposed the addition of tax credits and the provision of government matching money for a variety of "worthwhile" activities rather than lowering tax rates across the board. In other words, people who pay college tuition, families that care for elderly and disabled relatives, individuals who drive fuel-efficient vehicles, and those who save for retirement would receive new tax breaks. Gore also proposed a major increase in the standard deduction and in the EITC, increasing the latter by approximately $500 over 10 years. Other conservative and liberal politicians have proposed even more dramatic, even extreme, changes to the federal income tax, including the elimination of taxes altogether.

The second largest federal category of taxes is for social insurance. Taxes in this category are also called earmarked **payroll taxes,** because they are deducted directly from your paycheck or paid by your employer to fund various social insurance programs. The worker and the employer are taxed an equal amount for the two major social insurance programs, Social Security and Medicare. These two programs provide income to retired workers and their dependents, disabled workers, and survivors of deceased workers as well as hospitalization and basic medical care for the retired and disabled. All social insurance taxes together represent 34 percent of federal government tax revenue. They are discussed in greater detail in Chapter Twelve on Social Security.

Corporate profits are taxed according to the corporate income tax. The corporate income tax generates about 10 percent of federal tax revenue. **Excise taxes,** operating like sales taxes but levied only on particular goods and services, bring in approximately 4 percent of federal tax revenue.

A miscellaneous category includes various other taxes as well as assorted inter- and intragovernmental transactions. This category represents the other 4 percent of the total federal tax revenue and includes estate (inheritance) and gift taxes and **tariffs,** which are taxes on imported goods. A proposal by President George

Exemption
An amount of money that can be deducted from household income before tax rates are applied.

Standard deduction
A fixed amount of income that taxpayers can deduct from their taxable income when calculating their personal income taxes, if other deductions are not claimed.

Tax credit
An amount of money by which the amount of income taxes payable to the government can be directly reduced. A person or business must meet certain criteria to be eligible for the credit.

Earned income tax credit (EITC)
A federal tax credit for eligible low-income working individuals and families.

Refundable
A refund is available even if an income-earner does not pay taxes, as long as he or she files a tax form.

Payroll taxes
Taxes based on earnings from work and usually deducted directly from the paycheck.

Excise tax

A tax applied to the purchase of a specific good or service.

Tariff

A tax on an imported good.

W. Bush would eliminate the estate tax, thereby returning billions of dollars to the public. Because high-income people receive the bulk of the value of taxable estates, most of the return would go to the nation's highest-income earners.

State and Local Taxes

Different state and local governments use various taxes and place different emphasis on one tax or another. Figure 16-2 displays the various state and local taxes, and shows the overall relative importance of each type of tax in 1999.

As revealed by Figure 16-2, sales and excise taxes bring in the second largest share of state and local tax revenue (25 percent). Sales taxes are levied on goods and services sold within the state, locality, or both. Some states exempt certain items, such as medicine and food. Other states do not. Excise taxes are placed on the sale of goods such as gasoline, tobacco, and alcohol (state and local excise taxes are often placed on the same products as federal excise taxes). Alaska has the highest cigarette tax, at $1.00 per pack. Virginia has the lowest tax, at 2.5 cents per pack. Why do you think Virginia has such a low cigarette tax?

FIGURE 16-2   Revenue from State and Local Taxes as a Share of Total State and Local Tax Revenue, 1999

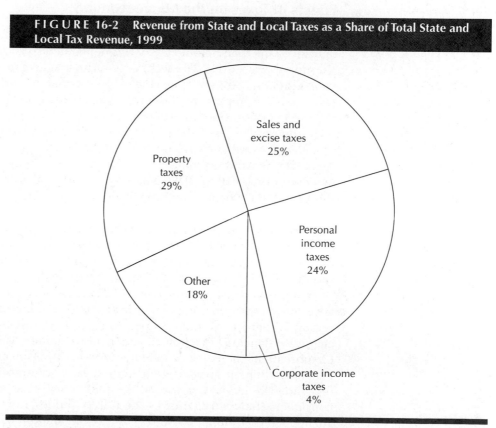

Source: U.S. Census Bureau, Department of Commerce, http://www.census.gov

Personal income taxes are also usually levied at the state (and sometimes local) level and bring in approximately 24 percent of total state and local tax revenue. In some states there are different tax brackets and rates, as at the federal level. In other states one rate applies to all people's income. Note that various exemptions, deductions, and credits apply to state personal income tax systems as well as at the federal level. Many states also have a corporate income tax, which brings in 4 percent of total state and local tax revenue.

Property taxes are levied by local governments and bring in the highest (29) percent of combined state and local tax revenue. These taxes are levied directly on owners of houses and land and depend on the value of this property. Economists usually assume that much of the property tax is passed from owner to renter (in the form of higher rents) in the case of rental housing. Property taxes are used to fund local public schools, as is discussed in greater detail in Chapters Six and Ten. Because property values are low in low-income school districts, educational opportunities are often poor in these areas.

The remaining portion of state and local taxes comes from various fees, licenses, and other miscellaneous collections.

Effects of Taxes on the Macroeconomy

Recall the aggregate demand curve of Chapter Fifteen. Remember that aggregate demand is the total output (U.S. GDP) demanded by all sectors of the economy, at alternative price levels. The sectors comprising aggregate demand include individual consumers, business firms, the U.S. government, and foreigners. Government taxes have an impact on the buying decisions of people within some of these groups. Let us consider the effect on individual consumers.

Suppose that the federal government increases spending on public parks by $1 million. As we know from Chapter Fifteen, this greater spending will increase aggregate demand, as indicated by the arrow in Figure 16-3, Panel A. Real GDP increases from GDP to GDP'. Now suppose that the government wishes to finance this $1 million expenditure through an increase in personal income taxes. Consider what happens when the government raises these taxes. As you and I pay more of our income to the government, we have less after-tax income to spend as we wish. As a result, our consumption spending goes down. As the consumption component of aggregate demand decreases, aggregate demand decreases as well, as shown by the lower arrow in Panel B of Figure 16-3.

Even though aggregate demand falls, it will not fall as much as the increased government spending on public parks caused it to increase in the first place. The reason is that the $1 million spent on parks represents a direct component of aggregate demand. The initial increase of $1 million will be magnified as a result of subsequent increases in spending due to rising incomes that result from the expansion. These increases will cause a fairly substantial increase in aggregate demand. The increase in taxes of $1 million will cause a decrease in spending by consumers, but initially not by the full $1 million. The reason is that we rarely change our consumption spending by the full amount of an income change. If our income goes up by $100, we may go out and spend an additional $80. We will save

Panel A shows the increase in aggregate demand that occurs as a result of the increased government spending on parks. A relatively large increase in GDP results. Panel B shows the impact of the increased government spending on parks, assuming that this spending is financed by increased government taxes. Aggregate demand increases as a result of the increased government spending, but it shifts back somewhat as a result of the increased taxes, which result in lower after-tax income for consumers, thereby reducing some of their consumption spending. The net increase in aggregate demand is very small, resulting in just a very small increase in GDP.

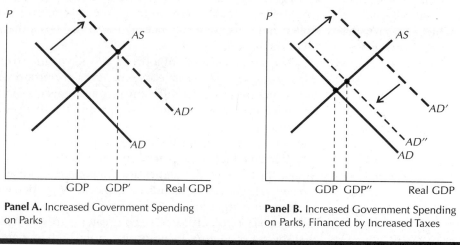

Panel A. Increased Government Spending on Parks

Panel B. Increased Government Spending on Parks, Financed by Increased Taxes

the rest. When the income of consumers goes down by $1 million, they will reduce their spending by less than $1 million. Thus spending initially may fall by $800,000 rather than the full $1 million. Subsequent decreases in spending will occur as well, as incomes fall due to the contraction of the economy.

The point of this discussion is that the rise in aggregate demand through increased government spending will be substantially offset by the decline in aggregate demand through decreased consumer spending when taxes go up. This offset will not be a total offset. That is, the combined effect of the increase in government spending *and* taxes will be a small net increase in aggregate demand. A small expansion in the economy will be accompanied by some small increase in GDP (from GDP to GDP″ in Panel B).

The important point is as follows: if the government finances increased expenditures through increased taxes, a moderate expansion of the economy will occur. A moderate expansion may be appropriate if the economy is operating at a high level of capacity; too much expansion would put undesired upward pressure on the price level. On the other hand, if the goal of government is to substantially expand the economy, raising taxes to finance increased expenditures is not the most effective way to proceed. As we shall see shortly, financing of government expenditure by borrowing would be preferable.

Effects of Taxes on the Income Distribution

In addition to their effect on the macroeconomy, taxes have an important impact on the distribution of income. Indeed, taxes can be designed specifically for this purpose. When economists consider the redistributive effect of taxes, they usually classify taxes according to three basic types: progressive taxes, proportional taxes, and regressive taxes. Each of these will have a different impact on the income distribution.

Progressive tax

A tax that takes a greater percentage of income from high-income people than from low-income people.

As we noted in Chapter Eleven, a **progressive tax** is one that takes a larger percentage of income from high-income people than from low-income people. Note that the key phrase is *percentage of income*. We are not concerned here with absolute dollar amounts; we are concerned with the taxes that people pay relative to their incomes.

The prime example of a progressive tax is the structure of the federal personal income tax rate. Many state income taxes are progressive as well. A progressive tax rate structure relies on different income brackets. As we previously discussed, the first portion of a person's income goes into the first tax bracket and is taxed at a corresponding tax rate. The next portion of income goes into in a higher tax bracket and is taxed at a higher tax rate. This procedure continues until the last increment of a person's income is placed into the highest appropriate tax bracket. Thus the higher the income, the higher are the tax rates applied to increments of income. As a result, a higher-income individual pays a larger percentage of his or her income to the government; a lower-income individual pays a smaller percentage of his or her income. This type of tax places a greater burden on the higher-income individual, thereby redistributing income away from high-income households. Recall that the 1986 tax reform bill greatly reduced the progressivity of the income tax rate structure by reducing the number of brackets and by lowering the maximum tax rate. President George W. Bush's proposals would further lower these tax rates and the number of tax brackets. Also note that once various exemptions, deductions, and tax credits are taken into account, the actual income tax may be less progressive, or perhaps no longer progressive at all because many of these tax breaks may be targeted to the middle- and upper-income class, not to the poor. (The deduction of mortgage interest, discussed in Chapter Eleven, is a case in point.)

Proportional tax

A tax that takes the same percentage of income from people of all income levels.

A **proportional tax** is one that takes the same percentage of income from people of all income levels. An example of this type of tax is the flat-rate personal income tax levied by various state governments. Some have proposed that a flat rate income tax be used at the federal level as well. Because a flat-rate tax takes the same percentage of income from people of all income levels, it does not redistribute income. Again, bear in mind that the proportionality of actual flat-rate taxes will depend on the existence of various exemptions, deductions, and credits combined with the taxes. The overall result may well be a regressive tax.

Regressive tax

A tax that takes a greater percentage of income from low-income people than from high-income people.

A **regressive tax** is one that takes a larger percentage of income from low-income households than from high-income ones. Most of the taxes in our country are regressive. Does this surprise you? Our regressive taxes include sales taxes, most excise taxes, property taxes, and the Social Security tax. Because some of these taxes are not levied directly on income, seeing why they are regressive is sometimes difficult. Let us consider a state sales tax as an example.

TABLE 16-1   Effects of the Sales Tax on Two Hypothetical High- and Low-Income Families in One Year

	HIGH-INCOME FAMILY	LOW-INCOME FAMILY
Income	$100,000	$10,000
Purchases of taxable goods	$50,000	$8,000
Sales tax rate	5%	5%
Amount of sales tax paid	$2,500	$400
Amount of sales tax paid as a % of income	$2,500/$100,000 = 2.5%	$400/$10,000 = 4.0%

Suppose that a state levies a sales tax of 5 percent of the value of taxable goods purchased within the state. The 5 percent is the tax rate, whereas the value of taxable goods is the tax base. Actual percentage rates vary by state, and the taxable goods covered by the tax vary as well. Let us consider two typical families, a high-income family with an annual income of $100,000, and a low-income family with an income of $10,000. The situations of these two families are outlined in Table 16-1.

Although the numbers chosen are made up, they provide realistic results. Note that the high-income family spends $50,000 per year on taxable goods, whereas the low-income family spends only $8,000. A low-income family can be expected to have smaller consumption expenditures than a high-income family. But note that the low-income family spends a larger *percentage* of its income on taxable consumer goods. The reason is that low-income families need to spend their income on necessities and have little income left over for saving. Higher-income families, on the other hand, can afford to save a larger share of their income, thereby "consuming" a smaller share. Because the higher-income family does spend more money on taxable goods, in absolute terms, it will also spend more money on the state sales tax, again in absolute terms. When these tax amounts are expressed as percentages of family income, however, we see that the lower-income family pays a higher percentage of its income (4 percent) on the tax, whereas the higher-income family pays a smaller percentage: 2.5 percent. The 5 percent sales tax results in the lower-income family paying a higher percentage of its income on the tax. Thus the tax is regressive.

Property taxes and excise taxes are regressive for very similar reasons. Low-income families tend to spend a larger percentage of income on goods covered by excise taxes and on housing (either owned housing or rental housing) than do higher-income families. Assuming that property taxes are passed on to renters in the form of higher rent, low-income families end up paying a larger percentage of their incomes on excise and property taxes than do higher-income families.

The Social Security tax is also highly regressive, but for different reasons. First, the Social Security tax is levied only on income earned by working: that is, on wages and salaries. Because lower-income families earn most of their income in the form of wages and salaries, all of this income will be taxed. On the other hand, most of the income of high-income people may be in the form of interest, capital gains, dividends, and so on. Therefore, most of their income may not be taxed for

Social Security purposes. The Social Security tax rate on eligible income is 6.2 percent. (Medicare is taxed separately.)

Social Security taxes also are regressive in that they are assessed on earnings only up to a certain limit. Beyond this limit, earnings are not taxed. In 2000, this earnings limit was $76,200. Any income earned beyond this level will not be taxed for Social Security purposes. Therefore, all of the income of low-income earners may be taxed, whereas most of the income of high-income earners may not be.

As a result of the earnings limit and the taxation of only work-earned income, low-income families pay a much larger share of their income on the Social Security tax than do high-income families. Remember that once Social Security benefits are taken into account, the overall Social Security system can no longer be described as regressive. This situation was discussed more completely in Chapter Twelve.

Regressive taxes redistribute income in favor of the rich and to the detriment of the poor. Progressive taxes do the opposite. Over the course of the 1980s and 1990s, a number of factors helped to make our overall tax system increasingly regressive. Large cuts made during the Reagan Administration in personal and corporate income tax rates, the two most progressive taxes, have reduced the significance of these two taxes as tax revenue sources. In addition, large increases in Social Security, excise, sales, and property taxes have occurred over the same time period. Thus we are seeing less emphasis on progressive taxes and increasing emphasis on regressive ones. Proposed changes by President Bush would also result in a more regressive tax system. President Bush's proposed tax rate cut would further reduce the significance of our principal progressive tax, the federal personal income tax, while providing the largest tax reductions to those who are better off. Elimination of the estate tax would overwhelmingly benefit the extremely rich. Other people's proposals, such as replacing the current federal income tax structure with a flat-rate tax structure and replacing the federal income tax with a national sales tax would also clearly make our overall tax structure more regressive.

Effects of Taxes on the Microeconomy of Individual Markets

Excise and property taxes affect markets for specific goods. Consider an excise tax in a hypothetical local market for gasoline.

Demand and supply for gasoline are indicated by the curves D and S in Figure 16-4. Without any excise tax, equilibrium occurs at point E; equilibrium quantity equals 100 gallons, and equilibrium price equals $1.00 per gallon. Now consider the imposition of an excise tax of $.50 per gallon. We can view this excise tax as an additional cost of production because the supplier of gasoline must actually hand the tax dollars to the government. Just as the supplier must pay wage costs, energy costs, rental costs, and so on, it now must pay an additional cost of $.50 per gallon on each gallon of gasoline sold. Recall that any increase in the costs of production will cause supply to decrease. The supply curve with the excise tax is indicated by curve S'.

With the imposition of the excise tax, a new equilibrium is established at point E'. Equilibrium quantity has fallen to 75 gallons, and the equilibrium price has

A $.50 per gallon excise tax will shift back the supply curve for gasoline. At the new equilibrium *E'*, the price is $1.25 per gallon and the quantity of gasoline is 75 gallons. The excise tax of $.50 per gallon is paid by the suppliers of gasoline to the government. Because consumers pay more and suppliers keep less, both groups bear part of the burden of the excise tax.

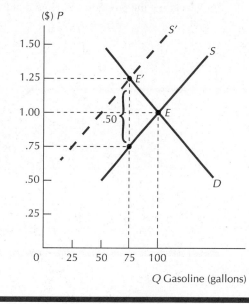

risen to $1.25 per gallon. What has happened is that supply has decreased, causing gasoline prices to rise. In response to higher prices, consumers have moved back up along their demand curve, reducing the quantity they wish to buy. Both quantity demanded and quantity supplied are now at the lower level of 75 gallons.

Why has the price risen to $1.25, and not by the full $.50 per gallon? The actual price increase is the result of demand and supply. Note that the vertical distance between the two supply curves (measured on the price axis) represents the $.50 per gallon excise tax. The cost of supplying each gallon of gasoline has gone up by exactly this amount. But the market price of gasoline has risen by only a portion of this amount, in this case by $.25 per gallon. The implication is that the **burden of the tax** has been borne by suppliers and consumers alike. Consumers bear a portion of the full burden of the tax in the form of the extra $.25 they must pay for each gallon of gasoline that they purchase. Suppliers bear a portion of the full burden in the form of lower profits; they now must pay an additional $.50 per gallon that they sell (the tax), but receive only an additional $.25 from consumers. The difference comes out of their pockets.

The results of this exercise are fairly typical. As a consequence of the imposition of the excise tax, a smaller quantity of the product is produced and sold, the

Burden of the tax
The impact of the tax that is felt by producers and consumers. Consumers bear the burden in the form of higher prices paid for the product; producers bear the burden in the form of lower profits.

The property tax on rental housing will shift back the supply curve, resulting in a new equilibrium at *E'*. At the new equilibrium, the rental price of housing has increased from $200 to $250, but the landlord must pay $100 to the government in property tax. Because the tenant pays more and the landlord in effect receives less, both groups will bear part of the burden of the property tax. Note that the equilibrium quantity has decreased.

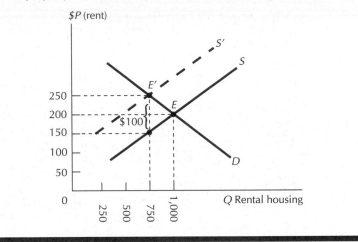

price is higher, and both consumers and suppliers share the burden of the tax. Realize, however, that the burden need not be shared equally by these two groups. The price of a product upon which an excise tax is imposed could rise substantially, perhaps even the full amount of the tax. In this case, consumers will bear the entire brunt of the tax. Likewise, the price could rise only negligibly. In this event, suppliers will bear the greater burden. The appendix to this chapter will consider some of the circumstances that determine which group will actually bear the greatest burden of any particular excise tax. Generally, consumers will bear a large share of the burden of the gasoline excise tax.

Property taxes can operate in a similar way. Consider a local market for rental housing, depicted in Figure 16-5. Demand and supply determine an equilibrium quantity of housing of 1,000 units and a market rental price of $200 per unit per month. The $100 per month property tax can be viewed as an additional cost of supplying the housing, as property *owners* themselves must hand the tax dollars to the government. The higher cost will be reflected in a backward shift of the supply curve to *S'*. A new equilibrium will be established at point *E'*. Quantity has decreased to 750 units, and the market rent has gone up to $250 per unit. Recall our earlier assumption that at least a portion of property taxes is passed along to *renters*. The analysis indicates how and why a portion of the burden is redirected. As mentioned in the appendix, the renter may indeed bear most of the burden of the tax.

Neither a lender nor a borrower be.

Old proverb

Despite this well-meaning advice, individual people and families do borrow money. In doing so, they go into debt. The debt may be good or bad for the family, depending on a number of factors. But what about the government? Is the country well-served or poorly served when the government borrows money and in doing so goes into debt? The next several pages will help us answer this question.

Recall that the government can finance its expenditures not only through taxes but also by borrowing. The latter process occurs as the government issues securities. Anyone can purchase a government security: another level or agency of government, a bank or other financial institution, a corporation or other form of business, and individual people like us. When I purchase a government bond, I am lending my money to the government. At some specified point in the future, I will receive my money back, plus interest. Because no coercion is involved, presumably this deal is a good one for both the government and me. Is it a good deal for the economy?

To answer this question, we need to consider the impact of government borrowing in a couple of respects. We will analyze the impact on the macroeconomy, on income distribution, on interest rates, and finally on the government budget and national debt.

Effects on the Macroeconomy

Recall our earlier scenario in which the government wishes to increase spending on public parks by $1 million. As indicated before, the higher spending will cause aggregate demand to shift forward, as we see in Panels A and B of Figure 16-3 on page 359. This time taxes will not increase, as the government is obtaining financing by borrowing. Thus there is no reason for the aggregate demand curve to shift backward once again. The final impact of the transaction is indicated in Panel A. A significant economic expansion has occurred. Again, whether this result is desirable depends on the state of the economy. If the economy is operating at high capacity, the expansion is most likely to bring unwanted price rises in its wake. On the other hand, if the economy is operating well below capacity and perhaps is in recession, the expansion is exactly what the doctor ordered. Financing by borrowing will expand the economy more than financing through increased taxes.

Effects on the Income Distribution

If I buy government bonds, I will benefit from this decision. The government will repay me at some future time, with interest to boot. Who will finance the interest payment? One possibility is that the government will merely borrow again to finance interest expenditures. There is nothing wrong with this practice. Unlike you and me, the government can borrow indefinitely. Alternatively, the government may increase taxes to finance my interest payment. If you pay the additional tax and I receive the interest benefit, income is redistributed from you to me. I will be happy, but you will not.

The redistribution of income that occurs in this process may in fact further increase income inequality in our country. Bond owners tend to be middle- to upper-income people; rarely do low-income people have the means to participate in this type of investment activity. On the other hand, we have seen that our tax system has become increasingly regressive. To the extent that low-income people bear a greater burden of tax payments, and high-income people receive a greater benefit from interest receipts, income redistribution occurs.

This redistribution does not mean that government borrowing is bad, per se. We *can* alter the impact of government borrowing on income distribution without reducing the government's borrowing ability. We can devise means to restructure government securities in ways that make them more accessible to low-income people. And of course, we can alter our national system of taxation to achieve greater progressivity, if we have the desire to do so. The negative impacts of government borrowing on income distribution could be dealt with directly in this fashion. Finally, we know that both tax revenue and money borrowed by the government can be used to finance policies and programs in ways that foster greater or less equality, depending on the nature of the policies and programs.

Effects on Interest Rates

Interest rate
The percentage of borrowed funds that must be paid to the lender (or investor) for the privilege of using the funds.

Loanable funds
Money that is borrowed and lent.

We can analyze the impact of government borrowing on **interest rates** if we view market interest rates as simply the price of **loanable funds.** An interest rate is the percentage of borrowed funds that must be paid to the lender (or investor); loanable funds refers to money that is borrowed or lent. To see how interest rates are determined, we must consider the market for loanable funds. This task is not difficult because our demand and supply analysis will work in the market for loanable funds just as easily as it does in the market for rental housing, automobiles, or corn.

Figure 16-6 shows the market for loanable funds. The price axis is labeled i, for the market interest rate. The quantity axis Q represents the quantity of loanable funds. The demand curve for loanable funds represents all who wish to borrow money: business firms, individuals like us, and, of course, our government. The curve is downward sloping, indicating that we are more willing and able to borrow money at low interest rates than at high interest rates. The supply curve for loanable funds represents all who wish to lend money: commercial banks, the local savings and loan, and individuals who place money in savings accounts (so that banks may lend it out) or purchase government securities (lending money to the government). The supply curve is upward sloping, indicating that we are more willing to lend (or save) as the interest rate that we can receive becomes higher. Note that we are simplifying by talking about "a market interest rate." In fact there are many rates, depending on types of securities, lengths of maturity, and whether you are borrowing or lending. We are ignoring these differences, and perhaps looking at what might be an average market interest rate. Equilibrium will occur at

The demand for loanable funds curve D represents the demand for borrowed funds by consumers, businesses, and government. If the government wishes to increase its spending on goods and services, and chooses to finance these expenditures by borrowing, the demand for loanable funds will increase to D'. This increase in demand will cause an increase in the interest rate from 10 percent to 12 percent, and an increase in the amount of money borrowed and lent to Q'.

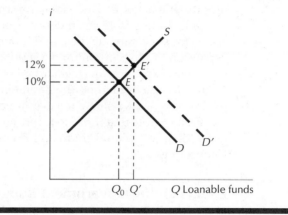

point E, with quantity Q_0 being borrowed and lent, and a market interest rate of 10 percent.

Now suppose the government wishes to finance expenditures by issuing securities—that is, by borrowing money. The demand for loanable funds will thereby increase, as reflected in the new demand curve D', resulting in the new equilibrium E'. In this new equilibrium, the quantity of funds both borrowed and lent has increased to Q', and the market interest rate has risen to 12 percent. What has happened is simply that the demand for loanable funds has gone up, causing an increase in the "price" of loanable funds. Lenders have moved up along their supply curve, increasing the quantity they are willing to lend to match the increase in quantity demanded.

As a result of government borrowing, interest rates go up. The amount depends on the state of the economy and the market for loanable funds. The most serious concern about rising interest rates is their impact on business and consumer spending. As we've noted before, when interest rates are high, business firms are less likely to purchase factories and other capital equipment, and individuals are less likely to purchase big-ticket items like cars, houses, and appliances. We simply are less willing and able to pay the higher costs of borrowing. Economists refer to this situation as **crowding out.** Government spending, financed by borrowing, has caused interest rates to rise. As a result, those in the private economy choose to borrow less and therefore spend less. Government spending has partially crowded out private spending. Those who wish to see a reduced role for government in our economy, and consequently an increased role for the private sector, are particularly concerned about crowding out.

Crowding out

A situation in which government spending, financed by borrowing, causes interest rates to rise, which results in less spending by the private economy.

Crowding out is certainly an issue, but we must keep it in perspective. First, crowding out is never complete, at least in the short run. Suppose that the government borrows and increases spending by $1 million. This government borrowing of $1 million does not mean that there is $1 million less for the private sector to borrow and spend. Remember that the rising interest rates have increased the willingness of people to lend; thus more funds are available for everyone. Second, rising interest rates need not occur. Recall that monetary policy can be used to control these rates. An increase in the money supply will cause interest rates to fall, offsetting the impact of the increased government borrowing on interest rates. Whether this policy is desirable again depends on the state of the economy. In an overheated economy, simultaneous fiscal and monetary expansion will probably cause an overexpansion of the economy and a serious threat of inflation. In a less active economy, economic expansion may again be just what the doctor ordered. Economists, like politicians, are divided on the desirability of the various options. But understanding the impacts of the policy choices is important to forming an intelligent opinion.

Finally, note that a rise in interest rates, for any reason, will have some implications for international trade and finance. These implications were considered in Chapter Five.

Effects on the Government Budget and the National Debt

> The federal government is too big and it spends too much money. [We need] a constitutional amendment that mandates a balanced budget.
>
> President Reagan, 1988

> We must bring the federal budget into balance.
>
> President G. H. W. Bush, 1989

> We have an obligation to leave our children a legacy of opportunity, not debt.
>
> President Clinton, 1996

> My plan pays down an unprecedented amount of our national debt. And then, when money is still left over, my plan returns it to the people who earned it in the first place.
>
> President G. W. Bush, 2001

One of the major issues of the new millennium is the government budget. Until the late 1990s, our national concern was how to manage government budget deficits. With the turn of the century, our concern is how to manage government budget surpluses.

Budget deficit
The difference between federal government spending and federal government tax revenue in any one year.

The **budget deficit** is simply the difference between federal government spending and federal government tax revenue in a particular year. If the government spends $1,500 billion and brings in tax revenue of $1,300 billion, we have a budget deficit of $200 billion. The deficit is the amount by which the government is currently in the red: that is, the amount that the government must borrow to make up the difference. The budget deficit is an annual concept: that is, it represents the difference between spending and taxes over the course of any one year.

The opposite of a budget deficit is a **budget surplus.** If the government brings in tax revenue that is greater than government spending in a year, we have a budget surplus. Thus if the government spends $1,500 billion and brings in tax revenue of $1,700 billion, we have a budget surplus of $200 billion. Just like the budget deficit, the budget surplus is an annual concept.

In 1998, the last year of a federal budget deficit, the deficit was approximately $22 billion. By 1999, government tax revenue exceeded government spending by about $69 billion. The budget deficit had turned into a budget surplus. The year 2000 surplus was approximately $237 billion.[1] The surplus seen in the new millennium so far has ushered in vast disagreement over the best use of this money. The government might use it to finance increased spending on programs and transfers; or it might, as proposed by President Bush, use the bulk of the surplus to finance tax relief. Others argue that the surplus should be used to shore up the Social Security program. In the absence of deliberate decisions such as these, the surplus would automatically go toward reducing the national debt.

National debt
The total amount of money owed by the federal government. It represents the accumulation of all funds borrowed by the federal government that have not yet been repaid.

The national debt is different but closely related to the budget. The **national debt** is the *total* amount of money owed by the federal government. It represents the accumulation of all funds borrowed by the federal government, up to the present, that have not yet been repaid. A budget deficit in any one year will increase the size of the national debt (and, as indicated, a budget surplus will decrease the national debt). Hence the concern over government borrowing. Is there anything wrong with the government running a budget deficit and incurring an increasing national debt? Most politicians say yes. Most citizens also say yes. People often make an analogy between government and individual households. They say that we ought to be responsible. We ought to spend within our means. We ought to repay prior debts before borrowing more. We cannot borrow forever. Eventually a day of reckoning will arrive; eventually there must be repayment or bankruptcy. If we individually must exhibit financial responsibility, certainly our government should do the same.

This analogy is not appropriate, however. As we noted before, the government can continue to borrow indefinitely. Unlike individual households, the country does not have to answer to the frowning face of the bank loan officer. With no limit on borrowing, the government can continually "roll over" its debt; that is, it can continue to borrow money to repay previously borrowed money. No day of reckoning will arrive. There will be no day of bankruptcy. No shortage of people and businesses willing to lend to the government will occur.

Does this mean that the national debt causes no problems? Many of our politicians and many of our citizens believe it does cause problems. To analyze their concerns, we should begin by considering the actual size of the debt, the owners of the debt, and the impact of the debt on our economy.

THE NATIONAL DEBT

The Size of the National Debt

Recall our discussion of gross domestic product (GDP) in Chapter Fifteen. We recognized that any variable that is expressed in dollar terms and compared over different years must first be adjusted for inflation. Otherwise, increases in the value of the variable may simply express a rising price level, not a rise in the real variable itself. The same care is necessary when considering the size of the national debt. If we are comparing its size over time, we must adjust for inflation to eliminate the impact of rising prices. Often when the size of the national debt is reported in newspapers and compared over different years, the writer neglects to adjust for inflation. This failure results in reporting of a grossly exaggerated increase in the size of the debt.

It is also important to use an appropriate benchmark when considering the size of the debt. Gross domestic product represents one such reference. A simple illustration should demonstrate why we should be interested in the size of the debt relative to GDP (which is really our capacity to produce and repay), and not just in the debt's size alone. Consider a simple economy with the following budget deficit in a particular year:

$$
\begin{aligned}
GDP &= \$100,000 \\
\text{Government Spending} &= \$20,000 \\
\text{Government Tax Revenue} &= \$18,000 \\
\text{The Budget Deficit} &= \$2,000 \\
\text{The Budget Deficit Relative to GDP} &= \$2,000/\$100,000 = 2\%
\end{aligned}
$$

In this example, the budget deficit is $2,000. This deficit represents 2 percent of gross domestic product. This $2,000 is contributing to the size of the national debt.

Now suppose the economy has doubled over time:

$$
\begin{aligned}
GDP &= \$200,000 \\
\text{Government Spending} &= \$40,000 \\
\text{Government Tax Revenue} &= \$36,000 \\
\text{The Budget Deficit} &= \$4,000 \\
\text{The Budget Deficit Relative to GDP} &= \$4,000/\$200,000 = 2\%
\end{aligned}
$$

The size of the budget deficit has doubled, from $2,000 to $4,000. Yet nothing in this example should alarm us. As GDP doubles, it appears quite natural for government spending to double (as all sectors' spending probably doubles), for government tax revenue to double, and for the size of the deficit to double as well. Relative to GDP, however, the deficit has not grown; it remains at 2 percent. Although an enormous doubling of the budget deficit would appear to contribute to an enormously rising national debt, this example suggests no cause for concern. The national debt will grow, but we should be more interested in the size of the debt relative to GDP, just as we are interested in the size of the budget deficit relative to GDP.

What it all means is this: if we wish to accurately consider the growing size of the national debt, we need to adjust the data for inflation and we need to consider the size of the debt relative to GDP. Table 16-2 displays the data in this fashion for the time period 1960 to 2000.

We see from Table 16-2 that the size of the national debt relative to GDP was 53 percent in 1940, increasing to 122 percent in 1946. This dramatic increase in the national debt was due to huge government spending during World War II. The

TABLE 16-2   The Size of the National Debt Relative to Gross Domestic Product, Selected Years, 1960 to 2000

YEAR	NATIONAL DEBT/GDP	YEAR	NATIONAL DEBT/GDP
1940	53%	1995	68%
1946	122%	1996	69%
1960	56%	1997	67%
1970	38%	1998	65%
1980	33%	1999	64%*
1990	56%	2000	63%*

*Estimate.

Source: U.S. Department of Commerce, Bureau of the Census, *Statistical Abstract of the United States: 1999* (http://www.census.gov/statab).

http://www.fms.treas.
gov/bulletin
This Web site for the *Treasury Bulletin* presents data on the U.S. government budget, including expenditures, tax revenue, size of the deficit or surplus, and the national debt.

debt relative to GDP was quite low in 1980, but it increased steadily, especially over the decade of the 1980s, until 1996. Recall that the 1980s was a time of tax cuts. Nevertheless, spending on Social Security and national defense soared. The money had to be borrowed, thereby increasing the debt. Since 1996, the size of the debt relative to GDP has steadily decreased, as government budget deficits have fallen and surpluses have arisen.

Who Owns the National Debt?

Recall that anyone can purchase government securities. Buyers of these securities are the owners of the national debt. Table 16-3 indicates the percentage of the national debt that is owned by (owed to) various groups. Note that our government and government agencies own approximately 56 percent of the national debt (calculated by adding the first three items in Table 16-3). Thus more than half of the federal debt represents transfers among different levels and agencies of

TABLE 16-3   Who Owns the National Debt? (2nd quarter, 2000)

HOLDER	SHARE OF NATIONAL DEBT (%)
U.S Government and Federal Reserve banks	47
State and local governments	5
Pension funds owned by state and local governments	4
Pension funds owned privately	3
Depository institutions	4
Insurance companies	2
Mutual funds	6
U.S. savings bonds	3
Foreign and international owners	22
Other miscellaneous investors	4

Source: Based on data from the U.S. Treasury Department, *Treasury Bulletin* (http://www.fms.treas.gov/bulletin).

government. Depository institutions (such as commercial banks) and insurance companies own 6 percent of the total, and U.S. savings bonds represent 3 percent. Also note that a substantial, though relatively small, share is owed to foreigners. This group concerns many people the most. As interest payments are made to foreign owners of the national debt, a transfer of real resources out of the United States occurs. This circumstance is the only one in which such a transfer occurs in terms of the debt.

The Impact of the National Debt

The implications of the national debt are really the implications of government borrowing that we have already considered. The negative effects of government borrowing involve inappropriate income redistribution and rising interest rates. The interest payments made to foreign people generate particular concern for some, as they represent a real transfer of income out of the United States. Some people are also concerned about a potential burden passed on to our children. This burden would take the form of taxes imposed on future generations to make interest payments.

On the other hand, government borrowing has some positive consequences. It enables the government to expand the economy as needed and to make expenditures that can specifically benefit our society. Whether these are programs benefiting us directly in the present, such as Social Security and poverty reduction, or programs that invest in future generations, such as programs of health and education, benefits accrue to our nation. These benefits must be considered whenever we concern ourselves with potential problems with the national debt.

PROPOSALS TO REQUIRE A BALANCED BUDGET

No discussion of budget deficits and the national debt is complete without a discussion of the many proposals that would require a balanced budget by the federal government. An annually balanced budget would mean no government borrowing, hence no addition to the national debt. It would mean that all government expenditures must be financed by tax revenue and that any government spending increase must be matched by an increase in tax revenue.

Unlike politicians, economists see many problems with a requirement that the federal government balance its budget. First, balancing the budget in any given year is extremely difficult. Too many variables are unknown. Suppose, for example, that the nation must deal with extensive flooding or tornado destruction. By declaring a national emergency, the federal government is committed to spending additional amounts to assist in the cleanup. Or even more to the point, suppose that the nation goes to war and must increase its defense spending. These unplanned events would create a budget deficit. It's true that the government could change the tax code or establish additional taxes, but such measures would not be feasible on a regular basis. It's also true that the government could reduce its spending on other programs, but funds may have already been committed. (Halting highway construction already under way, denying Social Security benefits

As you might suspect, conservatives and liberals hold disparate views on the issues of government taxes and borrowing. Conservatives generally favor reductions in government taxes for several reasons. First, they prefer to see income remain in the hands of the private economy, rather than turned over to the government. They prefer to see private-sector spending rather than public-sector spending. Second, they worry about the effect of various taxes on incentives. They believe that if personal income taxes are too high, people will work less. If business taxes are too high, businesses will produce less. If income from savings is taxed, people will save less. And the list goes on. On the other hand, liberals are more comfortable with government taxes and spending, as long as the taxes do not heavily burden the poor and the middle class. They also like to use tax credits and government matches to support what they consider worthwhile activity, such as spending on higher education or the care of elderly people.

Government spending financed by government borrowing is a serious problem for conservatives. They are concerned that attendant increases in interest rates will crowd out private spending. And they are concerned about the increased government spending that government borrowing permits. Although still favoring high defense expenditures and reductions in taxes, traditional conservatives have nevertheless argued in favor of a balanced budget. For liberals, the size of the budget deficit (and the national debt, for that matter) is less of a concern than the spending reductions for government social programs that would result from major budget reductions.

already promised, or closing federal prisons just because the budget is headed into deficit would be inappropriate!)

Second, suppose that our nation is entering a recession. As you will recall from the discussion of fiscal policy in the previous chapter, the government would like to pull the nation out of the recession by increasing government spending or reducing government taxes. In the context of a balanced budget requirement, the government can do neither because each would create a budget deficit. The government's hands are tied, as it can no longer use fiscal policy to correct the economy.

Now let's take this discussion one step further. During a recession, people lose their jobs. When people lose jobs, their incomes decline. When people's incomes decrease, they pay fewer taxes. They also are more likely to receive unemployment compensation and welfare assistance. For these reasons, an economy in recession creates an automatic decrease in government tax revenue and an automatic increase in government spending. Together this revenue decrease and spending increase create an automatic increase in the budget deficit. (The opposite would be the case in an expansion of the economy.) Now, according to a balanced budget requirement, the government must eliminate the deficit by initiating an increase in taxes, a decrease in government spending, or some combination of the two. Although difficult, carrying out these measures is possible. But they represent exactly the *wrong* policy prescription for a nation in recession! What the government needs to do to correct the recession is increase its spending or decrease taxes. In other words, complying with the balanced budget amendment would exacerbate the recession and create even greater instability for the economy.

The proposals for a balanced budget requirement have come in the form of proposals for new legislation and proposals for a constitutional amendment. The proposals have varied somewhat: those that allow exceptions for periods of recession, and those that require the budget to be balanced over several years rather than one, mitigate some of the problems we have cited. We should keep in mind that concerns about government spending, borrowing, and the national debt have motivated proposals that require a balanced budget. These proposals reflect the conservative viewpoint that less government involvement in our economy is best.

SUMMARY

The U.S. government has two means of acquiring financing for its expenditure programs: taxing and borrowing. The largest source of federal government tax revenue is the personal income tax. Other federal taxes include social insurance taxes, the corporate income tax, excise taxes, estate and gift taxes, and tariffs. Individual state and local governments commonly levy sales and excise taxes, personal income taxes, corporate income taxes, and property taxes. Government expenditure programs that are financed by taxes will have a moderate impact on the macroeconomy in terms of expanding gross domestic product. In addition, taxes will have important implications for income distribution, depending on whether they are progressive, proportional, or regressive. The federal personal income tax—and some state personal income taxes—have progressive rate structures. Sales and excise taxes, property taxes, and social insurance taxes are all regressive. Finally, excise and property taxes will have an impact on the markets for specific goods such as gasoline, alcohol, cigarettes, and rental housing. They will generally cause prices (and rents) to rise and quantity consumed to decrease.

Government borrowing occurs whenever the government issues government bonds and treasury bills. When you and I purchase a government bond, we are in effect lending our money to the government. Government expenditures, financed by borrowing, cause the greatest expansion of the macroeconomy in terms of increasing gross domestic product. Government borrowing also has an effect on income distribution in that it primarily benefits owners of financial securities (in terms of their interest return) and harms taxpayers as they finance these interest payments. Finally, government borrowing has the effect of raising interest rates, which may serve to reduce private investment expenditures within the economy. This process is referred to as "crowding out."

The budget deficit is the difference between government spending and government tax revenue. The deficit is an annual concept; it represents the amount that the government borrows in a particular year. Similarly, the budget surplus is the difference between government tax revenue and government spending. When the budget is in deficit, politicians argue about how to reduce the deficit. When the budget is in surplus, politicians argue over how to spend the surplus. The national debt is the total amount of money owed by the government. A budget deficit in any one year will increase the size of the national debt.

The size of the national debt is exaggerated when we do not make adjustments for inflation and properly compare the debt with the nation's gross domestic product. Much of the national debt is owed to various levels and agencies of government; smaller shares are owed to businesses and financial institutions, individuals, and foreigners. Any negative effects of government borrowing and the national debt must be considered relative to the positive results of government borrowing. These results include expansion of our economy and spending on government programs that may benefit us directly.

NOTE

1. U.S. Census Bureau, Department of Commerce (http://www.census.gov). These statistics include revenue through Social Security taxes.

DISCUSSION QUESTIONS

1. *Consider recent proposals to replace the federal income tax structure with a flat-rate tax structure or replace the income tax with a national sales tax. How would these actions affect income distribution?*

2. *How do you feel about the elimination of the estate tax? an increase in the earned income tax credit? a tax credit for tuition for higher education? Why do you feel this way?*

3. *Should the Social Security tax be overhauled to reduce its regressivity? Why or why not?*

4. *Why does the government place excise taxes on goods such as cigarettes and alcohol? Is it because these products are "sinful"? (These taxes are often called "sin taxes.") Do you feel that we cut down on our consumption of these goods by very much as a result of excise taxes? What does our response imply for the amount of government excise tax revenue?*

5. *What sort of tax system do you feel is the fairest? What are the advantages and disadvantages of regressive, progressive, and proportional taxes?*

6. *Are you concerned about the national debt? Why or why not? Has your opinion changed as a result of what you have learned in this chapter?*

7. *Visit the Census Bureau Web site (http://www.census.gov) to find current information on federal government spending and tax revenue. What is the major spending category? What is the major tax revenue source?*

8. *Visit the* **Treasury Bulletin** *Web site (http://www.fms.treas.gov/bulletin) to determine the current size of the budget surplus and of the national debt. How have these figures changed, if at all, from the 1999 data in this textbook?*

9. *How do you propose that the current budget surplus be spent? Should it fund expanded government programs and transfers? Should it be used to shore up the Social Security system? Should it be used to reduce the national debt?*

Chapter Sixteen Appendix:
Impact of Excise Taxes with Inelastic Demand and Supply

We have already considered the impact of an excise tax on gasoline and the closely related case of a property tax on rental housing. Let us consider a few additional cases of excise taxes to further "observe" the workings of our economy.

Consider a hypothetical market for cigarettes. In Figure 16-7, an extreme assumption is made. The supply curve is drawn with its usual shape, but the demand curve is perfectly vertical. Consider what this vertical demand curve means. Although price is free to move up and down, the quantity demanded will always remain fixed. That is, people wish to buy a particular quantity of cigarettes and refuse to adjust this quantity merely because of a price change. Economists refer to this lack of adjustment to price changes as a **perfectly inelastic demand.** Of course, perfectly inelastic demand isn't entirely realistic. Although many people are so addicted to cigarettes that they appear willing to pay almost any price for the product, at least some smokers (particularly teenagers) will adjust quantity demanded in response to price changes. But their response probably will not be very large, especially if we consider a reasonable range of market prices. We can assume for simplicity here that cigarette smokers will pay any price, as long as they can get their desired quantity of cigarettes. Equilibrium occurs at point E, with a market price of $1.50 per pack, and an equilibrium quantity of 5,000 packs of cigarettes.

Perfectly inelastic demand

Demand in which buyers are completely unresponsive to changes in price.

FIGURE 16-7 Effects of an Excise Tax in a Hypothetical Market for Cigarettes with Perfectly Inelastic Demand

An excise tax of $.50 per pack of cigarettes will cause a backward shift in the supply curve from S to S'. At the new equilibrium E', the price of cigarettes has increased from $1.50 to $2.00 per pack, the full amount of the tax. Consumers will bear the full burden of an excise tax when the demand curve is perfectly inelastic.

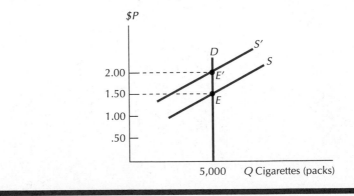

Now consider the imposition of a $.50 per pack excise tax. As you know, this tax will result in a backward shift of the supply curve to S'. A new equilibrium results at E', at which point a higher price is charged for the cigarettes. Recall that the vertical distance between the two supply curves represents the amount of the tax. Note that the price has gone up by the full amount of the tax, from $1.50 to $2.00 per pack. Equally important, the quantity of cigarettes bought and sold has not changed at all.

What has happened is that supply has decreased, pushing up the market price of cigarettes. But consumers have not responded in the usual fashion; they have refused to cut down on their purchases of cigarettes. As a result of this inflexibility (inelasticity), they incur the full burden of the tax. They pay the full additional $.50 in the form of a higher price; suppliers bear no cost whatsoever.

Although this case is an extreme and somewhat unrealistic one, it does demonstrate an important principle. As consumers are more unresponsive to price changes (that is, as they have a more inelastic demand), they will bear the larger burden of any excise tax. This is also true in the case of excise taxes on gasoline and alcohol, and the similar case of property taxes on rental housing.

Now let's consider an opposite case, shown in Figure 16-8. Let's analyze the local farmers' market in your town, where local growers try to sell their tomatoes. On any given day, let's assume that growers have a fixed supply of tomatoes. This quantity is available for sale, regardless of the price it can command, because the tomatoes have already been picked. No others are available on this day, and those

FIGURE 16-8   Effects of an Excise Tax in a Hypothetical Market for Tomatoes with Perfectly Inelastic Supply

An excise tax of $1 per pound of tomatoes would ordinarily be reflected in a backward shift of the supply curve. When supply is perfectly inelastic, we can express this shift as a vertical extension of the original supply curve. Equilibrium remains at point E, and the price remains at $2 per pound. Because the supplier must pay $1 per pound to the government, but receives no increase in the price paid by the consumer, the supplier bears the full burden of the excise tax when supply is perfectly inelastic.

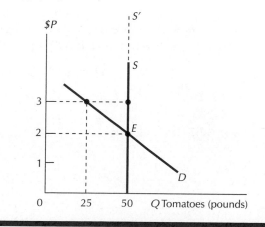

already picked cannot be saved for another day (let's assume they turn into mush on day two). This kind of situation will result in a market for tomatoes in which the demand curve has its normal slope, but the supply curve is now perfectly vertical. Equilibrium occurs at point E, with a market price of tomatoes of $2 per pound and an equilibrium quantity of 50 pounds of tomatoes.

Now consider an excise tax imposed by local authorities on the sale of tomatoes. Let's suppose this tax is $1 per pound. We would like to shift the supply curve by the vertical distance of the tax. There is no way to go but up, however. We cannot shift the curve in the usual fashion; we can indicate the shift merely as a vertical extension S'. The equilibrium remains at point E, with no change in quantity or price.

Why doesn't the price change? Why don't the growers say to heck with the market (or something similar), and raise their price by $1 anyway? Well, they're certainly free to do that. But look at the problem that would result. At a price of $3 per pound, quantity demanded falls to 25 pounds, but quantity supplied remains unchanged (as we know it must). A surplus of tomatoes is the result. The natural process we considered in Chapter One will result in a bidding down of prices as the only means of eliminating the surplus. Farmers are stuck with the realities of the market; their inability to alter their quantity supplied means they are stuck with the entire burden of the tax. They pay an extra $1 to the government, but they receive not one extra penny from consumers. This time, producers have the **perfectly inelastic supply.** This extreme example gives way to the more general result that the more unresponsive suppliers are to price changes (that is, the more inelastic their supply), the greater the burden of the excise tax they will bear.

The results of the cigarette and tomato cases can be generalized in a number of respects. First, the group—be it consumers or producers—that is more unresponsive (inelastic) to price changes will bear the greater burden of any excise tax. This principle applies to any situation in which production costs increase, whether because of excise taxes, government regulations for safety or pollution standards, increased energy prices, or whatever. When rising production costs reduce supply, price will rise in association with the costs, depending on the relative elasticity of demand and supply. The more inelastic the demand, the more the increased cost will be passed on to consumers in the form of increased prices. The more inelastic the supply, the more the cost will be borne by producers in the form of lower profits, and the less probable it is that prices will rise.

Perfectly inelastic supply Supply in which producers are completely unresponsive to changes in price.

CHAPTER 17

Globally Free Markets for the Twenty-First Century?

Year after year in Washington, . . . debates seem to come down to an old, tired argument: on one side, those who want more government regardless of the cost; on the other, those who want less government, regardless of the need. We should leave those arguments to the last century, and chart a different course.

George W. Bush, *Address of the President to the Joint Session of Congress*, February 27, 2001

More government or less government: that has been the debate throughout the last century, as well as throughout this textbook. As indicated in the quotation opening this chapter, George Bush believes this is a "tired" debate, one that should be left behind in the future. As we shall see, however, the world has recently embraced a direction decidedly in favor of globally free markets—markets characterized by minimal government involvement. But what about the future?

The title of this chapter ends with a question mark. Although the direction of change is clear, there is no reason to expect that free markets will work for all countries and all times. There is also no reason to assume that the transition to free markets will go smoothly for all nations or that a return to policies of the past will not occur.

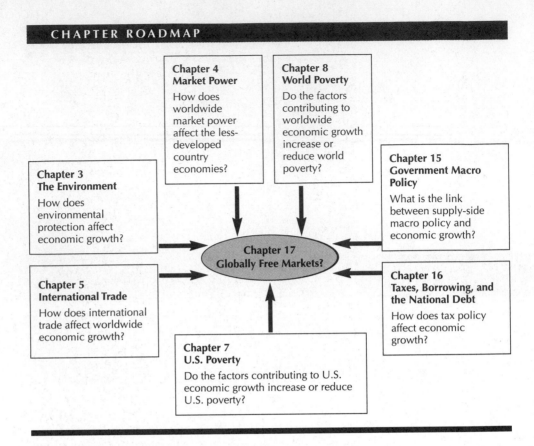

Chapter 4
Market Power

How does worldwide market power affect the less-developed country economies?

Chapter 8
World Poverty

Do the factors contributing to worldwide economic growth increase or reduce world poverty?

Chapter 3
The Environment

How does environmental protection affect economic growth?

Chapter 15
Government Macro Policy

What is the link between supply-side macro policy and economic growth?

Chapter 17
Globally Free Markets?

Chapter 5
International Trade

How does international trade affect worldwide economic growth?

Chapter 16
Taxes, Borrowing, and the National Debt

How does tax policy affect economic growth?

Chapter 7
U.S. Poverty

Do the factors contributing to U.S. economic growth increase or reduce U.S. poverty?

MARKETS

Throughout this book, we have made repeated reference to demand and supply and the workings of markets in general. We also have made repeated reference to government intervention in the economy. The proper role for government versus the proper role for the marketplace has prompted heated discussion between economists and politicians for decades. The respective roles for government and market have been the focal point for the Viewpoint sections throughout this text. In terms of economic philosophy and in U.S. terminology, those who favor a limited role for government are generally referred to as conservatives, whereas those who favor a greater role for government are regarded as liberals. The conservative view maintains that free markets are efficient and provide the proper incentives for economic prosperity and growth to occur. Government interference in properly functioning markets can only create inefficiencies and restrict growth; limiting the government role as much as possible is best.

This conservative view was evident in the discussion of supply-side policy in Chapter Fifteen. Supply-side economists favor reductions in government regulations, taxes, programs, and transfers. Their view is that the marketplace works efficiently; we need to untie the hands of businesses and consumers to enable them to make their own private decisions, and the economy will be better as a result.

Liberals, on the other hand, see the marketplace as imperfect. In their view, markets are *not* necessarily equitable, and sometimes not even efficient. Furthermore, society has goals, such as environmental protection, care for the poor and elderly, and economic stabilization, that cannot be met by the marketplace operating freely on its own. Liberals believe that the government must intervene in markets to achieve these goals.

Most economies have some combination of markets and government involvement. Some countries are more heavily capitalist, whereas some are predominantly socialist. Under **capitalism,** economic decisions are made by the private sector (individuals and private business) via the marketplace, and the means of production (factories, equipment, and land) are owned by this private sector. Under **socialism,** by contrast, economic decisions are made by the public sector (the government), and the means of production are owned or controlled by this public sector. Under capitalism, consumers and producers interact through the marketplace, responding to market-determined prices. Under socialism, the government has a more prominent role in determining which goods will be produced, how they will be produced, and what their prices will be.

Keep in mind that capitalism and socialism refer to economic systems. They imply nothing about political systems, such as democracy and communism. Certainly, a socialist economy may exist under either communism (Vietnam) or democracy (Chile); and a capitalist economy may exist under communism (Hong Kong) or democracy (the United States). In this text, we are discussing economic systems only.

The movement toward free markets is a global phenomenon, the direction entailing different circumstances in different parts of the globe. We will consider each of the three major regions of the world in turn. We will define the **Western industrialized world** as the industrialized capitalist countries of the world, including the United States, Canada, most of Western Europe, and other countries (including Japan) that have achieved high economic performance through predominantly market conditions. We will define the **formerly socialist industrialized world** as the industrialized ex-socialist countries of Eastern Europe. These countries include the former Soviet Union and much of the rest of Eastern Europe. Finally, the **less-developed world** encompasses all of the less-developed countries (LDCs), including most countries of Africa, Asia, and Latin America. These countries are often referred to as Third World countries.

One more term should be clarified. Economists often refer to the changes taking place in the formerly socialist and less-developed countries as **liberalism** (or sometimes neo-liberalism). This term is confusing, because it refers to a movement toward markets with less government intervention, rather than the traditional liberal philosophy we have described. The word "liberalism" refers to its root, liberty (that is, minimal government interference—no state religion, no absolute monarchy, and so on—and maximum personal liberty). Do not confuse the words "liberal" and "liberalism." The first implies government involvement in the economy; the latter implies change toward free markets.

Capitalism
An economic system wherein the economic decisions are made by the private sector via the marketplace, and the means of production are owned by the private sector.

Socialism
An economic system wherein the economic decisions are made by the public (government) sector, and the means of production are owned by the public sector.

Western industrialized world
The industrialized capitalist countries of the world.

Formerly socialist industrialized world
The industrialized ex-socialist countries of Eastern Europe.

Less-developed world
The less-developed countries of the world.

Liberalism
A movement toward freer markets.

Conservative Republicans controlled the U.S. presidency for the 12 years from 1981 to 1992. And although a Democrat became president in 1993, conservative Republicans took control of both houses of Congress in 1994. A conservative Republican once again took the presidential office in 2001, with an administration that includes conservatives from prior Republican administrations. President George W. Bush's views toward tax policy, education, the environment, and government regulation reflect the familiar undercurrent of supply-side economics and a philosophy of free markets with a minimal economic role for government.

This undercurrent and philosophy have not been unique to the United States. In many of the larger democracies of the Western industrialized world, a conservative philosophy has resulted in restricted government involvement and more market-based economies. Even the Social Democrats in Germany have moved to reduce transfer programs and the general role of government in the economy, although these efforts have run into significant resistance. Members of popular "populist" movements in the Scandinavian countries are demanding less government involvement, but they have not yet changed the overall role of government in these economies. Throughout Western Europe, it is argued that markets create economic growth, whereas too much government interference stifles it. Economic growth drives the Western industrialized world in the new century.

Economic Growth Rates

Economic growth
A sustained increase in production, represented by an outward shift of the production possibilities curve. An increase in GNP (GDP) or GNP per capita (GDP per capita) over an extended time period.

Economic growth is defined as a sustained increase in production. One standard measure of economic growth is the annual growth rate of GDP, averaged over a period of several years. (An alternative measure, the growth rate of GDP per capita, was used in Chapter Eight.) Table 17-1 displays average annual GDP growth rates for selected Western industrialized nations for the time period 1990 to 1999.

TABLE 17-1   Average Annual Economic Growth Rates, Selected Western Industrialized Countries, 1990–1999

COUNTRY	AVERAGE ANNUAL GROWTH OF GDP, %	COUNTRY	AVERAGE ANNUAL GROWTH OF GNP, %
Ireland	7.9	France	1.7
Australia	3.8	Belgium	1.7
United States	3.4	Germany	1.5
Netherlands	2.7	Sweden	1.5
Canada	2.3	Japan	1.4
Spain	2.2	Italy	1.2
United Kingdom	2.2	Switzerland	0.5

Source: Data from World Bank, *World Development Report 2000/2001* (New York: Oxford University Press, 2001).

As revealed by the data, these growth rates generally range from about 1.0 to 4.0 percent per year. The United States ranks at the high end, with an average growth rate of 3.4 percent per year.

The increase in GDP that underlies the growth rates in Table 17-1 can be discussed in the framework of aggregate supply (in the short run) and production possibilities (in the long run).

Aggregate Supply and Production Possibilities

Supply-side philosophies are based on the idea that reductions in government regulations, programs, taxes, and transfers create incentives for greater productivity, thereby increasing aggregate supply. This forward shift in the aggregate supply curve would be associated with an increase in gross domestic product. Figure 17-1 summarizes the desired effects of supply-side policy.

Supply-side policies are intended to increase GDP, but a sustained expansion of GDP requires additional policies that create long-term changes. These fundamental changes can be analyzed in the context of the production possibilities curve discussed in Chapter One.

Recall that the production possibilities curve shows the alternative combinations of the maximum amounts of output that an economy can produce if all of its resources and technology are fully and efficiently utilized. The economy can achieve higher levels of production if the production possibilities curve shifts outward over time. We have defined economic growth as a sustained expansion of output. The factors that cause this outward shift in production possibilities include an increase in the quantity or quality of society's resources or an improvement in technology. These factors can generate a sustained expansion of output—that is, economic growth.

FIGURE 17-1   Effects of Supply-Side Policy on the Macroeconomy

Supply-side policy is designed to cause an increase in aggregate supply, as shown by the shift of the aggregate supply curve *AS* to *AS'*. The result is an increase in GDP to GDP' and a reduction in the average price level from *P* to *P'*.

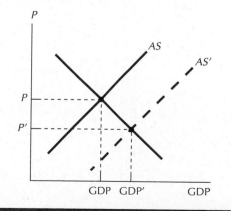

Policies to Achieve Economic Growth

This production possibilities curve from Chapter One is repeated below in Figure 17-2. Let us consider four factors contributing to economic growth. These factors are central to current discussions of economic growth; they are an increase in capital, an improvement in technology, an improvement in labor productivity, and a decrease in unnecessary regulation. As we examine these factors, we can consider government policy with respect to each of them.

An Increase in Capital

Economic growth can occur if there is a sustained increase in the quantity of physical capital: that is, an increase in our nation's stock of factories, equipment, machinery, and the like. This increase in capital is made possible by an increase in investment, and investment is made possible by saving—either private saving by households and businesses, or public saving through government taxes.

Savings rate
Gross domestic product minus private and government consumption spending, relative to gross domestic product.

High investment activity necessitates a high **savings rate,** which is defined here as the difference between GDP and consumption spending (private plus government), relative to gross domestic product. (Government consumption spending refers to government purchases of goods and services that do not represent government investment activity.) The current U.S. savings rate is 17 percent, up from 15 percent in 1990. The U.S. savings rate is among the lowest in the Western

FIGURE 17-2   Production Possibilities with Economic Growth

Points A through F show alternative combinations of bread and roses that the economy can produce. More of both bread and roses can be produced when the production possibilities curve shifts outward as a result of economic growth.

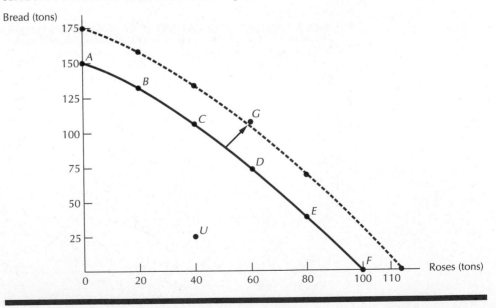

http://www.worldbank.
org/data
This is the introductory page
for The World Bank data. It
provides information on
worldwide economic and
social indicators, including
information on savings rates,
standards of living and international debt. To obtain data
quickly, use the Country at a
Glance tables.

Capital gains
The income earned when
an asset is bought at a
particular price and sold
at a higher price.

Consumption tax
A hypothetical tax on
income that is spent on
consumer goods and
services, as opposed to
income that goes
into savings.

Technology
Ways of using available
resources to produce
output.

industrialized world, along with that of Greece, Portugal, and the United Kingdom. Savings rates in the 20–29 percent range are typical for most countries in this
grouping, but several countries (Ireland, Japan, and Norway) have even higher
rates.[1] The relatively low rate of the United States has concerned many economists.

An increase in the savings rate in the United States is expected in the twenty-
first century for two reasons. First, the baby-boomer generation will be growing
older, enjoying higher incomes, and finishing their payments for houses and education for their children. Second, as pressures and policies result in lower government budget deficits, the negative savings by government will go down. (When the
government spends more than it brings in through tax revenue, it engages in negative saving, which is the opposite of saving.) These phenomena should serve to
raise the national savings rate.

Numerous efforts and proposals have been made to increase the national savings rate through supply-side policy, These efforts and proposals have been aimed
at increasing incentives for households and businesses to save and invest. The 1981
tax law accelerated tax write-offs for new investment by businesses, greatly reducing corporate income taxes. The 1981 and subsequent tax laws provided tax
breaks to households placing income into individual retirement accounts (IRAs)
and 401(k) accounts. There have also been repeated efforts to reduce the capital
gains tax. A **capital gain** is the income earned when one sells an asset at a higher
price than was paid for the asset. Proposals to cut the capital gains tax have been
controversial because the majority of the tax benefits accrue to the wealthiest
Americans, the ones who are more likely to receive capital gains.

Finally, there have been repeated proposals for a **consumption tax** to replace
our current personal income tax. Like a national sales tax, a consumption tax
taxes only the share of household income that is spent on consumer goods and
services; it does not tax the portion of income that is saved. Although the goal is to
provide greater incentives for saving, this tax would place the greatest burden on
low-income individuals, who by necessity must spend virtually all of their incomes
on consumption. This would represent a very regressive tax (recall the definition
of a regressive tax in Chapter Sixteen) unless deductions, credits, or a progressive
rate structure were built in to relieve the poor.

If these types of policies prove successful in increasing savings, we would
expect to see an expansion in investment in our nation's stock of physical capital.
The expansion of our nation's factories, equipment, and machinery would result
in an expansion of gross domestic product—that is, in economic growth.

While most of the conservative emphasis has been on providing incentives for
increased private saving and investment, liberal interest in increasing government
investment should not be overlooked. The government can play an important role
by investing in highways, mass transit, and airports, as well as schools and health
care facilities. Since all of these forms of investment can improve the business environment as well as the productivity of workers, they can enhance both the physical
and human capital of our nation.

An Improvement in Technology
Technology can be thought of as ways of using available resources to produce output. Improvements in technology enable us to produce more output, given our

limited resources. These improvements are embodied in new and more efficient machines, new products, and new methods of production.

Technological advance depends on research and development (R&D). Some 3,700 scientists and engineers are engaged in R&D per each million people in the United States. In this respect, the United States ranks third only to Sweden (with 3,800 scientists and engineers conducting research per million people) and Japan (with 4,900 per million).[2]

Government policies can again be used to encourage research and development. The government can increase university funding available for research and offer tax breaks for businesses that engage in research and development. The government also can provide patent protection to developers of new products. A **patent** is a government grant of exclusive rights to use or sell a new technology for a period of time. Without patents, other businesses might copy the new technology, thereby creating profits for themselves at the expense of the developer. Without patents, businesses have little incentive to develop new products. Patents have been extremely important in areas such as pharmaceuticals, communications technology, and consumer goods.

Nowhere has technological advance been more prominent than in the area of computers. Indeed, investment in information technology, including computers, software, communications networks, and Internet infrastructure, has contributed to a large share of economic growth in recent years. The United States has the largest number of personal computers per 1,000 people in the world: 459. It also has the highest number of Internet hosts per 10,000 people (close to 2,000).[3] Computer technology has enabled U.S. business to produce more and better products at the same or lower costs of production. It has also been a major factor in improving labor productivity.

Patent
A government grant of exclusive rights to use or sell a new technology for a period of time.

An Improvement in Labor Productivity

Labor Productivity
Total output per average work hour, calculated as GDP divided by the number of work hours.

Labor productivity is defined as total output per average work hour, calculated as gross domestic product divided by the number of work hours performed. Annual U.S. labor productivity growth, which lagged in the 1970s and 1980s, has soared to around 3 percent per year currently. Labor productivity hinges on the type and amount of capital and technology used in conjunction with labor, and these of course have improved in recent years. Keep in mind, however, that labor productivity also depends on human capital. Human capital includes the skills and abilities of people. Once again, government support for training programs, education, health, and nutrition all remain important for ensuring high levels of human capital.

A Decrease in Regulation

The government regulates business in a variety of ways, including protections for consumers of pharmaceuticals, food, and manufactured goods; safeguards for workers in industry; and protection of the environment. In light of recent deaths due to unsafe tires and pharmaceutical drugs, the necessity for wisely developed government regulations is clear. On the other hand, unwise and unnecessary regulation merely increases business costs and decreases output. Therefore, cutting unwise regulation is a desirable policy and is conducive to economic growth. The problem, of course, is recognizing which regulations are harmful and which are beneficial.

Generally speaking, economic conservatives prefer less government regulation, whereas economic liberals prefer more. The supply-side policies of the 1980s and 1990s included widespread cuts in government regulations. Environmental protection is a good case in point. Presidents Reagan and Bush greatly reduced government regulations in this area. Many of President Clinton's proposed regulations met a hostile Congress and were not passed. President George W. Bush has indicated he will continue the trend toward less environmental regulation and seek a more industry-friendly environmental policy. Although this policy may provide some short-run benefit to the economy through a reduction in the compliance costs of business and a resulting forward shift of aggregate supply, the long-run costs might outweigh this benefit. Just as an increase in productive resources will shift the production possibilities curve outward over time, a decrease in our natural resources due to environmental damage and resource depletion will shift the curve inward. The capacity of our nation to produce and grow will be compromised, and the quality of life of our citizens will decline.

As suggested in Chapter Three on the environment, environmental protection is a global necessity. Deforestation and the burning of fossil fuels contribute to global warming and loss of precious biodiversity. Acid rain destroys crops, waterways, and capital structures across countries. Use of certain chemicals destroys the ozone layer. Air and water pollution knows no boundaries.

In the final days of his administration, President Clinton considered but ultimately decided against an executive order that would have protected nearly 60 million acres of U.S. forested area by prohibiting oil exploration in Alaska's Arctic National Wildlife Refuge. President George W. Bush's plans for oil exploration there is a central part of his energy policy. Clearly a battle looms ahead between the president and environmental advocates in Congress. Similarly, an international battle hovers over the issue of global warming. President Bush has indicated his opposition to the 1997 Kyoto Treaty, signed by President Clinton, which forces industrial nations to reduce greenhouse gases. This treaty is seen as critical to reducing the problem of global warming.

Implications of Growth for the Twenty-First Century

The market-oriented growth policies of the Western industrialized world are likely to persist for at least the near future. However, there may be a cyclical movement of philosophy from a restricted government role to an expanded government role and back again, as dissatisfaction with the drawbacks of either extreme become evident. In the United States, post–World War II economic growth did little to mitigate extremely high poverty rates. The War on Poverty and the Civil Rights movement of the 1960s addressed the needs of the population for which the prosperity of the 1950s did not trickle down. Yet the policies of the 1960s and 1970s brought forth a conservative backlash, as politicians in the 1980s and 1990s sought to reverse years of affirmative action and antipoverty policies. In the twenty-first century, concern for the people left behind from the prosperity of worldwide economic growth may well again precipitate a greater call for government response.

THE FORMERLY SOCIALIST INDUSTRIALIZED WORLD: ECONOMIC TRANSITION

The recent changes in Eastern Europe are nothing short of revolutionary. The Cold War has ended. Germany is reunified, and the Berlin Wall is down. The Soviet Union no longer exists; it has been divided into some 15 independent nations (the largest of which is Russia). And finally, the formerly socialist economies of Eastern Europe are now undergoing an economic transition toward capitalism.

This transition has achieved varied levels of success, as evidenced by diverse economic growth rates. Table 17-2 displays the variation in growth rates for selected countries of the formerly socialist industrialized world over the period 1990–1999. More successful countries such as Slovenia and Albania have the highest average annual growth rates of 2.4 percent and 2.3 percent, respectively. Less successful countries such as Moldova and Ukraine have growth rates of –11.5 percent and –10.8 percent, respectively. Russia also has a negative average annual growth rate: –6.1 percent for the time period. A negative growth rate means that the production of goods and services is declining.

The most prominent elements of the transition to capitalism are the movement toward market-determined prices and the process of privatization, as well as the development of entrepreneurship. Russia has experienced some of the difficulties inherent in the transition process. Nevertheless, in terms of entrepreneurship,

> there is no question that everyday Russian citizens have embraced entrepreneurial activities; whether in the form of kiosks lining the streets of Moscow's famous Arbat and metro stops, babushkas selling homemade fast foods and household articles at every bus stop, teenagers selling gasoline along highways near the long lines at gas

TABLE 17-2   Average Annual Economic Growth, Selected Formerly Socialist Industrialized Countries, 1990–1999

COUNTRY	AVERAGE ANNUAL GROWTH OF GNP, %	COUNTRY	AVERAGE ANNUAL GROWTH OF GNP, %
Slovenia	2.4	Armenia	–3.1
Albania	2.3	Lithuania	–3.9
Austria	2.0	Belarus	–4.3
Hungary	1.0	Russia	–6.1
Czech Republic	0.9	Georgia	–10.3
Romania	–1.2	Ukraine	–10.8
Bulgaria	–2.7	Moldova	–11.5

Source: Data from World Bank, *World Development Report 2000/2001,* (New York: Oxford University Press, 2001).

stations, professionals moonlighting as translators and drivers, and residents seeking Western partners in Russian joint ventures.[4]

Problems in Russia are more evident in the area of prices and privatization.

Market-Determined Prices

Recall the efficiencies associated with market-determined prices. Demand and supply equate so that shortages and surpluses are eliminated. (It is when the government intervenes by setting rental ceilings in housing or price supports in agriculture, for example, that we end up with shortages or surpluses.) In a free market, the high prices of scarce goods encourage consumers to be frugal in their use of the goods and encourage suppliers to expand production of the goods. Shortages do not result. On the other hand, the low prices of plentiful goods encourage consumers to use the goods more extensively and encourage suppliers to produce fewer of these goods and shift production away from these goods and toward a greater number of goods more desirable to consumers. Surpluses are thus prevented.

Under socialism, the government sets the prices of goods and services. Prices have traditionally been set artificially low in the socialist economies of Eastern Europe. For example, consumers have been able to afford to buy basic items of food, clothing, and gasoline. Artificially low prices operate like price ceilings, however, and shortages are the result. So although people could afford to purchase needed items, these goods were often unavailable in stores. People would expend considerable time and energy standing in long lines and leaving their jobs to rush to stores whenever new supplies arrived.

These shortages are largely relics of the past. Prices of most items have been allowed to rise to market-determined levels in most Eastern European countries. In other words, **decontrol of prices** has occurred. Government no longer sets the prices. Because wages have typically not risen as rapidly as prices, the purchasing power of consumers has declined. Supplies are now plentiful, but people cannot afford the goods.

Price decontrol in Russia was abrupt. Within days, prices on 80 to 90 percent of wholesale and retail goods were decontrolled.[5] The rise in prices of so many goods and services naturally caused a sudden rise in the average price level. The inflation rate soared, peaking at approximately 1,353 percent per year at the height of price decontrol in 1992. Inflation has since subsided but is still considered to be a serious problem. (The inflation rate in 1999 was 86 percent, up from 28 percent in 1998.)[6]

Privatization

Privatization refers to the sale of government enterprises to the private sector. Throughout Eastern Europe, governments have owned everything from industry and businesses to agricultural land, energy facilities, agricultural marketing boards, and transportation networks. The process of privatization presumes that private ownership of the means of production enhances efficiency and growth.

http://www.imfsite.org
This Web site is the home page of the International Monetary Fund. It provides links to countless statistics, reports, and other global information, including the transformation of countries to capitalism.

Decontrol of prices
Removal of government control of prices.

Privatization
Sale of government-owned enterprises to the private sector.

Once again, Russia presents an interesting example of this process of privatization. The Russian privatization program started in April 1992 with the sale of municipally owned shops. At the same time, the government began the process whereby state and collective farms would convert to private ownership. In June the government began to convert large and medium-sized firms into shareholding companies (meaning that individuals may own shares in the company). Finally, in October the government began to issue to all Russian citizens a voucher that can be used to purchase shares in such companies.[7] (Your author even managed to purchase a voucher, a "piece of Russia," in a secondary market to a secondary market—that is, a hallway outside of an auction site.)

The Russian privatization program has not been without difficulty. First, different elements of the Russian government have disagreed greatly over the pace of privatization. Second, small businesses, mostly shops and services, have been sold off more rapidly than larger enterprises. The largest enterprises are far more difficult to privatize. Third, machinery and equipment in many Russian enterprises are outmoded and in poor repair. Productivity in these enterprises is very low. As privatized businesses have become more profit-oriented, and as government subsidies to these businesses have declined, many firms have gone bankrupt, resulting in worker layoffs. Fourth, Russian enterprises tend to be monopolies. Before the transition, Soviet planners had categorized industry into 7,664 "product groups." Of these product groups, 77 percent were produced by single firms.[8] Even as these government-owned monopolies become privatized, there remain the problems associated with monopoly that were discussed in Chapter Four. Finally, nearly 15 percent of Russia's industries were defense-related. Since the end of the Cold War, Russian demand for defense-related products has been low.[9] All of this suggests that Russia will face serious hurdles in the forms of privatization, de-monopolization, and defense conversion.

Effects of the Transition

The objectives of the transition from socialism to capitalism throughout the formerly socialist industrialized world are greater efficiency and growth. But this transition has posed many problems for people. Inflation has made it difficult for consumers to afford basic necessities. Farmers have been hard hit by increases in the prices of inputs such as fertilizer, and the prices that they receive for their food products often still remain artificially low. Workers have been laid off in defense industries, government jobs, and privatized businesses. Other workers have received no paychecks for months. Corruption is often widespread, and organized crime is often rampant. Whereas most people have been struggling to make do in light of these difficulties, some have been profiting from liberalization. The masses of people are deeply troubled by this blatant inequality. Alcoholism and suicide rates in some countries have been rising, and life expectancies have even declined. A quotation from a young Russian woman studying in the United States summarizes some of these difficulties.

The situation in Russia is very difficult for the ordinary citizen. My father recently lost his government job, though he was soon hired into a different job. My mother, who works at a bank, did not lose her job but she was not paid for seven months. Imagine, a bank with all that money, and my mother not being paid! Lost jobs and non-payment of wages are common. People get by by moonlighting. Old women beg or sell home-made food, used clothing, or anything that anyone will buy. Pensions are often very small, as low as $30 per month (900 rubles) or less. This will buy maybe a loaf of bread and a bottle of milk each day, plus a little bit of meat each week. With wages falling behind prices, it now takes about seven days of work at a typical wage to purchase a tube of mascara, and two months of work to purchase a good pair of shoes. Twenty rubles will buy a bottle of bad vodka. Many people drink. In the meanwhile, middle-aged men flaunt their wealth and drive their Mercedes, Audis, and BMWs. It is easy to recognize the Mafia.[10]

The Twenty-First Century?

The twenty-first century is a question mark. Although policies of liberalization will undoubtedly continue, the struggles and dissatisfactions of ordinary people may slow down or change the nature of the transition. In some countries the transition may even be reversed. In Russia, the rise in power of politicians who wish to return to the policies of the past exemplifies the dissatisfaction of people with the current political and economic situation. Opinion polls show that large shares of the popu-lation wish to return to the "old days," when they were provided with housing, jobs, child care, and health care. In other formerly socialist countries, such as Poland and Belarus, some policies of liberalization have been reversed and some socialist-leaning politicians have been elected. In other Eastern European coun-tries, significant minorities favor the return to socialist economies.

One of the critical issues in the transition to freer-market economies in East-ern Europe is a safety net for people. Under socialism, governments *had* guaran-teed jobs, housing, child care, and medical coverage for all citizens. As ordinary citizens now experience a loss of jobs and purchasing power, governments need to ensure that their basic needs are met. Otherwise, the transition will proceed nei-ther smoothly nor successfully.

THE LESS-DEVELOPED WORLD: ECONOMIC REFORM

Economic reform
Change in policies and institutions that moves economies to freer markets.

Much of the less-developed world is undergoing a process referred to as **economic reform.** This means that developing countries are adopting policies that move their economies toward freer markets. The economic growth rates reported in Chapter Eight indicated much variation in the success of less-developed countries in increasing GDP per capita. The economic reforms predominant in the 1990s and 2000s have their roots in the international debt crisis of the 1980s. And that crisis has its roots in the world economic conditions of the 1970s.

The 1970s: Oil Crisis

The most significant economic events of the 1970s began with the restriction of oil supplies by the Organization of Petroleum Exporting Countries (OPEC), the Arab oil embargo, and the quadrupling of oil prices between 1973 and 1974. The OPEC countries experienced massive increases in their export earnings, and the non-oil-exporting, less-developed countries suffered huge increases in their spending for oil imports. The effects of the oil shock were threefold. First, the OPEC nations began a process of "recycling" the revenue earned through their international sales of oil. That is, they deposited much of their oil revenue in U.S. and European financial institutions. These **petrodollars** greatly enhanced the lending capacity of these commercial banks and other financial institutions. Second, the oil price increase caused a generalized inflation, and subsequent recession, throughout much of the world. Ultimately, the worldwide recession caused a decline in demand for exports from less-developed countries and a consequent decline in the export earnings of these countries. And finally, the combination of reduced export earnings and increased oil import expenditures forced the non-oil-exporting developing countries to borrow from the **International Monetary Fund (IMF),** as well as from commercial banks. At the time, the cost of borrowing was low due to low real interest rates, and the lending capacity of Western financial institutions was large.

The next stage of the debt crisis began in 1979, when OPEC and the Iranian oil embargo again sent oil prices soaring. (This event was described as an example of cost-push inflation in Chapter Sixteen.) Along with this second oil shock came another phase of petrodollar recycling. The commercial banks were now quite capable and willing to make even larger loans to developing countries. Many non-oil-exporting countries borrowed heavily to finance their oil imports. Several other oil-exporting developing countries, such as Mexico, borrowed to develop their oil sectors and diversify their economies. Most of these new loans came from private commercial banks, rather than the IMF, which by now was running low on lending funds. For a variety of reasons that we will discuss, this second phase of borrowing placed developing countries in a situation even more precarious than the first phase.

The Early 1980s: U.S. Reaction

The second phase of borrowing occurred at a time of great concern in the United States over the inflation that was partly generated by the escalating oil prices. High inflation rates persisted until the early 1980s, when the Federal Reserve engaged in **contractionary monetary policy** (recall the discussion in Chapter Fifteen on macro policy in the early 1980s). Inflation was brought under control, but at the expense of skyrocketing interest rates and consequent U.S. recession that later spread worldwide. An outcome of LDC borrowing from commercial banks, as opposed to the IMF, was that larger proportions of lending agreements now stipulated variable interest rates. This meant that as market interest rates rose, interest payments of LDC borrowers increased as well.

Rising interest rates in the United States had a secondary effect of pushing up the value of the dollar. The rising dollar made developing countries' payment for oil imports even more difficult because oil is valued in dollars. It also made repaying predominantly dollar-denominated debt more difficult for developing countries. Less-developed-country debt was now a full-blown crisis.

Petrodollars
Money earned from the sale of petroleum. Petroleum prices are denominated in dollars.

International Monetary Fund (IMF)
An international organization, largely funded by Western industrialized countries, that provides conditional loans and financial assistance to needy countries.

Contractionary monetary policy
Reductions in the nation's money supply that serve to raise interest rates and reduce aggregate demand.

The 1980s: International Debt Crisis

By 1988, the less-developed countries had borrowed more than a trillion dollars, and the number was increasing. They borrowed for a variety of reasons, including those related to the oil market, which we noted earlier. Many less-developed countries borrowed for a variety of laudable purposes, including investment in infrastructure and industry and development of agricultural and export sectors.

In other countries, borrowed funds were grossly misused. Countless stories tell of funds that were squandered on grandiose but inefficient government projects, on luxury goods for the rich, and on the coffers of wealthy businesspeople and government officials. For example, Tyler Bridges, then a writer for the *Washington Post,* examined Venezuela's use of borrowed funds in the mid-1980s. He wrote:

> . . . I discovered that the government hadn't kept track of where the money had gone, though various sources indicated that only a portion of the money was invested in projects fostering long-term growth. [I found that Venezuela] borrowed heavily from abroad in the late 1970s to finance food imports and to subsidize domestic food prices. As food imports soared, however, local agriculture was neglected and production declined. Once self-sufficient, Venezuela today imports about fifty percent of Venezuela's food. . . . [In another example] thanks in part to a presidential decree requiring that every public bathroom and elevator have an attendant, public-sector employment tripled from 1974–1984.[11]

Capital flight
A process whereby less-developed countries invest funds in foreign countries.

Another problem was that of capital flight. **Capital flight** is a process whereby borrowed funds are reinvested in financial markets or real estate abroad. Corrupt government officials or businesspeople with access to borrowed funds often invested these funds overseas, rather than using them for local projects. Capital flowed outward, profits and interest earnings accrued to wealthy investors, and developing countries failed to benefit from the borrowed money. When governments fail to invest borrowed funds productively, this naturally hampers the ability of borrowing countries to repay their debt. The fault may lie with an inefficient or corrupt government, but it is the residents of the borrowing countries who now bear the burden of the debt.

The enormous burden of the debt becomes clear when one carefully considers the process by which a country tries to pay off its debt. First, the amount of money that must service the debt (interest payment plus repayment of principal) represents a large expenditure in any particular year, meaning that a significant proportion of the income generated from the production of goods and services (GDP) must be transferred out of the country. Recall that the gross domestic product of developing countries is typically small. Thus the income generated from production of GDP is low as well. The demands on this limited income represent a bewildering array of choices in a typical low-income country trying desperately to develop. Large expenditures must go to satisfying the basic consumption needs of people: food, shelter, and medical care. Government expenditures are also necessary for a variety of social services, public education, and infrastructure. With a population at the margin of subsistence and with a driving need for development, any expenditures diverted toward repaying the debt will directly harm the well-being of people. This state of affairs explains a commonly made observation: "In poor countries, the debt crisis has a child's face." The reallocation of expenditure toward servicing of debt has harmed the well-being of people, the most vulnerable of whom are typically the very young.

In addition to the problem of allocating income for debt servicing, there is the problem of the form that this transfer must take. Debt repayment must be made in the form of the currency initially borrowed; thus repayment must typically be in U.S. dollars or in the currency of major developed countries. We'll refer to this currency as foreign currency. Less-developed countries have very limited means of obtaining foreign currency with which to make their payments. They may earn foreign currency through their exports to other countries. Typically these export earnings are very limited, and they declined for many LDCs over the 1980s as a consequence of the U.S. and worldwide recession. (Do you recall the problem of LDC declining terms of trade discussed in Chapter Five?) A country may also acquire foreign currency through foreign investment by other countries and through international assistance. A final option, and one that has been increasingly chosen by LDC governments, is to continually borrow to repay past debts. Obviously the latter results in a vicious cycle of continuous borrowing in which LDCs have little hope of becoming debt free.

In a country with limited opportunity to earn foreign currency, such currency must be carefully spent. When that currency must be used for debt repayment, it cannot be used for other important activities such as the purchase of foreign capital or technology or the import of important food and energy products. Yet perhaps the most dire implications of debt servicing take place in the long term. Countries that are desperate for foreign currency earnings to service their debt will undertake overall development policies that are quite different from the ones they might normally undertake. Countries under pressure to acquire export earnings may feel forced to expand patterns of export cropping that worsen the income distribution, use up limited resources, and cause environmental problems. They may succumb to pressures to encourage indiscriminate foreign investment that may not be the most conducive to their overall development objectives. They may emphasize industrial over agricultural sector development. Under more ideal conditions, a country might well pursue very different, and more beneficial, paths to development.

The 1990s: Economic Reform

The final phase of the debt crisis occurred as many countries were forced by their inability to meet payment schedules to seek financial assistance from the International Monetary Fund. IMF assistance is helpful, but it has typically involved **conditionality,** forcing countries to undertake the economic reforms referred to earlier (often called "austerity measures") as a condition for assistance. These reforms include requirements that governments reduce their spending, reduce general inflation and wages, and privatize government enterprises. Governments are also required to allow food and other prices to rise to market levels and to reduce their controls on foreign trade and investment. In other words, they must move toward freer markets, reducing their role in the economy and allowing the market to determine prices. Some countries have voluntarily adopted economic reforms, but

Conditionality
The obligation to meet certain requirements in exchange for financial assistance.

This chapter has examined a conservative movement throughout the world toward capitalism and globally freer markets. Economists vary in their views of this movement. Market economies often lead to efficiency and growth, but issues of equity may be neglected. If this is the case, and if governments fail to provide adequate programs for the poor and the unemployed, the benefits of a market economy will fail to trickle down to the needy. In the new millennium the disparity between the rich and the poor may become greater. Liberals tend to be more concerned than conservatives about this equity issue.

On the other hand, if government interventions go so far as to reduce the usefulness of the price system and the incentives of the marketplace, economies may stagnate and fail to grow. Conservatives tend to be more concerned than liberals about these issues of incentives and efficiency.

Where is the balance between the conservative and the liberal view? You have studied this contrast throughout the course, whether the issue is agriculture, housing, or environment. You now have the information and insight you need to analyze this issue by yourself and to come to the policy conclusions that make sense to you.

most others have had these reforms forced on them. Some of these reforms have run counter to development policies and have created tremendous hardship for governments and residents alike. One African leader expressed his frustration this way:

> You do not talk of "austerity" to a [person] who has not tasted food for days, who can conceive of no more ecstatic pleasure than to have a few drops of water to wet his [or her] lips and tongue. . . . Enforced increases in food prices are meaningless mutterings to the mother brushing the flies off her baby's eyes, watching [the child] starve to death by the minute because there is no food or milk or water.[12]

The Twenty-First Century?

Less-developed countries have had mixed reactions to economic reforms. In many countries, such as Nigeria and other African countries, privatization has resulted in massive layoffs of public-sector employees. The private sector has not yet been able to restore employment adequately in these countries. In other countries such as Kenya and Indonesia, rising food prices have been met with riots by urban consumers. In still other countries such as Chile, economic reforms have created rapid economic growth and national prosperity despite the fact that large segments of the population remain abysmally poor. (Chile has returned to more socialist policies with the recent election of socialist President Ricardo Lagos.) It is hoped that economic reform throughout the less-developed world will lead to economic growth and that the benefits of this growth will trickle down to the poor, but at least in the short term, the poor are the ones who suffer most. Once again, a critical issue is the existence of an adequate safety net for the poor.

It remains to be seen how the less-developed countries, like the formerly socialist industrialized countries, will respond to the effects of economic reform. Some will undoubtedly move forward; others will react like Chile has to the hardships borne by their people. They will seek policies to soften, or even nullify, the policies of economic reform.

SUMMARY

The Western industrialized world, the formerly socialist industrialized world, and the less-developed world are all currently embarked on a movement toward freer markets for their economies. Much of the Western industrialized world has embraced conservative economic policies in the hope of generating economic growth. Most formerly socialist industrialized countries are experiencing a revolutionary transition from socialism to capitalism. And finally, large numbers of less-developed countries have adopted economic reform policies, voluntarily or involuntarily, that are designed to make their economies more market-oriented. The long-term success of these changes remains to be seen.

NOTES

1. The World Bank, *World Development Report 2000/2001* (New York: Oxford University Press, 2001). Savings rates in other Western European countries range from 12 percent in Greece to 17 percent in Portugal, 15 percent in the United Kingdom, 37 percent in Ireland, 30 percent in Japan, and 32 percent in Norway. Statistics are for 1999.

2. The World Bank, *World Development Report 2000/2001*. Statistics are for the most recent year available.

3. The World Bank, *World Development Report 2000/2001*. Statistics are for 1998 and January 2000, respectively.

4. Jacqueline Brux and Jacques Foust, "Doing Business in the Russian Economy in Transition," presented at the Midwest Economic Association meetings, Chicago, March 1994 (unpublished).

5. U.S. Department of Commerce, Business Information Service for the Newly Independent States (BISNIS), International Trade Administration, *Commercial Overview of Russia*, Moscow, January 28, 1993.

6. The 1992 inflation rate is reported in the International Monetary Fund, *World Economic Outlook* (Washington DC: International Monetary Fund, May 1995). The 1998 and 1999 inflation rates are reported in the Central Intelligence Agency (CIA), *The World Factbook* (http://www.odci.gov/cia/publications/factbook/geos/rs.html).

7. "Russia Reborn," *Economist*. December 5, 1992.

8. "Russia Reborn," *Economist*.

9. U.S. Department of Commerce, *Commercial Overview of Russia*.

10. Yana S. Yurgelyanis, in a conversation with the author.

11. Tyler Bridges, "Before Bailing Them Out, Plug the Leaks," *Washington Post National Weekly Edition*, March 22–April 7, 1989.

12. Bread for the World, *Africa: Crisis to Opportunity*, 1995.

DISCUSSION QUESTIONS

1. *Are you an economic liberal or conservative? What is your view of government social programs, taxes, and government regulation of business?*

2. *Consider the U.S. supply-side policies and proposals of the 2000s, such as proposals to change our tax system and environmental regulations. Do you expect these policies to achieve efficiency and economic growth? Do you expect the benefits of these policies to trickle down to all?*

3. *How might the U.S. government encourage greater research and development? How would R&D benefit the economy?*

4. *Suppose that the government of a formerly socialist country decontrols prices and permits them to rise to market levels. How can the government assist low-income consumers who might be unable to afford higher food and other prices?*

5. *Assume that the process of privatization continues successfully in Russia. Would all the problems of Russian industry by solved? What other policies may be necessary?*

6. *Use the Central Intelligence Agency (CIA) World Factbook (http://www.odci.gov/cia/publications/factbook) to look up the current economic situation in any one of the formerly socialist industrialized countries. Has GDP been increasing or decreasing? How high is the inflation rate? How do some of the standards of living (life expectancy, infant mortality rate, and so on) compare with those presented in Chapter Eight for less-developed countries?*

7. *How have international conditions outside the control of less-developed countries exacerbated the problem of international debt? Do you believe it is right for the IMF to stipulate conditions when providing financial assistance to debt-ridden less-developed countries?*

8. *Go to the International Monetary Fund Web site (http://www.imfsite.org) and click on Conditionality to learn more about the history, role, operation, and effectiveness of IMF conditionality (in the IMF view).*

9. *Use the World Bank Web site (http://www.worldbank.org/data) to look up debt information on a less-developed country of your choice. Look for the debt service ratio, which is the ratio between debt service (annual repayment of debt plus interest) and export earnings and is written as Total Debt Service/Exports. This ratio is the best indicator of the debt burden of an individual country.*

10. *What type of safety net is necessary for residents of formerly socialist and less-developed countries as they move toward market economies?*

11. *Do you believe that the global movement toward freer markets will continue into the twenty-first century, or will it reverse itself? Why or why not?*

You and the World around You

Now you have finished your study of economic issues in the world today. You have used economic tools to analyze a broad spectrum of social issues. And in the process you have learned techniques that you can use to analyze other issues. You have developed critical and analytical thinking skills that you can use all your life. You will be better able to understand how government policy affects you and your family. You have learned the vocabulary to understand what you read in the newspaper or see on the TV news. Indeed, you are now a better-educated citizen.

What does this mean? Are you a "better" person? Will you contribute to a more just society? Will you have a better quality of life? Will you make an impact on the world in which we live?

We hope your answer was yes to all of the questions above. Or at least we hope that you now have interest in improving the world around you. For all its imperfections, the United States is a rich, diverse country with one of the world's longest-lasting democratic governments. The U.S. GDP per capita in 2000 was more than $32,000, among the highest in the world. You will be among the 25 percent of the age-25-or-older population in this land of opportunity who have a college degree. What all of this means is that you have both the ability to affect policy and the responsibility to do so. You can inform yourself about social issues, exercise your right to vote, or contact your legislators.[1] You can campaign for a candidate who reflects your views or run for public office yourself. You can exercise your right to free speech by writing a letter to the editor of your local paper. You can demonstrate and carry a poster supporting a cause about which you feel strongly. You can agree with government policy, and you can disagree. You *can* make a difference in our society! You are an educated citizen.

The issues we analyzed in this book will not go away. You will finish your formal education (no one ever finishes learning), and you will go on to your career. We hope some of you will take more economics courses and perhaps even become economists. But you will be workers of all sorts: social workers, biochemists, teachers, accountants, doctors, nurses, controllers, and production managers. You may work in prisons or in foreign countries. Your investment in your education will make you a more productive worker wherever you go to work. We hope you will remain concerned about issues of poverty and discrimination, pollution, and abuse of market power. The real world forces you to take ethical positions on these issues as they are related to your workplace and your life.

Finally, you are a part of a global economy. Mexico's economic situation affects the United States. It influences our exports and imports. It affects our immigration policy. If Mexico does well, it adds to the health of the U.S. economy. And the economic situation in the United States affects the well-being of the average Mexican citizen. If our economy is healthy, we import Mexican goods and create jobs in Mexico, lessening the pressure on Mexican citizens to immigrate to the United States.

Mexico is only one example. The economies of the United States and Western Europe, and increasingly Eastern Europe as well, are intricately linked through foreign trade and foreign investment. The developed economy of the United States and the developing economies of Latin America, Asia, and Africa are becoming more and more interdependent through foreign lending, trade, and investment, as well as through cultural and educational exchange. As a citizen of the world, you will increasingly be called on to understand international issues, to work in businesses with international linkages, and very likely to travel in foreign countries yourself. The world has indeed become a global village. And you are a resident of that village!

NOTE

1. You may contact your U.S. senators at the U.S. Senate Office Building, Washington, DC 20510, and your U.S. representatives at the U.S. House of Representatives, Washington, DC 20515. You may leave a telephone message for either at (202) 224-3121. You may write the president at The White House, Washington, DC 20500, or leave a message at (202) 456-1111. You may also send an e-mail to the president at President@Whitehouse.gov. Web sites and e-mail addresses of members of the U.S. Senate and House of Representatives are available at http://www.senate.gov and http://www.house.gov, respectively, as is information about schedules, bills, committees, and so on.

GLOSSARY

A

Absolute advantage A situation whereby a country can produce a good at a lower resource cost than another country.

Absolute poverty A situation in which people experience the hardship of poverty according to some objective criterion.

Administered prices Prices regulated by the government.

Adverse selection Process by which insured people's choices lead to higher-than-average loss levels.

Affirmative action Mandated program to provide equal access to labor markets.

Aggregate demand The quantity of total output (GDP) demanded (purchased) at alternative average price levels.

Aggregate supply The quantity of total output (GDP) supplied (produced) at alternative average price levels.

Aid to Families with Dependent Children (AFDC) Our nation's former welfare program providing cash assistance to eligible low income families with children.

Antitrust Laws, agencies, and court system established to control monopoly in the United States.

Appreciate An increase in the value of one country's currency relative to another country's currency.

Appropriations Monies authorized by a legislative body to be spent for certain purposes.

Asset Property that is owned, such as land.

Average life expectancy The age to which a baby born in a particular year can be expected to live.

B

Barrier to entry Market characteristic that prevents new firms from entering the market.

Barter The direct exchange of goods and services for other goods and services rather than for money.

Block grant A lump sum of money given by the federal government to state governments to use as they wish within broad federal guidelines to develop programs to meet a broad category of need.

Budget deficit The difference between federal government spending and federal government tax revenue in any one year.

Budget surplus The difference between federal government tax revenue and federal government spending in any one year.

Buffer stock A mechanism for stabilizing agricultural prices, whereby an agricultural product is purchased and placed in storage during years of high production and released from storage and sold during years of low production.

Bumper crop Unexpectedly large crop resulting from good growing conditions.

Burden of the tax The impact of the tax that is felt by producers and consumers. Consumers bear the burden in the form of higher prices paid for the product; producers bear the burden in the form of lower profits.

C

Capital flight A process whereby less-developed countries invest funds in foreign countries.

Capital gains The income earned when an asset is bought at a particular price and sold at a higher price.

Capital goods Goods such as machinery and factories, which are used to produce other goods.

Capital-intensive technology Technology utilizing large amounts of capital.

Capitalism An economic system wherein the economic decisions are made by the private sector via the marketplace, and the means of production are owned by the private sector.

Cartel Price-fixing agreement and the firms who are party to it.

Certification License to produce a product that meets pollution standards or to use a technique that meets an environmental goal.

Closing costs Expenses paid at the time that a loan is finalized and the title is conveyed to the buyer.

Coinsurance payments Percentage of medical expenses remaining after the deductible, which the insured person must pay.

Collusion Price fixing.

Comparative advantage A situation whereby a country can produce a good at a lower opportunity cost than another country.

Composition of GDP The goods and services of which GDP consists.

Composition of GNP The items of production of which GNP consists.

Concentration The domination of a market or industry by a few large firms.

Concentration ratio The percentage of output produced by the four largest firms in an industry.

Conditionality The obligation to meet certain requirements in exchange for financial assistance.

Constant prices Prices that exist in a base year.

Consumer goods Goods that are consumed (or used) by consumers.

Consumer price index (CPI) A weighted average of the prices of a fixed basket of goods and services purchased by a typical urban household.

Consumption possibilities curve A curve that shows alternative amounts of two products that can be consumed within a country during a particular time period.

Consumption tax A hypothetical tax on income that is spent on consumer goods and services, as opposed to income that goes into savings.

Contractionary fiscal policy Fiscal policy that decreases aggregate demand, thereby contracting GDP.

Contractionary monetary policy Reductions in the nation's money supply that serve to raise interest rates and reduce aggregate demand, thereby contracting GDP.

Contractual right Right specified in contract between parties.

Control of essential raw materials Barrier to market entry resulting from a monopoly's ownership or control of an entire supply of a resource needed to produce its product.

Cost-benefit analysis Study that compares the costs and benefits of a policy or program.

Cost of living adjustment (COLA) An adjustment that automatically increases incomes or benefits when the average price level rises.

Cost-push inflation Inflation that occurs as a result of increases in the costs of production.

Cost shifting Practice of recovering the unpaid costs of some patients by charging higher prices to other patients.

Crowding out A situation in which government spending, financed by borrowing, causes interest rates to rise, which results in less spending by the private economy.

Current prices Actual prices of a particular year.

Cyclical unemployment Unemployment that results from a drop in economic activity in our economy as a whole.

D

Declining terms of trade A situation in which the price of a country's exports declines relative to the price of its imports.

Decontrol of prices Removal of government control of prices.

Deductibles Payments on an annual or per-service basis that must be made by the insured person before the insurance company's payments begin.

Defensive medicine Ordering of unnecessary tests and services solely to protect oneself from charges of malpractice.

Deficiency payment Target price minus market price, times the number of units sold.

Deflation A decrease in the average price level.

Deforestation The clearing of forested areas.

Demand curve A graph showing the quantities that consumers are willing to buy at alternative prices during a specified time period.

Demand-pull inflation Inflation that occurs when any sectors of the economy increase their demand for goods and services.

Demand schedule A table showing the quantities that consumers are willing to buy at alternative prices during a specified time period.

Depreciate A decrease in the value of one country's currency relative to another country's currency.

Deregulation The reduction of government regulations.

Desertification The encroachment of desert on previously fertile land.

Design standard Specifies both the required level of performance and the means of compliance.

Diagnosis-related-group (DRG) One of approximately 490 categories into which a medical diagnosis might fall. The DRG determines the prospective payment by Medicare.

Discouraged workers People who would like to work, but have become so discouraged in the job search that they have stopped actively seeking employment.

Discrimination Action that treats like individuals differently on the basis of some arbitrary characteristic.

Distribution of GNP Distribution of output (or income) generated from the production of GNP.

Distribution of income How national income is distributed within an economy.

Down payment Amount of home buyer's own money required by the lender for the purchase of a home.

Dumping Exporting goods at prices below the cost of production.

Durable goods Products with a life of longer than one year.

E

Early retirement effect Social Security's effect of increasing private savings by encouraging earlier retirements.

Earned income tax credit (EITC) A federal tax credit for low-income working individuals and families. The credit is available whether or not the worker pays federal personal income taxes.

Earnings Money received from labor market activities.

Economic development A multidimensional process that involves growth in GNP per capita, improvements in standards of living, and reductions in poverty.

Economic growth A sustained increase in production, represented by an outward shift of the production possibilities curve. An increase in GNP (GDP) or GNP per capita (GDP per capita) over an extended time period.

Economic reform Change in policies and institutions that moves economies to freer markets.

Economies of scale Decreasing long-run average costs.

Efficient Using resources in such as way as to maximize the output from them.

Effluent fee A tax on production causing water pollution.

Elastic demand Demand in which buyers are relatively responsive to changes in price.

Embargo Restrictions on trade with another country for political reasons.

Emissions fee A tax on production causing air pollution.

Employment discrimination Not hiring certain workers on the basis of some arbitrary characteristic.

Endowments Income-earning investments of a school.

Enrollment caps A maximum limit on the number of students allowed to enroll in a school.

Entitlement Payment to which eligible citizens have a right by law

Equilibrium A state of balance; a point at which quantity demanded equals quantity supplied.

Equitable Fair.

Exchange rate The price of one country's currency in terms of another country's currency.

Excise tax A tax applied to the purchase of a specific good or service.

Exclusive franchise Governmental monopoly grant, accompanied by regulation.

Exemption An amount of money that can be deducted from household income before tax rates are applied.

Expansionary fiscal policy Fiscal policy that increases aggregate demand, thereby expanding GDP.

Expansionary monetary policy Monetary policy that increases aggregate demand, thereby expanding GDP.

Export cropping Agricultural production for export, rather than production of food for local consumption.

Exports The value of goods and services sold to foreigners.

Externality The cost or benefit of an economic activity that spills over onto the rest of society.

F

Fair market rent Amount determined by HUD to be reasonable rent for low-income housing.

Federal Reserve The U.S. central banking system.

Field surveillance Inspections for compliance with standards.

Fiscal policy The use of government spending and tax policy to shift the aggregate demand curve.

Flexible (floating) exchange rate system A system whereby exchange rates are determined on the basis of international demand and supply for a currency.

Formerly socialist industrialized world The industrialized ex-socialist countries of Europe.

Free rider problem Situation in which individuals who do not pay their share for a good or service nevertheless enjoy its benefits.

Frictional unemployment Temporary unemployment due to a normal time delay when a person seeks a first job, changes jobs, or reenters the labor force after an absence.

Full employment A situation in which there is no cyclical unemployment; all unemployment is frictional or structural.

Fully funded Having sufficient reserves to pay all expected liabilities; legal requirement of private insurance.

G

General Agreement on Tariffs and Trade (GATT) An international trade agreement, first negotiated in 1947, that has included efforts to reduce tariff barriers among member countries of the world. It is now replaced by the World Trade Organization.

Gentrification Conversion of low-cost apartments into middle- and upper-middle-class housing.

GNP per capita Gross national product, per person, on average. Calculated by dividing total gross national product by total population.

Government securities Government bonds and treasury bills.

Gross domestic product (GDP) A measure of the total output (and income) produced in a nation in one year.

Gross national product (GNP) The market value of all final goods and services produced *by* the economy in a given time period (usually one year).

Group of Eight (G-8) A group of eight countries (the United States, Canada, Britain, France, Italy, Germany, Japan, and Russia) that coordinate policies in an effort to influence exchange rates.

H

Health maintenance organization (HMO) A health insurance plan under which the covered care is limited to designated providers and the use of services is coordinated by a patient's primary care physician.

Homeowner's insurance Insurance that covers the replacement cost of a house and its contents.

Housing voucher Housing subsidy in the amount of the difference between fair market rent and 30 percent of a poor family's income.

Human capital discrimination Anything that prevents certain groups from acquiring the level or quality of education to which other groups have access.

Hyperinflation Extremely high inflation, whereby money becomes almost worthless.

I

Imports The value of goods and services purchased from foreigners.

Incidence of poverty Who the poor are, and which groups of people have a greater likelihood of being poor.

Income Money received from all sources.

Income distribution The division of total income in an economy among people of different income groups.

Income transfer A cash transfer from the government to an individual, for which no good or service is provided to the government in return.

Index of dissimilarity Measure of segregation.

Indigenous People who are of native-born ancestry in a country.

Individual equity Principle that benefits received are proportional to amounts paid in.

Indivisible Characteristic of public goods in that they are impossible to divide into units sufficiently small to be sold in private markets.

Inelastic demand Demand in which buyers are relatively unresponsive to changes in price.

Infant mortality rate The number of babies who die within their first year of life, per 1,000 live births.

Inflation A rise in the average price level in the economy.

Informal employment sector An employment sector consisting primarily of service occupations in an unofficial setting.

Infrastructure Social overhead capital, including facilities for transportation, communication, marketing, and extension services.

In-kind transfer A transfer of goods or services (or access to goods or services) from the government to an individual, for which no good or service is provided to the government in return.

Interest rate The percentage of borrowed funds that must be paid to the lender (or investor) for the privilege of using the funds.

International Monetary Fund (IMF) An international organization, largely funded by Western industrialized countries, that provides conditional loans and financial assistance to needy countries.

Inventories Unsold goods and materials.

Investment in human capital Spending that is designed to improve the productivity of people.

Investment-in-human-capital theory The theory that people invest in education in the same way that businesses invest in machines, by calculating the investment's return, or profit rate.

L

Labor force All people age 16 and over who are working for pay or actively seeking employment.

Labor force participation rate The ratio of the number of people in the labor force to the number of people age 16 or over in the population.

Labor-intensive technology Technology utilizing large amounts of labor.

Labor productivity Total output per average work hour, calculated as GDP divided by the number of work hours.

Law of demand There is an inverse (negative) relationship between price and quantity demanded.

Law of supply There is a direct (positive) relationship between price and quantity supplied.

Less-developed world The less-developed countries of the world.

Liberalism A movement toward freer markets.

License Permit to operate in a trade or profession.

Limit pricing Practice whereby established firms take less than the maximum possible profit and thus keep price low enough to retard new entry into their market.

Literacy rate The percentage of the population that can read and write.

Loanable funds Money that is borrowed and lent.

Lorenz curve A graphical technique that exhibits the income distribution.

Luxury good A commodity for which demand is highly sensitive to changes in income.

M

Macroeconomics The study of the total economy.

Macroeconomy The total economy.

Malpractice insurance Insurance carried by health care professionals to protect them from large malpractice damage awards.

Marginal cost The extra cost of removing an additional unit of waste.

Market power The ability to influence the market price of a product.

Market price The retail price of a product plus any sales and excise taxes paid by the consumer.

Maternal mortality rate The number of deaths of women for pregnancy-related reasons per 100,000 live births.

Means-tested Benefits depend on low-income status as defined by law.

Medicaid A government program providing medical coverage for eligible low-income people.

Medical savings account Type of insurance in which the purchaser makes payments into an account that can be drawn against in times of illness.

Medicare A government program providing medical coverage largely to elderly people.

Menu costs The costs associated with reprinting menus, revising cost schedules, adjusting telephones and vending machines, and so on, when inflation occurs.

Microeconomics The study of individual areas of activity within the total economy.

Minimum efficient scale The smallest quantity at which the lowest possible average cost is reached.

Minimum wage A legally imposed minimum price (wage) for labor.

Minority Group with lesser access to the prerequisites of society.

Monetary policy Changes made in the nation's money supply to shift the aggregate demand curve.

Money income All household income from any source, including income transfers, calculated before taxes.

Monitoring Testing to check that standards are being met.

Monopoly Market in which one firm produces a product with no close substitutes.

Mortgage insurance Insurance that pays off a mortgage if the borrower defaults.

N

National debt The total amount of money owed by the federal government. It represents the accumulation of all funds borrowed by the federal government that have not yet been repaid.

National health insurance Government program ensuring universal and comprehensive coverage of the population.

Natural monopoly Market with significant economies of scale.

Negative income tax A taxation system that taxes people with incomes above a certain level and pays people with incomes below that level.

Net benefits The excess of benefits over costs.

Newly industrializing countries (NICs) Singapore, South Korea, Taiwan, and other countries achieving rapid growth through industrialization.

Nominal GDP GDP calculated at current prices.

Nondurable goods Products with a life of less than one year.

Nonexcludable Characteristic of public goods in that their benefits cannot be kept from persons who do not pay for the goods' provision in a private market.

Nonrivalrous Characteristic of public goods in that use by one person does not prevent use by others.

Normal profit Minimum profit needed to keep resources invested in a firm (an opportunity cost of production).

Normal retirement age Minimum age at which workers can retire with full Social Security benefits.

North American Free Trade Agreement (NAFTA) An agreement between the United States, Canada, and Mexico allowing more equal access to one another's markets. The agreement went into effect on January 1, 1994.

O

Occupational crowding Crowding some groups of workers into a limited number of jobs.

Occupational discrimination Not hiring some groups of workers for particular jobs, resulting, for example, in men's jobs and women's jobs or black jobs and white jobs.

Oligopoly A market in which only a few large firms exist.

Opportunity cost The best alternative forgone to produce or consume something else; what you give up to get something else.

Overallocation of resources The production of more than the socially optimum amount of a good or service.

P

Patent A limited-term government grant of exclusive rights to use or sell a new technology intended to encourage innovation and technological change.

Pay-as-you-go program Program in which current taxes pay current benefits.

Payroll taxes Taxes based on earnings from work, usually deducted directly from the paycheck.

Perfectly inelastic demand Demand in which buyers are completely unresponsive to changes in price.

Perfectly inelastic supply Supply in which producers are completely unresponsive to changes in price.

Performance standard Specifies the required level of performance but not the means of compliance.

Personal Responsibility and Work Opportunity Reconciliation Act of 1996 (PRA) Legislation that eliminated AFDC and replaced it with state programs that require work. It also tightened eligibility for and reduced the benefits offered by other social assistance programs.

Petrodollars Money earned from the sale of petroleum. Petroleum prices are denominated in dollars.

Physician sovereignty Medical doctors' control of demand for medical procedures.

Points Fees charged by a lender at the time it grants a mortgage.

Pollution Waste that is not recycled.

Pollution permit Tradable permit to produce a given amount of pollution.

Poverty line A level of income below which a household is considered poor.

Poverty rate The percentage of the population that is poor.

Preferred provider organization (PPO) A health insurance plan under which a group of medical providers contract to provide the insured patient's medical care at discounted rates.

Prejudice Prejudgment on the basis of stereotypes and hearsay, plus the refusal to credit evidence that conflicts with prejudgment.

Premiums Payments to purchase and keep in force an insurance policy.

Price ceiling A legalized maximum price for a good or service.

Price discrimination Charging different groups of buyers different prices when price differentials are not justified by cost differences.

Price floor A legally imposed minimum price for a good or service.

Price leadership Form of collusion in which firms follow the price increases of a leading firm.

Price maker Firm that can influence its own price.

Price supports Legally fixed minimum prices.

Price taker Firm that is not able to influence its own price.

Primary commodities Unprocessed raw material and agricultural products.

Private Individual people and businesses.

Private goods Goods provided by business firms.

Private insurance Program provided by for-profit insurance companies and funded by premiums. Its purpose is the pooling of risk of losses.

Private schools Schools that are not operated by the government and are mainly financed by student tuition.

Privatization Returning government functions to the private sector.

Product differentiation Creation of image on part of consumers that one firm's product is different (superior in some way) from others.

Production possibilities curve An economic concept explaining scarcity and the need for choices; a graph showing alternate combinations of the maximum amounts of two different goods that can be produced during a particular time period if the economy's resources are efficiently and fully employed.

Profit Total revenues minus total costs.

Profit-push inflation Inflation that occurs when businesses use market power to restrict output in order to push up prices and profits.

Programs to restrict supply Policies to decrease the amount produced and offered for sale.

Progressive tax A tax that takes a greater percentage of income from high-income people than from low-income people.

Property taxes Taxes levied by local governments to fund services such as education and police protection.

Proportional tax Tax that takes the same percentage of income from people at all income levels.

Prospective payment Flat rate paid a hospital by Medicare to treat a particular patient for a given diagnosis.

Protective tariffs Taxes placed on imported goods to protect domestic producers.

Public Government.

Public goods Goods often provided by the government because their unique characteristics make it unlikely that the private market will provide them in sufficient quantity.

Public housing Housing units owned and operated by a local public housing authority but federally subsidized and often federally regulated.

Public schools Schools that are financed by tax revenues and operated by the government.

Purchasing power The ability to buy goods and services.

Pure competition Market in which many independent producers compete to sell a standardized product to many independent buyers.

Q

Quota A restriction on the quantity of an imported good; rigid numerical requirement in hiring.

R

Rate of return Profit rate computed by dividing profit by investment.

Rationing function of price Ability of flexible market price to clear the market of shortages and surpluses.

Real GDP GDP calculated at constant prices.

Real price Price adjusted for the effects of inflation.

Recession Decline in a nation's gross domestic product (output) associated with a rise in unemployment.

Redlining Lending institutions' refusal to make loans on property in areas dominated by minorities.

Refundable A refund is available even if an income-earner does not pay taxes, as long as he or she files a tax form.

Regressive Taking a larger percentage of lower incomes than of higher incomes.

Regressive tax A tax that takes a greater percentage of income from low-income people than from high-income people.

Relative poverty A situation in which people are poor in comparison with other people.

Remedies Fines or other penalties for noncompliance with standards.

Rental ceiling (rent control) A legally set maximum rent on an apartment.

Replacement rate Percentage of worker's last working year's earnings that is replaced by Social Security retirement benefits.

Resources Land, labor, machinery, and other inputs used to produce goods and services.

Retaliation A situation in which one country responds to the trade restrictions of another country by imposing trade restrictions of its own.

Reverse discrimination Discrimination against white males.

Rural–urban migration The movement of people from the rural sector to the urban sector, often in search of better living conditions.

S

Savings rate Gross domestic product minus private and government consumption spending, relative to gross domestic product.

Scarcity Limited resources relative to wants and needs.

Services Activities (such as hair cuts, health care, and education) that are consumed (used) by consumers.

Shortage A situation in which quantity demanded is greater than quantity supplied.

Six Markets Group (Asian G-6) A group of six (original) countries (the United States, Japan, China, Singapore, Australia, and Hong Kong) that coordinate financial policies.

Social adequacy Principle that benefits are sufficient to provide a minimum level of economic security to the population as a whole.

Social costs of production The total costs of production, including private costs and spillover costs.

Social insurance Government program funded by earmarked payroll taxes of employers, employees, or both. Its purpose is the pooling of risk of losses. A person need not have low income to qualify.

Socialism An economic system wherein the economic decisions are made the public (government) sector, and the means of production are owned by the public sector.

Social (public) assistance Any government program that is targeted to aid low-income people.

Social Security A federal program that provides income transfers to retired workers, the survivors of deceased workers, and disabled workers.

Social Security wealth effect Tendency of the population to substitute Social Security for private saving, thus decreasing private saving.

Specific standards Standards that are individualized to certain situations and firms.

Spillover Cost or benefit of private market activity shifted onto society at large.

Spillover benefit A positive externality in which benefits are shifted from the private market onto society.

Spillover cost Negative externality in which costs are shifted from the private market onto society.

Stagflation Simultaneous inflation and recession.

Standard deduction A fixed amount of income that taxpayers can deduct from their taxable income when calculating their personal income taxes, if other deductions are not claimed.

Standards Acceptable levels of performance.

Statistical discrimination Judging an individual on the average characteristics of his or her group.

Statutory right Right specified by law.

Structural unemployment Unemployment that results from structural changes in our economy, such as changes in demand or technology.

Subsidies to developers Government payments to landlords who build housing for the poor.

Subsidize Pay part of the cost.

Subsidy A payment from the government for some given action, such as recycling.

Subsistence food crops Crops grown primarily as food for the family. A small amount may be marketed.

Supply curve A graph showing the quantities that suppliers are willing to sell at alternative prices during a specified time period.

Supply schedule A table showing the quantities that suppliers are willing to sell at alternative prices during a specified time period.

Supply-side policy The use of various tools to shift the aggregate supply curve to the right.

Surplus A situation in which quantity supplied is greater than quantity demanded.

T

Target prices Support program in which farmer swill be paid the difference between the target and the market price.

Tariff A tax on an imported good.

Tax base Value of income, earnings, property, sales, or other variables to which a tax rate is applied.

Tax credit An amount of money by which the amount of income taxes payable to the government can be directly reduced. A person or business must meet certain criteria to be eligible for the credit.

Tax rate Percentage of the tax base that must be paid to the government as tax.

Technology Ways of using available resources to produce output.

Temporary Assistance for Needy Families (TANF) A block grant from the federal government to state governments to be used in state welfare programs in compliance with federal guidelines.

Third-party payment Health care payment made by someone other than the patient's family.

Tokenism Hiring minorities to comply with law, not for their abilities.

Trade balance The value of a nation's exports minus its imports.

Trade deficit The amount by which a nation's trade balance is in deficit (imports exceed exports).

Trade surplus The amount by which a nation's trade balance is in surplus (exports exceed imports).

Trickle-down philosophy The view that supply-side policy will generate economic growth and prosperity, the benefits of which will eventually "trickle down" to all.

Trust fund Taxes invested to pay future Social Security benefits.

U

Underallocation of resources The production of less than the socially optimum amount of a good or service.

Underemployment A situation in which people work limited hours or with low productivity.

Unemployed person A person aged 16 or over who is actively seeking employment but who is unable to find a job.

Unemployment A situation in which resources are not fully used in production.

Unemployment rate The percentage of the labor force that is unemployed.

Uniform standards General standards covering a wide range of situations and firms.

Universal entitlements Payments (or programs) to which eligible citizens have a right by law.

Usury laws Laws establishing a maximum legal interest rate.

V

Variable rate mortgages Mortgage loans on which interest rates are periodically adjusted.

W

Wage discrimination Paying equally productive workers different wages on the basis of some arbitrary characteristic.

Western industrialized world The industrialized capitalist countries of the world.

World Trade Organization (WTO) The organization that replaced GATT in 1995 and continues to pursue GATT's agenda to reduce barriers to trade among member countries.

INDEX